THE UNIVERSITY OF MICHIGAN
CENTER FOR SOUTH AND SOUTHEAST ASIAN STUDIES

MICHIGAN PAPERS ON SOUTH AND SOUTHEAST ASIA

Ann Arbor, Michigan

EXPLORATIONS IN
EARLY SOUTHEAST ASIAN HISTORY:
THE ORIGINS OF SOUTHEAST ASIAN STATECRAFT

Edited by:
Kenneth R. Hall
and
John K. Whitmore

Ann Arbor
Center for South and Southeast Asian Studies
The University of Michigan
1976

Michigan Papers on South and Southeast Asia, 11

Open access edition funded by the National Endowment for the Humanities/ Andrew W. Mellon Foundation Humanities Open Book Program.

Library of Congress Catalog Card Number: 76-6836
International Standard Book Number: 0-89148-052-8

Printed and bound by CPI Group (UK) Ltd, Croydon, CR0 4YY

ISBN 978-0-89148-011-2 (paper)
ISBN 978-0-472-12799-3 (ebook)
ISBN 978-0-472-90195-1 (open access)

To our Southeast Asian friends

Contents

Maps

Charts

The Authors

NIDHI AEUSRIVONGSE is a recent Ph.D. in Southeast Asian History at the University of Michigan, having completed a dissertation entitled "The Intellectual Elite and Modern Literature in Indonesia." He was awarded a B.A. and M.A. by Chulalongkorn University, Bangkok, and is a member of the history faculty at Chiengmai University.

MICHAEL AUNG THWIN was born in Burma, but was brought up in India. His education has taken him to Doane College for a B.A., the University of Illinois for an M.A., and he is currently working toward his doctorate in Southeast Asian History at the University of Michigan. During 1973-74, he studied in London, South India, and Southeast Asia under a John D. Rockefeller 3rd Fund Research Grant. His dissertation, "The Nature of State and Society in Pagan (1200-1300 A.D.): Saṅgha-State Relations and the Dynamics of Burmese Institutional History," expands on the essay he has contributed to this volume. Publications: "The Problem of Ceylonese-Burmese Relations in the 12th Century and the Question of an Interregnum in Pagan: 1165-1174 A.D.," Journal of the Siam Society (January, 1976).

KENNETH R. HALL, born in Niles, Michigan, received a B.A. from Albion College, an M.A. from Northern Illinois University, and completed a Ph.D. in pre-modern South and Southeast Asian History at the University of Michigan. He is currently a Lecturer in the University of Michigan's Department of Asian Studies. Hall has conducted field research in Southeast Asia and southern India, and participated in the 1974 Sumatra Expedition of the Indonesian Archeological Institute. Publications: "Toward an Analysis of Dynastic Hinterlands: The Imperial Cholas of 11th Century South India" (with George W. Spencer), Asian Profile (February, 1974); "Khmer Commercial Development and Foreign Contacts under Sūryavarman I," Journal of the Economic and Social History of the Orient (Fall, 1975).

KEITH TAYLOR comes from Cadilac, Michigan. He studied as an undergraduate at Hope College and was graduated from George Washington University. After serving with the United States Army in Vietnam, he began a Ph.D. program at the University of Michigan in 1972. His dissertation is entitled "The Birth of Vietnam: Sino-Vietnamese Relations to the 10th Century and the Origins of Vietnamese Nationhood." Taylor has reviewed several books on Vietnamese history for the Journal of Asian Studies.

JOHN K. WHITMORE completed a B.A. at Wesleyan University and received an M.A. and a Ph.D. in Southeast Asian History from Cornell University. He is Assistant Professor of Early Southeast Asian History at the University of Michigan and a specialist in the history of Vietnam. His book, The Transformation of Vietnam: Politics and Confucianism in the 15th Century, is forthcoming.

Foreword

While following the probes of foreign individuals into various obscure parts of Southeast Asia over the centuries is a diverting and entertaining pastime, the purpose of this volume is to investigate this past with the mind, to question and postulate upon the historical patterns that have developed from earlier study of the area, and to bring concepts from other areas and disciplines to bear on the existing information. The product of this effort, as it is encompassed in this volume, is not an attempt at the definitive study of any of the topics. It is rather a series of speculations on the directions feasible for the further study of the Southeast Asian past. As such, the answers proposed in these essays are really questions. Are the ideas presented here true within the specific historical contexts for which they have been developed? If so, can we use these ideas, or variations of them, to interpret the history of other parts of Southeast Asia? If not, what other ideas may be brought to bear on these situations in order to understand them? The ultimate aim of this volume is thus a challenge to the profession at large not only to criticize what we have done, but also to go beyond our postulations and create new ones.

The studies included here have not been based on the primary source materials in their original forms, with one exception (Aung Thwin). The authors have utilized a variety of available materials, generally in translation (in both European and modern Southeast Asian languages), and have applied certain concepts derived from a number of different directions to put forward their proposals. Both Taylor and Hall, in the second and third essays, operate by careful analogy from 19th and 20th century ethnological data in order to provide a cultural framework of understanding for the earlier material. As Hall shows, epigraphic and ethnological detail can be fitted together to construct a viable model for the indigenous political structure of the times. In the second essay, Taylor also brings to bear linguistic theories in the attempt to gauge patterns of change and continuity. In both this essay and the fifth one, he makes a fundamental use of mythological material to gain a generic sense of local development and to see how this sense presents insights into the historical events.

This resurrection of what might be called the folklorist approach of French scholars in the first decades of this century, when combined with other source material, proves itself to be a most fruitful form of inquiry.

In the same way, Aeusrivongse has utilized theories of religion developed by earlier Dutch archeologists and art historians for the distant past of Java and Bali in his attempt to penetrate the mysteries of the Devarāja cult and thereby explore the indigenous belief system which formed its core. Aung Thwin, on the other hand, draws on the more modern anthropological theories of Polanyi and Sahlins, Leach and Spiro to propose a dynamic structure for the state of Pagan which involves economic, social, religious, and political patterns. His basic questions, which must now be applied to the other classical states, are: what occurred socially and economically, with the formation of an empire? was it more of the same? or did a totally new structure emerge? Taylor, in the seventh essay, brings a "Southeast Asian" historical frame of analysis to bear on Ceylon and additionally uses a genealogical approach to understand its political events. The other pieces, my own "Note" and the essay by Hall and myself, attempt to fill in areas of historical investigation that have heretofore been generally ignored, while Hall's "Introductory Essay" both sets the stage for the following explorations and integrates the latter's finding into a general discussion of the classical Southeast Asian state and its form.

Behind these postulations is the solid use of more traditional textual and historical approaches. Aung Thwin and Taylor (essay no. 5) are doing work in their own areas of doctoral research, utilizing inscriptional and chronicle materials respectively. The other essays by Hall, Aeusrivongse, and Taylor are based on English and French translations of a wide range of local Southeast Asian materials combined with sources from the Mediterranean, the Middle East, India, and China. The results they have produced will indicate the fact that much remains to be done even in terms of utilizing already translated primary materials, much less plunging into untranslated sources. A key point here is the lack of study on Java, relatively the least studied area in Southeast Asia in these centuries vis-a-vis the amount of

indigenous materials available. The need, of course, is for
the continuation of such efforts as these and the encouragement
of students to exercise their minds and explore the fascinating
possibilities of early Southeast Asian history.

John K. Whitmore
Ann Arbor
February, 1976

Symbols Used in the Notes

AA	Artibus Asiae (Ascona)
BEFEO	Bulletin de l'École Française d'Extrême-Orient (Hanoi-Paris)
BSEI	Bulletin de la Société des Études Indochinoises (Saigon)
BSOAS	Bulletin of the School of Oriental and African Studies (London)
CHJ	Ceylon Historical Journal (Colombo)
CJHSS	Ceylon Journal of Historical and Social Studies (Colombo)
CSSH	Comparative Studies in Society and History (Leiden)
EZ	Epigraphia Zeylanica (London)
FA	France/Asiae (Paris)
IC	Inscriptions du Cambodge (Hanoi-Paris)
JA	Journal Asiatique (Paris)
JAOS	Journal of the American Oriental Society (New Haven)
JAS	Journal of Asian Studies (Ann Arbor)
JBRS	Journal of the Burma Research Society (Rangoon)
JCBRAS	Journal of the Ceylon Branch of the Royal Asiatic Society (Colombo)
JESHO	Journal of the Economic and Social History of the Orient (Leiden)
JMBRAS	Journal of the Malayan Branch of the Royal Asiatic Society (Singapore)
JRAS	Journal of the Royal Asiatic Society of Great Britain and Northern Ireland (London)
JSEAH	Journal of South-East Asian History (Singapore)
JSS	Journal of the Siam Society (Bangkok)
PA	Pacific Affairs (Vancouver)
PI	Prasasti Indonesia (Bandung)
TP	T'oung Pao (Leiden)

An Introductory Essay

on Southeast Asian Statecraft

in the Classical Period

With the exception of O. W. Wolters' publications on
the Malay world, very little innovative research focusing on
the ancient history of Southeast Asia has appeared in print in
this country during the last decade. As a result, methods,
hypotheses, and early research in this field have remained unchallenged. One can point, for example, to the Heine-Geldern
work entitled Conceptions of State and Kingship in Southeast
Asia, written over a generation ago,[1] which has often been
criticized but never revised in a major way. George Coedès'
Les États hindouisés d'Indochine et d'Indonésie, the standard
text for ancient Southeast Asian history, makes use of all the
research available when it was written, much of it done by
the author himself, but represents little response to scholarship which has taken place since the 1950's.[2]

In an attempt to encourage new approaches to the
historiography of Southeast Asia, Harry J. Benda's 1962
essay, "The Structure of Southeast Asian History: Some
Preliminary Observations," criticized earlier scholarship as
being externally oriented and suggested that future research
should take a "generic" or internal approach to regional
history:

The structural, generic approach to Southeast Asian
history should commence with the endeavor to discover,
or reconstruct, a set of social, economic, and
political relationships during the classical era.
Periodization will logically coincide with major
structural changes affecting these relationships, and
thus need not necessarily correspond to mere shifts
in the political fortunes of this or that dynasty or
ethnic group.[3]

1

Earlier historiography, as depicted by Benda, used external factors to define the structure of the area's history. Thus historicans spoke of the "Hinduized" and "Indianized" states of early Southeast Asia, regarding them as mere extensions of India's culture. Similarly, when writing about early Vietnamese history, historians have depicted a "Sinicized" culture, disregarding the fact that at least until the fifteenth century Vietnamese civilization was more indigenous in character than Chinese. The ultimate extension of this type of interpretation was the historiography of the colonial period which interpreted Southeast Asia's history almost totally within the context of the European experience. Thus it was at one time believed that such monuments as central Java's Borobudur could never have been a creation of an indigenous civilization because Southeast Asians were held to be incapable of such a sophisticated effort. [4]

In fairness it should be pointed out that these great epigraphers and historians laid the foundation for future research. Quite naturally, since the source material was often in Sanskrit or in any case was imbued with Indic (or Sinic) cultural forms, the first task of these men was to bring the fruits of the vast Indic and Sinic scholarship to bear on the deciphering and interpretation of the documents and to elucidate the relationship of these people to Indic and Sinic culture. But in order to accomplish this, and indeed as an end in itself, the task of scholarship on classical Southeast Asia then became one of defining indigenous culture beneath what was increasingly suspected of being a mere veneer of Indic or Sinic patterns.

Early historical interpretations have proposed that in the first centuries A. D. Southeast Asia was subjected to a period of colonization by Indians or that traders from India came to Southeast Asia and spread Hindu culture by inter-marrying with the local populations and becoming rulers of the earliest Southeast Asian states. This view has been criticized on the ground that maritime traders were neither intellectuals nor an elite and were thus incapable of transmitting a culture. [5] The initial supposition was thus that cultural interchange occurred only in one direction, with

Indian Brahmans, the custodians of India's Hindu tradition
and of certain principles of social organization bulwarked by
cosmic sanctions, coming to Southeast Asian and bringing
the people of the area into a wider universe of common symbols
and attachments. These Brahmans, with their ability to read
and write, brought Indian religious texts which they applied to
give the developing states an Indian framework for their
statecraft.

As opposed to such externally oriented analysis,
recent scholarship has suggested that there was an indigenous
pattern into which these newcomers were integrated. The
first two papers in this volume, for example, make such an
attempt to identify the system of organization prevalent in
Malay society prior to the formation of the classical state of
Srivijaya.[6] As the first essay demonstrates, existing Malay
culture was incapable of generating the development of a
state larger than the small groups of Malay boatmen.
Something was necessary to institute development beyond this
level of organization. It is within this context that we may
examine the adoption of Indic and Sinic culture, suggesting
that developing indigenous states utilized these foreign patterns
for their own advantage.

In identifying this foreign/indigenous dichotomy, the
external trappings of items seemingly of Indic or Sinic origin
are misleading. For example, our second paper discusses
the stone on which an oath of allegiance to the Srivijaya
state's king has been engraved. On this stone appears the
seven-headed nāga (snake spirit) which is well-known in
Indian iconography. It could well be concluded that in this
instance a wholesale borrowing of an Indic image had taken
place as a foreign symbol--the seven-headed nāga--had
become an important part of the new system of statecraft.
Yet the Srivijaya essay suggests that there was a pre-existing
snake cult in Sumatra, such that we may see the seven-headed
nāga as something which fits well with the belief system of the
local culture. Another example of selective borrowing may
be examined in the Khmer domain where existing veneration
of mountains resulted in the selection of features of Indic
cosmology which fit with the developing mountain cult of the

new Khmer state. Although the location of the world of the ancestors varies in Indian thought, it is never put on top of a mountain, and such an association must thus be considered a Khmer feature. Yet to pass over Indic culture--which gives a certain coherence to the development of classical statecraft-- in silence would suggest a unity of indigenous Southeast Asian culture which is as yet only partially tenable. On the other hand, the state of existing scholarship is such that in order to understand the process of synthesis more fully we must identify what is Indic or Sinic and what is Southeast Asian.

Benda believed that the most important issues to be researched in the 1960's involved further analysis of statecraft itself, in particular the relationship of ruler and ruled. This volume, in answer to Benda's appeal, studies the classical centers of power and their problems in ruling their domains. In attempting to suggest how such centers of power controlled their own people, two forms of classical states are examined: the coastal state (as represented by Srivijaya), and the lowland wet rice state of the mainland. In both forms the objective of local statecraft seems to have been the control of people, not land. Indeed, manpower was seemingly the basis of political power. This volume thus defines a state in terms of its control over population centers within a system in which claimed control and actual control were quite different.[7] Herein the classical state showed a consistent inability to absorb the regions beyond its "core" domain.[8]

People of various regions were brought under the state's control. Yet, although a people was engulfed by a state, even for several centuries, with the decline of that state this same group of people and their traditions were capable of reemerging. One example of this phenomenon is the Mon tradition of the Dvāravatī region, which was engulfed by the Khmer in the mid-tenth century and administratively annexed in the following century, but which reemerged as a recognizable cultural entity in the fourteenth century.[9] A clue to the nature of this relationship is provided in a Khmer inscription from Pimai (1041), where reference is given to an animal dating cycle associated with later Thai practice and nowhere else encountered in Khmer epigraphy.[10]

This is probably an example of a local practice which was retained under Khmer hegemony. The Srivijaya empire's history, too, is marked by a fluctuating relationship with the peoples of the Sumatra and Malay coasts which has been documented in Chinese dynastic histories. In times when Srivijaya's center was weak, the various ports acted independently, as seen in the registration of their individual embassies to the Chinese court--efforts which were intended to develop their own trade with Chinese commercial centers. In times of the center's strength, however, no such independent efforts were attempted as only embassies from the center itself were recorded. 11

The apparent key to a center's control over manpower was its ability to form "lord-subordinate" alliances with such local peoples. A king, acting from a center of authority, fragmented his potential enemies by reaching agreements in which these potential opponents became subordinates of the state. Eleventh century Khmer inscriptions show that Sūryavarman I, whose rule (1002-1050) marked a high point in Khmer administrative development, was particularly adept at incorporating the chiefs of peoples on the outer edges of his personal domain. After "conquering" a territory with his armies, local chiefs of the "defeated" peoples were recruited as district chiefs (khloñ viṣaya), and their power status changed little. In Khmer inscriptions from Pimai, which was such a peripheral area to Sūryavarman's core, there is evidence that this type of alliance was formed with the local elite. The inscription from Pimai which gives reference to the animal dating cycle (1041) also names a kholñ viṣaya for this area. Since the inscription makes no special reference to the chief's status, as was common when an individual with royal ties was appointed, it would seem to indicate that this figure may well have been a chief of the local population whose traditions were being retained. On the other hand, a Lopburi inscription from the same period, which registers the extension of the Khmer administration into the old Dvāravatī region, contains evidence that a khloñ tamrvac viṣaya, a royal "inspector"--a person with ties to the center-- was assigned by Sūryavarman to oversee this western area. 12 Yet there is no evidence of a massive influx of Khmer

administrators into Lopburi, suggesting that the local Khmer
government incorporated many of the indigenous elite.

Early historiography on the classical period depicted
the capital as being formed by the king and his elite sitting
on top of a social pyramid, with little contact between them
and the people below.[13] Sūryavarman's state seems, however,
to have had a more intense relationship between the center
and the local populations. The Khmer state protected regional
interests by incorporating the local status quo into its formal
structure. It further benefited local communities by using its
army to guard the state, maintaining the orderliness of the
regions under its control and protecting its domain from
invasion. Inscriptions indicate the physical presence of
royal officials to administer the transfer of land--apparently
to confirm that the exculsive rights of the previous owner had
changed hands with the land[14]--as well as local visits made
by the royal retinue (kamsten). The kamsten was a mobile
body of state administrators who traveled from place to place
within the realm, acting on disputes which could not be solved
locally or on affairs which were considered to be within the
state's area of interest.[15] The kamsten was thus a visible
symbol of the king's administration.

In some cases the classical state provided its own
governors to administer key provices. In Cambodia the
region of the state's core was under direct royal
administration.[16] In Java, the kingdom was divided into a
large number of autonomous areas each governed by a rakryan,
and the sons of kings were placed in key rakryan positions.[17]
As expressed in the Telagu Batu inscription, certain areas of
the Srivijaya empire were ruled by royal dātus (chiefs),
while others were ruled by dātus of non-royal background.
The distinction between the two is not entirely clear, although
it can be speculated that the Srivijaya king was quite willing
to accept strong local elites as his subordinate dātus. As
described in the essay below on early Srivijaya, the versions
of the Telagu Batu inscription found in Karangbrahi (Jambi),
Kotakapur (Bangka), and Palas Pasemah (West Lampung)
were not as elaborate in their demands for local loyalty to
the state apparently because they were erected in areas

outside the Srivijaya king's core. In such areas the king's power was not direct. Thus passages in the Telagu Batu inscription which applied only to that region which was considered to be under the king's personal control were omitted from the three versions which were erected in centers of local power.

The Telagu Batu inscription also describes an oath of loyalty which was administered to all state subordinates. This was an oath expressing one's personal devotion to the king. If one broke the oath, divine retribution was threatened. A similar oath was administered to Sūryavarman's Khmer subordinates in 1011, nine years after he had actually claimed the Khmer throne.[18] It would appear that only in that year was Sūryavarman's succession to the Khmer throne unchallenged such that he could legitimately administer this oath.[19] Khmer subordinates swore to become the local eyes of Sūryavarman, pledging to feed the center with information about local activities.

Moreover, Khmer statecraft utilized an elaborate royal cult to integrate subordinates with the center.[20] In devarāja ideology, there was an interaction of the human and the divine in the person of the king. Traditional symbols of divinity and power, such as the liṅga and the mountain, merged local ancestor cults and the cosmological symbolism of Indian religious theory to form an ideological basis for Khmer kingship.[21] Royal ceremony generated the king's powers. The royal court, its activities, and its style recreated a world of the gods--in theory a heaven on earth. Here all greatness and glory were concentrated. By successfully fulfilling his role as the hypothetical focus of all sanctity and power, the king maintained the orderliness of the world.

The king's court appears to have been ritually linked to its subordinate centers of power as the subordinate centers sought to imitate the style of the center.[22] This ritual unity was probably more important than administrative control in maintaining the state's dominance over areas outside its core. For a lasting state, territorial unification was not

sufficient to sustain the empire. This was attained by
successfully integrating indigenous folk traditions, symbols,
and religious beliefs into a cult which was visibly concentrated
in the center.[23] Local deities and, of most consequence,
local ancestor worship became focused in the state's religious
ceremony. In the indigenous belief system of Cambodia, for
example, death was held to represent the passage of the
spirit into the realm of the ancestors. Local death rites
ushered the spirit into this world of the dead. In return for
faithful worship of the dead, the ancestors granted a certain
life-power to the living. Under the Khmer kings this ancestor
worship and its traditional symbols, the liṅga and the mountain,
the former representing fertility and the latter the abode of
the dead, were subordinated to a state level cult. External
deities such as Śiva, Viṣṇu, and the Buddha were merged
with indigenous devarāja deities and were installed at the
center of the king's capital to represent the king's control
over the protective forces of the ancestors. The significance
of this synthesis is depicted in the Khmer oath of loyalty
to Sūryavarman I. In this instance, the state's subordinates
requested that, in return for their faithful service, their king
first maintain their family ancestral cults; and then, secondly,
that he sustain their families. By properly observing the rites
to the ancestors, the subordinate's kin would be guaranteed
the forces necessary for a prosperous life.[24]

While in a theoretical sense the king's only duty was
to maintain the world order, legally it involved the practical
application of such laws which regulated land and labor.
Khmer epigraphy records the use of a state court system
to maintain land borders and to settle land disputes.[25] The
extent of the state's legal intervention seems to have been
enforcing land grants and edicts sent out, and arbitrating
disputes unable to be settled at the local level.[26] In an
inscription from central Java dated 860, for example, state
administrators (rakarayan mapatih) were asked to intervene
in a local dispute when the village elders and a certain
individual, who probably represented a religious foundation,
could not resolve the method of repaying a considerable debt
owed to the local community. In this case the state
administrators ruled in favor of the local community.[27]

From such an examination of Southeast Asian epigraphy, one
receives the sense that the state preferred to remain above
such conflicts, discouraging all but major disputes from
clogging the state's administrative system. This encouraged
the continuity of local custom, which the state generally left
untouched as long as it was not disruptive to state harmony.

The king also took an interest in his state's economic
activity. In addition to being the ideological center of the
state, the king's capital was the economic center of his
domain. The economic resources of the state's core were
very important to the state's ability to maintain its power.
In Burma, the Pagan system of statecraft was established
after the conquest and settlement of the agriculturally rich
Kyauske area and was then extended to encompass the old
Mon economic center at Minbu. The agricultural output of
these areas, and thus the state's economic base, was increased
by land endowments to Buddhist monasteries, made by Pagan
kings and private individuals, which provided for the building
of water tanks, irrigation of land, and economic development
in general. While the donor acquired merit in return for his
generosity, the kingdom received both social and material
benefit. [28]

In the Khmer core large local estates were integrated
into the state's ritual system via a network of local temples;
local "kin" temples seem to have been consolidated into a
structured relationship with ten large state-level temples
which were administered by functionaries who were shadowy
representatives of the state. [29] Local temples were often
established by the founders of local estates, many of whom
were originally given their land by royal grant. In return for
recognition as a legitimate temple, which was expressed by
allowing the priests of the local temple ritual privileges in
a central temple, the local temple paid the central temple
treasury a set percentage of the annual yield of its endowed
lands. Such a network may well have dictated some royal
control over the uniformity of ritual style. An inscription
for Sūryavarman I's reign (1027), for instance, records an
order placing four religious institutions solely under the
authority of an "inspector of royal service." [30] In addition to

providing the basis for ritual unity, this temple network
insured that local landholding would remain fragmented. This
was done by forbidding miśrabhoga, the joining of the lands
of more than one local estate's temple, unless by the approval
of the king himself. [31] Such a practice prevented a situation
such as the Pagan court faced in the late twelfth century,
when the consolidation of the Burmese saṅgha's landholding
rights gave the church sufficient power to resist the state's
efforts to control land. [32]

Similarly, rich wet rice agricultural centers could be
found around the capitals of the classical states which
developed near Prambanan in central Java and at Thăng-long
in the Red River Delta of Vietnam. In Java, rather than an
actual concentration of manpower in one or two centers, the
population seemingly was spread among the various villages.
To develop economically peripheral lands, reward loyal
followers, and extend the control of the throne, land grants
known as sīma ("freehold") were given. [33] Although such land
was considered to be beyond the administrative powers of
the king--freeing it from royal demands for taxes and
service--a ceremony dedicating the sīma land grant
emphasized that the grantee was expected to remain loyal to
the Javanese state. This ceremony involved an oath in which
the grantee pledged his loyalty, and it culminated with the
pronouncement of a curse by a religious official. [34]

In Cambodia, with the absence of natural conditions
which would have allowed the development of an economic base,
an artificial base was created by the state. An elaborate
system of state controlled irrigation works was constructed
around the Khmer capital at Angkor. The first artificial
lake, the east baray, was constructed in the 890's by
Yaśovarman I at the time when the capital was being
established at Angkor. It has been estimated that the
construction of the second baray to the west, which was
probably initiated by Sūryavarman I in the eleventh century,
at least doubled the amount of cultivated land in the Angkor
region and provided the necessary economic wealth for the
dramatic expansion of the Khmer state at that time. [35] The
resulting economic prosperity is reflected in an urban

development that took place in the tenth and eleventh centuries. In the epigraphy of this period, urban development becomes noticeable in the reign of Rājendravarman II (944-968) and continued under Jayavarman V (968-1001), but reached its fullness only under Sūryavarman I. For example, the epigraphy mentions only twelve place names ending in -pura, a Sanskrit term used to identify urban areas, during the reign of Jayavarman IV (928-942), twenty-four in the period of Rājendravarman II, twenty under Jayavarman V, but forty-seven--more than double those of his immediate predecessors--in the reign of Sūryavarman I.36

The prosperity generated by the Khmer empire was shared by merchants who were active in the Khmer domain. There are over twenty specific references to merchant activity in the period from the reign of Harṣavarman I (922) to that of Harṣavarman III (1071). Commercial growth seems to have culminated during Sūryavarman's rule, as the new commercial opportunities available from the extension of Khmer administrative control into the region north of the Dangrek mountain range and into the former Dvāravatī area in the west resulted in the development of new commercial networks. Although the Khmer state was an inland wet rice state, anything useful to the economic strength of the realm was encouraged. Thus Sūryavarman himself seems to have been active in furthering Khmer commercial aspirations by attempting to establish regular commercial intercourse with the Cōla state in southern India and the Lý state in Vietnam.37

Although different in nature, the economic center of the Srivijaya state appears to have been functionally similar to those of the wet rice producing states. As proposed in our essay on Srivijaya statecraft, Palembang served as a center of economic redistribution, fulfilling roles both as a trade entrepôt and as the central treasury for a series of ports. Because the Srivijaya state's economic base was more vulnerable than those of the land based states, it placed more emphasis on oaths of loyalty and physical force than was probably true in the agrarian states. The Srivijaya capital's control of its peripheral areas was similar to that maintained by the land based states. Areas which were distant from the capital were difficult to administer directly. A state thus relied on either physical force or an alliance relationship, symbolized by the oath administered to state subordinates, to maintain its hegemony in such areas. While a royal "navy" of sea nomads maintained Palembang's position as the dominant port on the Sumatra coast, a network of alliances allowed a flow of goods from the interior to the ports--giving Srivijaya its economic and thus its political strength.

Each of the classical states thus attempted to draw in the resources of its realm--in the form of tribute, talent, men, and goods--to its center. In the Khmer domain, as has been pointed out, even estates in the core area were kept fragmented by legally preventing the consolidation of their temple lands and by requiring local temples to relinquish a certain percentage of their annual harvest to support the state's central temples. Srivijaya ports were probably also required to send a percentage of their port revenues to the central treasury in Palembang. The central Javanese state expected both taxes and labor service from its subjects.[38] Resources acquired from its own core, when added to certain required tribute which was extracted from peripheral areas, supplied the centers with large quantities of wealth. This wealth was then redistributed to maintain loyalties to the state. One type of investment was the construction of large temple complexes which emphasized the state's theoretical powers. In such instances the investment also provided for economic development in the vicinity of the temple and, as was the case in Pagan, allowed the growth of an indigenous artisan class. Payments to various state armies were another important revenue outlay of the state. In the process of concentrating as many resources as possible at the center, military power was essential. Military strength allowed the establishment of the economic base, the administration of oaths, and the formulation of the various royal cults.

To insure this flow of revenues which supported the classical state, a system of record keeping was developed, and a council of state administration was formed to handle it. This royal administration was composed of a group of administrators who were generally literate and were capable of dealing with a variety of matters.[39] These state administrators also participated in the various state ceremonies. In a system of statecraft in which ritual links were an important tool of integration, it was essential that the ritual at the center was performed by an elite who knew how to conduct the required ceremonies properly. With such a dual responsibility of administrative function and ritual performance the royal administrators could well have become a secondary force within the state, with their own hereditary rights. The importance of such officials would have been further enhanced when rival branches of the royal family became imbedded in disputes over legitimate succession. In such a crisis the state's administrative and religious elite would thus have come to hold the key to legitimacy--or the power to bestow legitimacy--via their control of court ritual. As shown in Sūryavarman I's inscriptions, the bestowal of legitimacy in Cambodia was not performed until a king's claim to the throne was unquestioned.[40] To consolidate his power and to settle the succession dispute, Sūryavarman married his daughter to the major Brahman family which controlled the devarāja cult. This gave Sūryavarman access to the legitimacy symbolized in that cult and insured his proper investiture as king. Under Sūryavarman's rule these religious technicians were made the king's hereditary hotars (religious advisors) and were allowed to assume civil functions in the Khmer administrative system. It might be suggested that one of the effects of the major Cham raid on Angkor in 1177 was the elimination of such a group of the administrative elite--perhaps by carrying them off to the Cham court, a typical practice in classical Southeast Asian warfare[41]--resulting in a crisis in the continuity of the Khmer statecraft tradition. This may explain the efforts of Jayavarman VII, who occupied the Khmer throne after that raid and made significant changes in the Khmer religious and ceremonial tradition. If the administrative elite was the stabilizing force in the system of Khmer statecraft and was indeed able to provide continuity to the classical state even in the face of dynastic crisis, then Jayavarman's efforts to create a new system of legitimacy as symbolized in his construction of the Bayon (a temple complex

of quite different style and religious patronage than earlier
Khmer monuments--a fact which has long puzzled historians)
may well have been necessitated by the Chams' removal of
the old Khmer administrative elite and their system of
legitimacy.

The first four papers in this volume argue that at
the heart of this classical system lay indigenous ideas of
chieftainship, its sacred nature and its duties, which had
previously served as the basis of earlier forms of political
organization. Here it is demonstrated that a coming to terms
with one's own culture was the first concern as developing
Southeast Asian states attempted to consolidate their hold
over their people. For instance, Taylor's paper on the
wāqwāq presents a Malay legend which explains why Malay
society was fragmentary by nature. The Srivijaya paper
suggests that to counteract this problem early kings designed
an oath which specifically emphasized the coming together of
the various factions under that state's control. This oath
was administered to all the subordinates of the Srivijaya
king. It was a product of the local culture and was taken on
a stone on which appeared the seven-headed nāga, representing
the various religious forces which were being invoked to seal
the oath. Cambodia's devarāja cult was also such a receptical
for the flow of indigenous elements of the past into the
present. Traditional ancestor worship was used to define
the systematic integration of the Indian cosmology into a
new, yet characteristically Khmer polity. At the same time
local religious spirits were unified under a supreme "spirit
of the mountain."

An explanation of why later Vietnamese historians
regarded Đinh Bộ Lĩnh and not the Ngô kings as the tenth
century heir to the ancient political traditions of the
Vietnamese monarchy is provided in Taylor's essay on the
origin and development of the Vietnamese state. By renewing
folk symbols such as water and mountain spirits and a claw
myth, the Hoa-lu' monarchy was able to exploit the theme of
the expulsion of the Chinese and the re-emergence of
indigenous traditions. Under the Lý kings of the eleventh
century this political base was broadened; the systematic

incorporation of local ancestor worship and the patronage of the Buddhist saṅgha provided a way for royal authority to penetrate and incorporate the local political structure. The skills of the educated Buddhist clergy were channeled into state service as monks became technicians in the royal administration.

Here too we encounter the early blending of the Confucian cult into the Vietnamese system of statecraft. During the 1070's and 1080's, we read in the Vietnamese chronicles of the establishment of the Confucian Temple of Literature, the first examinations, the National College, the Han-lin Academy, and the nine-level civil service hierarchy. These striking innovations led merely to the formation of a rather peripheral Confucian cult within the Court. Such literati were needed for the handling of the Chinese texts and ritual and for diplomatic purposes, but in all probability they were very few in number and their duties were confined to the capital. Throughout the Lý period (to 1225) the "Confucian scholar" was most likely a man of Buddhist background who was part of a small group kept for the maintenance of the Confucian cult at the Court. His was a religious, not a political or administrative function. [42] Indeed, so contrary to the Chinese system of statecraft was the character of the Lý state that, as Whitmore notes, Confucian commentators found the non-Confucian reality of the period difficult to comprehend.

Pagan Burma was also a Buddhist state which systematically blended local religious cults, Buddhism, and traditional patterns of chieftainship to organize a polity, as the old order was maintained, but reoriented to support the new state. Yet, when the Burmese state shifted to a different form of organization in the thirteenth and fourteenth centuries, as it changed internally in a qualitative sense, the old order would not work. Aung Thwin has depicted this process as a transformation in the patterns of socio-economic control as control over the produce of the land in the Pagan nucleus shifted to the Burmese saṅgha and away from the central government. With no control over the economic resources in its domain, Burmese kingship was forced to redefine its structure, resulting in a new pattern of statecraft.

Although not usually considered a part of geographical Southeast Asia, Taylor's paper on the Polonnaruva period of Singhalese history has been included because it too shows an end to a classical system of Buddhist kingship. The political and religious aspects of the end of one system of Singhalese kingship are emphasized, but the origins of a new age are also examined. Here, as in Burma, internal changes of a qualitative sense made the old state structure impractical, or impossible to maintain. A new state was organized around a new Theravāda Buddhist elite and in a new physical setting.

Both Aung Thwin and Taylor have responded to Benda's suggestion of letting internal "structural change" define periodization. In Burma, there was a significant shift of socio-economic power away from the king to a counter power group, the saṅgha. Such an explanation for the structural change of the Burmese state, that is, an internally generated change, is totally different from the reason proposed by George Coedès in his Les États hindouisés d'Indochine et d'Indonésie for the decline of the Pagan state. Coedès explained the thirteenth century change in Burmese statecraft as being the result of a raid by the Mongols into Burma in 1287 A.D. --which is a good example of searching for an external explanation for significant internal change. In Ceylon, there was a transition from one set of state religious elite to another, which necessitated a structural change in the relationship of the king to his elite. Likewise, it has been suggested in this essay that the twelfth century Khmer empire experienced a similar transition of state elite after the 1177 Cham raid on Angkor. Here, too, Jayavarman VII's response was to attempt a structural change which was symbolized by his shift to a syncretic Buddhist cult. The massive, incomplete artistic style of the Bayon was a break from the past and suggests the immediacy of his problem. The decline of the Khmer state following Jayavarman's death indicates the failure of his attempt to revive Angkor's statecraft, suggesting that internal decay may well have contributed to the state's collapse. It remained for the fourteenth century Thai state which developed in the old eastern Mon region of Dvāravatī to restore political cohesion on the mainland by successfully blending the Khmer and Theravāda Buddhist styles of statecraft.

Our final paper returns to the first paper's suggestion that there was a relationship between the channels of communication and the trade routes of Asia and that cultural interchange along these routes had an impact upon Southeast Asia's statecraft. By the late eleventh century, the Straits of Malacca were no longer the focal point of Southeast Asian trade. Burma and the upper Malay Peninsula had withdrawn from the earlier patterns of trade to develop a more regionally centered communications network connecting Ceylon to Pagan and Angkor. Tensions caused by Burmese efforts to dominate this route resulted in the Singhalese raid on lower Burma of the 1160's. During the twelfth century the way was reopened and rapidly became a path for the spread of Theravāda Buddhism on the mainland. Developments inside the Southeast Asian states provided openings for such formerly peripheral forms of belief as Theravāda Buddhism, Neo-Confucianism, and Sūfi Islam, and they became a part of the transition phase from the "classical" form of Southeast Asia polity to the "post classical."

In such a way is this volume an attempt to apply Harry Benda's "generic" approach to the "classical" system of statecraft. During the 1972-73 academic year, Professor John K. Whitmore and his students organized a graduate seminar for the specific purpose of reexamining the assumptions on which prior research concerning Southeast Asia's classical history had been based. The students suggested new interpretations and methods for the examination of the available data. Under Professor Whitmore's encouragement, the seminar papers were revised over the past two years to form the text of this book.

It is hoped that the essays contained here will generate additional thought and research on the classical period. To encourage others to continue the type of research presented, a topical bibliography of suggested published sources relating to the classical history of Southeast Asia has been included in an appendix. This bibliography has served not only as

18

the basis for our individual research interests, but also has provided a solid and basic understanding of the comparative aspects of Southeast Asia's historiography. For this reason the bibliography has also been organized so that it may be adapted by others as a course outline.

As co-editor of the volume, I would like to express my gratitude to each of the contributors for their willingness to see this project through to its completion. In some cases this has involved putting aside current dissertation research taking place in London, Bangkok, Palembang, and Madras to concentrate on something of past interest. In other cases the essays are an initial presentation of ideas which are now being tested and expanded in doctoral research. The final revisions have incorporated this continuing scholarship whenever possible.

Professor Whitmore deserves much of the credit for this volume. Not only did he conceive the idea of publishing these papers, but he has continued to supply encouragement and guidance throught the completion of the project. I also acknowledge the various criticism received from other scholars at the University of Michigan and elsewhere. Among these Dr. Thomas R. Trautmann, Dr. Alton L. Becker, and John K. Musgrave deserve special recognition for their editorial advice. The Center for South and Southeast Asian Studies (Professor Alton L. Becker, Director) at the University of Michigan provided both its facilities and its financial assistance during the final drafts of the text. Finally, to my wife Vicki I pay special tribute for her ability to live with me through the various frustrations of preparing such a book.

Kenneth R. Hall
Ann Arbor, Michigan
February 1975

19

NOTES

1. Robert Heine-Geldern, "Conceptions of State and Kingship in Southeast Asia," The Far Eastern Quarterly, 2 (November, 1942), pp. 15-30; reprinted as Cornell Data Paper 10 (Ithaca, New York, 1956).

2. George Coedès, Les États hindouisés d'Indochine et d'Indonésie, 2nd edn. (Paris, 1964).

3. Harry J. Benda, "The Structure of Southeast Asian History: Some Preliminary Observations," Journal of Southeast Asian History, 3 (March, 1962), pp. 103-138, as reprinted in Robert O. Tilman, ed., Man, State, and Society in Contemporary Southeast Asia (New York, 1969), p. 24.

4. F. D. K. Bosch, "The Problem of the Hindu 'Colonization' of Indonesia," Selected Studies in Indonesian Archaeology (The Hague, 1961), p. 5.

5. Ibid.

6. See O. W. Wolters, Early Indonesian Commerce (Ithaca, New York, 1967), pp. 154-158, for another presentation on this theme.

7. See George W. Spencer and Kenneth R. Hall, "Toward an Analysis of Dynastic Hinterlands: The Imperial Cholas of 11th Century South India," Asian Profile, 2, 1 (February, 1974), pp. 51-62, for a discussion of claimed versus actual control as reflected in the distribution of Chōla inscriptions.

8. The "core" is defined as that area of land, usually near the capital, which was administered directly by the state's central administration. The king was usually a major landholder in this "core," but the landholding rights of others were also protected. In some cases others were

granted land to develop in the core--these might be royal
service grants or religious grants. What I have called
"peripheral areas" are those areas bordering the core.
Peripheral areas seem to have been in more of a tributary
relationship to the state. Although the state might claim
to have administratively annexed these areas, its real
control was probably minimal as local elites remained
in power while paying homage to the center. For a
definition of what I have included in the Khmer "core,"
see Kenneth R. Hall, "Khmer Commercial Development
and Foreign Contacts under Sūryavarman I," JESHO,
(forthcoming).

9. The fact that Dvāravatī was included in the title of the
Thai Ayuddhya kings in later centuries leads us to believe
that the tradition survived. On the survival of Mon
traditions see H. L. Shorto, "A Mon Genealogy of Kings:
Observations on The Nidāna Ārambhakanthā," in D. G. E.
Hall, ed., Historians of Southeast Asia (London, 1962),
pp. 163-172. In a recent article O. W. Walters has noted
that "South East Asia comprised many little regions, whose
inhabitants had a stubborn sense of their group identity,
and documents yield sufficiently numerous examples of
ancient and persisting place-names...." Among these
he cites Barus, Dvāravatī, and Malayu as familiar examples
and then provides a list of some thirteen Khmer toponyms
which lingered for centuries. See O. W. Wolters, "North-
western Cambodia in the Seventh Century," BSOAS, 37, 2,
(1974), p. 370.

10. George Coedès, IC (1942-1966), 7, pp. 124-126.

11. O. W. Wolters, The Fall of Srivijaya in Malay History
(Ithaca, New York, 1970), pp. 39-48.

12. George Coedès, Recueil des inscriptions du Siam (Bangkok,
1961), ii, pp. 13-18.

13. Heine-Geldern, loc. cit.

14. See IC, 4, pp. 149-150, and M. C. Ricklefs, "Land and

the Law in the Epigraphy of Tenth-Century Cambodia,"
JAS, 26, 3 (1967), pp. 411-420.

15. IC, 3, pp. 57-64; IC, 4, pp. 140-150; IC, 6, pp. 225-227.

16. Though under direct administration, local landholding
patterns included land granted as estates to various
individuals and their families as well as land granted to
temples. Ricklefs believes that outside of the capital
itself the Khmer countryside was largely under the control
of private, non-royal persons. See Ricklefs, op. cit.,
p. 419.

17. Buchari, "A Preliminary Note on the Study of the Old-
Javanese Civil Administration," Madjalah Ilmu-Ilmu
Sastra Indonesia (1963), pp. 122-133.

18. H. de Mestier du Bourg, "La premier moitie de XI[e]
siecle au Cambodge: Suryavarman I[er], sa vie et quelques
aspects des institutions a son epoque," JA, 258, 3-4,
pp. 291-293.

19. It is noteworthy that after administering this oath,
Sūryavarman sent an embassy to the Vietnamese court,
quite possibly to inform the Vietnamese that his power
was secure. Seventeen years later, a Vietnamese monarch,
son of the founder of the Lý dynasty, after a fierce struggle
with his brothers, also was installed with such an oath on
his ascension to the throne. See R. Deloustal, "Code de
Lê," BEFEO, 10 (1910), pp. 21-22.

20. See Nidhi Aeusrivongse's paper in this volume.

21. The significance of the mountain is seen in each of the
three classical mainland states. In Cambodia, Mount
Mahendra became the home of the devarāja in the cult of
Jayavarman II. As the traditional abode of ancestor spirits,
the mountain was already considered sacred by indigenous
tradition. By incorporating the external god Śiva, who was
known in Indian philosophy as the "Lord of the Mountain"
and for his association with fertility, the king's position
was reinforced. It remained for Khmer kings to associate

themselves with this mountain and thereby symbolize their
ability to guarantee the flow of life-power from the realm
of the ancestors to their subjects. In Pagan, the various
Nat spirits were integrated into a similar cult which also
came to be focused in a "Lord of the Mountain," the
Mahāgiri spirit of Mount Popa. In Vietnam, kings were
regarded as descendants from the union of the nāga (water)
spirit and a maiden who resided on the mountain inhabited
by the mountain spirit.

22. See Clifford Geertz's model of the "theatre state" in C.
Geertz, Islam Observed (New Haven, 1968), pp. 36-39.

23. The necessity of this process of incorporating indigenous
folk belief is well shown in the case of Vietnam where the
Sino-oriented elite of the upper Red River Delta failed in
its attempts to form a lasting state because it never
integrated local folk traditions into its ideology. See
Keith Taylor's paper in this volume.

24. Sūryavarman's association with the realm of the dead is
further reinforced by his posthumous name "Nirvānapada,"
which indicated that he was the way to the abode of Nirvāna.
See Nidhi Aeusrivongse's paper in this volume.

25. Ricklefs, op. cit., pp. 416-419.

26. H. de Mestier du Bourg, "La proces dans l'ancien droit
Khmer," JA, 256, 1 (1968), pp. 37-53.

27. J. G. de Casparis, PI, II (1956), pp. 330-338.

28. Such large grants of state land to the Buddhist institutions,
as Aung Thwin points out in his paper, eventually
undermined the state's economic base as the Buddhist
saṅgha ultimately controlled more land than the state.
The late Pagan period was marked by a resulting struggle
between the Pagan court and the monastic institutions for
control over land near the capital.

29. L. A. Sedov, "On the Problem of the Economic System in
Angkor Cambodia in the IX-XII Centuries," Narody Asii

23

i Afriki, Istoriia, Ekonomika, Kul'tura (ANSSSR, 1963),
6, pp. 73-81. The author has used a translation of the
Russian done by Antonia Glasse for Professor O. W.
Wolters of Cornell University.

30. IC, 2, pp. 25-39.

31. Ricklefs, op. cit., p. 415. See also Joan L. Beckham,
"Pre-Angkorian Society in the Lower Course and Delta of
the Mekong," Ms. (Itaaca, New York, 1969).

32. See Michael Aung Thwin's essay in this volume.

33. Boechari, "Epigraphy and Indonesian Historiography,"
in Soedjatmoka, et al., An Introduction to Indonesian
Historiography (Ithaca, New York, 1965), pp. 50-60.

34. Unfortunately, very little has been written on classical
Javanese statecraft since the early 1950's, despite the
considerable amount of evidence which has since been
accumulated by Indonesia's very capable archeologists.
My comments on Javanese statecraft are based on J. G.
deCasparis, PI, I and II (1950 and 1956) and the work of
the Indonesian epigraphist Buchari. The Candi Perot
inscription (850) may be of particular use in the
reconstruction of the ninth century Javanese state
hierarchy. See deCasparis, II, pp. 211-243.

35. Bernard P. Groslier, Angkor et le Cambodge au XVIe
siècle (Paris, 1958), pp. 108-112.

36. Du Bourg, "La premier moitie de XIe siecle...," p. 308.

37. See Kenneth R. Hall, "Khmer Commercial Development
and Foreign Contacts under Sūryavarman I," loc. cit.

38. DeCasparis, op. cit., pp. 211-243.

39. As opposed to a modern bureaucracy which is composed
of specialists who deal with specific responsibilities.

40. Sūryavarman claimed membership in the eastern Khmer house of Iśanapura by the inter-marriage of a local house to the maternal line of the royal house. As a member of this eastern branch of the royal family, Sūryavarman made his claim to the vacant Khmer throne against the western Khmer house and its candidate Jayaviravarman, the maternal nephew of Jayavarman V, by bilateral succession. See IC, 7, pp. 164-189.

41. This is much the same as another aspect of classical warfare: the victor carrying off or destroying the linga of his opponent, symbolizing the victor's desecration of the loser's source of mystical power, and thus in a theoretical sense his legitimacy.

42. This information has been supplied by John K. Whitmore from his paper "The Confucian Scholar in Vietnam and his View of Early Vietnamese History," which was presented to the Association for Asian Studies, 1971.

Madagascar in the

Ancient Malayo-Polynesian Myths

by
Keith Taylor

I

The fourth largest island in the world (after Greenland,
New Guinea, and Bornea), Madagascar lies about 250 miles
off the East African coast; yet the languages and the culture
of this island are Malayo-Polynesian in origin.[1] The
relationship of Madagascar to Africa is best viewed in the
larger context of the influence of Malayo-Polynesian culture
in Africa. A pioneer study on this subject is A. M. Jones'
Africa and Indonesia.[2] Although Jones' research was chiefly
in the field of music and particularly in the distribution of
the xylophone with its various tuning scales, he also touched
on a number of other cultural factors which tie large areas of
the African continent, in particular the Congo Basin and West
Africa, to the Indonesian Archipelago. The theme of Jones'
book coincides with the views of the anthropologist Leo
Frobenius who, in the 1920's, hypothesized that, sometime
before the first century A.D., native cultures in large areas
of the African continent had been radically changed by
considerable cultural stimuli from across the Indian Ocean
over an extended period of time.[3] H. A. Wieschoff, an
archeologist who studied the ancient kingdoms of East Africa,
opposed Frobenius' theory on the grounds that a number of
customs associated with East African royal houses were
indigenous and owed nothing to foreign influence.[4] However,
some of the customs Weischoff identitied as purely African
can be identified with Malayo-Polynesian culture as well,
such as royal incest and necrophagy.[5] Frobenius' view that
the Malayo-Polynesian influence spread across Africa overland
via two routes (one from the Somali coast to the West African
coast, a second from the Mozambique coast to the Congo
Basin) possibly could be supported by the observation of a

25

British surveyor in West Africa during the early eighteenth
century who spoke of seeing "Malayans" who left their
homeland to escape Dutch rule and, reaching the Somali
coast, became engaged in the slave trade resulting in their
taking long journeys across the African continent.[6] Such a
phenomenon in the eighteenth century could be construed as
evidence that similar developments had taken place much
earlier.[7] A more satisfactory view, however, in the light
of cultural evidence extant in Africa as well as what is known
of the seafaring predilections of the ancient Malayo-
Polynesians, is that the Malayo-Polynesians reached the
Congo Basin and the West African coast by sea.[8]

Aside from musical instruments and tuning scales,
Jones also finds convincing evidence of cultural identity in
the areas of shipping and canoes, board games, the bellows,
artistic patterns, the use of bronze, names of metals,
ethnographic traditions, funeral rites, and head-hunting.[9]
In addition to the cultural items listed by Jones, the following,
presently confined to Madagascar, are provided by H.
Deschamps: wet rice agriculture, clothing styles, cooking
utensils, jewelry, harpoons and the assagai (a kind of spear),
the blowgun, freedom and high position of women, geometric
designs, ancestor worship, spiritual "possession," taboos,
and tomb styles.[10] Thus it would appear that the survival of
Malayo-Polynesian culture on Madagascar is simply the most
visible witness of a cultural world that once stretched as far
as West Africa.

Modern scholarship[11] has made it clear that mythic
themes represent thought patterns structured by relationships
among men and between men and their natural environment.
Myths arise from the application of particular thought patterns
to categories of knowledge which are important within a
specific culture. Like any form of expression, myths are
symbolic abstractions; they express values which explain and
legitimize a particular cultural orientation. If a culture
develops certain attitudes toward political authority, the
forces of nature, the miracle of birth, or whatever, these
attitudes must be expressed in order to validate the day to
day usages upon which these attitudes are based; such was
the necessity of ancient myth, it quenched the thirst for

cultural direction and was comparable to what we in modern times call an ideology. Thus, if similar mythic themes have survived in several different localities, it can be concluded that they are linked to a common cultural base.

In an article published in 1925, Jean Przyluski compared myths from India, China, and all regions of Southeast Asia which share the theme of sovereignty being transmitted by a woman who originates from the sea.[12] Pointing out that this theme is directly opposed to the continental and patriarchal cultures of the Indo-Aryans and the Chinese, Przyluski attributes it to a prehistoric maritime civilization in Southeast Asia "whose hearth was not localized but whose force of expansion was considerable," which spread into southern and eastern China and into the Indian sub-continent exclusive of the Indus Valley. A later modification of the same mythical theme dates from the spread of Indo-Aryan and Chinese culture east and south until they reached their respective geographical limits on the central coast of modern Vietnam; these myths share the theme of the marriage of a powerful newcomer with a local princess, thus founding a royal dynasty. This second theme seems to reflect the imposition of a more patriarchal concept of political organization upon the earlier myths. Vestiges of this theme come from the Former Han of China, the "barbarians" of South China, the Nan-Chao kingdom of Yunnan, the Viets of the Red River Delta, Champa on the central coast of modern Vietnam, Fu-nan in the Mekong Delta, the Khmer Empire, Laos, the Thai of the Menam Basin, the Mons of Pegu and Thaton, the Burmans of the Irrawaddy Basin, the Munda of northeast India, the Pallava and Cōḻa dynasties of South India, and the Srivijayan traditions of the island world. If the myths examined by Przyluski represent the interaction of Malayo-Polynesian peoples with the Asian continent, what can be said of Malayo-Polynesian myths that have survived in more isolated spots?

Traditions concerning the Malayo-Polynesian migrations to both Madagascar and to Easter Island have been preserved. Geographically, the two traditions represent the furthest expansion of the surviving Malayo-Polynesian peoples to the west and to the east. Chronologically, there is good reason to believe that the origins of the traditions were relatively contemporaneous. Culturally, the underlying themes of both traditions fit with what will be described as the sea-oriented nomadic culture of the ancient Malayo-Polynesians.

The indigenous myth concerning the discovery and settlement of Easter Island, as related by a native informant in 1934, [13] contains four aspects which can be usefully compared with the Malagasy myth; these are the reasons for migration, the procedure of discovery, the theme of fertility, and the concept of chieftainship.

Hotu-Matua, a chief of an island to the west of Easter Island, was forced to flee after being defeated in a war in which his brother played an ignoble role. A tattooer in Hotu-Matua's entourage had a vision of an island with six men standing on the beach. In an attempt to re-enact the vision, Hotu-Matua ordered a canoe with six men to search for the island. After the six men had discovered an island which fit the description in the vision, Hotu-Matua arrived with his entourage in a double canoe. At the moment of debarkation, the wife of Hotu-Matua and the wife of his second-in-command gave birth to a prince and princess respectively. However, Hotu-Matua's old enemy, Oroi, had stowed away aboard the canoe and fled into the rugged interior from where he frequently emerged to plague the followers of Hotu-Matua by stealing or destroying goods and ambushing unwary wanderers. Peace was established when Hotu-Matua eventually caught and killed Oroi.

The Malagasy myth is found in several versions and fragments in a number of Arabic-Malagasy texts and in Flacourt's seventeenth century Histoire de la grande isle Madagascar, which is presumably based on indigenous accounts current at his time. Gabriel Ferrand has written a fifty page article examining the myth from a textual, chronological, geographical, and genealogical point of view. [14] The chief difficulty in dealing with this myth is that the versions in which it presently exists have been Islamicized to varying degrees. There are numerous reasons, however, for regarding the Islamic elements of the myth as later accretions

to a tradition which concerns migration from Southeast Asia
to Madagascar during an earlier, pre-Islamic, period.[15]

In contrast to the Easter Island myth, there is no
question of a vision or an exploratory expedition to identify
the destination of the migration. It can be assumed that the
myth dates from a time after which Madagascar was already
well known to the migrating peoples. This may indicate that
Madagascar was familiar to the migrating peoples as part of
a trade route long before significant colonization took place;
or, as seems more likely, if trade and colonization occurred
simultaneously, the migratory tradition represents either
the lore of a particularly powerful group of colonists or the
blending of many traditions into a synthesized whole. The
reason for migration in the Malagasy myth is virtually
identical with that of the Easter Island myth; the various
versions all agree on the immediate cause being either a
defeat in war or a crisis of succession to the chieftainship.[16]
Both the Easter Island and the Malagasy myths include the
aspect of fraternal rivalry; the significance of this may be
related to an ambivalent concept of chieftainship.

A second theme shared by both myths is fertility. In
the Malagasy myth, the successful leader of the expedition
gains ascendance over rival chiefs who followed in other
canoes by tricking them into throwing their infants into the
sea to calm a tempest; he himself pretended to do the same
while merely throwing rocks overboard, thus insuring the
posterity of his entourage.[17] This concern for insuring the
posterity is paralleled by the dual births at the moment of
arrival on Easter Island.

Finally, the concept of chieftainship in both myths is
similar in that they both contain the idea of a personal
nemesis. Corresponding to the Hotu-Matua/Oroi conflict of
the Easter Island myth is the rivalry between the brothers
Racoube and Rahazi in the Malagasy myth; Racoube and his
entourage are followed by Rahazi, in fear of whom Racoube
strikes inland once he reaches Madagascar and sets himself
up in the mountains of the interior.[18]

One element of the Malagasy myth not shared with the

Easter Island myth, yet significantly shared with the myths
signalled by Przyluski is that both Racoube in the interior
and Rahazi on the coast take a local princess as a consort
and thus found a new royal house.[19] Since it is generally
agreed that the Island of Madagascar was uninhabited prior
to the arrival of the Malayo-Polynesians with their slaves
taken from the East African coast, the existence of local
princesses is further evidence that the Malagasy myth is
in a tradition originating after contact was well established
between Southeast Asia, the East African coast, and
Madagascar.

David Lewis' recent book, We, the Navigators,
examines the nature of the seafaring capabilities of the
ancient Malayo-Polynesians and the importance of these
capabilities to their culture. His conclusions, based on
personal voyages with several possessors of the old oral
navigational traditions of Polynesia and Micronesia, show
that the geographic and navigational conceptions underlying
this oral tradition, while foreign to the European mind,
are directly related to experiential observation, are at
least as effective as the more mathematical-scientific
navigational technology developed in Europe, and in many
cases are much more effective, particularly in the matter
of finding land.

An important element of the ancient art of landfinding
was the concept of "island blocks." The basis of this concept
is that swell and wave patterns, cloud formations, winds,
and bird and sea life are recognizably different in near
proximity to land and that this zone in which signs of land
can be distinguished is called an "island block." Lewis
defines an "island block" as including a 30 mile radius of
water around each island.[20] Thus, two or more islands
less than sixty miles from each other would combine to form
large "island blocks" easily distinguished by an experienced
navigator. Applying this concept to the Indian Ocean, at
least three important "island blocks" can be identified on the
route from Southeast Asia to Madagascar and the East African
coast. These are the Maldive Islands off the south-west
coast of the Indian sub-continent, the Chagos islands
approximately 500 miles south of the Maldives, and the

Seychelles approximately 950 miles west of the Chagos.
Between the northern coast of Madagascar, the East African
coast, and the Seychelles lies the Comore archipelago. The
Maldives stand midway between Sumatra and the Somali
coast, a little over 1250 miles distant from each. From what
is known of ancient navigation in Polynesia, these distances
would not have been beyond the capabilities of the ancient
Malayo-Polynesians. [21]

Lewis' most interesting chapter for our purposes is
the one in which he attempts to formulate a complex of
motivations for the voyages of the ancient Polynesians and,
in so doing, indicates important aspects of ancient Malayo-
Polynesian culture. [22] It appears that this culture was one
in which the act of taking to the sea served numerous social,
political, economic, and personal functions and was performed
with ease. An important political, economic, and social unit
was the "boatload," a relatively small group of people very
likely united by common ancestry under the quasi-democratic
rule of a council of elders which included a quasi-hereditary
chief and a number of experienced navigators. Such a group,
after reaching an uninhabited island, would tend to perpetuate
the seagoing values which had successfully carried it thither.
On the slightest pretext, whether for political, economic,
religious, or personal reasons, one or more "boatloads"
would break off and take to the sea following directions pointed
out by previous exploration or by spiritual visions. [23]

The assumption that there was a common cultural
base underlying the phenomenon of Malayo-Polynesian peoples
dispersing more than half-way around the globe by sea
provides a helpful context in which to place textual and
linguistic evidence. Our discussion so far indicates specific
elements of this culture. First, the culture can be referred
to as "oceanic nomadism." The ancient Malayo-Polynesians
had developed an orally preserved navigational technology
equal to the pattern of embarking on oceanic migrations in
response to economic, political, social, religious, and
personal needs. Second, this nomadic character was
complemented by political atomization. The very concept of
chieftainship contained seeds of discord and division; the basic
political unit was highly susceptible to being split into two or

32

more groups. There was a cultural antipathy to the amalgamation of manpower and a decided preference for the nomadically useful "boatload" as a political unit. Finally, because the culture was based on such atomized groupings of people and because of the hazards of oceanic travel, itself an integral part of the culture, the importance of fertility and of insuring the existence of a viable posterity was necessarily raised against the threat of extinction.[24]

II

Chinese, Arabic, and, to a lesser degree, Greek texts contain numerous references to the Malayo-Polynesian peoples. These references, however, are far from being immediately intelligible. Gabriel Ferrand has made an exhaustive study of Chinese and Arabic references, yet not without tending to be somewhat immobilized by the sheer weight of textual, linguistic, and geographical detail. However, using his studies as a point of departure and adding to them some recent conjectures of J. Innes Miller drawn from Mediterranean texts, a brief survey of the textual evidence can be assembled. Three terms found in the texts as nomenclature for Malayo-Polynesian peoples can be distinguished; these are K'un-lun, Qumr (or Komr in the now outdated transcription utilized by Ferrand), and Wāq-Wāq (or Uāq-Uāq, or Wāk-Wāk).

The name K'un-lun is found exclusively in Chinese sources except for a single passage in the Periplus of the Erythrean Sea, which dates from the middle of the second century A.D. The earliest textual appearance of the name K'un-lun [崑 崙] is in "The Tribute of Yu" of the Shu-ching, in which it appears as the name of western mountain and of a tributary tribe of barbarians who are called by the name of the mountain.[25] By no later than the third century B.C. K'un-lun had become an island in the southern seas, usually volcanic and invariably endowed with marvelous and potent powers. Into the seventh century A.D., Chinese texts referring to Fu-nan and Lin-yi (Champa) used K'un-lun variously as a linguistic and literary designation, an ethnic designation, a term of political vassalage (for peninsular dependencies of Fu-nan), a court title, a dynastic name, and a geographic feature (mountain in the case of Fu-nan, island in the case of Lin-yi). Buddhist pilgrims who travelled to India by sea in the seventh century invariable spent several years in Sumatra learning not only Sanskrit but also the "K'un-lun language." What is most significant in these texts is the frequent use of K'un-lun to designate an oceanic people who built and crewed sea-going vessels engaged in international trade.[26] It is in this same role as oceanic commercial carriers between China and the West that the K'un-lun appear in the Periplus.[27] Post-T'ang texts use the name K'un-lun with a significant shift of emphasis. Rather than referring specifically to Fu-nan (which, in any case, has passed from the scene by this time), to Champa, or to Srivijaya (Sumatra), the K'un-lun peoples and the various mountains, islands, and oceans called K'un-lun are now located farther out from the coasts into the sea. Locations east of Champa and of Java and far to the south-west (described in such a way as to make an identification with East Africa and Madagascar unmistakable) reveal that by this time, the Chinese notion of the K'un-lun is essentially that of peoples and places off the beaten track, just beyond the normal sea routes.[28] Thus, to the Chinese, K'un-lun was originally a tribal name associated with a western mountain in the vicinity of present day Tibet. It later became associated with coastal and island peoples of Southeast Asia, often in the proximity of a volcanic island, who were adept at oceanic navigation. Finally, the K'un-lun fade into the sea to distant isles, including Madagascar, just beyond the reach of ordinary travel.

The Qumr of Arabic sources provides an interesting comparison with the Chinese K'un-lun. However, as the etymology of the name Qumr is unusually complex, a few introductory remarks are in order. Ptolemy recorded a Greek transcription of a Bantu name to designate the mythical mountain at the source of the Nile River. The original Bantu name included the meaning of "moon." This meaning was transmitted via Ptolemy to the Arabs who transcribed the pertinent name as Qumr. In the way, the Arabs knew the mountain at the source of the Nile as the Mountain of Qumr (Mountain of the Moon). Furthermore, the Arab name for Madagascar was the Island of Qumr (Island of the Moon);

for reasons not explicit, the Arabs associated Madagascar
with the region at the source of the Nile. In addition, the
Arabs confounded the Khmers of Cambodia with Qumr of
Africa and Madagascar. Finally, the Arabs designated the
Qumr/Khmers as ethnic brothers of the Chinese.[29] With
these few prefatory remarks, the Arab story concerning the
origins of the Qumr people can be understood. The story is
as follows. Both the Chinese and the Qumr are descended
from a grandson of Noah who reached the Far East by sea
in a boat modelled on the more famous vessel built by his
grandfather. The Chinese and the Qumr lived together on
the mainland of Asia until discord and division resulted in
the Qumr being chased to the coastal and island regions
where they dwelt for a time under a king with the title of
Ḳāmrūn. After a time, discords and divisions arose, and
the faction not belonging to the royal family took to the sea
and migrated to the Island of Qumr (Madagascar). Further
discords and divisions resulted in many of them migrating
to the East African coast and hinterland where they gave their
name to the mountains at the source of the Nile.[30]

This story contains three important points of contact
with themes previously mentioned in this discussion. First,
the theme of political discord and atomization corresponds
with the migratory traditions from Madagascar and Easter
Island as well as the ambivalent concept of chieftainship
found in those traditions and the causes given for the
migrations. Second, the Arab story concerning the origins
of the Qumr and their association with the African continent
fits with the cultural evidence assembled by Jones et al.
indicating a significant Malayo-Polynesian penetration of
the continent itself. Finally, the theme of the Qumr migrating
off the Asian continent after an unhappy relationship with
the Chinese, sojourning for a time in the coastal and island
areas under a king named Ḳāmrūn, and finally splitting up
with one faction migrating to Madagascar and East Africa is
paralleled by the K'un-lun of the Chinese texts who first
appear as a tributary tribe in the western mountains, then
as the coastal and island peoples associated with Fu-nan,
Lin-yi, and Srivijaya, and finally as dispersed peoples who
reached as far as Madagascar and East Africa. Ferrand
believes that an etymological connection can be made between

Ḵāmrūn and K'un-lun.[31] He also points out that the Arabs
knew Ḵāmrūn as the name of a king who ruled in Cambodia.[32]
He further believes that the Arabs confused the later Khmer
peoples with their predecessors in the Mekong delta and
adjoining areas, the K'un-lun of Fu-nan and Lin-yi; this
confusion naturally arose from the phonetical similarity of
Khmer and Qumr as well as from Arab notions of geography
discussed below.[33]

The origins of the word Qumr, however, continue to
be unclear. The use of Qumr by the Arabs to designate
ethnic brothers of the ancient Chinese and their use of this
designation to explain the name of the mountain at the source
of the Nile, a name seemingly derived from indigenous Bantu
via Greek, would seem to be unexplainable without assuming
that the Arabs had specific reasons for associating areas of
East Africa with peoples of Asian origin. For reasons
already considered, such an assumption poses no difficulty.
A remaining question, however, is what, if any, significance
can be drawn from the meaning of Qumr as "moon." Like
the Chinese K'un-lun, the Arabic Qumr can designate either
a mountain or an island, but there is no evidence that the
meaning of K'un-lun has anything to do with "moon." Other
than as a geographic, linguistic, or ethnic name, it appears
that K'un-lun held no more than the connotation of the color
black to both the Chinese and Japanese (for instance, the
Japanese name for eggplant in the literary style is the
"K'un-lun gourd"). The Vietnamese Côn-lôn appears only
as a proper name derived from the Chinese classics. It is
likely that the "moon" idea is local to East Africa and
Madagascar insofar as the Bantu word from which the Greek
and Arabic Qumr is derived does mean "moon" to this day.[34]
The Qumr of the Arabs, then, coincides with the K'un-lun of
the Chinese as what can be taken to be a linguistic and cultural
term descriptive of peoples who took to the sea at an early
date, provided the human resources for the kingdoms of
Fu-nan, Lin-yi, and Srivijaya, and, displaying a tendency
toward political atomization, dispersed across the sea as
far as Madagascar and East Africa. Chinese sources indicate
that the K'un-lun were also found to the east of Java, the
only textual reference to the long trail leading to Easter
Island.

Map 1:

PTOLEMY'S OCEANUS INDICUS

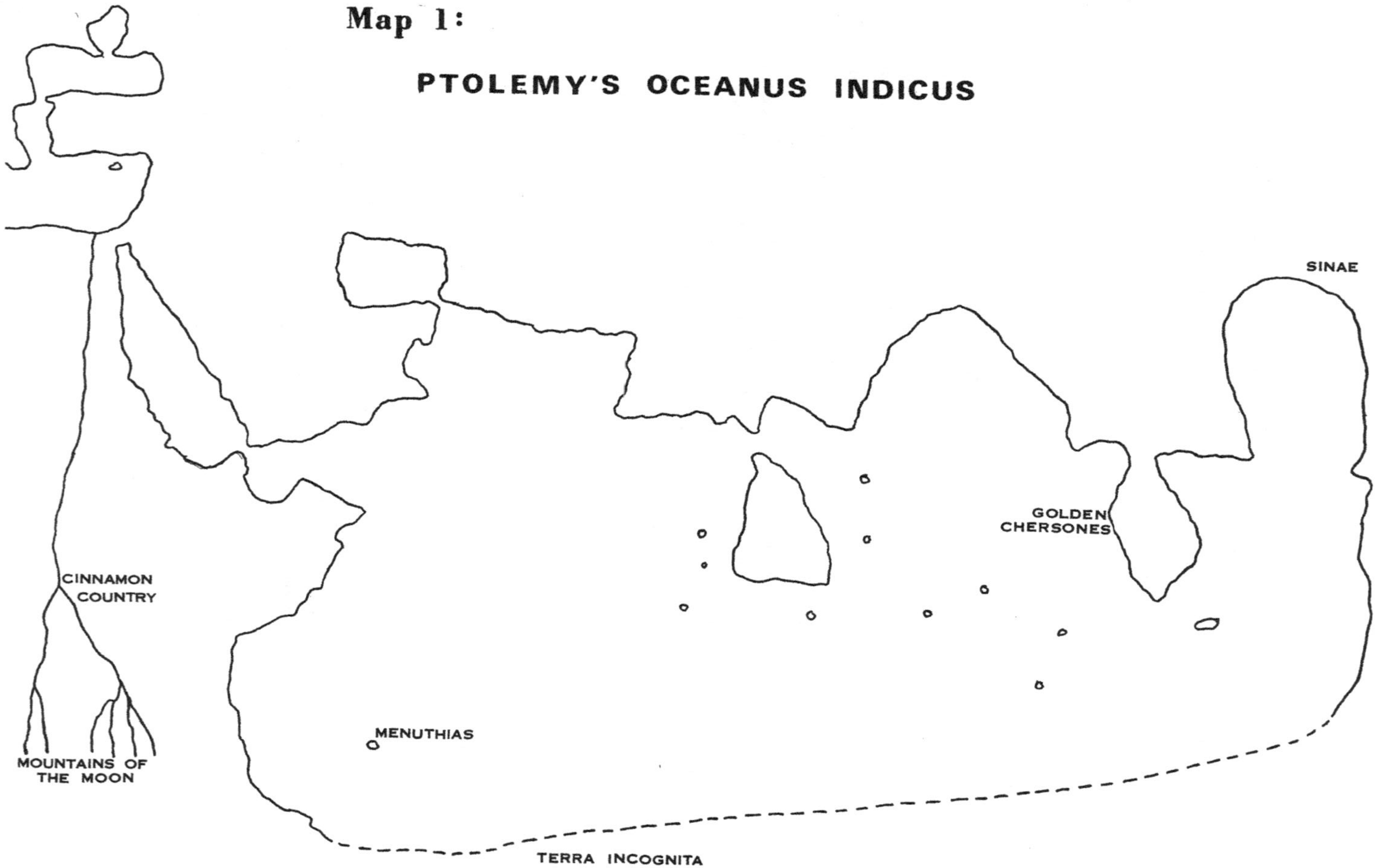

SINAE

GOLDEN CHERSONES

MENUTHIAS

CINNAMON COUNTRY

MOUNTAINS OF THE MOON

TERRA INCOGNITA

The Arab term Wāq-Wāq appears later than Qumr and persists after Qumr has fallen into disuse. The basic idea behind Wāq-Wāq appears to be geographic and is closely related to the prevailing Arabic conception of the Indian Ocean and the various islands and coasts found in and around it. Arab geographers, until the penetration of the Indian Ocean by the Portuguese, conceived of the Indian Ocean in Ptolemaic terms as a closed sea with Africa and Asia meeting in its southern extremities. [35] This geographical concept is illustrated in Map 1, which represents Ptolemy's view of the extremities of Africa and Asia and their juncture in a southern "terra incognita." [36] The Arabs improved on Ptolemy's map by adding to it their knowledge of the islands of Southeast Asia and of Madagascar with the smaller islands in the western part of the ocean. [37] However, they retained the basic notion of a closed sea. The implication of this was that the regions lying at the extreme limits of their knowledge in both Africa and Asia tended to be placed together. This meant the use of a single name to designate both Madagascar and Japan: the name was Wāq-Wāq.

Wāq-Wāq apparently had its origin as the Arabic transcription of a native Malagasy tribal name which also meant "kingdom, people, subjects" in the Malagasy language. [38] Wāq-Wāq subsequently became the Arabic transcription of the Cantonese name for Japan. [39] The coincidence of the two names was not only phonetic; it also fit well with the Arabic notion of geography. Wāq-Wāq eventually became the designation for all the little-known islands thought to extend between Madagascar and Japan just beyond the normal trade route, including Borneo and the Philippines. [40] This use of the name Wāq-Wāq is paralleled by the utilization of Qumr to designate not only Madagascar but also Sumatra, Java, and other islands of the Indonesian Archipelago and the tendency to equate both Qumr and Wāq-Wāq with Khmer; this equation was made not only on what were thought to be geographic grounds, but also on what are described as ethnic and cultural grounds. [41] The confusion of a volcanic island off the east coast of Africa with Krakatoa in the Sunda Straits further demonstrates the nature of Arab geographical notions. [42] To the Arabs, then, Madagascar was considered to be in the immediate vicinity of, if not

actually a part of, the Indonesian Archipelago at the same
time that it lay not far off an African coast which curved to
the east such that somewhere south of China it faded into a
"terra incognita" which lay behind a heavy screen of isles
called Wāq-Wāq. [43]

J. Innes Miller's recent book, The Spice Trade of
the Roman Empire, contains discussions based on
Mediterranean texts. In connection with Madagascar, Miller's
most pertinent postulation is a "cinnamon route" extending
directly by sea between Southeast Asia and the East African
coast over which Malayo-Polynesians were bringing cinnamon
of South Chinese origin as early as the late second millenium
B.C. The main points of Miller's argument are, briefly,
as follows. Botanical authorities agree that no species of
cinnamon is indigenous to Africa nor was it commercially
cultivated there at any time. [44] Ancient Egyptian texts as
well as Phoenician sources and Hebrew texts dating from the
late second millenium and early first millenium B.C. refer
to the importation of cinnamon from locations along the east
coast of Africa. [45] The Greek word for cinnamon is derived
from Malayo-Polynesian through Phoenician and pre-Exilic
Hebrew literature. [46] The specific terminology used to
designate the cinnamon of these early texts indicates that its
origin is in South China. [47] Herodotus (5th century B.C.)
designated the upper Nile (Ethiopia) as the source of cinnamon
yet states that the spice itself grew in a land to the east.
Strabo (early Roman Empire) located the so-called "cinnamon-
bearing country" in eastern and central Africa near the source
of the Nile. [48] (It is noteworthy to compare the cinnamon
country of Herodotus and Strabo with the Arabic association
of this very region with Madagascar and Southeast Asia by
use of the name Qumr.) Pliny (1st century A.D.) wrote that
cinnamon was obtained in Ethiopia from traffickers who had
bought it from their neighbors; these in turn obtained it from
others, who, in Pliny's words,

> bring it over vast seas on rafts which have no rudders
> to steer them or oars to push or pull them or sails or
> other aids to navigation; but instead only the spirit
> of man and human courage. What is more, they put
> out to sea in winter around the time of the winter

solstice, when the east winds are blowing their
hardest. These winds drive them on a straight
course, and from gulf to gulf. Now cinnamon is the
chief object of their journey and they say that these
merchant sailors take almost five years before they
return and that many perish. In exchange they carry
back with them glassware and bronze ware, clothing,
brooches, armlets, and necklaces. And that trade
depends chiefly on women's fidelity to fashion. [49]

Miller identifies Pliny's "raft-men" with the Malayo-
Polynesians and their "rafts" with the double outrigger canoe
which persists to this day along the coast of East Africa
opposite Madagascar. [50] Finally, Miller finds no evidence
that the particular cinnamon in question was ever an element
of trade via Ceylon or South India prior to the fourth century
A.D. [51] Previous to this time, the sole source was from the
Malayo-Polynesians of Madagascar and East Africa; Arabian
merchants controlled the coastal cinnamon trade between
the Malayo-Polynesians and the Red Sea while the overland
trade passed from people to people, eventually reaching the
Nile valley. [52] Miller's postulated cinnamon route is the
only textually based argument for the presence of Malayo-
Polynesians in East Africa prior to the time of Christ.

An Arabic text dating from the thirteenth century is
apparently a remembrance of early Malayo-Polynesian
penetration of the western waters of the Indian Ocean. It
states that at the time of the decline of the Egyptian Empire
of the Pharaohs, Aden (commanding the southern entrance to
the Red Sea) was inhabited by fishermen until the arrival of
the Qumr (Malayo-Polynesians) in vast fleets of outrigger
canoes who expelled the fishermen, took possesssion of the
cape, established a cult on a mountain (similar to Fu-nan),
erected numerous monuments, and maintained direct (as
opposed to coastal) sea contact with Madagascar and/or
Southeast Asia. Eventually, these Qumr grew weak, lost
their seafaring skills, and were overpowered by neighboring
peoples. [53] Equating the declining Egyptian Empire of the
text with Ptolemaic Egypt, about the time of Christ, both
Ferrand and Dahl date this Qumr invasion in the first
centuries of the Christian era. [54] It would seem that the

Malayo-Polynesians must have already been well established
on Madagascar and/or the adjacent African coast prior to
carrying out the invasion of Aden; the size of the attacking
fleet and the ability to possess the land indicate a less remote
base of operations than Southeast Asia. Aden was a strategic
location for international trade and its colonization by the
Qumr is further evidence of the commercial nature of
Malayo-Polynesian expansion across the Indian Ocean. [55]

III

The lexicostatistical and glottochronological methods
of linguistic analysis have not yet established themselves as
unambiguously reliable guides. A major problem with work
done on the Malayo-Polynesian languages is that the quality
of available vocabulary lists has not always been equal to
the computer technology utilized. It must be remembered
that conclusions drawn on the basis of these methods are
still vulnerable to serious challenge within the linguistic
discipline. Such conclusions are worthwhile, however, when
their broad outlines are confirmed by evidence from other
disciplines. Let us examine these linguistic methods and
their conclusions to see if they can be related to the cultural
and textual evidence already discussed.

In 1965, Isidore Dyen published the results of his
lexicostatistical classification of Austronesian languages. [56]
The lexicostatistical method is simply a comparison of
basic vocabulary shared by related languages to determine
a scheme of linguistic parentage (that is, a relative sequence
of linguistic diversification). Based on his classification,
Dyen concludes that the linguistic homeland of the far flung
languages in question lies in the area of the island of New
Guinea. However, a second possible homeland indicated by
his classification is the island of Formosa. In the current
state of linguistic theory, the Formosan hypothesis poses
more difficulties than does the New Guinea hypothesis,
though Dyen states that further research in the area of
phonological mergers may well strengthen the Formosan
claim. [57] Dyen theorizes that the earliest distribution of
the Austronesian languages extended from Formosa to

New Guinea and included most of Micronesia and Melanesia.
From the area of New Guinea, the only significant sub-class
of Austronesian, the Malayo-Polynesian sub-class, spread
east into Polynesia (classified as Heonesian), west into the
Moluccas, and north-west into the Sulu Sea (North Borneo
and the southern Philippines), the latter being designated as
the Hesperonesian sub-class of the Malayo-Polynesian sub-
class. It is from Hesperonesian that the languages of the
Philippines are derived. Hesperonesian itself spread south
and west giving rise to all of the Malay and Dayak languages,
Bugi (Celebes), Cham and related languages found in present
day southern Vietnam, and Malagasy.

Malagasy, however, along with its closely related
sister language in south-central Borneo, Maanyan, occupies
a unique position in Hesperonesian. Malagasy and Maanyan
are together called the Malagasic Cluster. The Malagasic
Cluster appears to be a link not only between mother
Hesperonesian and the daughter languages of the Philippines
and of North Borneo but also between Bugi and the Malay
languages of Java, Sumatra, the Malay Penninsula, and the
Southeast Asian mainland.[58] Furthermore, more than any
other Hesperonesian language, the Malagasic Cluster has
retained the fundamental vowel system of old Austronesian.[59]
It is in this respect that the Malagasic Cluster presents an
interesting comparison with Easter Island. Both Malagasy
and Easter Island represent an archaic development stemming
from an early split and geographical isolation from its
nearest linguistic neighbors and thereby the retention of
more characteristics of the mother language; Dahl, in his
study of the Malagasic Cluster, compares this phenomenon
with the independent development of Icelandic with respect
to the Scandinavian languages.[60]

Dyen's lexicostatistical classification suggests that
Malagasy differentiated from the mother Hesperonesian sub-
class prior to the differentiation of its surviving sister
languages of the Southeast Asian mainland and archipelago.
Dyen attempts to explain this by postulating a late migration
from Borneo to Madagascar by a people who had remained
linguistically isolated for an extended period of time.[61]
The existence of Maanyan on Borneo might appear to support

this view if no attempt is made to explain how a people isolated
in the interior of a large island for centuries suddenly acquired
seafaring skills, took to the sea, and settled on the far side
of the Indian Ocean while remining linguistically untouched
by sister languages existing along the route. It would seem
that the existence of Maanyan in the interior of Borneo can
only represent the retreat from the sea and subsequent
isolation of a people whose kin had already disappeared into
the western waters. Borneo is thought to be the home of all
the Malayo-Polynesian (more specifically, Hesperonesian)
languages found in the Western Indonesian Archipelago and
the Southeast Asian Mainland.[62] The implications of Dyen's
classification is that the surviving languages thus derived did
not significantly differentiate until after the departure of
Malagasy from Southeast Asia; or, more accurately, they
differentiated after the isolation of the Malagasic Cluster.
As we shall see, the differentiation of modern Malayo-
Polynesian languages in Southeast Asia and the isolation of
the Malagasic Cluster may have been aspects of a single
phenomenon: the arrival of Sanskritic civilization.

Andrew Pawley has recently applied glottochronology
to Dyen's classification. In Pawley's words, glottochronology
is "a technique for dating linguistic splits based on the
assumption of a stable rate of basic vocabulary
replacement."[63] On the basis of glottochronology, Pawley
concludes that the original dispersion of the Austronesian
languages from the region of New Guinea took place no later
than 3000 B.C. and possibly much earlier.[64] By 1000 B.C.,
the Malayo-Polynesian sub-class had differentiated and the
differentiation of its three sub-classes (the languages of
Polynesia, the Moluccan languages, and Hesperonesian)
was already well advanced.[65] Pawley then concludes that
sometime after 1000 B.C. Malayo-Polynesian traders
journeyed to Indian, Arabian, and East African ports,
eventually settling the previously uninhabited island of
Madagascar. Malagasy and Maanyan split around the time
of Christ.[66] It was also around the time of Christ, or within
a few centuries, that Easter Island was settled and its language
thus differentiated from its Polynesian neighbors.[67]
Concerning the idea of New Guinea as the homeland of these
languages, Pawley states that it is not clear whether or not

New Guinea was the primary dispersal point for all
Austronesian languages, but it is certain that it was a very
early dispersal center.[68] Based on Pawley's glottochronological scheme, it was roughly in the millenium just prior to
the time of Christ that Hesperonesian (the proto-language of
the Philippine languages, the Chamic languages of the
Southeast Asian Mainland, the Bugic languages of the Celebes,
the Malay and Dayak languages of the western archipelago
and penninsula, and Malagasy) dispersed from its center in
Borneo and reached the limits of its present day geographical
distribution. A parallel development is seen in the dispersal
of Hesperonesian's sister sub-class of Malayo-Polynesian,
Heonesian, during this same millenium and the first few
centuries of the Christian era, from its departure point in
Fiji and Tonga throughout Polynesia.[69] Linguistic development
during this millenium is, of course, obscure; and the
hypothesized dates assigned to the earliest developments
cannot be regarded as anything other than a vague
approximation. However, the surviving languages found
farthest from the dispersal center (Malagasy and Easter
Island) both display an archaic development, partly imposed
by their geographic isolation from sister languages, indicating
a split from the mother language prior to the differentiation
of surviving languages located closer to the dispersal center.
The time period for the differentiation of both Malagasy and
Easter Island is in the first few centuries of the Christian
era.[70] The implication of these conclusions is that the
ancient Malayo-Polynesian seafaring nomadic culture described
near the beginning of this discussion was already well
developed by 1000 B.C. and experienced the peak of its
expansion in the few centuries preceding and following the
time of Christ. It is in this context that the K'un-lun of the
Chinese texts and the Qumr of the Arabic texts can be
placed. It is in this same context that the dispersion of
mythical themes examined by Przyluski can be placed. And,
most importantly for this discussion, it is in this context
that the Malayo-Polynesian penetration of Africa and
Madagascar can be understood. Jones' view that the Malayo-
Polynesians were in significant contact with the West African
coast is not surprising. If the Malayo-Polynesians could
reach such an improbable location as Easter Island, following
the coast of Africa would pose no problem once they had

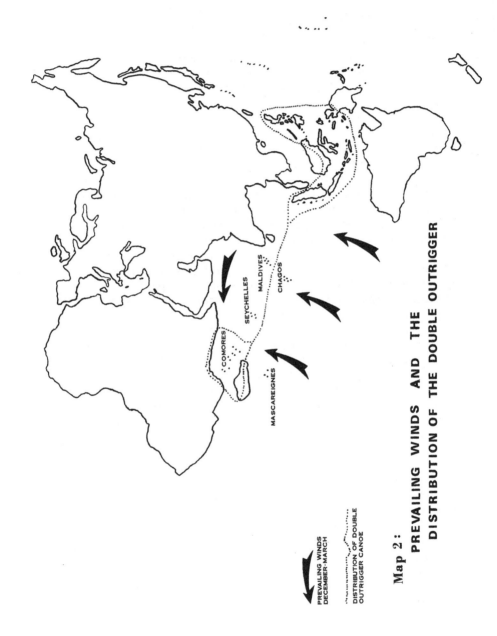

Map 2 : PREVAILING WINDS AND THE
DISTRIBUTION OF THE DOUBLE OUTRIGGER

MASCAREIGNES

COMORES

SEYCHELLES

MALDIVES

CHAGOS

PREVAILING WINDS
DECEMBER-MARCH

DISTRIBUTION OF DOUBLE
OUTRIGGER CANOE

reached Madagascar and East Africa.

Pliny's description from the 1st century A.D. of the
"raft-men" (Malayo-Polynesians in double outrigger canoes)
includes the information that they "put out to sea around the
time of the winter solstice, when the east winds are blowing
their hardest; these winds drive them on a straight course...
from gulf to gulf." Pliny's information dates from a time
when the sea route between Southeast Asia and East Africa
was well established and regularly used for commercial
purposes. How long this route had been in use before
Pliny's time and how the route came into use remain matters
of conjecture, though Miller's argument tends to support
an earlier date than has previously been considered possible.
The route as described by Pliny, however, is itself not
difficult to trace. Map 2 illustrates the winds in the Indian
Ocean during the season indicated by Pliny as well as areas
in which the outrigger canoe survives to this day. The east
wind referred to by Pliny is the south-east monsoon. This
wind would persist until one was well past the Maldives and
Chagos Islands at which point it would give way to a north-
easterly wind blowing off the Indian subcontinent towards
the East African coast north of Madagascar.

The route postulated by Miller displays an unwarranted
preference for a straight line to Madagascar, as opposed to
the East African coast in the vicinity of Zanzibar which Miller
himself identifies as the ancient entrepot of the pertinent
coastal trade between the Malayo-Polynesians and the
Arabs.[71] Linguistic evidence indicates that the earliest
habitation of Madagascar was on its west coast.[72] This
favors the view that the Malayo-Polynesians did not come
directly to Madagascar from Southeast Asia but rather
reached the island subsequent to their exploration of the
East African coast. The ancient navigational concept of
island blocks described by David Lewis would also favor a
more northern route via the Seychelles and Comores Islands.
Three further factors discount a direct route to Madagascar.
First, the Mascareignes Islands to the east of Madagascar
were uninhabited and bereft of any evidence of human
habitation at the time of the discovery by Europeans.
Second, the outrigger canoe is not found on the east coast

of Madagascar. Third, the south-east monsoon would tend
to encourage a more northerly route. Pliny's reference to
a straight course "from gulf to gulf" could imply knowledge
of a route which avoided the Bay of Bengal and the Arabian
Sea, or, perhaps, skirted the outer limits of these bodies of
water. The first part of the journey from Southeast Asia to
the island blocks of the Maldives or the Chagos poses no
difficulty. As for the last part of the journey, Ferrand, who
lived for many years in Madagascar, prefers a route from
the Maldives (or the nearby Ceylonese and South Indian
coasts) directly to the East African coast north of the
Comores, perhaps, but not necessarily, by way of the
Seychelles. [73]

Attention has already been drawn to the temporary
Malayo-Polynesian occupation of Aden; Ferrand believes
that other such probes along the Arabian and African coasts
may have occured and draws from this the conclusion that
the original route was along the coasts and that oceanic routes
were later developed to provide more direct contact between
the coasts thus discovered. [74] This idea is certainly
reasonable, but it should be remembered that in Polynesia
the Malayo-Polynesians required no guiding coastline to
lead the way; on the other hand, there were no guiding
coastlines in Polynesia whereas in the Indian Ocean one would
tend to see no reason to go the hard way into unknown waters
as long as there was a handy coastline. However the sea
route was first developed, whether by oceanic exploration or
by coastal exploration and subsequent development of the
route to connect the coasts, it appears that it reached
Madagascar from the north and west rather than from the
east.

Ferrand states that monsoon navigation between the
Maldives, Madagascar, and the Aden/Somali region at the
entrance to the Red Sea is a natural pattern. [75] This may
explain the attempt of the Malayo-Polynesians to occupy
Aden. In any case, once Madagascar was discovered by
the Malayo-Polynesians, it undoubtedly became their primary
center of settlement. Uninhabited prior to their arrival and
isolated from potential threats, the Madagascar settlements
would not have faced the dangers from hostile neighbors

such as overtook the Aden colony. From what is known of
the navigational talents and exploratory impulses of the
Malayo-Polynesians in Polynesia, there is nothing surprising
about the idea of contacts radiating from the Madagascar base
to all the coasts of sub-Sahara Africa. Any attempt to probe
north of this would, like the Aden colony, eventually fall
prey to Mediterranean-connected powers; this factor in itself
can explain the existance of a sea route which avoided the
Arabian Sea.

To return to linguistic analysis, one final area needs
to be examined; this is the presence of thirty words of
Sanskritic origin in the Malagasy language. Otto Dahl is
the most recent linguist to compare Malagasy with Maanyan
and other Malayo-Polynesian languages. Dahl separates
the thirty words of Sanskritic origin into three categories.
Thirteen words are of a religious or political nature and
imply some form of court life. [76] Ten words are calendar
words (names of months and seasons) and display a connection
with Sanskritic loan words in Old Javanese. Seven words can
be described as commercial terms; these are: ten thousand,
debt, balance or remainder (of a sum of money), glass or
bottle, betel, lemon/acid/vinegar, and ginger. [77] Malagasy
shares all of these Sanskritic loan words except ginger with
other Malayo-Polynesian languages of Southeast Asia. [78]
This exception may be an indication of the commercial nature
of the expansion to Madagascar. Whereas the Greek word for
cinnamon, as noted above, is of Malayo-Polynesian origin,
the Greek word for ginger, like the Malagasy, is derived
from Sanskrit. [79] Dahl concludes on the basis of the small
number of Sanskritic loan words in Malagasy as compared
with the much larger number of such words in other Malayo-
Polynesian languages of Southeast Asia that "the migration"
to Madagascar occurred at the very beginning of Sanskritic
influence in Southeast Asia. [80]

The least enlightening discussions in the scholarly
literature on Madagascar have centered on "the migration"
from Southeast Asia to Madagascar. I suggest that there was
no such thing as "the migration"; rather, there was a long
period of at least a millenium during which many migrations
took place, or more correctly, during which continuous

contact between Southeast Asia and Africa was maintained both in the nature of trade and of colonization. A single great migration is not necessary to explain the linguistic break occurring about the time of Christ; rather, this break reflects the impact of Sanskritic civilization on the Malayo-Polynesian people. The direction of the Sanskritic thrust was into Southeast Asia where the major entrepots were located; pre-Sanskritic tradtions survived only in the isolated interior of Borneo and in Madagascar off the African coast. But let us consider the notion of a single migration.

Assuming that "the migration" came directly from Borneo (on the grounds that Borneo is where Maanyan is presently found), Dahl then points to the earliest Sanskrit inscription found in Borneo as the key to dating the migration. He does this because the Yupa inscriptions found at Kotei in East Borneo list the names of three succeeding rulers, the first of which is of Malayo-Polynesian origin and the second and third of which are Sanskritic. Assuming that the inscriptions date from the beginning of Sanskritic influence, inasmuch as they display a transition from non-Sanskritic to Sanskritic royal names, the date of "the migration" would seem to depend on what date could be assigned to the inscriptions.

The only detailed study of these inscriptions available in a language other than Dutch is that of Vogel who, writing over fifty years ago, assigned the approximate date of A.D. 400 on palaeographical grounds. Of more interest than his self-admitted questionable chronological assignment, however, is Vogel's comparison of the Kotei inscriptions with earlier Cham inscriptions and later Javanese inscriptions. Vogel concluded that the Chams played an important role in spreading Sanskritic influence into the islands.[81] The first Sanskrit inscription of Champa can possibly be dated as early as the second century A.D.[82] On palaeographical grounds, Vogel sees a direct line of Sanskritic influence leading from South India to Champa, from Champa to East Borneo, and from East Borneo to West Java over a hundred year period.[83] Since the Malagasy language did not separate from its mother Hesperonesian until about the time of Christ and it was not until this time that significant differentiation of other

Hesperonesian languages took place, it can be postulated that in the initial period of Sanskritic influence, the languages spoken by the Malayo-Polynesians of Champa, East Borneo, and West Java were not extremely dissimilar. To select the fourth century Kotei inscription over the second century Cham inscription, then, is unwarranted on linguistic grounds in spite of the isolated survival of Maanyan in the interior of Borneo, which by itself only means that it, like Malagasy, was at an early date isolated from its sister languages.

The value of the Kotei inscriptions to our discussion is that they appear to date from the time of the Sanskritic penetration of East Borneo and thereby perhaps, but not explicitly, are contemporaneous with the isolation of Maanyan in Borneo's interior; the relevance of these inscriptions to Madagascar is simply that as Sanskrit penetrated Southeast Asia, Madagascar began its independent linguistic development. Furthermore, Hebrew literature indicates that commercial terms of Sanskritic origin were current in the Mediterranean and the Red Sea as early as the tenth century B.C.[84] Since we know that Malayo-Polynesians were in contact with the Mediterranean world as early as this time, it makes little sense to wait until Sanskritic influence filtered back from the vanguard into the home region to date this influence, particularly when the language in question, Malagasy, is itself the surviving witness of the vanguard. Compared with the Malayo-Polynesians, Indo-Aryan and Dravidian seafaring tendencies were notably low; in light of this, it might make more sense to see the Malayo-Polynesians going to India and coming back with Sanskrit than to invent Indian Sanskritizers radiating through Southeast Asia. The truth of the matter can be expected to lie somewhere between these bald extremes.

Those Malayo-Polynesians who continued beyond India to the frontier of the Mediterranean could be expected to experience some Sanskritic influences unfelt by those left behind as well as to escape other influences experienced in the lands of departure. Thus we see the Sanskrit word for ginger added to Malagasy even as it was to Greek, though not to Southeast Asian languages, as direct evidence of commercial contacts in the Arabian Sea. On the other hand, Malagasy escaped the full brunt of Sanskritic influence as it penetrated Southeast Asia. It is not until about the time of Christ or shortly thereafter that ginger is known to the Greeks.[85] Postulating a similar date for the adding of Sanskritic ginger to Malagasy coincides with Pawley's glottochronological conclusions. Thus it can be concluded that, with regard to Sanskrit as in all other regards, Malagasy began to experience a separate development from its sister languages about the time of Christ.

IV

In prehistoric times, before the Indo-Aryans appeared in North India and before Chinese civilization emerged from the headwaters of the Yellow River, a maritime civilization germinated among the peoples inhabiting the seas and islands lying between Australia and the Asian continent; these peoples became the Malayo-Polynesians. Sometime before the end of the second millenium B.C., the Malayo-Polynesians spread onto the coasts and up the river villeys of Asia and Africa introducing to these continental lands all of the distinctive characteristics of their civilization from the tuning scales of the xylophone and the outrigger canoe to the intellectual life of their mythic thought. The ancient Egyptians, Phoenicians, and Hebrews sent naval expeditions to the entrance of the Red Sea and down the East African coast to obtain exotic goods from India and beyond brought thither by the Malayo-Polynesians. As Arab power extended down the coast of East Africa during the millenium before Christ, the Malayo-Polynesians avoided the Arabian Sea and sailed directly to the African coast just beyond the reach of the Arabs from where they continued their trading activities. During this time, Madagascar became the home of Malayo-Polynesian peoples.

In the last two centuries before the Christian era, the Roman Empire united the Mediterranean while Ch'in and Han China marched down to the South China Sea. The Kushan dynasties which controlled the land routes between these two great empires were patrons of Sanskritic civilization. All of this martial energy being expended on the Eurasian and African continents had its effect on Malayo-Polynesian civilization. As Sinic civilization spread south and as Sanskritic civilization spread south and east, they encountered a maritime civilization which lacked the coercive political institutions needed to resist alien pressures, whether military or cultural.

The Chinese conquest of the northern and northwestern shores of the South China Sea was preceeded by the founding of short-lived syncretic states, Âu-Lạc in the Red River Basin and Nan Yüeh (Nam Việt) in the West River Basin, both of which to varying degrees utilized Sinic political and military concepts in the cultural environment of a maritime civilization. The mythical themes accompanying the absorption of Âu-Lạc by Nan Yüeh are, according to Przyluski, simply a Sinic version of the myth accounting for the foundation of Fu-nan in the Mekong Delta, which has been preserved in Sanskritic garb; likewise, the same myth grew out of the introduction of Sanskritic civilization into South India as well as the Isthmus of Kra and adjacent regions to the north, eventually being sculpted in bas-relief on the Bayon of Angkor Thom. The unity of these surviving myths is derived from their being rooted in Malayo-Polynesian civilization.

At the time of these developments on the Asian continent, Madagascar experienced a linguistic break (fixed by glottochronology and by the incidence of Sanskritic loan words) from Malayo-Polynesian peoples to the east. While this could be explained by a significant movement of peoples to Madagascar, the more likely explanation is a significant decrease or alteration in communication between Madagascar and the east. The spread of Sanskritic civilization into South India may suffice to account for the linguistic isolation of Madagascar at this time, but this was simply part of a larger development encompassing most of Southeast Asia. As Sanskritic civilization spread through the mainland and islands of Southeast Asia, the pre-Sanskritic linguistic traditions were retained only in the interior of Borneo where, as on Madagascar, Malayo-Polynesian peoples were isolated from the Sanskritic tide. The mythical tradition concerning migration to Madagascar is solidly within the sphere of Malayo-Polynesian civilization, a civilization whose very existence presupposes continuous seaborne migrations; we need not look for a single great migration. Madagascar's myth has as much in common with Easter Island's as it does with those of South and Southeast Asia.

Prior to the Christian era, Malayo-Polynesian peoples had advanced eastward only as far as the Tongo and Samoan Islands, on the border of modern Melanesia and Polynesia.[86] It had taken nearly a millenium to advance the 600 miles from Fiji to Samoa. The 3800 miles from Samoa to Easter Island, however, were covered by 400-450 A.D. This sudden move across the Pacific, contemporaneous with the arrival of Sanskritic civilization in Southeast Asia, seems to reflect the vigor of Malayo-Polynesian civilization at this time.[87]

Are we justified in speaking of a Malayo-Polynesian civilization? I believe that we are. Whenever we attempt to describe Southeast Asian culture we are driven to such terms as "substratum," "Little Tradition," or "indigenous," by which we mean something distinctively "Southeast Asian." Yet, like an aqueous essense, this distinctive "something" has left traces in nearly every region of Asia and Africa. The ethnological, mythological, textual, and linguistic evidence we have examined is only intelligible within the theory of a far flung prehistoric maritime civilization.[88]

Pursuing the mystery of Madagascar's Malayo-Polynesian origins lead us back to an age when the sea belonged to men who knew it intimately. In the words of one writer: "The early inhabitants of Oceana were essentially nomadic, traversing immense distances in accordance with the laws of their environment, of wind systems, currents and the migratory patterns of the animals upon which they were dependent, and discovering islands, not as Europeans discover them, by chance, but naturally where birds and fish led them."[89]

NOTES

1. The basic, though dated, study of the peoples and cultures
   of Madagascar is Alfred and Guillaume Grandidier,
   Ethnographie de Madagascar, 2 vols., Vol. IV of Histoire
   Physique, Naturelle et Politique de Madagascar (Paris,
   1908). This work, along with Arnold van Gennep, Tabou
   et Totemisme a de l'Ecole des Hautes Etudes, Sciences
   Religieuses (Paris, 1904), contains a vast amount of
   poorly interpreted detail. An extensive bibliography of
   works concerning relgious concepts and beliefs of
   Madagascar can be found in Pierre Colin, Aspects de l'Ame
   Malgache (Paris, 1959). Representative of these studies
   is Colin's book itself which is written from the perspective
   of a Christian missionary, albeit a missionary with
   knowledge of and respect for the Malagasy language and
   culture; Colin's main concern is to identify indigenous
   concepts and to relate them to a Christian cosmology.
   Another notable example is D. Ramandraivonona, Le
   Malgache, Sa Langue, Sa Religion (Paris, 1959), which
   is a unique application of linguistics to religion, resulting
   largely in various notions of geomancy.

2. A. M. Jones, Africa and Indonesia (Leiden, 1964).

3. Roger Summers, Zimbabwe (Cape Town, 1963), pp. 67-68,
   77-80.

4. Ibid., pp. 68-70.

5. Jones, op. cit., pp. 230-231. Gabriel Ferrand, "Les Iles
   Ramny, Lamery, WakWak, Komor des Geographes Arabes,
   et Madagascar," JA, X serie, 10 (1907), p. 433.

6. Jones, op. cit., pp. 232-233.

7. This theory is still popular among African scholars today:
   J. D. Fage and R. A. Oliver, eds., Papers in African
   Prehistory (Cambridge, 1970), pp. 67-68, 145-146, 148.

54

8. Ibid., p. 226.

9. Jones' conclusions accord with the suggestions made 25 years ago by the anthropologist J. H. Hulton concerning cultural affinities between West Africa and Indonesia (Ibid., p. 217). On the origins and distribution of the outrigger canoe, see James Hornell, Water Transport (Cambridge, 1946), pp. 253-271.

10. Hubert Jules Deschamps, Madagascar (Paris, 1951), p. 60; also Histoire de Madagascar, 3rd edn. (Paris, 1965), pp. 22-23.

11. Maurice Godalier, "Myth and History," New Left Review, 69 (Sept.-Oct., 1971), pp. 93-112. Henri Frankfort, Harry J. Carroll, Jr., et. al., The Development of Civilization (Glenview, Ill., 1961), pp. 41-47.

12. Jean Przyluski, "La Princesse a l'Odeur de Poisson et la Nagi dans les Traditions de l'Asie Oriental," Etudes Asiatiques (Publications, Ecole Francaise d'Extreme-Orient, vol. 19-20, 1925), vol. II, pp. 265-285.

13. Robert C. Suggs, The Island Civilizations of Polynesia (New York, 1960), pp. 173-174.

14. Gabriel Ferrand, "Les Voyages des Javanais a Madagascar," JA, X serie, 15 (1910), pp. 281-330.

15. Ibid., p. 330; Ferrand (1907), op. cit., pp. 441-445.

16. Ferrand (1910), op. cit., p. 319.

17. Ibid., pp. 290-292.

18. Loc. cit.

19. Ibid., pp. 295-296.

20. David Lewis, We, the Navigators (Honolulu, 1972), pp. 153ff.

21. Ibid., pp. 302-305. Deliberate navigation between Tahiti and Hawaii in ancient times represents a much more astounding navigational feat than anything comparable in the Indian Ocean. The complex use of stars for navigation is treated in detail by Lewis, pp. 45-81.

22. Ibid., pp. 277-292.

23. Deschamps emphasizes the importance of the nomadic impulse in the culture of Madagascar. Describing it as a "supreme law" handed down by the Malagasy ancients, Deschamps uses it to explain the continual migrations from one part of the island to another by the Malagasy peoples throughout their long history. Hubert Jules Deschamps, Les Migrations Interieures passees et presentes a Madagascar (Paris, 1959), p. 41.

24. A modern survival of this culture might be seen in the Orang Laut of the lower Malay Straits region and the Badjau of the Sulu Sea. See: Jose R. Arong, "The Badjaw of Sulu," Philippine Sociological Review, 10, 3-4 (July-October, 1962), pp. 134-147; David E. Sopher, "The Sea Nomads," Memoirs of the National Museum, No. 5 (Singapore, 1965).

25. James Legge, Chinese Classics, Vol. III, part I, p. 127. The Kunlun Mountains of Tibet have retained this ancient nomenclature. The Shu-ching dates from the middle of the first millenium B.C. but contains traditions of great antiquity.

26. Gabriel Ferrand, Le K'ouen-louen et les Ancienes Navigations Interoceaniques dans les Mers du Sud, extrait du JA (Paris, 1919), pp. 7-18.

27. Anthony Christie,, "An Obscure Passage from the Periplus," BSOAS, 19 (1957), pp. 345-353. The Greek κολανδ ιοφωντα corresponds to the Chinese K'un-lun po 崑 崙 舶 (K'un-lun boat).

28. Ferrand (1919), op. cit., pp. 18-28.

29. Ferrand (1907), op. cit., pp. 526-531.

30. Ferrand (1919), op. cit., pp. 115-116.

31. Ibid., p. 234

32. Ibid., pp. 110-111.

33. Ibid., pp. 229-239.

34. Miller's belief that K'un-lun originally derives from the Vietnamese Côn-lôn cannot be accepted inasmuch as the term first appears in the Shu-ching. See: J. Innes Miller, The Spice Trade of the Roman Empire (Oxford, 1969), p. 185. In addition to being the name variously of a continental mountain in China, of a volcanic island off the Southeast Asian coast or of peoples associated with these geographic features, the Vietnamese Côn-lôn also includes the idea of something hidden or hard to find. Trịnh yăn Thanh, Thành-Ngữ'Điên-Tích Danh-Nhân Tu'-Diên, Q. I (Saigon, 1966), p. 111.

35. Ferrand (1907), op. cit., pp. 450-451.

36. For a full discussion of Ptolemy's map of Africa and Asia, see: J. Oliver Thomson, History of Ancient Geography (Cambridge, 1948), pp. 273-278, 313-318.

37. Ptolemy's Menuthias Island (see Map 1) is most likely Zanzibar or Pemba; see: Ibid., p. 274.

38. Wāq-Wāq was also the Arabic transcription for the name of a particular tree found on Madagascar to which were attributed certain marvelous properties; see: Ferrand (1907), op. cit., pp. 483-493. Interestingly, this Malagasy tribal name also has etymological affinities with the Bantu-ized name ascribed to the people living on Madagascar at the time of the arrival of Rahdzi and Racoube in the legend already discussed; see: ibid., p. 481 and Ferrand (1910), op. cit., p. 297.

39. Ferrand (1907), op. cit., p. 474.

40. Otto Chr. Dahl, Malgache et Maanyan (Oslo, 1951), p. 363.

41. Ferrand (1907), op. cit., pp. 501-503, 542, 550.

42. Ibid., pp. 563-564.

43. Ibid., pp. 538-542. Ferrand deals briefly with one other term (Ramny/Lamery) which he identifies with Sumatra as the starting point for the migrations to Madagascar as described in the tradition already discussed; Ibid., pp. 440-450.

44. Miller, op. cit., p. 156.

45. Ibid., pp. 154-155, 171-172, 274-275.

46. Ibid., pp. 45-46.

47. Ibid., pp. 42-44.

48. Ibid., p. 155.

49. Ibid., p. 156.

50. Ibid., p. 158. Also see Map 2.

51. Ibid., pp. 158-159.

52. Ibid., p. 157. A general history of the East African kingdoms and polities through which Miller's postulated cinnamon route passed can be found in the second chapter of L. A. Thompson's Africa in Classical Antiquity (Ibadan, Nigeria, 1969), pp. 26-61.

53. Ferrand (1907), op. cit., pp. 139-147.

54. Ibid., p. 149; Dahl, op. cit., p. 364.

55. Raymond Mauny has signalled an Islamic reference to a Malay raid on the East African coast in the tenth century stemming from commercial motivations. Raymond Mauny, "The Wakwak and the Indonesian invasion in East Africa in 945 A.D.," Studia, 15 (May, 1965), pp. 7-15.

56. Isidore Dyen, A Lexicostatistical Classification of the Austronesian Languages, Memoir 19 of Indiana University

Publications in Anthropology and Linguistics, Supplement to International Journal of American Linguistics, Vol. 31, No. 1 (1965). Dyen describes the method and basic assumptions of his classification on pp. 14-25.

57. Ibid., pp. 55-57.

58. Ibid., pp. 43-44; Dahl, op. cit., p. 372.

59. Andrew Pawley, "Austronesian Languages," draft for an article to be published in the Encyclopedia Britannica, Working Papers in Linguistics, University of Auckland, Anthropology Department, January, 1971, p. 20.

60. Dahl, op. cit., p. 371.

61. Dyen, op. cit., p. 371.

62. Ibid., p. 55; Pawley, op. cit., p. 14.

63. Ibid., p. 6.

64. Ibid., p. 5.

65. Ibid., pp. 6-7.

66. Ibid., p. 14.

67. Ibid., p. 35.

68. Ibid., p. 23.

69. Ibid., p. 6.

70. Glottochronology indicates A.D. 400 as the time of differentiation for Easter Island (See: Roger Green and Andrew Pawley, The Linguistic Sub-groups of Polynesia, Polynesian Society Reprints No. 11, from The Journal of the Polynesian Society, Vol. 75, No. 1 (Wellington, 1966), p. 31.

71. Miller, op. cit., p. 165.

72. Dahl, op. cit., p. 365.

73. Ferrand (1919), op. cit., p. 150.

74. Ibid., p. 149, n. 5.

75. Ibid., p. 146, n. 2.

76. The thirteen words are: to work/do, royal/public palace/ pavillion, cloud, monster that causes eclipses by devouring the sun/moon, friend/servitor, slave/comrade/relative, arm/articulation/liason, particle denoting accomplishment/ superlative/because, paddy/pond/lake, to tell a story, to judge/deliberate, proper or correct behavior, to examine or survey.

77. Ibid., pp. 97-104.

78. Ibid., p. 367.

79. Miller, op. cit., p. 56.

80. Dahl, op. cit., p. 367.

81. J. Ph. Vogel, "The Yupa Inscriptions of King Mulavarman, from Koetei (East Borneo)," Bijdragen Tot de Taal-land-En Volkenkunde van Nederlandsch-Indie, 74 (1918), p. 187.

82. Ibid., p. 188.

83. Ibid., p. 231.

84. Miller, op. cit., p. 263.

85. Ibid., pp. 56-57.

86. This reconstruction of the Polynesian expansion is derived from Roger Green who based his interpretation on the work not only of the linguist Andrew Pawley and the archeologist Robert C. Suggs, but of numerous other scholars, anthropologists as well as archeologists and linguists. Roger Green and Andrew Pawley, op. cit., pp. 3-35.

87. On ancient navigation in the Pacific, see David Lewis, op. cit., and Jack Golson, ed., Polynesian Navigation, A Symposium on Andrew Sharp's Theory of Accidental Voyages (Wellington, 1963), especially pp. 11-63, 68-79, 125-131.

88. We have not discussed religious cults and beliefs but work done in this area confirms the broad outlines of the picture we have drawn. See: P. Mus, "Cultes Indiens et Indigenes au Champa," BEFEO, 33 (1933), pp. 367-410. J. H. Hutton has discussed cultural traits shared by Assam and the island world stretching from Madagascar to Samoa in "Assam Origins in Relation to Oceana," Journal of the Burma Research Society, 51, 2 (December, 1968), pp. 97-122.

89. Golson, op. cit., p. 63.

State and Statecraft in Early Srivijaya

by
Kenneth R. Hall

As depicted by O. W. Wolters, the prosperity of early
Southeast Asian trade centers was quite dependent on the
fluctuations of the international markets, expecially those of
China. Based upon his study of the pattern of tribute missions
to the Chinese court, Wolters has defined the response of
the international commercial environment to the opening and
closing of Chinese markets as a "rhythm of trade."[1] Between
the seventh and the eleventh centuries, Wolters portrays the
trading pattern as having been interrupted only when the
Chinese emperors were unable to control their port at Canton.
The Chinese government wanted east-west trade to flow
smoothly and viewed Southeast Asia an an area of barbarians,
an unstable region which presented a threat to the trade route.
In these times the island region of Southeast Asia was a key
zone in the international trade network connecting East and
West. Chinese officials thus looked for a dominant, strong
state in the area to maintain the flow of trade. As the Chinese
sought trade, the Southeast Asian states asked for political
assistance or the bestowal of legitimacy in return. A state's
ability to claim preferred treatment in commercial dealing
with China undoubtedly added to the prestige and power of
its ports.

Wolters' study of tribute missions indicates that
periods when many Southeast Asian states sent tribute
alternated with periods when only one state was sending
tribute. Periods of few Chinese missions indicated relative
stability of the area, while periods of many missions
represented times of political and economic competition when
several states appealed for Chinese patronage. In times when
China was especially interested in trade--when Canton was
controlled by a new and stable imperial government--local
Southeast Asian ports attempted to emerge as the "central
port" of their area.

61

GULF
OF SIAM

SOUTH CHINA SEA

MALAY

PENINSULA

STRAIT OF MALACCA

SUMATRA

Karimun Besar

RIAU ARCHIPELAGO

LINGGA ARCHIPELAGO

BORNEO

BATANG HARI RIVER

Muara Jambi

Jambi-
Malayu

Karang
Brahi

BANGKA

Kotakapur

N

MUSI RIVER

Bukit Segutang

Tanah
Abang

Palembang

Japara

JAVA SEA

Map 3:
WESTERN INDONESIA
IN THE EARLY
SRIVIJAYA PERIOD

Palas Pasemah

SUNDA STRAITS

Tjibuaja

JAVA

Prambanan

0 50 100 200 km SCALE

During the period 670-1025 A.D., the southern Sumatra
thalassocracy of Srivijaya appears to have been the power
which dominated maritime commerce passing through
Southeast Asia. Srivijaya gained control of the seas in the
vicinity of the Straits of Malacca, put down piracy and
competition, and established a cosmopolitan trading center
on the "favored coast" of southeastern Sumatra, a position
standing between the flow of international trade and the
wealth of Java and beyond. The ports of Srivijaya then
furnished supplies, local products, Chinese and western
goods, storage facilities, and hostelries for waiting out the
monsoon season to passing traders. China's trade with the
Malay Peninsula and beyond now came to be focussed on the
Srivijaya ports as the ports of the Kra Isthmus, the principle
entrepôts of earlier east-west trade, became secondary
and under a loose Srivijaya control. [2]

Wolters has described the classical maritime state of
Srivijaya as a "federation of trading ports on the fringe of
large areas of forest. . . . Srivijaya was not a state with
territorial boundaries, but a series of interlocked human
relationships among harbor principalities and pirate lairs
based on patronage, loyalty, and power." [3] In Wolters'
structure, there were three zones of dependencies: the Malay
Peninsula, where Srivijaya's dominance was not continuous;
the north and northeast coasts of Sumatra, which supplied
raw materials for international trade; and the east coast and
island area near Palembang which became the heartland of
the empire's power. This heartland was supported by a group
of sea nomads whose power was measured in the number of
ships under their control. Wolters' thesis is that a Southeast
Asian harbor area such as Palembang could, by the support of
a group such as the sea nomads, establish its autonomy
within its own domain and then spread its influence outward
along the sea coast to encompass other similarly structured
harbor ports. Civilized port zones were surrounded by tribal
peoples of the interior who supplied the ports with raw
materials, but were in general feared. Wolters notes that
the central Sumatran port of Jambi did not attempt to collect
taxes from the population outside its own town boundaries. [4]
In his analysis such ports had no need for an agrarian base.
The local ruler looked elsewhere for his revenues--

essentially to the sea.

Wolters' emphasis on the thalassocratic aspect of
Srivijaya is in the main correct, but tends to neglect the
important relationship between the Srivijaya ports and their
hinterland. For instance the Bukit Seguntang inscription, the
earliest of the known Old Malay inscriptions left by the
Srivijaya empire, states that on April 23, 683 A.D., the king
of Srivijaya embarked in a boat to go on a siddhayātra, and
that on May 19 he conducted an army of twenty thousand
men from one place and arrived at another. This army
included about 200 sailors and 2,000 foot soldiers.[5] Since
a force of 2,000 foot soldiers must have been recruited from
the interior, this inscription does not seem to indicate a lack
of interaction between the port city and its hinterland, but
rather the opposite.

As further evidence of a Srivijaya hinterland, the
Arab geographer Abu Zayd (916) stated in his observation of
the local settlement pattern that "the isle of the Maharaja has
one village after another" between the coast and the port city
of Palembang.[6] As one cock crowed another would pick up
the crow until the capital was reached. Abu Zayd also noted
that one could always find a spot to rest or a place to lodge.
This information is supported by the limited archeological
research that has been conducted in the area of Palembang
and its river estuaries. Remains of the Srivijaya period
indicate that Srivijaya's culture penetrated deeply into the
interior not only along the rivers which flowed to Palembang,
but also along those which flowed through other contemporary
commercial centers on both the island of Sumatra and the
Malay Peninsula.[7]

Both Arab and Chinese documents record that Srivijaya
was the source of forest products and aromatics,[8] yet the
southeastern Sumatra coast was not strategically located to
control the internal origin of these rich natural resources
which came from north and central Sumatra. The importance
of these products to the international commercial community
would have caused the shift of the center of trade to ports of
these other areas if Srivijaya failed to supply the demand.
Wolters, by his neglect, has implied that there were no formal

political alliances which generated the flow of products to Srivijaya's ports. Yet the nature of the goods required a regular, ongoing relationship with the hinterland to allow goods to reach the ports. The general ambiguity of foreign sources when describing the Sumatra interior suggests that visiting merchants did not make direct contact with the hinterland. Thus it may be assumed that the flow of goods to Srivijaya's ports was organized as either a tribute system in which subordinate chiefs were required to supply the Srivijaya ports with marketable commodities, or that Srivijaya came to control an indigenous trade cycle in which people of the interior exchanged forest products they had collected for the imported goods which were available in coastal ports.

We should thus examine Srivijaya's hinterland to determine if it was a significant part of the Srivijaya state and establish, if possible, the degree to which the Srivijaya king ruled in accordance with the traditions of this hinterland. The Srivijaya king was honored as "Lord of the Mountain" and "Mahārāja of the Isles," terms which seem to have much traditional content. The ability of the Srivijaya kings to synthesize hinterland cultural symbols to new systems of legitimacy is depicted in their inscriptions. The Ligor Plate inscription of 775, recording the dedication of a sanctuary near Nakhon Si Thammarat on the eastern coast of the Malay Peninsula to the Buddha and to the Bodhisattvas Padmapāni and Vajrapāni, refers to the Srivijaya king as "the patron of the nagas, their heads halved by the streaks of the lustre of gems."[9] We can see a similar association in the seventh century Telagu Batu inscription carved on a Buddhist ceremonial stone, the upper edge of which is canopied by the heads of seven serpents (nāgas). A funnel below the text drained water which was poured over the stone during the ceremonies.[10] Since the seven-headed nāga is a well-known symbol in Indian iconography it could well be argued that in this instance a wholesale borrowing of an Indic image had taken place and that it had become an important part of the Srivijaya system of statecraft. But local evidence suggests that the seven-headed nāga of Indic tradition fits with indigenous patterns of belief. The Srivijaya king may thus be seen syncretizing both local and foreign patterns in creating his own royal style.

According to Chau Ju-kua's early thirteenth century account, the Srivijaya king could not eat grain on a specific day of the year. If he did, the year would be dry and grain dear. Another instance of the Srivijaya monarch holding the fortune of his people is also reported: the king could only bathe in rose-water; if he should use ordinary water there would be a great flood.[11] It is interesting that a similar tradition was preserved into the nineteenth century among the Lampongs of southern Sumatra. As reported by William Marsden in the History of Sumatra, "The island people of that country are said to pay a kind of adoration to the sea, and make it offerings...deprecating its power of doing them mischief."[12] The Arab geographers Ibn Khurdadhbih (846) and Abu Zayd both spoke of the "Mahārāja" communicating with the sea. Daily the Mahārāja of Srivijaya propitiated the ocean by throwing a gold brick into the water, saying, "Look, there lies my treasure," and demonstrating his debt to the sea.[13]

One can postulate the effect of the 1025 Cōḷa invasion on Srivijaya's capital. If Srivijaya defined its position in traditional Sumatran terms as is being suggested, then the "destruction of the center" would have had a tremendous psychological impact. The Tanjore inscription of Rājēndra Cōḷa (1030/31) referred to the conquest of the Srivijaya capital and its treasury as if this symbolized the destruction of the source of Srivijaya's legitimacy and power.[17] The old prosperity and control were never regained. By 1079-1082, the capital had moved to the central Sumatra port of Jambi.[18] Java had become a "dominant port" area and the ports of northern Sumatra and the Malay Isthmus were beginning to function independently as alternative "centers." O. W. Wolters, in his analysis of the Sejarah Malayu, particularly its value in determining the rise of Malacca in the fourteenth and fifteenth centuries, suggests that Malacca genealogies were purposely connected to Srivijaya-Palembang and not to Srivijaya-Jambi.[19] This would substantiate the success of the Palembang monarchs in building a political network within the context of Malay-Sumatran culture. Despite its political demise, Srivijaya-Palembang was still a viable symbol of Malay unity and common prosperity.

This paper will focus on the earliest period of
Srivijaya's history--the late seventh century--to examine the
methods used by the Srivijaya monarch to appeal to the
indigenous population of Sumatra. It is from this period that
most of the inscriptions left by Srivijaya's kings have come.
There are only two known sources for the study of the
structure of Srivijaya's early statecraft. One is the extremely
generalized Arab account of the redistribution of gold bars
which had been thrown into the Palembang harbor at the death
of each Mahārāja.[20] According to this account the greatness
of a deceased king was measured by the number of gold bars
dredged from the water. These were divided first among the
royal family, then the military commanders, and finally
what remained was to be given to the king's other subjects.
While giving little elaboration of these "class" distinctions,
the hierarchy depicted in this account is consistent with the
Telagu Batu inscription which has served as the main source
for the analysis of Srivijaya's government. Hierarchy focused
on the king. The royal family ranked above all other families,
military commanders were recognized for their role in keeping
the empire together, and the king's other subjects loyally
served their monarch. J. G. deCasparis has provided us
with a most complete and accurate translation of the Telagu
Batu inscription, but has stopped short of using the inscription
to speculate on the system of statecraft established by
Srivijaya's early rulers or on the similarities between this
system and the indigenous patterns of Sumatra culture.[21]
The author's purpose is to explore the possibilities of such
an analysis.

Part I: Srivijaya's State Structure

DeCasparis' translation of the Telagu Batu inscription
offers a solid basis upon which one may attempt to reconstruct
the development of the Srivijaya state. As will be argued in
the next section, early Srivijaya statecraft reflected the
Sumatra culture from which it arose. Yet this culture appears
to have been incapable of generating a classical Southeast
Asian state until the mid-seventh century when inscriptions
record the rise of the Srivijaya thalassocracy in southeastern
Sumatra. Ancient Malay myth itself recognized the divisive

Map 4:
THE DISTRIBUTION OF SEVENTH CENTURY INSCRIPTIONS IN PALEMBANG

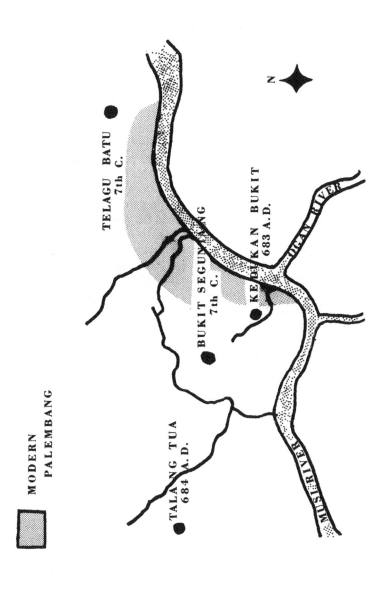

MODERN PALEMBANG

TELAGU BATU
7th C.

BUKIT SEGUNTANG
7th C.

KEDUKAN BUKIT
683 A.D.

OGAN RIVER

TALANG TUA
684 A.D.

MUSI RIVER

N

nature of its society.[22] One such myth records that as a boatload of Malays reached land they would almost immediately split into factions. Such a culture was capable of developing small groups, but needed some new principle of organization to allow it to generate something as politically sophisticated as a state. The Telagu Batu inscription's value is that it provides information on how this earliest Malay state was organized.

At the center of the Srivijaya state was the king himself who personally invoked the Telagu Batu inscription against all those under his command. It is significant that the text of this inscription is directed in the first person to the king's servants, as opposed to the Bangka inscription at Kotakapur (686 A.D.) and the Sumatra inscriptions at Karangbrahi and Palas Pasemah. These are usually considered equivalents and contemporaries of the Telagu Batu inscription,[23] but instead invoked a deity to initiate the necessary punishments on those subordinates of the king who revolted against the state. The distinction suggested by these inscriptions is that near the center of the Srivijaya king's domain his power was direct, yet in the state's hinterland the king was forced to emphasize the more theoretical and mythical aspects of his kingship because his power would seem to have been less direct.

The Telagu Batu inscription initially tells us about the organization of the core domain. Here we see the Srivijaya king surrounded by his kinsmen and his close associates. Immediately below the king in importance was the crown prince, the yuvarāja; the prince next in line for the succession was the pratiyuvarāja; then came the other princes of the royal family, the rājakumāra. These three levels of status were distinct from that of the rājaputra, "sons of kings born of lower queens," which appears in line three of the text.[24] In establishing a state hierarchy, as this inscription seems to be doing, the fact that these rājaputra were regarded as being of an inferior status in relation both to the king's other sons and to the royal family is very important. The inscription's stipulated graded spirituality would have permitted succession to the throne by the king's legitimate sons, but not to the rājaputra.

Chart 1

Srivijaya's State Hierarchy Based on the Telagu Batu Inscription

[Arrows indicate flow of authority in addition to that implicit in the hierarchical arrangement.]

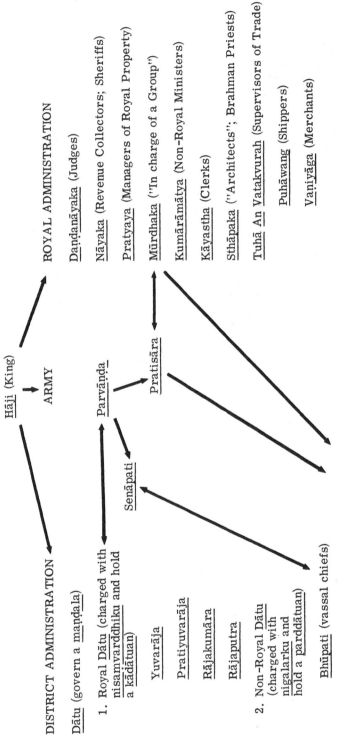

Surrounding the royal family and probably at the heart of the central administration were the various royal officials named in the text. Highest in status among this group were the daṇḍanāyaka, royal judges who exercised the king's powers of adjudication. Next were the nāyaka and pratyaya who are considered by deCasparis to have been two categories of administrators. [25] Nāyaka were revenue collectors, while pratyaya apparently managed the property of the royal family. It is interesting that pratyaya appears in compound with hāji, "the king," as hāji-pratyaya. DeCasparis believes that this compound distinguished a confident of the king, meaning that the pratyaya were in personal contact with the king and were probably very important members of the king's administrative staff. [26] If deCasparis' assignment of their function is correct, then it would appear that the Srivijaya monarch derived a notable amount of his revenue from some landed base. At the time of this inscription, when Srivijaya was consolidating its own power, it is not likely that revenues derived from the state's control over the China trade could have sustained the monarchy. The titles of administrative office listed in the Telagu Batu inscription suggest that the Srivijaya king was able to draw upon the resources of the land under his direct control in order to support his position as monarch as well as to expand his control over other rival centers of power in Sumatra and the Straits region. This royal economic base was probably populated by the hulun hāji, personal subjects of the king as defined by the inscription, who were controlled by their own local chiefs, mūrdhaka. [27] As inhabitants of the area surrounding the state's capital, they had undoubtedly been forced to subordinate themselves to the Srivijaya monarch.

Other officials of the center included kumārāmātya, "ministers not of the royal blood"; kāyastha, "clerks"; and sthāpaka, the "priests" or technical supervisors of the erection of divine images and the construction of buildings, who directed rather than actually worked on these projects. DeCasparis also notes that sthāpaka usually played important roles in royal inauguration ceremonies in contemporary Java. It should therefore be expected that these were Brahman advisors, religious specialists who advised the king in the Indian method of construction and in the proper

routine for performing religious ceremony--particularly
that of installation. If Indian ritual was of such importance,
then the Srivijaya monarch's attempts to consolidate his rule
may have included the systematic incorporation of Indian
cosmology to promote his own legitimacy. The Telagu Batu
inscription's assignment of Sanskritic titles to all those who
were subordinates to the king suggests that, as in other
developing Southeast Asian states during this era, the Indic
culture provided a certain unity and prestige to the new
system of statecraft. Brahman religious specialists, whose
educational background allowed them to assume useful roles in
a developing state as clerks or technical advisors to the
indigenous ruler, legitimized the rule of such a superior
"chief" who was able to distinguish himself from among
other local chiefs. [28] The organization of the earlier southeast
Sumatra port of Kan-t'o-li appears to have included Buddhist
advisors of the Brahman type. [29] In the Srivijaya period a
similar group seems to have supported the king of the new
dominant port, but by that time their status, as reflected in
the Telagu Batu inscription, was considered lower than that
of many other administrative and military officials.

Wolters views the ascent of Srivijaya in the seventh
century as arising from a challenge by Malayu to Kan-t'o-li's
position as dominent port in this part of the Straits region. [30]
It was thus necessary for the Srivijaya ruler to reestablish
the paramountcy of the southeastern Sumatra coast by forging
alliances with sea nomads and various hinterland chiefs until
he had surrounded the position of Malayu with Srivijaya allies.
The Kedukan Bukit inscription's reference to a force of 20,000
troops under the personal command of the King of Srivijaya
could well have been speaking of such an alliance. Only 2,000
troops were actually called upon for this expedition; it is
possible that only 2,000 troops could have been put in the field
under the direct command of Srivijaya at this time. The
remainder of the Srivijaya king's "army" may have been allies
who fulfilled their part of the alliance by remaining neutral or
by terminating their relations with Malayu. [31]

Such alliances forged to establish the rule of the
Srivijaya monarch were an integral part of the developing
empire. While Kan-t'o-li was a relatively isolated port-
state which had encountered few challenges to its position

due to the uncivilized character of the remainder of the
island, circumstances had changed by the seventh century.
The consolidation of T'ang rule in China presented new
opportunities for trade, attracting commerce to China from
the emerging port regions on the Sumatra coast.[32] Srivijaya
chose to cut off the expectations of these ports and to organize
them under the dominance of the Srivijaya capital. The
Srivijaya system of statecraft expanded from its limited core
domain to include assorted "vassal" relationships with a
wide range of subordinates who were allowed to retain varying
degrees of autonomy in relation to the center.

O. W. Wolters has suggested that Malay sea nomads
formed the initial military nucleus for the extension of
Srivijaya's control. An example of such a body of mercenaries
is provided in the geography of Ibn Rosteh, which mentions
an official known as a harladj who had an island named for
him and was "the head of the Maharaja's army."[33] This
island, situated in the Riau or Lingga Archipelago, was said
to have been famous for its camphor and to have possessed
a cliff. From it the island inhabitants could protect or harass
ships passing through the Straits region. In David Soper's
detailed analysis of such an island-based Malay chiefdom,
the role of a chief is seen as providing a land base, boats,
and munitions of war to a group of followers in return for
a share of any booty returning from a war campaign.[34]
Prestige was defined in terms of serving one's ruler.
These Malay sea peoples viewed a king as powerful and to
be feared.[35]

Relations between the Malay sea peoples and the
Mahārāja of Srivijaya were probably similar to those
established between the Srivijaya ruler and the military
leaders and chiefs of the Sumatra hinterland. The Mahārāja
was capable of investing power, as in naming the island of
Ibn Rosteh's reference in honor of his vassal. The attraction
of the center was its prestige. The King of Srivijaya was
both royal and rich and was known to promote the general
well-being of his people. To a military group, participation
in the division of the royal treasury meant a regularization
of income. This participation in the wealth of the center is
represented by the emphasis which the Arab geographers
place on the observation that at the death of a Mahārāja the

gold deposited in the Palembang harbor was divided first among the royal family and then among the military commanders.

Since Srivijaya did not initially dominate the power structure of either the Sumatra interior or the coast, the new state relied on military alliances with various subordinates who were willing, or forced, to accept the superiority of the Srivijaya monarch. Those unwilling to accept the position of the Srivijaya king were removed from office. This is expressed in "Palembang Inscription Fragment A," line 11, where the phrase bharu nirbhāra appears. DeCasparis translates this as "lords without a charge or function," probably indicating that those unfaithful to the king would be isolated by having their functions and thus their power taken away. Only those faithful to the king were rewarded. In line 24 of the Telagu Batu inscription there also occurs the phrase samaryyādamāmu, "your realms (or) your newly acquired regions." In deCasparis' opinion, this is a reference to pieces of ground or districts granted to loyal civil and military servants.[36]

In the list of people linked to the Srivijaya king, one finds two major classes of military commanders at the top of the hierarchy, well ahead of the priests (whose contributions to Srivijaya's statecraft were more theoretical than physical) and also above those who were regarded as members of the king's administrative staff. A parvvānda is described by deCasparis as being "a rather high official, in command of troops or of a small district...."[37] The fact that parvvānda appears in compound with nisamvarddhiku (nisamvarddhiku parvvānda) is of particular interest. Nisamvarddhiku also appears in the Telagu Batu inscription when the responsibilities of royal princes are described. Those charged with nisamvarddhiku seem to have been directly responsible to the king. In a Palembang inscription fragment, one nisamvarddhiku parvvānda had been personally charged by the king to bring a rebellious area under control.[38]

The Telagu Batu inscription also identifies the senāpati as a second category of important military commanders. While parvvānda commanded royal troops, senāpati may be seen as commanders in the private armies of the Srivijaya king's subordinate chiefs. Such an association is suggested in the inscription's text since senāpati appears with bhūpati, a term which deCasparis translates "vassal chiefs." Thus senāpati may be seen as military commanders of "vassal troops."

One further category of military commander appears in the state's hierarchy. Pratisāra is translated by deCasparis as "low ranking military commanders." The position of this group in the inscription suggests that they were subordinates of the two higher ranking military commanders. Since pratisāra is followed immediately in the inscription by the term hulun hāji, "the king's personal subjects," the two may well be connected in some way. Seemingly hulun hāji would have participated in Srivijaya's army and it is not unreasonable to expect that the pratisāra were their military commanders. As coordinators of royal troops the pratisāra would have been under the command of parvvānda rather than senāpati (see Chart 1).

Since it appears that local elite continued to maintain their own power base, it was necessary for the Srivijaya king to come to terms with these local chiefs and to integrate them into his system of statecraft. In doing so he was able to take advantage of the existing system of political organization by synthesizing his new style of kingship into it. The Telagu Batu inscription lists bhūpati, "vassal chiefs" to whom deCasparis assigns a high district level office, 39 in a position immediately following rājaputra, the "sons of kings born of lower queens," in the state's hierarchy. The bhūpati's district level office was that of dātu, the traditional Malay title corresponding to that of an important chief. A dātu, according to the inscription, held a parddātuan, a dātu province, which was distinguished from land belonging to the king personally, called kādātuan. Royal princes were usually appointed to a dātu position, probably governing kādātuan, and were charged with nisamvarddhiku. This was different from those of non-royal status who filled dātu positions and were charged with nigalarku. 40 As discussed by deCasparis, the distinction between the terms nisamvarddhiku and nigalarku is considered to measure the danger to the king posed by members of the royal family.

Royal dātu were believed to be potentially more dangerous to
the king than non-royal dātu. Since he was of royal blood a
royal dātu was a threat to the king's rule because he was a
legitimate heir to the throne. As a result, those dātu charged
with nisamvarddhiku were subject to far more severe
punishment than were those charged with nigalarku.

In line 21 of the Telagu Batu inscription the phrase
"purvvāna mulam kāmu," as translated by deCasparis,
presents the impression that as soon as the king received
information about suspect action by one of the royal dātu
"he would immediately take measures. He would organize an
expedition in order to have the culprit brought to the capital,
where he would be liabel to punishements; but, it is added,
the expedition would hardly be necessary; the culprits would
already have been killed by the effect of the imprecation,"
the curse associated with this inscription. [41] Not only was
the threat of a curse imposed upon royal dātu, but the king
also promised to order the immediate execution of anyone in
such a position who challenged the throne. To the dātu
charged with nigalarku there was no such threat of physical
retribution; only the threat of invoking the curse was held
against them. Thus, in the Kotakapur, Palas Pasemah, and
Karangbrahi versions of the inscription, the Srivijaya monarch
could merely invoke the curse and seemingly could undertake
no "other measures" to protect his position.

It would be extremely beneficial if one were able to
map the geographical distribution of those appointed and
charged with one or the other of the dātu positions. For
instance the Kotakapur inscription (line 4) states that the
rulers of Bangka were charged with nigalarku. As non-
royal elite, their position as a dātu in the Srivijaya system
did not demand total subservience to the center, but allowed
them considerable autonomy. The king did not hold out the
threat of direct force against them, submitting the threat of
the curse as a warning against potential disloyalty. In some
cases such local chiefs may have been in the process of being
assimilated into the Srivijaya administrative structure.
Line 13 of the Telagu Batu inscription also expressed the
king's fear that rebellion would break out in the frontier
regions of the empire. Here, too, emphasis was placed on

the curse taking its vengence rather than on a specific military response: "If you plot against me in the frontier regions of my empire, then you are not submissive and will be killed by the curse."

Apparently the proper function of a dātu was to serve as the king's "eyes" (line 6) in the areas outside the capital. Line 14 of the Telagu Batu inscription defines this duty, as translated by deCasparis:

"They [i.e. those persons known to you in your region who are committing the mentioned crimes] are not reported to me and to my empire [i.e. the authorities acting on my behalf all over the empire] ...." The passage would refer to those cases in which governors of provinces belonging to the Çrivijaya empire, or other authorities, know that insurrection is being prepared, but do not take the appropriate measures (which consist, among other things, of reporting to the king). This amounts to passive aid or complicity. [42]

After this warning that actions taken independently of the center in an attempt to build one's own base of power would be punished, line 15 then promises that if those persons who have attempted actions against the king are punished by the dātu, then "I shall not take measures against you."

Allied areas were probably allowed to retain their own power structures in response to the necessity of formulating a base for the empire itself. In lines 21-22 of the Telagu Batu inscription which speak of non-royal dātu, there is reference to the clans and descendants of these dātu who would suffer under the curse if a revolt against Srivijaya were supported. The indication is that in contemporary government it mattered who your ancestors were. A family endowed one with a particular status, as recognized in the inscription's elaboration of the royal family. Regional clans seem to have dominated certain areas of the Srivijaya empire. Rather than remove a dominant group from a powerful local area and then attempt to subjugate the remaining population, it was very important that Srivijaya incorporate this local elite.

Emphasis on family membership is given several times in
the inscription. In line 6 family ties are mentioned; in line
line 11 a warning is issued to those who "charge members of
your family to conspire"; line 19 places emphasis on the
joint responsibility of one's family for one's improper
actions: "[you] will be killed...with your wives and
children...your posterity will be punished by me...you will
be killed by the curse. You will be punished with your
children, your wives, your posterity, your clans, and your
friends."; finally, line 21 notifies state servants that if they
knew anything about their relatives' participation in a revolt
they would be punished, even though they themselves did not
participate.

Among the final groups recognized in the Telagu Batu
inscription were those people associated with commerce.
One first encounters the royal officials known as tuhā an
vatakvarah, "supervisors of trade and crafts." Next appear
the puhāwang, "shippers," and vaniyāga, "merchants."
The final two terms are given in their Indonesian form rather
than in the formal Sanskrit employed for the other titles
in the list, which may indicate that these were considered
indigenous traders and shippers who used the Srivijaya
capital as their home port and who were supervised by royal
officials with a specific jurisdiction over their activities--
officials such as the tuhā an vatakvurah. [43] An early
Palembang inscription refers to merchants in general as
"migratory men," comparing them with birds which traveled
over long distances. [44] In the Telagu Batu inscription the
shippers and merchants were included in the list of those
who were potentially dangerous to the king--probably because
of their contact with foreign powers. Merchants were
regarded as likely spies for the king's enemies. Thus the
movement of foreigners and their goods was undoubtedly
regulated in conformity with the requirements of the state.
In particular, foreign merchants would not have been allowed
to establish a commercial relationship dealing directly with
the interior sources of supply. But a policy of supressing
the foreigner was impossible. The advantage to be derived
from trade revenues, which Wolters has argued were an
important asset to the developing Srivijaya state, required
that hospitality be extended.

That trade was conducted under royal control, taking place in specific places under the supervision of royal officials, is suggested in the Telagu Batu inscription's reference to tuhā an vatakvurah, the "supervisors of trade and crafts." In economic terms we may suggest that the Srivijaya king utilized his hinterland relationship to collect goods at designated centers of exchange where goods met and flowed outward. This entire process would have been dependent on the system of statecraft developed by Srivijaya kings in the mid-seventh century, a system which may be regarded as an extension of the structure, or "code," of the indigenous society. [45]

Part II: The Srivijaya Monarch
as a Traditional Chief

Having analyzed the Telagu Batu inscription, we should reexamine specific points of the text as they relate to enduring features within the indigenous culture of Sumatra. Let us approach the ruler of Srivijaya as a product of his own culture. He was, in the earliest period of Srivijaya's history, an important chief who was able to forge alliances with other Sumatra chiefs. These alliances allowed his empire's expansion. On the everyday level, as indicated in the Telagu Batu inscription, the Srivijaya king fulfilled certain functions expected of a chief: he was a judge, he collected revenues, and he received the services of those under his control.

The Srivijaya king's role as an indigenous chief may be examined via analogy with that seen in the early ethnologies of Sumatra's society. E. M. Loeb considered the local rāja's power to investigate and settle local disputes as being the most important responsibility of a chief in Batak society. [46] According to William Marsden in his History of Sumatra, "The revenues of the chief arise principally from fines of cattle adjudged in criminal proceedings, which he always appropriates to himself; and from the produce of the camphour and benzoin trees throughout his districts...."[47] Chiefs administered justice and shared in the fines imposed as punishments (this share was known as a denda). When a chief arbitrated in civil matters he received compensation,

known as tahil amas. As stated by G. A. Wilken in his classic
nineteenth century ethnology on Indonesian society, "From
the nature of their office, the chiefs are charged with the
administration of justice, and as such they have a share of
the fines that are imposed as punishment. This profit is
not insignificant when one realizes... that all punishments
consist of fines."[48] The right of the Srivijaya king to collect
fines is expressed in the Telagu Batu inscription. In line 15,
the words "dandaku danda," "are fined by me with fine, "
appear. DeCasparis explains that in early Java, "free
villages" were given the special right to collect fines imposed
on certain crimes.[49] Normally these fines were considered
a part of the king's income. Indeed, deCasparis believes
that the Javanese dandaku danda system was borrowed from
the Srivijaya method of administration.[50]

The third major privilege of a chief's position was
his right to free labor from his subjects. Wilken noted that
this service was known as adat martolung among the Batak,
and wemendu among the Minahasa; both terms translate as
"payment in labor."[51] Among the Batak, a chief had a
claim to the assistance of his people in tilling his rice fields,
for planting, weeding, and harvesting his crop. His subjects
also were required to give assistance in the building of the
chief's house, at least in the chopping of wood and the
supplying of roofing material. A chief's subjects served as
his retainers when he traveled.[52] Marsden was impressed
by a retinue of seventy "well-armed men" who accompanied
their Batak chief to meet Marsden's party and escort them
to a Batak village.[53]

> The dependants are bound to attend their chief in
> his journeys and his wars, and when an individual
> refuses, he is expelled from the society, without
> permission to take his property along with him.
> They are supplied with food for their expeditions,
> and allowed a reward for each person they kill.[54]

We would associate the hulun haji of the Telagu Batu
inscription with this description of the traditional rights
exercised by a Sumatra chief over his retainers. The
inscription distinguishes between "my slaves" (hulun) and

"my lords" (tuhān). Hulun were the personal "slaves" of the king. Their main occupation was probably the farming of land over which the Srivijaya king held a land right. As chief of a regional unit, the Srivijaya king could expect the normal services a Sumatra subject was obliged to give his chief. In addition to providing labor and revenues to their "chief," the loyal "slaves" also would have served as the nucleus of the king's army. Hulun troops would have served beside the various professional and mercenary troops. All contributed to the success of the Srivijaya monarch.

The pratisāra of the Telagu Batu inscription may have been the commanders of these hulun hāji units. Another inscription found at Telagu Batu, also dated in the late seventh century, names the "commanders of an army of my slaves" as netā maddāsasenāyāh.[55] This lengthy praśasti had been issued on the occasion of a great victory by the king over his revolting subjects. An insurgent had led "an army of the king's proper slaves" against the king. This was stated to be "adharmena," employing a common Indian expression of being against the proper code of conduct for a certain person's status. As punishment for acting adharmena, the enemy troops had been wiped out. The fighting of this fragment is alluded to in deCasparis' fragment "C" as well. Troops of the enemies (ripuganam) fled or surrendered "at the approach of my army."[56]

As noted, the Telagu Batu inscription consistently places emphasis on the families of the ruler and his subordinates. Blood relationships, graded spirituality, the mythical aspects of genealogy, and the joint responsibility of a family for the actions of its members are stressed. Marsden stated that: "among the Sumatrans...a man without property, family, or connections, never, in the partiality of self-love, considers his own life as being of equal value with that of a man of substance."[57] Wilken's ethnology depicts the system of Sumatra chiefship as having originated in the village political system and as being based on the priorities given to family elders.[58] Institutions consistently encountered in the village were the communal granary and a council house. Both were controlled by an assembly of family elders. In Batak land, as elsewhere, a senior marga, a "clan," had

gained dominance over these village assemblies. Other
lineages became bajo-bajo, "subordinates," to the senior
lineage. Family loyalties, which took the form of a "joint
liability," were especially important in supporting a lineage's
role in local politics. Wilken describes oaths taken by entire
families in both the Menangkabau and Batak regions of
Sumatra.[59] In each case, a single member would take the
oath surrounded by the members of his family. The ceremony
stressed that revenge would seek out both the taker and his
family if the oath were broken.

Describing indigenous government, Marsden stated:

> The government of the Batta Batak country, although
> nominally in the hands of three or more sovereign
> rajas, is effectively...divided into numberless petty
> chiefships,...[which have] no appearance of being
> dependent upon any superior power, but enter into
> associations with those belonging to the same tribe,
> for mutual defense and security against any distant
> enemy. They are at the same time extremely jealous
> of any increase of their relative power, and on the
> slightest pretext a war breaks out between them.[60]

Regional units usually recognized the same dominant lineages
as the local villages. In southern Batak land, villages (huta)
under village chiefs (pamusunan) were organized by lineage
ties to a regional unit (pagaran) under the rule of a regional
chief (panusuk). As described by Wilken, villages tended to
split up when they reached a certain size, but new settlements
initially depended on the old village, forming a political
whole.[61] When it was necessary to set up an independent
government in a new village, the nearest blood relative of
the chief of the old village was appointed to become the new
village's chief. This process has been described by Diane
Lewis in her study of the hill peoples of the interior in Negri
Sembilan on the Malay Peninsula--a people who have much in
common with the indigenous populations of Sumatra.[62] Among
these hill tribes, hereditary right to the land was held by a
village chief. The chief allowed individuals to leave the village
to develop new lands and conferred a specific title upon the
person assigned the responsibility of organizing a new village.

The ties of the new village to the old were emphasized by elaborate installation ceremonies in which the superior chief of the original village, the mythical source of the new village's prosperity, performed the sacred acts of investiture.[63]

In Batak land, such a superior chief whose territory had greatly expanded was given the title dja ihuta, "radja commander."[64] This emphasis on the "commander" title may have great significance when relating the ethnologies to Srivijaya's system of rule. As stressed by Wilken, a central authority generally became important only in times of an emergency, such as a war, when a commander was needed to lead one local military unit against another. A commander of local forces who had successfully led expeditions several times exercised considerable influence in peacetime politics. Reinforced by the local kinship system and his own military accomplishments, a war chief could extend his influence over a wide area.

The process of going to war ("war adat") among the Batak seems little different from that of the Srivijaya inscriptions. According to custom, a chief ("commander") declared war on another chief. A formal declaration of war was made before the opening of hostilities. One chief formed a federation with his neighboring chiefs, attacked the village of his opponent, and, when successful, plundered cattle and made slaves of the survivors. As observed by Loeb, "wars were never fought for the purpose of land seizure, nor could the boundaries be altered."[65] One tried to obtain control over another chief's manpower. The Srivijaya inscription notes this process by speaking of "lords without function," meaning rulers, or chiefs, who had been deprived of their control over manpower. Loeb's description of the usual Sumatra method of forming war alliances reminds one of the language used in the Telagu Batu inscription:

> The aggrieved radja invited the friendly chiefs of the district to a conference in the Sopo. A cow or buffalo was slaughtered and all the radjas partook. Every chief who was present at the feast had to break off friendly intercourse with the hostile village, under penalty of being treated as a traitor, even though his own subjects took no part in the war.[66]

In the same sense a word which deCasparis translated as "traitor" (drohaka) appears in both the Kotakapur and Karangbrahi inscriptions. In the Telagu Batu inscription, dātus who ignored the rebellion against the king of peoples within their territories were reminded that they, too, were considered traitors and would be subject to the curse.

In the Kedukan Bukit inscription's description of the Srivijaya expedition against Malayu, the king, fulfilling the traditional Sumatra role of war chief, had forged alliances with surrounding chiefs to form a landed military force with a potential of 20,000 soldiers. He then led a force of 2,000 into battle against Malayu, establishing his control over the manpower of this territory and forcing it into submission. [67] Having proven his worth by ordeal, by gaining siddhayātra-- a mythical supernatural power which is mentioned in the Kedukan Bukit inscription--the Srivijaya king was then able to assume legitimately the traditional role of a Sumatra war chief, and was allowed to exercise considerable influence over peacetime politics. The Malayu expedition thus may be thought of as having been initiated as a quest for legitimacy in addition to its having been undertaken out of the concrete necessity of imposing Srivijaya's control over a rival port.

An example of the command of such a superior chief over his subordinate chiefs is given in Marsden's comments on Batak respect for the old Menangkabau kingdom's chief:

[They] have a supersitious veneration for the sultan of Menangkabau and show blind submission to his relations and emmissaries...even when insulted and put in fear of their lives, they make no attempt at resistance: they think that their affairs would never prosper; that their padi would be blighted, and their buffaloes die; that they would remain under a spell, for offending those sacred messengers. [68]

Wilken noted that the Batak prayed to this superior chief for the harvest; it was he who controlled the sun and the rain. [69] Loeb also related a similar legend about the Singa Mahārāja who resided among the Pak Pak Batak. If one looked at the chief's sword, one would suffer instant death. [70]

A consistent theme of the Srivijaya inscriptions is that the king was responsible for the common prosperity, or lack of it, for all his subjects. This theme is projected in the Telagu Batu inscription as buah, the Buddhist notion of fruit. Acts against the king were tālu (tālu muah), "subject to punishment."[71] The sense implied is that, if the proper code of conduct were not observed, the empire would "not reach its perfect state."[72] In the Kotakapur inscription, the king warns: "to them (who plan revolts) the fruits of the sins contained in their wicked deeds will be turned."[73] To those who follow the king, prosperity for the future was promised: vrddhi, "growth, prosperity"[74]; subhiksa, "prosperity"[75]; siddha, "arriving at a perfect state"[76]; and śānti, "eternal quietude of Nirvāṇa."[77] The Telagu Batu inscription also promises the secret formula of final liberation, tantrā-mala, to faithful subjects.[78]

Inscription fragment "A" expresses a curse against all those guilty of prohibited love, anger, and greed--kāma, krodha, and lobha.[79] Those who thus disturbed the system would be swallowed by a big river which was controlled by the Srivijaya king. The inscription also speaks of a battle in which the blood of the citizens (pauravirakta) ran red in the waters or soil near this river. The indication is that in the Srivijaya heartland the king held a magical control over the waters of the Sungai Musi or some other river. Wilken recorded a folktale from the Palembang region that the origin of local civilization occurred where the water of the various rivers was weighed and a settlement was made where the water was the heaviest.[80] The legend probably represents the practical notion that the people searched for fertile lands where the silt content of the water was right for sawah cultivation. It is interesting that the legend's emphasis is on the sanctity of water. The Bangka inscription invoked two gods: Ulu, old Malay for "high" and "mountain," conveying the traditional Southeast Asian value of the holiness of mountains; and Tandru n Luah, "the God of the Waters of the Sea."[81] The Srivijaya king's association with these two gods may be the basis of Arab references to the "Lord of the Mountain and Mahārāja of the Isles." The connection of the Srivijaya monarch with the magical powers of water was also observed by Arab sources. It was particularly noted that the Srivijaya Mahārāja had bewitched the crocodiles of his river to allow safe navigation to his estuary.[82] The geographers' legend about the daily propitiation of the estuary with gold bricks may have been a part of this same association of magical power over the water with the king.

It also appears that the Srivijaya king was considered responsible for the prosperity of agriculture in his domain. Abu Zayd remarked that the "Maharaja's island is extremely fertile...things always grow there."[83] Chau Ju-Kua's comments that the king could not eat grain on a specific day of the year for fear of the weather being dry and grain dear for the next year have previously been noted. In addition, were he to bathe in ordinary water a great flood would engulf the fields of his subjects.[84] In the Talang Tua inscription (684), the king expressed his concern "that all the clearances and gardens made by them (his subjects) should be full (of crops). That the cattle of all species raised by them and the slaves they possess should prosper...that all their servants shall be faithful and devoted to them...that, wherever they may find themselves, there be in that place no thieves, no ruffians, no assassins and no adulterers...that there arise among them the thought of Bodhi and love of the Three Jewels."[85] As Batak legend associated the king with the sun, so does inscription fragment "C" of deCasparis' collection.[86] The last two lines of this inscription may indicate that the rays of the sun were obscured when the king was away.[87]

The practical role of the king as dispenser of material wealth as well as his theoretical role as the source of moral and spiritual benefit would have been further reinforced by the mystical legend which seems to have surrounded the central treasury. We have speculated that Srivijaya fulfilled a role as a center of economic redistribution. Key to the operation of such a system was the ability of the Srivijaya monarch to acquire a share of customs duties and trade profits collected at the subordinate ports. The Cōla inscription from Tanjore dated 1030-31 gives reference to thirteen Southeast Asian ports conquered by the naval expedition of Rājēndra Cōla I (1024-1025).[88] Of these thirteen, eight seem to have been mentioned for their military strength, while only

Srivijaya-Palembang was noted for its "golden gates" and royal treasury filled with gold. The Arab legend about the Srivijaya monarch daily propitiating the estuary of his capital with a golden brick is further evidence of the awe of international opinion for Srivijaya's wealth. The Telagu Batu inscription makes specific reference to "a treasury of gold and property" which was situated at the center of the kraton.[89] This treasury was closely guarded from outsiders. The inscription makes reference to the efforts of the king's enemies to get information on the location of the gold and jewels kept in the treasury. If the treasury were robbed, the inscription warns, a curse would affect the district governors (dātu). What this may have meant was that, if the mythical treasure were stolen, then the entire empire would crumble. Line 11 clearly indicates that the stolen treasure would be spent by the king's enemies to buy troops and to destroy the kraton.[90]

As symbolized in the account of Abu Zayd, the treasury's wealth was shared by all the citizens of the king. Arab sources refer to the Mahārāja whose source of prestige was the prosperity of trade. Commercial revenues came into the center and were redistributed to the loyal following. Port wealth was shared by alliances with local land-based chiefs as well as with sea nomads. Charters of alliance with local chiefs guaranteed the safe passage of goods in different segments of the trade network. In return the local chiefs received a guaranteed income. The "privilege" of protecting trade was granted to a favored chief by the center. The system depended on a strong central ruler to enforce personal loyalties, as well as to prevent the jealousy of those chiefs not favored. As the central government had a vested interest in local markets, loyal subordinate chiefs had a vested interest in preserving the entrepôt as the source of their common prosperity. The Srivijaya chief was their common banker. His wealth was shared with his "family" of subjects.[91]

As the holder of his subjects' prosperity a Sumatra chief seems to have been subject to a cult of veneration. Nineteenth and early twentieth century observers of Batak culture were particularly interested in the "spirit houses"

which they found in important villages. Examining middle
and southern Sumatra culture, Harley Bartlett's study
emphasized that the Batak were particularly knowledgible
about the descent of their chiefs. Djoro, "ancestor houses,"
both temporary and permanent, were erected over the graves
of notable chiefs.[92] Graves of chiefs were often opened
after their bodies had decayed to remove the dead chiefs'
skulls. The skull was carefully cleaned and decorated with
gold and silver ornaments, wrapped in cloth, and preserved
in a special place of honor.[93] When a great chief died, his
remains were burned after the body had decomposed. His
ashes were tied in white cloth and placed in the arms of
the deceased's image or placed in a stone urn before the
statue of the deceased. Such a custom is undoubtedly in
continuity with the veneration of chiefs practiced by the
Srivijaya monarchs. It has been noted that Srivijaya statuary
may have been sculptured with the face of a king. The statues
bore inscriptions warning future generations not to melt the
statues down. The Telagu Batu inscription indicates that
such a personality cult may have been an important part of
the king's legitimacy. In line 13 reference is made to
rūpinaṅku, "my picture," meaning the material image of
the king or something attributable to the king, which was
used for magical purposes. The same type of reference was
made earlier in the inscription when the rebels placed special
emphasis on destroying the personal orders of the king as
symbolizing their attempt to destroy the king's magical powers
and replace them with their own. "Making people crazy" was
part of this plot.

This relationship of the chief to supernatural powers
is demonstrated in Bartlett's ethnology of the Batak. Bartlett's
study indicates that Batak chiefs were the caretakers for
the parsoeroan, "spirit houses," which were the scene of
great observances concerning all the subjects of a chief.
Parsoeroan were always placed on a right angle to the chief's
house and were constructed like a small replica of the middle
room of the chief's great room.[94] Here great drums[95] were
used to assemble the gods and ancestor spirits. It is
interesting that Loeb's study of the Batak assigns this function
of summoning spirits to a Batak shaman known as a dātu.
Loeb observed that the Batak dātu was either next to the chief

in local importance or very often was the chief.[96] Part of
the routine of summoning spirits included a symbolic death as
well as a nocturnal visit to the top of a mountain to
communicate with the ancestors.[97] Such magical aspects of
chieftainship might well have been utilized by a powerful
chief to justify his rule over an extensive territory. One
wonders if the journey of the Srivijaya monarch to obtain
siddhiyātra could be viewed as symbolizing the acquisition
of the magical powers expected of an important chief.
Religious emphasis on the magical powers of a king would
have reinforced political control. The threat of the king's
invoking a curse on disobedient subordinates had a very
real meaning.

Despite all these positive attributes--although the
Srivijaya king was a great military hero, a traditional chief,
and the holder of common prosperity--the Srivijaya monarch
still faced the problem of political fragmentation. Wilken's
statement that political unions took place only in times of
emergency recognizes that the very concept of chieftainship
contained elements of discord and division. After a successful
military campaign, a built-in cultural antipathy to amalgamation of manpower would generally cause a break down of the
combined forces. The successful war chief retained only an
influence over the various units of the former alliance.
Victory was not in itself sufficient to hold the loyalty of
one's followers. Even Chau Ju-kua's thirteenth century
account gives a hint of these divisive tendencies:

> When they [the people of Srivijaya] are about to
> make war on another state they assemble and send
> a force as the occasion demands. They (then) appoint
> chiefs and leaders, and all provide their own military
> equipment and the necessary provisions.[98]

How, then, did the Srivijaya monarch maintain continued
control over his broad domain?

As a response to these divisive tendencies and to
reinforce his alliances, the Srivijaya monarch was able to
call upon the act of "oath taking," which by the nineteenth
century had become deeply rooted in local society. Wilken's

study found the practice of oath taking in use among all the peoples of Sumatra:

> The oath primarily consists of a curse pronounced on himself by the person taking the oath and such being represented by some symbolic action. For instance, among the Batak a frog is cut up, among the Niassans a pig; among the Dayak the head is cut off a black chicken to symbolize the fate that one calls upon himself in case of perjury. . . .
>
> Another way of taking the oath among the Batak is that the person who has sworn the oath pours a little water on the ground as a symbolic representation of his blood, which will be shed in like manner in case of perjury. [99]

Wilken found that the most common way of taking the oath was to drink a little water in which certain objects of symbolic significance had been placed. [100] The water oath of the Telagu Batu inscription should be seen as part of this tradition. The inscription was carved on a Buddhist ceremonial stone, the upper edge of which was canopied by seven serpent heads (nāgas). A funnel below the text drained water which was poured over the stone during ceremonies. One is told of the sacred function of the oath in the first line of the inscription, as the magical formula, or word "Om" was invoked, followed by the oath itself. [101] The same oath occurs in the Kotakapur and Karangbrahi inscriptions.

Taking the oath symbolized one's allegiance to the Srivijaya monarch. "If you embellish this curse on this stone, whether you are of low, middle or high descent," warned the text, you would be struck down with calamity by being disloyal to the ruler: "you will be killed by the imprecation which is drunk by you (niminumāmu)."[102] The curse promised rewards, such as the secret formula for final liberation (tantrā-mala), to faithful subjects (nimākan), but to the unfaithful was promised more than death alone. This is elaborated in line 25:

If you transfer (the execution of) the actions, you

will be killed by this curse which is drunk by you.
However, if you are submissive, faithful (and)
straight to me and do not commit these crimes,
an immaculate tantrā will be my recompense.
You will not be swallowed with your children and
wives. 103

This reference to being swallowed may refer to the nāgas
sculptured on the head of the stone. One is reminded of
the Arab geographer Ibn Khurdadhbih's (844-848) comments
that in the mountains of the Mahārāja of Zabag (Srivijaya)
were snakes which devour men. 104 The mention of being
"swallowed by the water" in deCasparis' fragment "A"
may also symbolize this threat of the type of death one
could expect for being unfaithful.

Thus, the ultimate barrier to the divisive nature of
chieftainship was the appeal to the Srivijayan blend of
indigenous and Indic supernatural powers, which were all
symbolized in the act of oath taking. Lower level traditions
were incorporated into the ceremony, which culminated in
the sharing of a tantrā -mala guaranteeing prosperity and
security as long as the participant adhered to the terms of
the oath. In effect, this was an act of subjugation: by taking
the oath a local leadership accommodated its functional roles
and structural organization to the demands of the state.
Threats of dire magical consequence, when backed by the
real threat of military power, were probably sufficient to
convince a local elite that the change was beneficial. As
such, Srivijaya's military campaign against Malayu, the
strongest of Srivijaya's opponents, was probably the single
most important factor in allowing this oath to be administered.
Victory over Malayu allowed the Srivijaya king to claim
siddhayātra (the campaign had been explained as a "search for
siddhayātra"--a mystical prowess) 105 and thereby focused a
good deal of attention on the monarch as the stabilizer of
both the cosmic and the mundane worlds. As the Srivijaya
ruler had done previously in developing alliances with the
sea nomads and the indigenous tribes who formed the core of
his military strength, assurances of greater wealth and glory
under Srivijaya's rule were extended to the established elites
of the Sumatra coast, offering them a continued although

depreciated role in the developing thalassocracy.[106]

Conclusion

In making this analysis, the author recognizes the hazards inherent in applying nineteenth century ethnologies to a seventh century context; yet the unfortunate lack of either contemporary or intermediate data leaves little alternative. While it should be recognized that a culture is not static, it is the author's belief that there are certain elements in each culture which give it its own distinctive character, or "code," and which do not totally change. Despite twelve centuries of history, the culture of Sumatra experienced little external domination until the early twentieth century, when the Dutch began to penetrate the hinterland and bring it under their direct control. The results of this intrusion are reflected in Bartlett's essay, which notes with sadness the neglect of Batak ancestor houses. The nineteenth century ethnologies used in this essay report a different situation, recording the resilience of the indigenous culture to such external forces as the spread of Islam. Much of the material reported in Wilken's ethnology constituted the initial western studies of the civilizations of the Sumatra interior. The author has accepted this data as the best available and has attempted to show that, by the critical use of such information, one may give the historical records--such as the inscriptions used for this essay--a cultural perspective. Using these sources, we have tried to show in what ways early Srivijaya was a product of its own cultural base.

As opposed to existing models of ancient ports of trade which were politically and economically peripheral to land-based empires, the thalassocracy of Srivijaya depended on its ability to organize hinterland trade. "Srivijaya" referred to an illustrious group of ports. The name "Srivijaya" represented prestige in dealing with the Chinese and Indian markets; to trade in China, one would want to trade in the the name of the Srivijaya ruler. Using this prestige, Srivijaya was able to build an empire by blending the naval power and commercial skill of coastal ports with the land force potential of the interior populations. The benefits to the local communities may have included subsidized religious ceremonies, social pageantry, and wars, as well as the underwriting of the construction of public and religious edifices.

In the seventh century, Buddhism was grafted on to traditional Sumatran terminology. Traditional values such as reference to mountains, oaths, and a cult of dead chiefs, were integrated with Buddhist ideology. Buddhist piety was reflected in the seventh century Talang Tua inscription recording the dedication of a public park. In this inscription the sovereign expressed the desire that the merit gained by the deed and all his other good works should be shared with all creatures and should bring them closer to enlightenment. While using Buddhism to gain status in the international commercial community, it was necessary for the Srivijaya monarch to establish his legitimacy within his own system as well. Royal ideology was diffused to the various levels of society as the king's subjects were given a new blend of magical beliefs and rites.

Chieftainship was defined in traditional terms: the Srivijaya monarch was a Sumatra chief. The dealings of the Srivijaya "chief" with his subordinates would have existed within traditional structures of relationship. Srivijaya was able to integrate its external trade with the internal village networks using systems of alliance; the Srivijaya chief brought all the various internal networks together, connecting them to the international trade network. Srivijaya was able to define its relationship with foreign merchants in much the same terms, as "chief" of one people dealing with the "chiefs" of others. The State developed continuing "treaty" relationships with different groups of people who would have owed each other nothing. Trade transactions became social strategy; reciprocity between representative chiefs of the various peoples became the basis of continued prosperity. Maintaining the harmony of the social relationships was the key function of the state.

NOTES

1. O. W. Wolters, The Fall of Srivijaya in Malay History (Ithaca, New York, 1971), pp. 19-48.

2. Trade in the early centuries A.D. went across the Gulf of Siam from the Funanese port of Oc-eo, then proceeded across the Kra Isthmus from the Bay of Bandon to various west coast points of disembarkation. By the fifth century Malays had shifted the route south to the Straits of Malacca. See O. W. Wolters, Early Indonesian Commerce (Ithaca, New York, 1967), pp. 30-48.

3. Wolters, The Fall of Srivijaya, p. 9.

4. Ibid., p. 8 (quoting Chou Ch'u-fei).

5. K. A. Nilakanta Sastri, The History of Srivijaya (Madras, 1949), p. 113.

6. G. Ferrand, "L'empire sumatranais de Crivijaya," JA, 20 (1922), p. 57.

7. See F. M. Schnitger, The Archaeology of Hindoo Sumatra (Leiden, 1937), and Stanley J. O'Connor, Jr., Hindu Gods of Peninsular Siam (Ascona, 1972), assorted maps and discussions. As a participant in the 1974 Palembang archeological expedition of the Lembaga Purbakala dan Peninggalan Nasional (The Indonesian Archeological Institute), I was able to form my own impressions of the Palembang area. The terrain of this region is essentially low and flat. There is very little top soil in this part of Sumatra, as one quickly encounters a very hard red clay when excavating. Despite this natural handicap, local wet rice agriculture is an important source of food. One of the major rice producing areas lies between the two dated seventh century inscriptions: Kedukan Bukit and Talang Tua. The Kedukan Bukit inscription was found near the Kedukan Bukit River, which leads to the foot of Bukit Seguntang, the highest hill in the Palembang area and a major source of remains for the early Srivijaya

period. Moving toward the interior (and toward Jambi),
the next high ground is Talang Tua where, as the Talang
Tua inscription states, the king of Srivijaya dedicated
a deer park. Unfortunately, my survey of the area
between did not produce remains dating to this early
period. (See Map 4.)

One problem in identifying the pre-tenth century culture is
the lack of evidence--particularly of a walled city of the
Funan type, which the Buddhist pilgrim I-Tsing indicated
that Palembang had in 671, when he reported that in
"the fortified city of Fo-shih" there resided 1,000 Buddhist
priests (see J. Takakusa, op. cit.). Twelfth and thirteenth
century Chinese accounts also described Palembang as a
city surrounded by a brick wall. While traders dealt
inside the wall, the people either lived scattered about
outside the city, or on the water on rafts of boards covered
over with reeds [F. Hirth and W. W. Rockhill, Chau
Ju-kua: His Work on the Chinese and Arab Trade in the
Twelfth and Thirteenth Centuries, Entitled Chu-fan chi
(St. Petersburg, 1911), p. 60]. One would at least expect
to recover T'ang porcelain in the Palembang area since
deposits of this trade commodity have been found in north
central Java.

Yet our excavations at Palembang revealed none of this
supportive data. While we were able to identify the
fourteenth and sixteenth century population centers, we
did not discover a definite pre-tenth century site. The
reasons for this are varied, including the possibility that
Palembang was not the center of Srivijaya. For the present
I will explain our failure as being due to the dense
settlement pattern of modern Palembang and the expectation
that evidence of the old city is hidden under a layer of
asphalt. Also, it is likely that early settlement patterns
were similar to those of today, with people living in
wooden houses along the various small tributaries which
flow into the Musi River. Indeed, the Kedukan Bukit
inscription was found near one such waterway. As a
result, decomposition, fire, and yearly floods have
probably taken their toll on much of the archeological
remains of the early Srivijaya empire. For a complete

96

summary of the 1974 expedition see Teguh Aswar, Bennet
Bronson, et al. , Report on the 1974 Sumatra Expedition,
in Indonesian with an English summary (Jakarta, 1975).
I would like to express my gratitude to the Lembaga
Purbakala for allowing me to participate in this expedition.

8. Wolters, Early Indonesian Commerce, pp. 87-138.

9. Nilakanta Sastri, op. cit. , p. 120.

10. This inscribed stone is now on display in the Jakarta
Museum.

11. Hirth and Rockhill, op. cit. , p. 61.

12. William Marsden, The History of Sumatra (Kuala Lumpur,
1966 reprint), p. 301.

13. Ferrand, op. cit. , p. 57.

14. Schnitger, op. cit. , pp. 1-4. One could argue that
Srivijaya, in its patronage of Buddhism, was imposing a
new religious system which had little traditional content,
but was primarily intended to impress upon the state's
hinterland that the royal religious system was superior
to traditional systems of belief.

15. Hirth and Rockhill, op. cit. , p. 61. Bukit Seguntang is
the most likely place in the Palembang area to correspond
to this description. See Schnitger, op. cit. , pp. 1-4,
for a description of the various statues discovered at this
site. On the 1974 expedition we excavated on this hill and
seem to have discovered the foundations of several
buildings--including a small stūpa--and a large brick wall
about thirty centimeters below the earth's surface. These
may well be part of a Buddhist complex which was once
located on top of this hill. Unfortunately supporting
evidence, including refuse that one would expect a
community of 1,000 monks (see I-Tsing's account) to have
left behind, was not discovered.

We also excavated a new site called Sarangwaty, which is

97

located southwest of Telagu Batu (now known as
Sabokingking), where a standing Bodhisattva was recovered
as well as hundreds of small clay Buddhist stūpicas.
The stūpicas, which contain small clay punch-marked
seals--all roughly the size of a dime, were deposited in
a rounded hole under the statue site, seemingly to sanctify
the ground under the statue. This same practice of
depositing stūpicas under Buddhist statues has been found
at the Borobudur in central Java. Again, further
excavations in the immediate area contributed no supporting
remains from the pre-tenth century period.

16. O'Connor, p. 59. O'Connor notes a "Srivijayan style"
Mahāyāna Buddhist iconography on the Malay Peninsula
and suggests a connection between the statuary and the
portraits of deified individuals. He connects this practice
with the eastern Javanese bathing place at Jalatunda (977).
See also W. F. Stutterheim, "The Meaning of the Hindu-
Javanese candi," JAOS 51 (1931), pp. 1-15, where it is
proposed that Javanese candi statuary was shaped to
portray deceased kings in the form of a deity; and Alastair
Lamb, "A Note on the Tiger Symbol in some Southeast
Asian Representations of Avalokitesvara," Federated
Museums Journal 6 (1961), pp. 89-90, who describes
the distribution of Tantric Buddhist statuary which he
believes symbolized Srivijaya's control over the eastern
Malay coast.

17. Nilakanta Sastri, op. cit., p. 80.

18. Wolters, Early Indonesian Commerce, p. 266, n. 33:
"A Note on the capital of Srivijaya during the eleventh
century," Artibus Asiae Supplementum XXIII (Felicitation
Volume presented to Professor G. H. Luce, part I),
pp. 225-239. The decay of Srivijaya may well have pre-
dated the 1025 raid. Three tenth century inscriptions from
western Lampung Province probably reflect the entry of
the western coast as a participant in the patterns of Asian
trade. See. L. Damais, "Etudes d'epigraphie
Indonesienne," part 3, BEFEO 46 (1952), pp. 98-103,
No. 275 (Bawang), No. 283 (Batu Bedil), and No. 289
(Ulu Belu). One of these inscriptions is in Old Javanese;

one is in Old Malay, but seems to have a Javanese style;
the third is in 'Sanskrit, but is written in Javanese script.
All may reflect a Javanese orientation to this early trade.
Previous archeological research has virtually ignored
Sumatra's west coast, yet Bennet Bronson of the University
of Pennsylvania Museum, who conducted a preliminary
survey of potential sites during the summer of 1973, found
a considerable amount of surface material in the Barus
area--particularly pot sherds and Sung porcelain. In
1088, Tamil merchants were active at Lobo Tua near
Barus [see K. A. Nilakanta Sastri, "A Tamil Merchant
Guild in Sumatra," Tijdschrift voor Indische Taal-,
Land-, en Volkenkunde 72 (1932), pp. 314-327] . Such
evidence may well indicate that by the eleventh century
the Straits of Malacca was no longer the focal point of
the island trade as alternative routes were available and
were being used by the various maritime traders.

19. Wolters, Fall of Srivijaya, p. 6.

20. From the Arab geographer Abu Zayd, see Ferrand,
op. cit., p. 57.

21. J. G. deCasparis, PI, Part II (1956), pp. 15-16. One of
the problems in defining the relationship of the Telagu Batu
inscription to the Palembang area is the location where the
inscription was found. Telagu Batu, now known as
Sabokingking, was one of the residences of the post-1500
Palembang sultanate. Also found at this site were thirty
inscribed stones and several seventh century inscriptional
fragments (as noted in deCasparis), which appear to have
been collected elsewhere and brought to this site where
they were deposited near a sultan's grave, possibly
because they were considered to have some desirable
magical power. This was probably the case with the
Telagu Batu stone as well, which judging from its size
required no small effort to move. A similar plight may
well have befallen the other Palembang inscriptions and
remains. Geding Suro, a site between Sabokingking and
the river, was a major Muslim candi complex in the
sultanate period and was also the source of three pre-
tenth century standing Buddhist statues which are now in

the Palembang museum. Bukit Seguntang, another major
source for the earlier period, is now the site of a Muslim
cemetary and pilgrimmage center. In the latter cases,
either the Srivijaya remains were moved to these spots
or Muslim religious complexes were built on land which
was already known to have magical qualities.

22. See Chapter II, Keith Taylor's article, "Madagascar in the
Ancient Malayo-Polynesian Myths."

23. An equivalent of the Kotakapur inscription has been
discovered at Palas Pasemah, near the southern coast of
Sumatra and across the Sunda Straits from Java, but is
as yet unpublished. The author wishes to thank the staff
of the Lembaga Purbakala dan Peninggalan Nasional for
supplying information about this discovery. See Map 3
for the locations of these inscriptions.

24. DeCasparis, p. 19. DeCasparis believes that the rājaputra
may have been sons of concubines of the Srivijaya king.

25. Loc. cit. See Chart 1 for a possible depiction of the early
Srivijaya political system.

26. DeCasparis translates hāji-prataya as "royal sheriffs,"
indicating that their responsibility was probably to keep
peace among the commoners (hulun).

27. DeCasparis translates mūrdhaka as "somebody at the head
of some group," and its position in the Telagu Batu inscription
inscription suggests that the people they controlled were
commoners (hulun). This is undoubtedly an example of
assigning a respectable Sanskrit title to a previously
existing group of indigenous elite who are probably best
described as "chiefs."

28. F. D. K. Bosch, "The Problem of Hindu 'Colonisation'
of Indonesia," Selected Studies in Indonesian Archaeology,
(The Hague, 1961), pp. 3-22.

29. Wolters, Early Indonesian Commerce, pp. 221-223.

30. Ibid., pp. 229-253, and "Srivijayan Expansion in the Seventh Century," AA 24 (1961), pp. 417-424. With the discovery of the Palas Pasemah inscription and archeological evidence of an early settlement on the southeastern tip of Sumatra, the possibility exists that the old Kan-t'o-li port was located at Palas Pasemah, and that this area may well have been brought under Srivijaya's administrative control in a way similar to Malayu.

31. As will be discussed later, this is the Sumatra method of going to war.

32. Wolters, Early Indonesian Commerce, pp. 229-250.

33. Wolters, Fall of Srivijaya, p. 15. The island in the Riau Archipelago known as Karimun Besar is said to have an inscription dating to the Srivijaya period (see Map 3).

34. David E. Sopher, The Sea Nomads (Singapore, 1965), p. 93.

35. Ibid., p. 321.

36. DeCasparis, p. 45, n. 73.

37. Ibid., p. 42, n. 52.

38. Ibid., "Inscription Fragment A," p. 5, line 11.

39. Ibid., p. 37.

40. "charged by me with...." (line 15).

41. DeCasparis, p. 44.

42. Ibid., p. 42, n. 49. The oath administered in the Khmer empire also required more than the testimony of one's loyalty to the state, as one specifically swore to become the king's eyes, feeding local information back to the center. See Harry J. Benda and John A. Larkin, eds., The World of Southeast Asia (New York, 1967), pp. 33-34.

43. In Indonesian inscriptions vaniyāga is used to distinguish long-distance or seafaring merchants. Presumably it is derived from the Sanskrit vanij/vanik, "merchant."

44. DeCasparis, p. 2.

45. See Marshall Sahlins, Stone Age Economics (Chicago, 1972), for a definition of "code" and its suggested application to the study of societies.

46. E. M. Loeb, Sumatra: Its History and People (Vienna, 1935), p. 39.

47. Marsden, op. cit., p. 375.

48. G. A. Wilken, Handleiding voor de Vergelijkende Volkenkunde van Nederlandsh-Indie (Leiden, 1893), p. 344.

49. DeCasperis, p. 27.

50. Ibid., p. 28.

51. Wilken, p. 345.

52. Loeb, p. 39.

53. Marsden, p. 371.

54. Ibid., p. 375.

55. DeCasparis, p. 6.

56. Ibid., p. 8.

57. Marsden, p. 250.

58. Wilken, p. 337.

59. Ibid., p. 473.

60. Marsden, pp. 374-375.

61. Wilken, p. 340.

62. Diane Lewis, "Inas: A Study of Local History," Journal of the Malayan Branch of the Royal Asiatic Society 33, 1 (1960), pp. 65-94.

63. Ibid., p. 75.

64. Wilken, p. 341.

65. Loeb, p. 99.

66. Ibid., p. 32.

67. See also deCasparis, fragment "A," for an example of the king leading his troops.

68. Marsden, pp. 376-377.

69. Wilken, p. 612.

70. Loeb, p. 38.

71. Lines 8, 19, 21, and 22.

72. DeCasparis, p. 25.

73. Loc. cit.

74. Talang Tua, line 6, in Nilakanta Sastri, op. cit., p. 114.

75. Kotakapur, line 7, in ibid., pp. 115-116.

76. Kotakapur, line 6; Telagu Batu, line 28.

77. Kotakapur, line 7; Telagu Batu, line 26.

78. Line 25.

79. Line 16, deCasparis, p. 5.

80. Wilken, p. 80.

81. Sujipto Wirjosuparto, "Shrivijaya and Majapahit," Hemisphere 14, 9 (1970), p. 29.

82. Jean Sauvaget, trans., Les merveilles de l'Inde (Paris, 1954), p. 302.

83. Ferrand, op. cit., p. 57.

84. Hirth and Rockhill, op. cit., p. 61.

85. Nilakanta Sastri, op. cit., p. 114.

86. DeCasparis, p. 10.

87. DeCasparis translates this as "praising the absent king is like somebody trying to glorify the sun during an eclipse."

88. For a discussion of the Cōla raid see George W. Spencer, "Royal Leadership and Imperial Conquest in Medieval South India: The Naval Expedition of Rajendra Chola I, c. 1025 A. D.," unpublished Ph. D. dissertation (Berkeley, 1967), pp. 191-205.

89. Line 9.

90. "to divide into small parts... to spend the gold and jewels in order to destroy my keraton...."

91. This is indicated in the Arab legend, and symbolized in the redistribution of wealth at the death of a king. Abu Zayd's reference states that a king was remembered for the number of gold blocks left behind. The days of his reign, remembered by the number of gold blocks available for redistribution to his people, symbolized the king's ability to keep the system prosperous. According to Abu Zayd, it was for leaving great wealth behind that a king was rewarded with a place in history. Ferrand, op. cit., p. 57.

92. Harley H. Bartlett, The Sacred Edifices of the Batak of Sumatra (Ann Arbor, 1934), p. 7. This small book has recently been republished by the Center for South and Southeast Asian Studies, Ann Arbor, in a collection of

Bartlett's work, entitled Labors of the Datoe (Ann Arbor, 1973), pp. 209-304.

93. Ibid., p. 15.

94. Ibid., p. 7.

95. bedoek and taboew: both are considered to be of very old origin.

96. Loeb, p. 82.

97. Ibid., p. 83.

98. Hirth and Rockhill, op. cit., p. 60.

99. Wilken, pp. 469-470.

100. DeCasparis finds these words impossible to translate-- which is probably an indication that the words were part of a magical vocabulary reserved for such sacred occasions.

101. Ibid., p. 470.

102. Line 21.

103. DeCasparis, p. 45.

104. His later account of the method of extracting camphor from trees in Sumatra's interior adds veracity to his description. Ferrand, pp. 52-53.

105. "Kedukan Bukit Inscription," Nilakanta Sastri, op. cit., p. 113.

106. The Srivijaya king's perception of his new empire may well be represented in the Telagu Batu inscription's multiple reference to huluntahāṅku, "the domain of the conquered and common people (hulun) and the ruling class (tuhāṅ)," (deCasparis, p. 26). One could make a case that the Srivijaya king described in this essay could have easily been a member of an "alien aristocracy" who was able to

adjust his ambitions to the local Sumatra environment. Although this is possible, I would still cite the Telagu Batu inscription's emphasis that indigenous tradition was the basis for and defined the initial development of the Srivijayan empire.

The Devarāja Cult

and Khmer Kingship at Angkor

by
Nidhi Aeusrivongse

Introduction

Very few words in Cambodian epigraphy have inspired
as much scholarly speculation as the term devarāja in the
Sdok Kak Thom inscription (SDK) of 1050 A. D. Ever since
Pierre Dupont and George Coedès published a translation of
the inscription in the early 1940's, this term has been seen
not merely as a description of a cult but also as a form of
kingship. Dupont himself saw the cult in a rather vague way
as being a part of the trend of the "personal cult" that marked
the whole history of ancient Cambodia. This cult, according
to Dupont, was elaborated upon in later periods and probably
merged with the deification of the rulers. [1]

Coedès thought that the object of the cult was a liṅga
obtained from Śiva through the Brahmans. The cult was seen
by him as "the communion between the king and the god." [2]
The liṅga was supposed to contain the "royal essence"
(bhūpālabhāva), and Coedès saw the cult as being closely
linked to the ritual of installing, upon the accession to the
throne of a Khmer king, liṅgas bearing his name together
with the suffix īśvara. [3] Like Dupont, Coedès came to the
conclusion that the "personal cult" was connected with the
Devarāja and, if the term were used to denote Angkorean
kingship, it was divine kingship, "it was the king who was
the great god of ancient Cambodia." [4] The political implication
of the cult established by Jayavarman II was seen by Coedès
as a proclamation of independence from the universal monarch
of Java as Jayavarman asserted his equality because the
essence of the ceremony was the cakravartin consecration of
Jayavarman. [5] This view was also held by K. Bhattacharya[6]
and by L. P. Briggs who regarded the occasion as an
inauguration of the rule of divine right in Cambodia. [7]

107

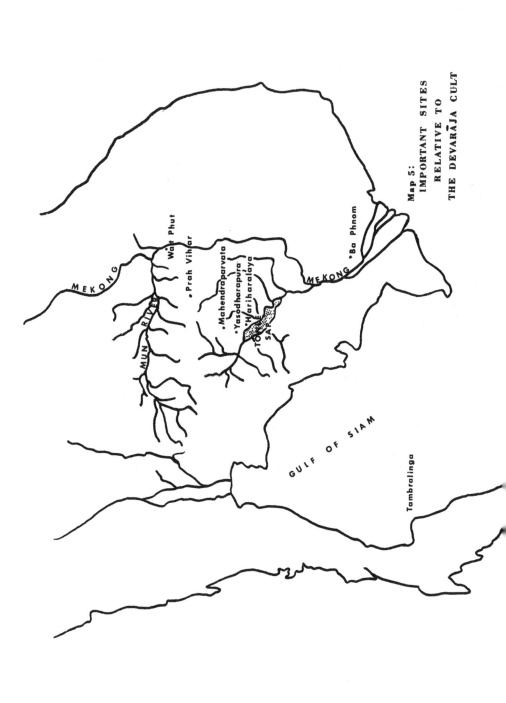

MEKONG

Wat Phut

Prah Vihar

MUN RIVER

Mahendraparvata

Yasodharapura

Hariharalaya

TONLÉ SAP

MEKONG

Ba Phnom

GULF OF SIAM

Tambralinga

Map 5:
IMPORTANT SITES
RELATIVE TO
THE DEVARĀJA CULT

Phillippe Stern largely accepted this view and even suggested that the cult was imported from Java by Jayavarman II himself.[8] In another study of Khmer art,[9] he was of the opinion that the ceremony mentioned in the SDK inscription was repeated in other reigns and that the Devarāja as a god was established in each reign or at least in each capital.[10]

The importance of the devarāja cult later declined in the opinion of some researchers, together with the status of Jayavarman II himself; in an article by Dupont, Jayavarman II's power was seen as having been limited to a small area north and west of the Great Lake. The marriage alliance with another "king," to Dupont, attested the invalidity of Jayavarman II's claim of being a universal monarch.[11] O. W. Wolters, however, basing his argument on a Chinese account not used by Dupont, convincingly shows that Jayavarman II was in fact a powerful monarch and that his proclamation of being a universal monarch was valid, at least in his successor's reign, if not his own.[12]

Nevertheless, the actual importance of the devarāja cult in the reign of Jayavarman II is not the key point to be examined here. The meaning of devarāja as used generally by scholars is not limited to one of the hundreds of "cults" found in the Cambodian inscriptions. It has been used to label a form of kingship found in ancient Cambodia, and even in its successor states. The interpretations of earlier scholars about apotheosis, personal cults, the Hindu theory of divine origin of kings, etc., have been drawn upon to form the content of the idea of devarāja kingship. This rather vague concept has tempted students of political history in their attempts to reconstruct from all these suggestions the story of Jayavarman's return from Java and the nature of the devarāja king as a cakravartin, "a universal monarch... the same as... the monarchs who were Buddhists of the Theravada school.... From his reign the pyramid-sanctuary marked the center of the royal city. At its summit, which was the center of the universe, the Devarāja entered into relationship with the divine world. He himself was the god to whom in his own lifetime the temple was dedicated." Even the expansionist policy of Angkorean kings after Jayavarman II is tied to the cult of cakravartin-devarāja in the SDK inscription.[13]

It was also very easy to adopt another viewpoint based on this vague description of Khmer kingship: that the Khmer government was a tyrannical despotism. This viewpoint was reinforced by the presumption that the gap between the masses and the ruling minority in a pre-mass education society such as Angkor was supposed to have been very wide. From this comes the conclusion that the gigantic monuments contemporary with Angkorean times--still existing in several parts of Southeast Asia--were products of a merciless conscription of free labor in order to fulfill the spiritual imagination of the ruling minority. One example of this viewpoint can be cited here:

> The great Khmer temples were not products of popular faith, like our cathedrals. They were princely buildings for the worship of kings and members of their entourage, deified in the form of one of the Hindu or Buddhist gods. It would be a serious mistake to think of these temples as similar to a modern church or pagoda. If the people were sometimes admitted to them on great occasions, it was not to offer prayers or sacrifices for divine mercy, but rather to prostrate themselves before the image of the god-king or the Buddha-king or other deified dignitaries.[14]

I. Mabbett in his article, "Devaraja,"[15] questions these conclusions. He points out that no Angkorean king had ever explicitly said in any inscription that he was a god and that the word devarāja itself, according to Sanskirt grammar, has several meanings, ranging from "a god as a king," "god of the king," to "king of gods." He believed that it was better to describe the concept in its original form; or, as done by Coedès himself, to translate the word directly as "god-king." Mabbett thinks that the devarāja cult, when performed, did not mean that the king was a god and thus had the right to rule, but that "he had the sole right to rule because he had a right ceremony performed for him." The aim of the ritual was to proclaim that the king had vassals but no overlord. Mabbett also emphasizes the ambivalent nature not only of the devarāja cult but of Khmer kingship in general. This ambivalence, he argues, was intentional so that the cult (which in its origin was the cult of the elite) and the aristocratic kingship could be meaningful both to the elite and to the masses. He suggests that the devarāja cult and its repercussions on the institution of kingship should be regarded as "the language of a society, employed to formulate ideas that were important to that society." This view that considers devarāja as the working principle of a society, not merely as a justification or ideology that concerned only the ruling minority, is very important since it helps us to look at Angkorean society in its entirety through evidence that is a product of the elite. However, Mabbett has not responded in his study to the vital questions of how the devarāja kingship was meaningful to the masses and how the ambivalence in the kingship institution secured "acquiescence of soldiers and conscripted labor."

This paper will explore answers to these questions. It provides the tentative answer that a section of the elite as well as the uneducated masses shared at least one belief in common, the belief in ancestral spirits. Ancestral worship in ancient Cambodia helps to explain how Khmer kings could acquire cooperation from their subjects through a common ideology. Needless to say, a common ideology is not the only means for a government to obtain mass cooperation, but our discussion is meant to explore this particular aspect. Information on Khmer ancestral worship is not complete, especially in the Angkorean period (the ninth to the thirteenth centuries). Following Coedès lead in drawing upon Javanese cases as analogies to help interpret Khmer funerary rites, [16] we shall take, as a point of departure, a description of Javo-Balinese ancestral worship given by Stutterheim's works. There is certainly disparity in the two cultures, but it is very useful to set the Javo-Balinese case as our frame of reference in order to get at least some vague idea about an underlying belief that might have supported Khmer devarāja kingship.

Ancestral Worship in Java and Bali

The Balinese, before being Hinduized, believed in the spirits of their ancestors which supposedly resided at the

hidden sources of the rivers on the mountain, without whose
waters no rice would grow. "They were the founders of the
village communities; they had established its customs and
cared for its growth."[17] The ancestral spirits of the Balinese
also dispensed the magic "life-power" which was the power that
brought life to man, animals, and plants.[18] The welfare of
a man or a community could be secured only when his or its
"life-power" was in a state of equilibrium. Since not every
man had an equal capacity to receive a large amount of this
magic "life-power," he who was considered to have the
greatest capacity had the sole right to make contact with the
ancestral spirits. He would be charged with the duty of
keeping the "life-power," not only of other members of a
community but of the community itself, in good balance so
that they would be in good health and the community would be
successful productively and have no disasters of any sort.

A temple of the village was supposed to be the place
where the sacred ceremony of contacting the ancestral spirits
was performed. The conductor of the ceremony would induce
himself into a state of trance and let the ancestral spirits
flow into him while the people knelt down before the incarnation
of the forefathers "who had descended from the mountains and
from the holy sources of the fertility-bringing rivers."
Their presence alone was sufficient to provide the community
with the absolutely necessary magic "life-power," "to further
the growth of rice, to calm the devastating overflowing
streams, to subdue epidemics afflicting the population."[19]

When village heads or priests died, their bodies would
remain unburied until no flesh remained on the bones. It
was then considered the proper moment to erect stone or
wooden figures of the deceased on the tombs of the buried jars
containing the bones. Feasts and ceremonies would be held
to restore the loss in the community's "life-power" caused by
the death of the village head. "The figure was intended to
represent the dead in a permanent way--an effort to retain
the person of the deceased in the community in place of the
corpse disappearing through decay. Simultaneously was
created a place which might at all times be recognized by the
soul as its own, so that it might be pleased to incarnate
itself there...."[20]

After Hinduization, the body of a Balinese king was cremated, and "rites were performed in order to convey his soul, liberated from earthly bonds, to heaven." With the completion of such rites, one more ceremony had to be held; it was to give to the dead king final and complete deliverance. To this end his soul was called to incarnate itself temporarily into a "flower-body" (puṣpaśarīra) which contained his ashes. Then another cremation of this body was performed and the ashes solemnly thrown into the sea. However, a part of the ashes was retained and buried under a stone monument dedicated to the god of whom the king had claimed to be a reincarnation. 21 In Hinduized Java, the cremation of a king almost exactly followed this pattern. The unburnt bones of a king's "flower-body," however, were stored in a stone coffin, the inside of which was divided into nine compartments, representing the eight mūrtis of Śiva which were supposed to be present in human bodies. The coffin was buried in a pit and an image-portrait erected over it with temples and walls to protect the image. When the image was consecrated, the "god-king" was able to make contact with descendants again through ritual. 22 A temple of this sort was usually built of permanent materials to perpetuate the contact between the living and the dead. 23

The Early Khmer Concept of Deities

There were at least two different concepts concerning gods or supernatural forces in Khmer society. One was associated with Sanskrit texts and Hindu theology, the other with folk beliefs. 24 The Sanskrit gods are represented in many invocations from a number of the Angkorean inscriptions. In this concept, Śiva was the one being who was surrounded by known mythology; his essence was universal, represented by liṅgas in several locations, but it stood for that one thing, the Absolute Śiva. The brahman who wrote the śloka in the stele of Toul Ta Pec undoubtedly intended to refer to this absolute Śiva when he said, "Homage to the linga of Śiva whose primordial light and sovereignty was produced at the beginning by the Creator, with the view to obtaining happiness and final bliss. "25

The Śiva in folk belief on the other hand was likely to be a more specific Śiva.[26] The Khmer undertook to make many representations of a single god under different names even in the same location. It is probable that each god with its individual name represented a specific local deity rather than an absolute god who was believed to be one and the same under different representations. This idea of specific local gods doubtless prevailed among the common people and was also held by the ruling elite. In 1048, King Sūryavarman I proclaimed that he had "obtained by the force of his asceticism [the knowledge] that Kamrateng Jagat Bhadreśvara of Liṅgapura has come to reign at Śrī Śikharīśvara [also another name of Śiva and the principal god of Prah Vihar] in order to manifest his power by the visible method so that the world may see him." His majesty then ordered all serfs of Bhadreśvara of Liṅgapura to move out of that place and come to serve the god at Prah Vihar.[27] In this case, Sūryavarman did not mean the absolute Śiva, who theoretically should have resided everywhere, especially in his own officiated representations, but a god whose name happened to have been Bhadreśvara and who formerly had resided in a liṅga at Liṅgapura. Certainly the ruler did not mean to include other Bhadreśvaras who resided in a large number of liṅgas in various locations in his empire.

Among the Khmers, there were many gods who resided in several places, on the top of some mountains, in religious foundations of villages and towns, in huge old trees, in caves, etc., and whose names might have been similar to those of the Hindu gods but who were local and bore no characteristic of universality at all. The description of this concept of the gods brings a statement of Stutterheim to mind about Hindu gods in Bali:

> For who indeed were the gods to whom the offerings were brought? Not Śiva, nor Brahma, nor Vishnu-- at least, not in the first place, nor exclusively. They were again the local gods, the deified founders of the village communities, --sometimes bearing names that sounded like Sanskrit.[28]

It is very difficult to distinguish the indigenous and

Indian elements in the religious beliefs of the Khmers. The
meaning of the Indian elements is limited to what can be found
in Sanskrit texts, and the difficulty remains formidable because
most of the evidence we have was made to bear the appearance
of Sanskritic culture. However, there is no question that
religious beliefs, as well as other social institutions in
Angkor, were the result of a syncretism that took place
perhaps from the beginning of contact between the two
cultures. Some vestiges of the syncretic nature of Angkorean
belief have been pointed out by Bhattacharya in his study of
iconography, as for example, the association of the Viṣṇu
at Prasat Kravan with a crocodile or lizard or the Naṭarāja
of Bantay Samre with two Asuras embracing his legs
(seemingly inspired by autochthonous mythology). "We are
on a more solid ground when we confront the transformation
of the nāga Ananta to a dragon, or again, the presence of
the rhino as vāhana of Agni."29

The origins of these specific gods, beneath the names
of the Hindu pantheon, were deities of local communities.
They had been revered by local people before classical Indian
culture arrived in Cambodia. Their names and, to a large
extent, their forms were transformed in the process of
Sanskritization. Even in the Angkorean period, the
transformation of names was not complete, as some gods
were still mentioned in the inscriptions under Khmer names.
The evidence we have comes from the entire period of the
seventh to the twelfth centuries. An inscription dated 611 A.D.
relates the merging of a god whose name ended in īśvara with
another god called Vrah Kamrateṅ An Kamratan Tem Krom
and also with the god Manīśvara. Coedès explained that the
Khmer name of the god signified a tree.30 This inscription
suggests very clearly one of the methods by which spirits of
indigenous beliefs came to be incorporated in the Hindu
pantheon. This Khmer spirit of the tree was mentioned
again not long after the first inscription, when the donations
given to it by a king were ordered merged with donations made
to other Hindu gods.31 Another inscription in the stele of
Tuol Nak Ta Bak Ka, the style of whose script is definitely
from the pre-Angkorean period, listed the names of several
gods to whom it would seem that a king had made donations;
among them there appeared a god whose name was Kpon
Kamrateṅ An Kamratan Slot.32

During the Angkorean period, we have two such inscriptions from the reign of Rājendravarman II. One is dated 956 A. D. and records a royal ordinance to a local chief ordering him to place an inscription for a god whose name was Kamrateṅ Jagat Pin Thmo.[33] The other reference is in the stele of Basak which shows a god whose Sanskritized name was Vakakākeśvara. Coedès was of the opinion that the name derived from a Khmer name and that it reappears again in the inscription of Vak Ek.[34] Also in this reign a donation was made in the same manner to Kanlon Kamrateṅ An Rājagūhā. Coedès pointed out that this name meant a deceased queen in the royal cave. The cave itself was, in Coedès' conjecture, the cremation ground of the queen.[35] More than a century later the same name reappeared in the inscription of Prasat Trau (1109). Although Coedès suggested that a specific person was being noted as the deceased queen in this particular case,[36] it is also probable that the name belonged to a Khmer goddess known to the local people through the centuries. The stele of Vat Phu, the sacred place which assembled many gods in the Angkorean period, relates the restoration by Jayavarman VI in 1103 of a god who was referred to in the inscription as being "the sacred image Vrah Thkval,"[37] a Khmer deity still maintaining his Khmer name.

It is thus possible to imagine that in the process of "Indianization," a number of local gods with Khmer names were "merged" with gods holding Hindu names, their figures (if they had any recognizable figure) being transformed to a liṅga or even an image. The cult surrounding the local gods was also instilled with new elements from Sanskrit texts which were introduced by indigenous or Indian brahmans. This process appears to have continued from the protohistoric period down to Angkorean times and to have left its vestige in the inscriptions.

Who were these gods originally? Two prominent types of spiritual concepts, of fertility and the ancestors, must have formed a large part of the Khmer pantheon. Trees were one of the best symbols of fertility, growing from the ground, productive, living, and full of "life-power." Megalithic monuments, another such symbol, became liṅga, especially the kind that was called the Svāyambhuva liṅga. This kind of liṅga stood directly on the ground without the normal yonī base. In India the Svāyambhuva liṅga was considered particularly sacred and was believed to have appeared naturally (as the name indicates) and to be able to exist to eternity.[38] This type of liṅga was very popular during the pre-Angkorean period. The liṅgapārvata, according to Bhattacharya, was probably a "natural liṅga" which "represented the top of the mountain."[39] One vocable of Śiva, Kedāreśvara, prevalent all over Cambodia during the period, was also linked to the Svāyambhuva liṅga because in India the name designated a place which possessed this type of liṅga; and an inscription from Toul Prah dated 673 relates the erection of a Svāyambhuva Mahāliṅga called Śrī Kedāreśvara. The interconnection of the fecundity spirit and ancestral worship as described by Paul Mus in the case of Champa can also be seen in the probable evolution of local megalithic monuments to the Svāyambhuva liṅgas.[40] Objects of fertility rites, these liṅgas had no yonī base and were thus able to impregnate the soil directly, at the same time that they represented the peaks of mountains, the source of "life-power" and the abode of the ancestors. The imperishability of the stone, corresponding to Hindu belief that Svāyambhuva liṅga were eternal, assured the Khmer of the continuation of the "life-power" of their communities in sufficient amount to make them secure and prosperous.

The site of burial or cremation was probably important to the Khmer. The name Kanlon Kamrateṅ an Rājaguha or a deceased queen of the "royal cave" was understood by Coedès to mean that the cave had been the cremation site of a "deified" queen.[41] In Angkor's successor states, the cremation sites or the death spots of princes or kings frequently became Buddhist temples. Examples are numerous in the Ayudhya chronicles. The installation of a stone figure on the site of a burial in Bali was closely related to this custom. The origin of Angkorean "mausoleums" can probably be traced back to an ancestral worship of the remote past which sanctified burial spots and cremation sites. The consecrated foundation on the site of a burial or cremation was the line of connection between the living and the dead.

Ancestral Elements
in Khmer Religious Beliefs

Among the many supernatural beings revered by the
Khmer during the pre-Angkorean and Angkorean periods,
ancestral spirits distinctly played a very significant role.
Bearing in mind the ancestral worship as described by
Stutterheim in Java and Bali, the Cambodian inscriptions
read more understandably to a modern man whose realms of
politics and religion are clearly distinguishable.

When a man died, his soul had to be liberated from
earthly bonds through certain rites. The information we have
about these rites came from those people who could afford a
rite which involved an establishment of figures, āśrama, or
other religious foundations or at least some concrete donations
to the gods. There might have been simpler and inexpensive
forms of the deliverance of ancestral souls but the
aristocratically biased information of the Cambodian
inscriptions makes no reference to them. However, it is
unmistakably clear that the deliverance of the decedant's soul
was the substance of the Khmer funerary rite. Information
from several inscriptions asserts that the purpose of
establishing certain religious objects was to "deliver the
deceased" to the next world. Evidence of this kind is
widespread, so only a few items will be cited here. An
inscription on the stele of Ta Keo, dated 639, contains this
passage in its Khmer text: "By devotion to the fortunate
Sambhū, for the deliverance of his parents, the (founder),
master of his senses, has erected it [the image of Devī
Caturbhujā] on the earth with the rites proper to Devī."[42]
A Vaiṣṇava official of Rājendravarman II declared in Sanskrit
verse, while supporting a Viṣṇu foundation for the favor of
his family, that "Having had erected here, for the joy of
his ancestors, two images of Śauri at the south and the north
respectively...," he donated various items.[43] The practice
was adhered to by kings as well. Jayavarman IV founded a
Śivaliṅga, "destined to obtain in the other world a just situation
in favor of his beloved brother, born from the same mother,
called by the fortunate and significative name of
Rājendravarman...."[44]

Again, there was another trend of thought derived from Sanskrit texts and believed by highly Indianized or Indian ascetics in the Angkorean empire. By one's own effort, one's soul could unite with the Absolute after death. An expression of this idea is explicitly exemplified by a eulogy in the inscription of the stele of Phum Da, dedicated to an ascetic Jñānapriya Āryamaitrin in 1054. He was praised since, during his lifetime, he was "devoted to the meditation of Śiva [and was] like the reality of Śiva Himself which had resided in him." After his death, "his purified soul now shared the supreme beatitude. [In his eyes] those who, tormented by the six enemies [senses], do not seek a refuge in the middle of forests in the sojourn of meditation are out of their minds."45

Ambiguity played a very important part in the declaration of soul deliverance; with the exception of this last eulogy, it is difficult to say definitely what the real meaning of the deliverance appearing in numerous inscriptions was. It might have meant, in a classical Hindu context, the deliverance of the deceased soul from earthly bonds in order to let it unite with the Absolute Oneness. But it may be interpreted, in an equal degree of validity, that the deceased's soul was delivered to an abode of the ancestors.46 The important place of the ancestors in the Cambodian inscriptions suggests that the second meaning was also significant in the Angkorean religious context, and it is very likely that the ambiguity was intentional. Such ambiguity may well have functioned as a device to embody diversified elements of the society, Indianized elite as well as the uneducated masses, within a social action that could be meaningful to everyone.

Thus, death in the Khmer system of belief was in fact not an extinction of being but a rebirth in the abode of the ancestors. The concept of death as a rebirth was shown in the figure of Rāhu or Kīrtimukha carved on stone coffins from the Angkorean period and on later Siamese and Cambodian urns. Rāhu was, in the carving, devouring the moon during a lunar eclipse. The scene represented the essential object of the funerary rites because it was the symbol of rebirth or resurrection.47 In studying modern Cambodian customs, Guy Porée pointed out that a large part of the ceremony for a

royal cremation very probably formed the rites of rebirth. [48]
Porée also thought that the idea of rebirth explained why the
royal body was put in the urn in a position resembling that of
the unborn fetus. [49]

The destination of the liberated soul or the place where
a person was to be reborn was an equivalent of the Javo-
Balinese ancestral homeland. It is probable (surmising from
the evidence available) that the place was believed by the
Khmers to be on a peak (or peaks) of a mountain (or
mountains). Coedès interestingly noted that the shape of the
spire above the pre-crematorial urn in later Siamese and
Cambodian funerary rites was similar to a mountain. A
modern Thai scholar has traced the origin of such an urn to
hem or the gold that enveloped a liṅga in twelfth century
Champa, but Coedès thought the word hem was an abbreviation
of Hemagiri or Mount Meru. [50]

The connection between ancestors and Śiva is obvious
since Śiva was said to be the king of the mountains. Both
Śiva and the ancestors resided on a mountain. The two main
features of "pre-Aryan" belief as seen by Paul Mus were the
fecundity cult and ancestral worship, and they were, in his
mind, closely connected though not always identifiable. [51]
These two aspects of Khmer belief were reflected in the
worship of the liṅga on the one hand and Śiva or the mountain
on the other. One of the earliest known gods of the Khmers
resided on the mountain at Liṅgapārvata. One of the earliest
known posthumous names for a king was "he who has gone to
the abode of Śiva,"[52] i.e., to the top of a mountain. Coedès
also found that the favorite posthumous name of pre-Angkorean
kings was "he who passed away to Śivapura," or the mountain-
city of Śiva. This name of Śivapura was the earlier equivalent
of the Śivaloka and Śivapada used in the Angkorean period. [53]
With remarkably few exceptions, all Khmer kings up to the
early fifteenth century are known to have been given the abode
of Śiva or a mountain top as their destination after death,
including Sūryavarman I whose posthumous name was
Nirvāṇapada. [54]

The mountain and its symbol remained very important
in the Angkorean state cult. Jayavarman II had the devarāja

cult performed on Mount Mahendra--itself named after the
Indian king of the gods (Indra). The mountain-temple of each
royal city was located at its center. The devarāja cult could
have been installed in this central "mountain" or prang as
indicated by a series of inscriptions at the Koh Ker group.[55]
In most cases, we do not know the exact location of the
principle devarāja cult of each reign, though there is evidence
to support the supposition that the principal cult of the reign
was installed in the central mountain as we see in the case of
the Bayon during the reign of Jayavarman VII.[56] To the
uneducated masses, the central temple-mountain undoubtedly
represented less the Sumeru than the symbol of the abode of
their ancestors, radiating their force of protection over all
the realm. The concept of the ancestral mountain would
have endured the change of the kings' personal religions.
Whether the king was Vaiṣṇavite, Śaivite, or Buddhist, he
could bring forth the protective force of the ancestors through
a central cult based on the mountain-temple.

Yet, if we may draw a parallel between the Khmer
concepts of specific deities and their ancestral spirits, it
is very probable that the spirits of the ancestors were not
seen as uniting with a single Absolute Ancestral Spirit on
the central mountain. Each village or community had its
own "ancestral spirit," as perhaps did each clan.[57] A village
community, a clan, or a person was protected by the spirits
of its or his ancestors. To deprive a community or a person
of their ancestral spirits would be to doom them. In order to
prevent damage to or the stealing of donations and religious
images, it was customary to condemn such a vicious person
and his ancestors in advance in the inscription that
commemorated the gift or the building of the foundation. A
few examples taken from many such passages is sufficient to
illustrate the point. The inscription of Tuol An Tnot, dated
681, condemned the "evil men who seize for themselves the
sacrifices of Śrī Khaṇḍaliṅga [to] go to the Avīci hell with
their ancestors and their parents."[58] Inscription D. 56 at
the Museum of Phnom Penh has a passage which reads,
"Those who rob these [donations to the god Śrī Bhadreśvara]
...these hells (names of Hindu hells), it is there that they will
rest with their father and mother."[59] Examples of this sort
come also from later periods, as in the inscription of

Prasat O Romduol dated 968.[60] In Khmer eyes, if a person's ancestors went down from a mountain to a hell, he was deprived of their protection and thus had to suffer all the dangers and miseries of the world even before his death. An inscription on a pedestal at Sambor, dated 683, expresses this idea more clearly because it puts aside any condemnation of the robbers and only describes what their ancestors were to receive: "This is an offer to Vrah Kamrateṅ An Suvarṇaliṅga...; those who cause the ruin of all of it, their male and female ancestors of seven generations will fall into the Raurava hell...."[61] There was no need to condemn the robber because, once his ancestors had departed from the ancestral abode, he could hardly live, let alone bear the suffering of the world, without the "life-power" from his ancestors.

In order to gain the proportionate "life-power" from its ancestors, the community concerned had to maintain a shrine by which it could communicate with their spirits and receive "life-power" through certain rituals. Chou Ta-kuan reported in the thirteenth century that each village had its temple or stūpa[62] which might be taken as a parallel of the Balinese temples. It is quite certain that many of the gods, liṅgas, and other religious objects mentioned in the Cambodian inscriptions were originally shrines of village ancestral spirits. And it is in this light that the request of the tamvrac made to Sūryavarman I, in return for taking an oath of loyalty should be read: they asked the king "to give orders for the maintenance of pious foundations in our 'sruk'" (the Khmer text reads, vrah punya sruk desa yen).[63] This request came before the one for the subsistence of their families. The ancestral shrines were very important to them because, without them, they would have been unable to sustain their own lives.

Among the aristocrats, the evidence we have suggests that they preferred to maintain their own family temples or shrines. Numerous inscriptions relate long stories of support to religious foundations by single families. The family temple and its gods linked the living to the bygone ancestors who had founded or donated to it in the past. At least one inscription explicitly expresses the special position

of a god in relation to its family. A yogin by the name of
Tribhuvanavajra in the late tenth century restored the image of
the god Jagadīśvara to whom his maternal grandfather had given
a slave. The god was qualified in the inscription as being
"Jagodīśvara of his family," explicitly referring to the yogin.
The yogin also had an image of the Mother of Muni
(Prajñāpārmitā) made, probably for his own deceased mother.
The religious foundation was thus the residence of gods related
in a direct way to his ancestors; as the inscription stated,
"Having restored here the foundation instituted in favor of the
gods of his family...."[64] The images of these gods remind us
of the stone or wood images in Indonesia made to represent the
deceased in a permanent way. The support of the family
shrines insured the supporter of his own prosperity. The
promise became reality in his life because he was legitimized
by the king in having the sole right of benefit from the offerings
and revenues of these gods. For example, in 627, Iśānavarman
nominated a brahman who, "for the service of the god, should
enjoy the revenues of the temple until the end of the world."[65]
It was customary for the founder of a religious foundation or the
donator of land to such a foundation to nominate his own son or
a close relative as the guardian of the temple and its revenue.[66]
The revenue of a god depended on the lands and slaves donated
to him and the offerings brought to him by his followers. As
long as he was strictly an ancestral spirit of a family, his
revenue from the second source tended to be limited.
Ambivalence in deity worship appears in this case also. The
ancestor became Indianized and its cult was officiated by
brahmans whose teachings were, to a greater or lesser degree,
applicable in a universal context. Thus the god came to have an
appeal for persons outside the family as well. At the same
time, however, the ancestral spirit could not be ignored
because the force of the belief remained strong and the Hindu
god was ambivalently related to the ancestors--male ancestors
with gods, female ancestors with goddesses. This ambivalent
relationship between Hindu gods and ancestral spirits is more
obvious when we deal with the ancestral elements in the
Angkorean state cults where more evidence is available.

The ancestral elements in Angkorean state cults can
be seen clearly in the funerary customs practiced by the
royal families. The idea of the ancestral cult also clarifies

the "deification" of dead kings which involved the construction of large "mausoleums." The latter could not have been done without the understanding and implicit approval of the conscripted people, and the ancestral worship that ran across the whole gamut of Khmer society helped facilitate government control and secure support for the royal power and its projects.

The tradition of kings erecting images of their ancestors goes back to the pre-Angkorean period. A Sanskrit inscription, dated 704, relates the erection of a Viṣṇu called Hari Śrī Viśvarūpa. The exact time of the erection was marked by astrological details. It was consecrated by a brahman by the name of Nāga, "who was well-versed in the Vedas, a receptacle of the diverse knowledges, devoted to his craft...." And Coedès saw in the name of the god, Viśvarūpa, the ancestor of Puṣkara and Jayavarman II whose pre-ordination name was also Viśvarūpa.[67] There is no difference in the nature of ambivalence in this case from that of the commoners' practice described above. The image represented simultaneously, in a restricted context, the builder's forefather named Viśvarūpa and, in a universal context, Viṣṇu. Better evidence about this practice becomes available in the Angkorean period when more inscriptions are left to us. The most spectacular case is perhaps an inscription written by Indradevī, the queen of Jayavarman VII, who related that her deceased sister, Jayavarman's first queen, had erected several figures of their parents, friends, brothers, and other members of the family. And she herself erected several statue-portraits of her deceased sister and the king in many towns.[68] The monument did not need to be a statue-portrait, since we know that Jayavarman IV erected a Śiva liṅga for his beloved brother, Rājendravarman.[69]

In the case of the king, it was the desire to gain "life-power" for his own prosperity by obtaining the "subtle self" of kingship from his predecessors. Understanding this "subtle self" in terms of Balinese ancestral worship, we may say that it was the ability to relay the "life-power" of the ancestors to other members of the community. This meaning was merged in two Sanskrit words, punya and dharma, for the pre-Angkorean and Angkorean periods respectively.

These two Sanskrit words were used ambivalently in the
Cambodian inscriptions. They contain two levels of meaning:
one is Sanskritic with a cosmic sense, while the other
specifies objects or piety or religious foundations. When
they were used the meaning remained intentionally ambivalent.
Dharma is thus, according to Coedès, "what the king, 'rich
in dharma' (dharmadhana), has received from his predecessors
and transmits to his successors; this is what assures the
transmission of the legitimate royal power (dharmarājya)
from the 'hereditary royal substance' (santatirājyasāra)."[70]
Coedès explained this dharma as being a bridge or a dike by
which the builder of a foundation or an image could link one
part of himself with the ancestors for whom he had erected
the images and the other part to his descendants to whom he
entrusted the maintenance of the foundation and the cult of
the familial images. In this way he could assure the
uninterrupted transmission of dharma "in which (he) had
worked hard...to entrap his 'subtle self' (sūkshmantarātman),
or his essence (bhāva)." That is the reason why Khmer kings
had to be sure that the foundations they built would be protected
by later kings. Rājendravarman's inscription of Pre Rup and
Jayavaraman VII's of Prah Khan attest to their deep concern
about this.[71]

It is proper here to introduce an analysis of Khmer
kingship, bearing in mind the ancestral elements of Khmer
culture in general, to show how its power was established
and legitimized.

Khmer Kingship

There were apparently two traditions of kingship in
ancient Cambodia which will be called here the Sanskritic
tradition and the Khmer tradition. Again, it should not
necessarily be inferred from the classification that a dichotomy
between Indian and indigenous culture is implied. The former
tradition of kingship has been preserved for us in Cambodian
inscriptions as well as in the Indian texts. The latter tradition
can be seen in both the Khmer and the Sanskrit sections of
the local inscriptions. De Mestier du Bourg has pointed out
the difference in the political power of the king as presented

in the two types of inscriptions. Brahmanical power tended to
be high in Sanskrit inscriptions, balancing that of the king,
while in Khmer inscriptions (or sections) the king's power
was obviously supreme.[72] Yet the two traditions were not
completely separable. The interaction between them was the
result of syncretic change in the process of Indianization.
"Followers" (if this is the right word to use) of either tradition
were able to resolve the dichotomy by basing their idea of
kingship on traditions of the other side. What seems to be
a conflict to us might have been a reciprocating reaffirmation
of their views to them. The qualities of an ideal king in the
two traditions, however, differed in the emphasis given to
particular aspects.

Eulogies of living and dead kings from several Sanskrit
inscriptions invariably praised their physical beauty. The
standard practice was to refer to the goddess of Love (Ratī)
who fell in chagrin because of their charm. The reference to
Ratī is a rather indirect metaphor based on Hindu mythology
about Śiva being tempted by Ratī. It is noteworthy that the
Cambodian inscriptions, probably without exception, do not
directly declare the divine nature of the king. The most
suggestive expression was that he was "like a god."[73] The
Indian tradition, on the other hand, was definite about the
divine origin of the king; in the Laws of Manu, it was asserted
that the king had been created by "eternal particles of Indra,
of the Wind, of Yama, of the Sun, of Fire, of Varuna, of the
Moon and of the Lord of wealth (Kubera)." Hence he
"surpasses all created beings in lustre....Even an infant
king must not be despised, (from an idea) that he is a (mere)
mortal; for he is a great deity in human form."[74] What
prevented the outright declaration by the Khmers that the king
was a human deity probably came from the idea that, since
the ancestors alone were the source of "life-power" and were
thus comparable to the gods, a living king was not the source
of "life-power"; rather he was the bearer and transmitter
of that power.

Instead the king was the possessor of worldly fortune,
being he "to whom the fickle goddess of fortune, Lakṣmī, is
firmly attached."[75] He was fortunate in two senses: always
victorious in battles and wealthy. Generosity came with

wealth and the king demonstrated his riches by giving fees to priests on the occasion of sacrifices to the gods (daksiṇās) and by giving "success to solicitors."[76] This quality of the king was confirmed by Indian political philosophy which stated that the Lord had commanded the Kṣatriya to bestow gifts and to offer sacrifices, etc.[77]

Naturally the king's bravery was unbounded: he rigorously "brings terror to the rebels";[78] he was the conqueror of the circle of his enemies; in combat he was a living incarnation of Victory, Vijaya.[79] This quality corresponds with the demand in the Laws of Manu that the king be the protector of the world and of all its creatures.

The king supported the law by punishing "those who deserve being punished with regard to the Law, protecting without respite the honorable people."[80] The Laws of Manu has a section on the duty of the king[81] of which the essence corresponds to these eulogies. The Cambodian king was also the master of arts, singing, musical instruments, and dancing. He was the possessor of the various forms of knowledge. The Indian ideal king was ordered to study the Vedas thoroughly.[82]

One thing differed, however; the Cambodian inscriptions do not emphasize a very important quality of the king in Indian philosophy, his self-control and moderation in pleasure. The Laws of Manu warned kings to shun the ten vices: gambling, greediness, drunkenness, sexual pleasure, etc.[83] The Cambodian kings could justify their spiritual superiority in other terms than abstention from vice, so this quality was not emphasized, although it was referred to on occasion.

On the other hand, the Khmer king was supposed to possess certain mystical powers that hardly find any parallel in the Indian concept of kingship. The eulogy in one of the Sanskrit inscriptions of Sek Ta Tuy implies certain rituals performed by the king to regulate rains in his land. The passage reads: "Śrī, taken by Śauri (Viṣṇu) who is awakened only at the beginning of each rainy season, has been praised each month by the orations of the king all the time of his awakening."[84] The king's mystical power becomes clearer in Khmer inscriptions, while in Sanskrit inscriptions it

remains ambivalent as in the above case which might be taken
as meaning that the king dutifully paid homage to Viṣṇu during
the rainy season. However, the references to rain, to Śrī
being "taken" by Viṣṇu, and to periodic sacrifice by the king
compel us to be aware of a deeper meaning which was mystical
and had a connection with the fertility cult.

The Khmer inscriptions generally deal with the names
of slaves donated and with land belonging to religious
foundations. It is clear that these inscriptions in Khmer or
Khmer sections of bilingual inscriptions served as titles to
the lands and property of the religious foundations or
individuals concerned. Exposition of the ideal kingship was
consequently rather rare in such inscriptions. However, one
quality of the king stood out prominently: he was able to
communicate with the gods through, according to the evidence
we have, dreams and asceticism. The Khmer inscription of
Prah Vihar, dated 1048 (quoted above), declared the power of
Sūryavarman I in obtaining knowledge about the shift of the
residence of the god Bhadreśvara from Liṅgapura to Prah
Vihar under the form and name of the god Śrī Śikharīśvara.
The inscription makes it clear that the king achieved this
power through his asceticism. He then ordered all people in
the different hermitages to revere Śrī Śikharīśvara, to behave
themselves as the commands engraved in a stone pillar
directed, and "not to have doubt (on the question of his
knowledge)."[85]

Another inscription in Khmer, from the second half of
the eleventh century, relates the origin of a religious
foundation. The story went back to the year 850 A. D. when
Jayavarman III lost his elephant in a forest. In the night, he
dreamt that he met Vrah Kamrateṅg An Vaiṣṇava who asked
for his promise to erect a statue of the god and give a cult to
it if the god were to return the elephant to him. The next day
the elephant was found, and the statue of the god was
subsequently erected under the name of Śakabrāhmaṇa,[86] the
title of a Vaiṣṇava text.

Keeping in mind the idea that Hindu gods in Cambodia
also represented ancestral spirits, the ability of the king to
communicate with them was necessary because only then

could he bring the "life-power" to flow upon the Khmer community.

The connection between kings and ancestral spirits belonged quite strictly to the Khmer tradition of kingship. This fact can be seen in the custom of assigning posthumous names to dead kings. With extremely few exceptions, the posthumous names were referred to only in Khmer inscriptions while the Sanskrit counterparts, as a general practice, referred to dead kings by their regnal names.[87] Some bilingual inscriptions clearly indicate strict adherence to this rule. For example, the stele of Trapan Don On gives the reigning names of Udyādityavarman II, Harṣavarman III, Jayavarman VI, and Dharaṇīndravarman I in the Sanskrit section, while these kings, in the Khmer section, were respectively referred to as Udyādityavarman (for some reason he had no posthumous name in Cambodian inscriptions), Sadāśivapāda, Paramakaivalyapāda, and Paramaniṣkālapāda respectively.[88] The case of Yaśovarman referred to above has the same kind of distinction made in the two languages. The Sanskrit section called him by his reigning name and the Khmer section by the name of Paramaśivaloka.[89]

Much has been said about the deification of Khmer kings. That such occurred cannot be easily refuted but qualifications must be attached to the assertion. The posthumous names of kings do not explicitly indicate that they were gods; rather the titles suggest the idea of a place by adding the word loka, "world" or "abode," or the idea of mobility with the word pāda, of which the essential meaning is "to go."[90] When the king died, it could be said that he did not become a god but went to reside in the ancestral abode; his new status was then described in terms of Hindu gods which were probably beings ambivalently related to the ancestors of the Khmers. A Sanskrit inscription from the tenth century, instead of calling the dead kings by their reigning or posthumous names expresses their new status using phrases which definitely describe their destination after death: His Majesty the king who has gone to Viṣṇuloka (Jayavarman III), His Majesty the king who has gone to Paramaśivaloka (Yaśovarman), His Majesty the king who has gone to Paramarudraloka (Īśānavarman II), and His

Majesty the king who has gone to Paramaśivapāda
(Jayavarman IV).[91]

There was another custom which is generally seen as
a form of apotheosis of the dead, i.e., the erection of statue-
portraits of the dead under the combined names of gods and
the deceased. The statue-portraits were supposed to be
revered in the manner rendered to the gods, sometimes with
cults created specially for them. This custom should be
viewed in the context of ancestral worship. The state was,
in Coedès' words, a bridge connecting the living with the dead
and the future generation. It was also part of the ritual to
deliver the dead from earthly bonds, so that the souls could
attain the ancestral abode and then make contact with their
descendants in order to give them the necessary "life-power."
Although a personal name was attached to the statue, that
person did not gain any special position in the pantheon of
ancestors. Even the naming itself was not absolutely
important. The living name of a deceased guru (probably of
Jayavarman VII) was inscribed among names of other "deified"
dead, including Jayavarman VII himself, in the pediments of
a monument in Bantay Chmar.[92] In some other cases, the
names of the statue-portraits had no resemblance to the
deceased's names. In Pre Rup where Rājendravarman
assembled statues of gods relating to his family, the one for
his aunt was just Umā, another name of Pārvati, and the one
for Harṣavarman II was Rājendravarmadeveśvara.[93]
Whatever their names, the deceased formed part of the source
of "life-power" if they were "delivered" through the proper
ritual.

The royal ancestral temples themselves were dedicated
not only to the direct ancestors of the builders but to all the
kings and mythical kings who were supposed to have reigned
over Cambodia.[94] The search for genealogy via both
patrilineal and matrilineal succession was thus not merely an
attempt by one king to link himself to his predecessors; rather
it was the effort to channel the "life-force" of these powerful
individuals down through the ages into the Kambuja of his own
day. By doing so through himself, the king demonstrated his
personal capacity to receive this "life-force," thus
legitimizing his claim to the throne. In such a way, we may

see the Khmer claim of descent from the Lunar line of Soma and Kauṇḍiṇya on the one hand, and the Solar line of the Maharṣi Kambu Svāyambhuva and the Apsaras Mera (a gift of Śiva) on the other, as the ultimate effort to bring the full ancestral power of their land, including that of their Funanese predecessors, to bear in their own day. [95]

An image of a god depicted the portrait of a particular person so that his soul could recognize and incarnate it in the statue. A name which was believed to bear the essence of the man was given to a liṅga for the same purpose. At the same time, these monuments also represented the whole enumeration of the ancestral spirits of the land. The custom practiced by the king indicated the existence of the contrasting ideas: the universal nature of the god and the localized nature of the god. The dichotomy was left unresolved with the former, which naturally worked for the benefit of the king's political power, being emphasized in the devarāja cult.

To perpetuate the communication, or the "bridge," between the ancestral spirits and the king was to assure that the kingdom would be continuously endowed with "life-power" from the ancestors and that the prosperity of the land would continue. The cult should not be regarded as the glorification of the person of the deceased king but as a guarantee of the prosperity of the kingdom for the common interest. The promise of prosperity was materialized in actuality because the Khmer temples were normally surrounded by complicated and efficient irrigation systems. [96] Stern notes that the sequence of construction in a reign was always or almost always initiated by construction of public works, then of the temples for the ancestors, and finally of the central mountain-temple itself. [97] The sequence of construction in a reign that saw the building of ancestral temples before the establishment of the mountain-temple had a reason in the ancestral cult. The ancestral souls had to be relieved of their earthly bonds before they could go to the ancestral land and consequently communicate with their descendants via the devarāja cult or its equivalent.

Devarāja Cult and Devarāja Kingship

In the Cambodian inscriptions, the word devarāja was primarily the name of a god and was more frequently referred to by the Khmer name, Kamrateṅ Jagat ta Rajya (Lord of the Universe who is Royalty). Like other gods in ancient Cambodia, this god possessed more than one shrine; serfs, lands, and villages were donated to him by dignitaries as well as by kings. How popular he was throughout the Angkorean period is difficult to determine from the inscriptions because the references to him are not scattered evenly in every reign. Jayavarman IV, a usurper, was very concerned with this god, at least during the first few years of his reign. The king had a sruk (district) founded for the god in 928. The next year the Bhagavan (probably an official in charge of the cult for the god) informed the king of the donations made to the god.[98] In 930, the king made donations to Kamrateṅ Jagat ta Rajya again, and the list of villages belonging to the god in that year were recorded in the inscription. The king donated more serfs to the god in 932.[99] No mention of the god comes in the same group of inscriptions until 1001 A. D. when Udyādityavarman ordered certain officials to donate a number of serfs for the enjoyment of the god-king.[100] There is no evidence to show that the god enjoyed such continuous favor from all reigning kings as he did from Jayavarman IV. In addition, the god might have assumed other names and resided in other shrines with the resulting diversity of names and forms making it difficult to measure his popularity. As noted, one of the inscriptions from the Koh Ker group gave another Sanskrit name to the god-king, Tribhuvaneśvara. We can identify him because the Khmer section of the inscription mentioned Kamrateṅ Jagat ta Rajya in its place.[101] Jayavarman IV, whose concern about the god-king has been noted above, proclaimed in one of his inscriptions that the god who was responsible for making him king was Tribhuvaneśvara.[102]

Mabbett has pointed out the ambivalent meaning of the word devarāja, and indeed it must have had several meanings among the different classes of the Khmer people. But, considering that ancestral worship involved the largest number of people and even cut across the whole spectrum of the Cambodian social structure, devarāja meant primarily the king of the gods, while also being the chief ancestor who had power over all the ancestral spirits. [103] A Sanskrit inscription from the reign of Jayavarman V makes it clear that this meaning was accepted in Cambodia. The inscription gave a genealogy of kings from Jayavarman II who "arrived at the royal power in the year marked by...[802 A. D.]. Jayavarmadeva, with full-blown wisdom, giving prosperity to those who honored him, to such comes the king of the gods for the protection of the land...."[104] The Sanskrit word for the king of gods here is devādhipendra which Coedès had no hesitation, as he had in the case of devarāja, in rendering in French, le roi des dieux. The author of the passage undoubtedly tried to make an allegorical comparison between the Devarāja and Jayavarman II by indirectly alluding to the famous cult on Mount Mahendra.

The worship of this god, once instituted, was not monopolized by the king. The god also obtained donations from such dignitaries as Śivācārya, a guru of Jayavarman III.[105] From all the evidence we have, it should not be far from the truth that the god-king, like other gods in Cambodia, enjoyed the worship of several groups of people. The main difference from other deities was that, from his inception, there had been an attempt to make him "universal," to place him above all local deities; this feature is attested by his name and by the details in the first cult established for him by Jayavarman II.

It is clear from the SDK inscription that Jayavarman II had the ceremony performed to proclaim himself a Cakravartin. By that time, his power over Cambodia was quite established, by conquest as well as by marriage alliance.[106] He was then not the "prince" of a local region but a great king whom all regions had to obey, at least nominally. This "universal" power had been absent from the experience of the Khmers for generations since the decline of Chenla. The proclamation was thus couched in a way most likely to be understandable to his subjects, that of ancestral cults. Jayavarman instituted a chief of all local ancestral spirits and had a special relationship established between himself and that chief spirit by means of ritual. The idea of a universal god was not new to Cambodia in the ninth century, since it was present in Hindu texts. But the idea did not belong to the Khmer tradition of deity-worship. It was, perhaps unconsciously, identified with Hinduism and the beliefs of the brahmans. The use of brahmans and Indian texts in the devarāja ceremony would then have reinforced the universal nature of the god-king. So a "great Brahman, sovereignly intelligent" who had "respectfully displayed to the king, his magical power that none knew" was invited to conduct the ceremony. The four śāstras, probably of Tantric origin, were recited. [107] Jayavarman II became a source of legitimacy not only to later Khmer kings who referred to him in their genealogies, but also to families that claimed their right of occupancy over lands, positions, ranks, and labor service from Jayavarman II's (possibly legendary) grants. [108] Whether or not Jayavarman was really a powerful monarch of Cambodia is less important to us here than the fact that he initiated a cult which was elaborated upon by later kings and was used as the ideology of the state for hundreds of years. To the aristocratic Khmers of the tenth to the thirteenth centuries his position in the history perceived by them was vital; there is no doubt that, like other great Southeast Asian kings, he was by then already surrounded by legend.

The devarāja cult was repeated in other reigns. We have evidence that Indravarman I had the cult conducted, again by brahmans, on Mount Mahendra in the year of his accession. [109] Mountains always stood prominently in the cult because they implied the abode of the ancestors. In Indravarman I's reign, Kamrateṅ Jagat ta Rajya resided in the summit of a prang which was the mountain-temple of the state in the period. The Devarāja himself was represented by a huge liṅga of great height. [110] In reading a series of inscriptions from the Koh Ker group, Coedès found that the height of the prang where the king of gods resided (according to an inscription) corresponded exactly with a prang west of Prasat Thom in the Koh Ker group and concluded that the prang was the mountain-temple. [111] In Pre Rup, where Rājendravarman II placed statue-images of his family as well as a liṅga which contained his "subtle self," there is no mention of the king of the gods in the inscriptions. At the center, the liṅga was named Rājendrabhadreśvara, a combination of his own name and that of the god Bhadreśvara, a very popular god from the establishment of the sanctuary of Vat Phu.[112] It is not certain whether the Devarāja of the reign resided in this particular linga or whether it had a separate one of its own, now unrecorded. However, it is highly probable that the Devarāja god, in one form or another was connected with the king and that one of the god's representations resided in the central temple-mountain of the capital city since a close predecessor and a successor are both known to have established the cult.[113]

The "subtle self" linga usually had the combined names of the king and -īśvara. What this custom of combining the name of a builder of a linga or a god's image with the name of the god Śiva really meant is difficult to determine. One possible meaning was that the builder's "subtle self" (or bhūpālabhāva, "the essence of kingship") was contained in the god. The king in Indian philosophy was created from particles of the gods. However, if this were the only meaning, the custom would be limited to kings alone. On the contrary, people outside of the royal family practiced the custom too. In 883 A. D. the master of Indravarman's hotars, Nandikācārya, installed a fire god and gave the name Nandikeśvara to the god.[114] Saṅkarṣa, a nephew of Udayādityavarman II, did the same thing when he gave the name Saṅgarseśvara to his restored linga. Examples are numerous both for commoners and for the royal family, and it is rather imprudent to conclude that the custom meant that the king was a god, or that it had this meaning exclusively. Allowing the installation of such a linga or god to ordinary people indicated that the Hindu meaning of divine kingship was not very prominent, if ever tolerated at all.

Jayavarman VII's arrangement of his central temple, the Bayon, is interesting as an example of how the chief ancestral spirit of Devarāja reigned over both the local ancestral spirits of the realm and the specified ancestors of kings whose souls had been delivered as well as how the Devarāja god was related to the reigning king. Indeed, we might almost see the Bayon as the physical manifestation of the ancestral realm of the Khmer belief system, a statue consecrated by the sacred items contained within it. Images (possibly reproductions) of famous deities from all over the kingdom including

Parameśvara from Hariharālaya (the statue portrait of
Jayavarman II), Śrī Jayamahānātha (the statue portrait of
Jayavarman VII) from Ratburi and Petburi in modern Thailand,
and interestingly enough Kamrateṅg Jagat ta Rajya, were
assembled in the Bayon.[115] Jayavarman VII thus collected
all the "life-forces" of the realm under one chief spirit,
which in his case might have been the Buddha-rāja. His own
portrait was depicted in the faces of Avalokiteśvara smiling
beneficently (in a trance?) and radiating peace and prosperity
from the four sides of the tower throughout the "universe."
His (or Avalokiteśvara's) power derived from the amassed
essence of "life-power" of the gods to mankind, again
reminding us of the village heads in Bali,who, in a trance,
relayed the "life-power" from the ancestors to the community.
In this role, a Khmer king could command respect from and
justify his rule to his mass of subjects. Conscription of
labor was not seen as oppression and drew no resistance
because the idea behind the massive construction was
communicable and acceptable among both rulers and ruled.
Wolters effectively sums up the interconnection between
religion and government in early Southeast Asian history in
his statement, "Great leaders in early Southeast Asia were
perceived by their contemporaries as agents of divine power,
and royal service could be valued as a source of religious
merit."[116]

Conclusion

Ancestors, as the source of "life-power," formed a
large part in the world-view of the Khmers. The ancestral
cult was connected with fertility rites. Some of the village
deities represented the ancestral spirits of that community.
Hindu mythology was syncretized with the folk beliefs and
ancestral gods obtained Indian names, but they still
represented local, specific spirits of the communities in
which they were located. Hinduism with its gods of universal
character probably existed only among ascetics and some
Indian immigrants. The dichotomy between the Hindu concept
of the gods and the Khmer's belief in local spirits was
resolved in ambivalence. Each god represented many different
characteristics that were sought after by his clients of

different social and educational backgrounds.

Under Jayavarman II, a cult was established for him
in which he claimed a special relationship with a newly
created spirit or god called the king of the gods, or in Khmer,
"Lord of the universe who is royalty." This god was also
a resolution of the religious dichotomy as he allowed
ambivalence to emerge. To a brahman and ascetic, the god
might have represented Śiva, who is supreme among the gods;
to an ordinary Khmer, he might have been the chief spirit of
all the ancestral spirits of the land. His Khmer name, unlike
those of other local spirits, was not submerged in later
inscriptions under the Sanskrit term devarāja, which indeed
was essentially created to fit the Khmer situation and had no
real parallel in Sanskrit mythology. Each term was used in
its own section of the inscriptions. The god was thus held up
as special for the Khmers in the rituals performed for him,
retaining his own Khmer name. His Sanskrit name has thus
been properly used as a description of Angkorean kingship,
which also had the characteristic of ambivalence, basing
its legitimacy on Sanskrit philosophy as well as on the
mystical power of a Khmer chieftain.

The two ideas of deities and kingship presumably lived
together in peace. Jayavarman II crystalized the ambivalent
resolution into an institution which was subsequently elaborated
upon by later kings. However, the idea that the king had a
special relationship with the Devarāja god possibly remained
unchanged. Among several justifications of the Khmer kings'
rule, probably the most prominent one that acquired approval
and acquiescense from the largest number of the Khmer
people was that the king acted as intermediary between the
source of "life-power" and the community. He materialized
the promised prosperity to the land through irrigation systems
and the promised peace to the people through administration.

Late in the thirteenth century, a Chinese visitor
recorded after long residence in Angkor and possible contacts
with the common folk, this "other" idea of kingship, not
clearly represented in the aristocratically biased inscriptions
of Cambodia. Chou Ta-kuan preserved for us a form of the
intermediary role of the king as well as the king's mystical

power as perceived by the people of that great empire when he reported that the king had to have intercourse with a spirit formed like a serpent with nine heads, "which is Lord of the entire kingdom," every night for the prosperity of the realm.[117]

NOTES

1. George Coedès and Pierre Dupont, "Les stèles de Sdok Kak Thom, Phnom Sandak et Prah Vihar," BEFEO, 43 (1943-46), pp. 63-64.

2. George Coedès, The Indianized States of Southeast Asia (Honolulu, 1968), pp. 100-101.

3. Ibid., p. 119.

4. George Coedès, Angkor, An Introduction (Hongkong, 1963), p. 31.

5. Coedès, The Indianized States, p. 100.

6. K. Bhattacharya, Les religions brahmaniques dans l'ancien Cambodge d'après l'epigraphie et l'iconographie, EFEO Publication 49 (Paris, 1961), pp. 27-28.

7. L. P. Briggs, The Ancient Khmer Empire (Philadelphia, 1951), p. 89.

8. P. Stern, "Temple-montagne khmer, le culte du linga et le Devaraja," BEFEO, 34, 2 (1935), p. 614. Coedès, with careful reservation, had suggested the idea in "La tradition genealogique des premiers rois d'Angkor d'après les inscriptions de Yaçovarman et de Rajendravarman," BEFEO, 28, 1-2 (1928), p. 117.

9. P. Stern, "Diversité et rythme des fondations royales khmers," BEFEO, 44, 2 (1954), p. 653.

10. Stern also referred to Coedès' later interpretation of the SDK inscription that the Devarāja was misinterpreted as having been shifted with the capital. Dupont's idea that the devarāja liṅga was not replaceable is thus rejected. The parallel between the devarāja figure and the royal regalia of later Southeast Asian states should not be drawn without some clarification. The regalia, including the white parasol, were sacred in themselves because they

were the symbols of the sacred kingship. The devarāja liṅga was sacred after being consecrated; it was not a symbol but firstly a god and secondly a bearer of the royal essence. To both characters, the liṅga of the Devarāja god was revered and received sacrifices made not exclusively by kings but also by persons outside the royal family. Yet, in comparing the functions of the two, there was one common feature: both attested to the status of the "possessor" and "founder" as being a universal monarch.

11. P. Dupont, "Les débuts de la royauté angkorienne," BEFEO, 46, 1 (1952), pp. 167-169.

12. O. W. Wolters, "Jayavarman II's Military Power: The Territorial Foundation of the Angkor Empire," JRAS (1973), pp. 21-30.

13. D. G. E. Hall, A History of Southeast Asia, third edition (London, 1970), pp. 101-103.

14. Coedès, Angkor, pp. 31-32. On the other hand, an ordinance of Yaśovarman to the temple police in the ninth century has a section which reads: "Gentlemen or gentlewomen ['L'homme de bien ou la femme'...the meaning here, I think, was intended to refer to the general public rather than a group of high social status. Another inscription from the same monarch quoted below confirms this interpretation. So it can read: 'men and women of good conduct....'] who desire to honor the divinities can enter devotedly with the offerings proportionate to their fortune." The stele of Thnal Baray from Yaśovarman's reign prohibited "girls of the common [prostitutes?] (or) whose conduct is notorious" from entering a temple. Groslier concludes from these ordinances that "The religious temples of the Khmer were open to the public, and naturally the rules were meticulous about how to dress, how to enter, etc." See G. Groslier, Recherches sur les Cambodgiens (Paris, 1921), pp. 330-331.

15. I. Mabbett, "Devaraja," JSEAH, 10, 2 (1969), pp. 202-223.

16. See George Coedès, "La destination funeraire de grands

monuments khmers," BEFEO, 40 (1940), pp. 315-344.

17. W. F. Stutterheim, Indian Influence in Old Balinese Art (London, 1935), p. 2.

18. On Java and other islands, parts of the ancestors' bones were kept in stone jars and stored in a small spirit house present in every home. There was a relationship between ancestral worship and fertility rites as seen by the cult surrounding the "rice granaries" in Java. See W. F. Stutterheim, "Some Remarks on Pre-Hinduistic Burial Customs on Java," in W. F. Stutterheim, Studies in Indonesian Archaeology (The Hague, 1956), pp. 74-90.

19. Stutterheim, Indian Influence, pp. 2-3.

20. Ibid., pp. 4-5.

21. Ibid., pp. 22-23.

22. Stutterheim, Studies in, pp. 69-74.

23. Stutterheim, Indian Influence, p. 24.

24. It is very tempting to assert that the two concepts of the divine differed because one was derived from Indian culture while the other came from indigenous culture. However, incorporation of folk belief has also existed in India since time immemorial and is very present in the Indian classical religion, as we can see in the incorporation of local legends into the purāṇa literature.

25. George Coedès, IC, 5, pp. 244-269.

26. Paul Mus said that the state cult of Champa emphasized relativity. When a king was deified as Śiva, he was a special Śiva not the one known in Sanskrit texts. See Paul Mus, "Cultes Indiens et indigenes au Champa," BEFEO, 33, 1 (1933), pp. 367-410.

27. IC, 6, pp. 267-270.

142

28. Stutterheim, Indian Influence, p. 24.

29. Bhattacharya, p. 169.

30. IC, 2, pp. 21-23.

31. Ibid., p. 117.

32. IC, 5, pp. 73-74.

33. Ibid., p. 114.

34. IC, 2, p. 58.

35. IC, 3, pp. 72-75.

36. Ibid., pp. 97-99.

37. IC, 5, p. 293.

38. Bhattacharya, p. 77. The nature of the Svāyambhuva liṅga corresponded with the belief in Svāyambhu, the god who was self-created, hence a natural god, and who brought forth the world and all its beings from his desire. See G. Bühler, The Laws of Manu (New York, 1969), pp. 1-18.

39. Bhattacharya, p. 21.

40. Mus, pp. 367-410.

41. IC, 3, p. 75.

42. IC, 2, p. 71.

43. IC, 5, p. 123.

44. IC, 1, p. 61.

45. IC, 3, pp. 178-179.

46. Indian culture recognizes ancestor worship, complete with a "World of the Fathers"; but though the cosmic location of

the world varies, it is never put on top of a mountain, which must therefore be a Khmer feature. The author wishes to thank Professor Thomas R. Trautmann for bringing this to his attention.

47. Coedès, "La destination," p. 319. In Indian philosophy rebirth and resurrection (mokṣa) are distinct ideas.

48. Guy Porée and E. Maspero, Moeurs et coutumes des khmers (Paris, 1938), p. 151.

49. Ibid., p. 147.

50. Coedès, "La destination," p. 319, n. 1.

51. Mus, p. 367f.

52. Briggs, p. 42.

53. IC, 4, p. 56.

54. For Sūryavarman I's religion, see Hubert de Mestier du Bourg, "La premiere moitie de XIe siecle au Cambodge Suryavarman 1er, sa vie et quelques aspects des institutions a son epoque," JA, 258, 3-4 (1970), pp. 281-314. It should be noted here that there had been another idea about the location of the ancestral land which may have prevailed among the Funanese. The pictures engraved on the bronze drums of the Dong-son culture suggest that the deceased's spirit was carried by boat to another shore. The similarity of the Dong-son culture with that of the later period found in the island world of Southeast Asia explains in part the similarity of the myths about the initiation of civilization in those islands. In many parts of maritime Southeast Asia the man or the spirit who caused civilization to begin came from or had connection with the sea. It is quite likely that these myths express the idea of the ancestral spirits protecting and making the living communities prosperous rather than preserving for us any story about the civilizing expeditions of the Indians. In Funan, the story of Kauṇḍinya should be placed in this category. The Khmer carried with them from their homeland in the Mekong

basin (or further west) to the Mun and southern Korat plateau the idea that their ancestral abode was on the top of a mountain [see George Coedès, "Nouvelles donnees sur les origines du royaume khmer," BEFEO, 48, 1 (1954), pp. 209-220]. They then adopted the Funanese myth about Kauṇḍiṇya in an attempt to link the reigning Khmer kings with all the dynasties ever to have reigned over the land. See Coedès, "La tradition," pp. 138-139.

55. IC, 1, pp. 70-71.

56. The Devarāja god might have had other Sanskrit names; for example, one of the Sanskrit inscriptions from the Koh Ker group gives the name Tribhuvaneśvara in correspondence with the Khmer inscription where Kamrateng An Jagat ta Rajya is used.

57. The Buddhist inscription of Prasat Plan blesses those who "conserve, abstain from robbing, and lavish wealth on that good deed will obtain with their clan [using the word gotra in Sanskrit which implies both the living and the dead] a favorable condition,...." (IC, 5, pp. 156-157.) Since the passage was written in Sanskrit, the importance of one's clan might have been overemphasized to impress the highly Indianized who were its expected readers (Coedés, "Nouvelles donnees," pp. 209-220).

58. IC, 2, pp. 39-44.

59. IC, 5, pp. 83-84.

60. Ibid., pp. 143-146.

61. IC, 2, pp. 89-91.

62. Chou Ta-kuan, Notes on the Custom of Cambodia (Bangkok, 1967), p. 38.

63. George Coedès, "Le servent des fonctionnaires de Suryavarman I," BEFEO, 13 (1913), pp. 11-17; and IC, 3, pp. 205-216.

64. IC, 2, p. 205.

65. L. Finot, "Nouvelles inscriptions du Cambodge," BEFEO, 28, 1-2 (1928), p. 46.

66. This is also seen in the case noted in the stele of Prasat Trapan Rung. Ibid., p. 58.

67. IC, 3, p. 129.

68. Coedès, "La destination," pp. 320-321.

69. IC, 1, p. 61.

70. Coedès, "La destination," pp. 324-328.

71. Ibid., pp. 327-329.

72. De Mestier du Bourg, p. 281f.

73. See for example the stele of the foundation of Prah Ko and Bakon, IC, 1, p. 34.

74. Bühler, pp. 216-217.

75. A eulogy to Jayavarman I, which is quoted in Briggs, p. 54.

76. Finot, p. 53.

77. Bühler, p. 24.

78. Finot, p. 53.

79. Briggs, p. 54.

80. A eulogy to Jayavarman VII, which appears in IC, 4, p. 224.

81. Bühler, pp. 219-239.

82. Ibid., p. 24.

83. Ibid., pp. 222-224. Though Manu counsels kings to be

self-controlled and free of vice, Indian inscriptions
regularly stress the king's sexual attractiveness and sexual
prowess. While Manu's view is conservative and
puritanical, Indian inscriptions stress the warlike and the
erotic.

84. Finot, p. 54.

85. IC, 6, pp. 269-270.

86. IC, 4, pp. 167-169.

87. See for example IC, 2, p. 106, in which Harṣavarman was
called Srī Harṣavarman; ibid., p. 12, in which
Rudravarman was referred to under his reigning name;
IC, 3, p. 11, in which Harṣavarman was referred to in
1036 as Śrī Harṣavarmadēva, a standard practice of adding
deva to kings' names, either living or dead; and ibid.,
p. 201, a Sanskrit inscription dated 910, in which no
posthumous name was given to Yaśovarman either.

88. IC, 3, pp. 180-192.

89. Ibid., p. 203.

90. In Sanskrit pāda, "foot," suggests motion.

91. IC, 5, p. 103.

92. IC, 3, p. 71.

93. Coedès, "La destination," p. 321.

94. Stern, "Diversité et rythme," p. 654.

95. See Briggs, pp. 39-40, 61, 81, and 209. and P. Dupont,
"La dislocation du Tchen-la et la formation du Cambodge
Angkorien, VIIe-IXe siecle," BEFEO, 43 (1943-46),
pp. 24-25.

96. B. P. Groslier, Angkor et le Cambodge au XVIe siecle
d'après les sources Portugaises et Espagnoles (Paris,
1958), pp. 107-121.

97. Stern, "Diversité et rythme," pp. 654-655.

98. IC, 1, p. 50.

99. Ibid., pp. 48-49.

100. Ibid., pp. 50-51.

101. Ibid., pp. 70-71.

102. R. C. Majumdar, Inscriptions of Kambuja (Calcutta, 1953), p. 165.

103. That this was explicitly a Khmer concept may be seen in the fact that the supreme Indian god is Indra, Mahendra, etc., who is never considered as either a chief ancestor or king of the dead (Yama). The author thanks Professor Trautmann for this information.

104. IC, 5, p. 167.

105. IC, 6, p. 179.

106. See Wolters, pp. 21-30.

107. Coedès and Dupont, p. 96; Bhattacharya, p. 27.

108. See for example an inscription dated 1064, IC, 3, pp. 94-96.

109. IC, 1, pp. 17-36.

110. Coedès, The Indianized States, p. 116.

111. IC, 1, pp. 70-71.

112. Coedès, The Indianized States, p. 119. Since the name of Bhadreśvara is found quite early in Cambodian history in a Chinese record and since his popularity has been well attested to in several inscriptions, it is tempting to describe him as the "national" god of the Khmers. However the concept of a "national" god still, I think, demands more evidence than we have to prove that it existed in ancient

148

Cambodian society. Bhadreśvara was always represented by a linga; his first appearance in history reflects a non-Brahman cult which involved human sacrifices, ritual in which an Indian brahman could not participate (Bhattacharya, p. 23). His popularity, although great in a large part of ancient Cambodian history, was not uninterrupted. In the early twelfth century, Jayavarman VI was asked by a number of official brahmans to reclaim the property of this god. He did and revived the cult of Bhadreśvara (IC, 5, p. 293). The passage indicates the lapse of his cult, at least at Vat Phu, during the previous reigns (Coedès, IC, 5, p. 289).

113. Jayavarman IV is said in an inscription to have brought the Devarāja along when he established himself in Chok Gargyar (Briggs, p. 116). Briggs quotes the Sdok Kak Thom inscription to show that when Rājendravarman returned to Yaśodharapura he brought back the Devarāja from Chok Gargyar (Briggs, p. 124). In the following reign (that of Jayavarman V), Tribhuvaneśvara, the god identified with the Devarāja in the reign of Jayavarman IV, is found at Bantay Srei (Briggs, pp. 135 and 137).

114. IC, 4, p. 46.

115. IC, 3, pp. 193-198.

116. Wolters, p. 29.

117. Chou Ta-kuan, p. 22.

The Rise of Đại Việt

and the Establishment of Thăng-long

by
Keith Taylor

During the tenth century, Vietnam evolved from a
dependency of the T'ang Empire into an independent monarchy.
In the first half of the eleventh century, the Lý Dynasty
institutionalized the power of the court and gave Vietnamese
civilization a form which endured for four centuries. In this
brief article, I will examine this century and half of
development, providing not only a historical narrative but also
a sense of how the events of this period reflected older political
traditions while creating new ones.

Under the T'ang Dynasty, Vietnam was divided into five
major administrative regions. Giao, Phong, and Trường were
located in the Red River Delta; Ái lay to the south in the delta
of the Ma River while Hoan was on the extreme southern
frontier in the delta of the Ca River.[1] The census of 742
was as follows[2]:

	Hearths	Heads
Giao	24,230	99,652
Phong	1,920	5,110
Trường	628	3,040

These figures represent the settled population most closely
associated with Chinese administration. Located where the
land and sea routes from China met in the fertile plains of the
upper Delta, Giao contained 85 to 90% of the settled population
and was the center of Chinese administration. Phong was the
strategic mountain frontier where the Red River and its
tributaries entered the Delta; here was the headquarters for
overseeing the surrounding mountain peoples.[3] Trường was
located along the lower Red River between the sea and the
mountains; at its southern extremity was the ancient canal
which cut through the mountains at the edge of the sea to

149

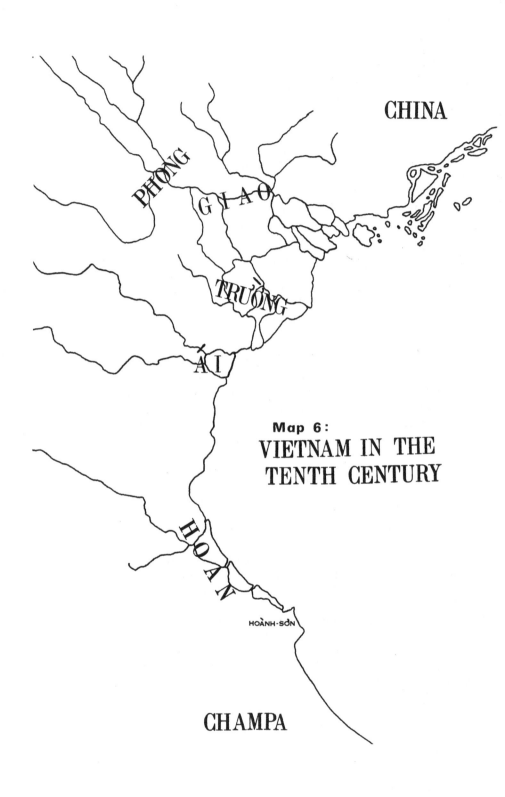

CHINA

PHONG

GIAO

TRƯỜNG

ÁI

Map 6:
VIETNAM IN THE
TENTH CENTURY

HOAN

HOÀNH-SƠN

CHAMPA

provide access to Ái.[4] Ái and Hoan, not included in the census, were notable as centers of rebellion and as the scene of periodic raids by the Chams from the south. During the many years of colonial status under the various dynasties of China, Vietnam remained a frontier region, open to non-Chinese influences and susceptible to revolt.

In the ninth century, there were a number of rebellions against T'ang authority. These rebellions reflected internal divisions within Vietnam as much as they did the broader theme of resistance to Chinese rule; or, more to the point, the issue of Chinese control was viewed from different perspectives by the Vietnamese, depending on the degree to which individual Vietnamese had learned to accept the process of Sinicization. Chinese influence was by far the strongest in the densely populated area of Giao. Giao contained schools which trained Vietnamese in the Chinese classics and prepared them for service in the local administration.[5] Giao was also the center of Vietnamese Buddhism which by the ninth century had important cultural ties with China. The areas of Phong, Trường, Ái and Hoan were more strongly oriented toward the mountain frontier. In these areas non-Sinic traditions remained important and resistance to Chinese rule was more easily aroused.

In 819, a military man from Hoan named Dương Thanh seized the governing citadel of Đại-la and killed more than one thousand Chinese including the governor and his family. Dương Thanh then closed the frontier and defied the empire.[6] The Chinese responded by getting in touch with those elements in Vietnam from whom they could expect co-operation; these were the civil officials and the Buddhist communities of Giao. In 820, a Chinese monk arrived in Vietnam and founded a new Buddhist sect, the Vô Ngôn Thông Sect.[7] This sect may have mobilized pro-Chinese elements against Dương Thanh's radicalism. By the end of 820, Dương Thanh had been deposed by his subordinates and the gates of Đai-la reopened to the Chinese.[8]

Dương Thanh's rebellion opened four decades of political instability in Vietnam. During this time, the conflict between pro-Chinese elements and anti-Chinese elements remained

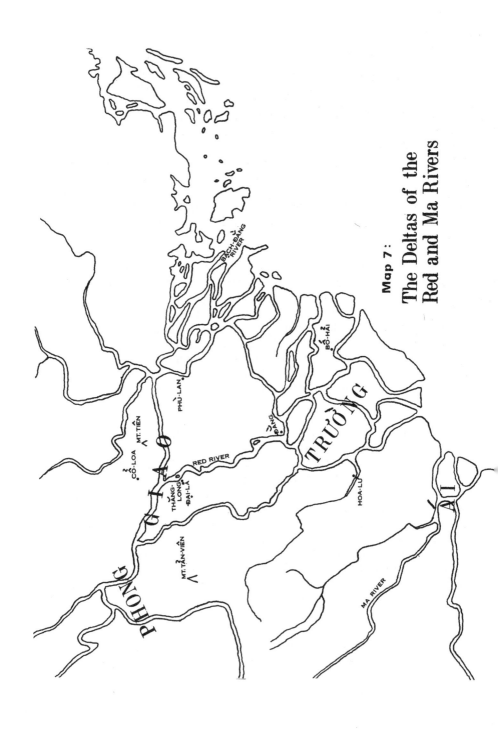

Map 7:

The Deltas of the Red and Ma Rivers

PHONG
GIAO
CHÂU
TRƯỜNG
ÁI

MT. TIÊN
CỔ-LOA
PHÙ-LAN
BỐ-HẢI
ĐẰNG
RED RIVER
THĂNG-LONG
ĐẠI-LA
HOA-LƯ
MT. TẢN-VIÊN
MA RIVER
BẠCH-ĐẰNG RIVER

unresolved. In 828 and in 843, Chinese governors were driven out by short-lived rebellions. [9] A memorial on Vietnam dated in 845 from the Chinese archives states: "At every stream, cave, marketplace, everywhere there is stubbornness. Repression is necessary. Once every three years soldiers have to be taken out to patrol and repress, then to report the situation." [10] In the 850's, anti-colonialists looked to the mountain kingdom of Nan Chao, on the Yunnan plateau, for help. In 858, only the presence of an able Chinese general prevented Vietnamese leaders from allying with Nan Chao armies against the Chinese. [11] In 860, just such an alliance captured Đại-la and drove out the governor. [12] In the resulting warfare, Vietnamese anti-colonialists were swallowed up by the armies of Nan Chao. By 863, these armies were in undisputed possession of Vietnam; they imposed a regime of plunder which made the return of Chinese armies in 865 a welcome sight to the Vietnamese. [13] The man who led these Chinese armies was to earn a special place in Vietnamese history. His name was Kao P'ien; he was a fine military strategist and a gifted political leader. Kao opened a new era of peace and prosperity which paved the way for Vietnamese independence.

The Nan Chao War had left Vietnam in a state of devastation. Kao initiated a broad program of reconstruction; roads, bridges, dikes, canals, public resthouses, shrines and temples were constructed or rebuilt. Kao was remembered most, however, for his rebuilding of Đại-la. The new citadel was four and a half miles in circumference; walls thirty feet high were enclosed within an eighteen foot dike. Over five thousand buildings were constructed within the walls. [14] But of deeper significance than the physical reconstruction was the spiritual reconstruction of Vietnam. According to local tradition, Kao honored the indigenous heroes of the Vietnamese and on several occasions reported personal visitations by powerful spirits of the land. [15] He commemorated an interview with the spirit of a third century B.C. figure in Vietnamese history by composing the following poem:

> The land of Chiao Chou (an ancient name of Vietnam)
>   is beautiful;
> So has it been from eternity.

> The worthy men of old extend their welcome;
> Then one is not ungrateful to the spirits. [16]

Kao left Vietnam in 868, but his policy of encouraging
and contributing to the development of Vietnamese cultural
traditions was carried on by his grandson, who governed from
868 to 878, and by his aide-de-camp during the Nan Chao War,
a man named Tseng Kun. Tseng became governor in 878; he
recorded local traditions in a book, now lost, which was used
by early Vietnamese historians. [17] A poem from Tseng's
brush reflects the new spirit prevailing in Vietnam, which he
prophetically refers to as the Southern Kingdom. Rather than
a source of oppression, the Dragon Spirit of imperial China
has become a guardian of peace and prosperity:

> The mountains and rivers of the Southern Kingdom
> are beautiful;
> The place where the Dragon Spirit dwells is blessed.
> Chiao Chou has ceased to be pressed down;
> From now on there will be peace and prosperity. [13]

This renaissance of Vietnamese culture had important
consequences for the post-colonial period. It can be assumed
that Buddhism prospered. Kao P'ien built a stupa at Mount
Tiên where the Buddhist leadership of the following century
would be based. [19] In the political arena, these developments
were accompanied by the emergence of a Sino-Vietnamese
aristocracy which united all the regions of Vietnam under the
imperial umbrella by means of marriage ties and class
interest. When, in 880, the era of Kao P'ien and his associates
came to a close, this class was ready to play a larger role
in politics.

In 880, Huang Ch'ao's rebellion in China provoked a
mutiny of the T'ang garrison at Đại-la. Tseng Kun hastily
departed for China and Chinese soldiers returned north in
small groups on their own initiative. [20] Thereafter, Chinese
control of Vietnam was virtually at an end as the T'ang Empire
crumbled irretrievably into ruin. The Sino-Vietnamese
aristocracy, however, depended on the imperial world for
justification of its ruling position. Consequently it was careful
to maintain a nominal connection with the empire.

The inability to cut loose from the imperial mentality characterized the Sino-Vietnamese aristocracy well into the post-T'ang period and, while a tribute to Kao P'ien, explains why it was unsuccessful in consolidating Vietnamese independence.

In the final years of the T'ang dynasty, Chu Wên was building up a position in north China from which he would found the Later Liang dynasty in 907.[21] The next Chinese governor in Vietnam after Tseng Kun was Chu Wên's elder brother, Chu Ch'üan-yü. Chu Ch'üan-yü was apparently out of his element among the ambitions of the emerging Sino-Vietnamese aristocracy. He was recalled in 905, ostensibly because, although "sincere," he was "simpleheaded and without talent."[22] He had probably been reduced to a cipher in the hands of the local aristocracy. His replacement was in Vietnam for only a few months before a local man named Khúc Thừa Dụ gained the title of governor.[23] In 907, Chu Wên named a governor in Canton; thereafter, his dynasty concerned itself no further with the south. In 917, the Cantonese governor's family founded the Southern Han dynasty[24]; this local dynasty was the only threat to Vietnamese independence until the rise of the Sung later in the century.

Whether the Khúc family was of Chinese or local origin is unknown; the Khúc had in any case been established in eastern Giao for several generations. Remembered as "ambitious and shrewd," they bore the title of governor and succeeded in holding Vietnam while claiming loyalty to the Later Liang as a check on Southern Han expansionism.[25] When the Later Liang dynasty fell in 923, the Southern Han invaded Vietnam, defeating and capturing the last of the Khúc.[26]

The Khúc had given Vietnam a measure of stability without challenging the imperial ideals inherited from the T'ang period. Southern Han aggression, however, unleashed forces in Vietnam which led to the abandonment of these ideals. A Khúc vassal in Ái, a man named Dương Đình Nghệ, led an army against the Southern Han following the Khúc defeat in 923. After negotiations, Đình Nghệ returned to Ái with a Southern Han title. The officials subsequently sent to

administer Giao were advised by the Southern Han ruler:
"The people of Giao often rise in revolt; therefore, a tight
rein must be maintained." The Southern Han held on for
eight years. During this time, Đình Nghệ built up an army
of three thousand men. In 931, he moved out from his base in
Ái and took possession of all Vietnam, independently naming
himself governor.[27]

With the rise of Dương Đình Nghệ, Vietnam entered a
period in which imperial ideals lost their meaning. While
Đình Nghệ claimed the title of an imperial governor, there
was no empire or even semi-empire to which Vietnam was
attached. The Khúc had maintained relations with the Later
Liang of North China. But the fall of the Later Liang followed
by Southern Han aggression had forced Vietnam back upon its
own resources. Colonial Vietnam began to crumble beneath
the weight of political anarchy in China, but more importantly
under the pressure of indigenous anti-colonial forces which
emerged from the frontier areas, in particular the region
of Ái.

In 937, this unstable situation came unglued with the
result that imperial ideals were abandoned altogether. Đình
Nghệ was killed by a man from Phong named Kiều Công Tiễn.
Whether this was a reaction of the more Sinicized elements
against the ascendence of Ái or simply an act of personal
ambition is unclear. In any case, when Đình Nghệ's son-in-
law and commander of Ái, a man from western Giao named
Ngô Quyền, marched against Công Tiễn, Công Tiễn called on
the Southern Han for aid. By the time the Chinese arrived
late in 938, Quyền had disposed of Công Tiễn and was prepared
to meet them. In what was essentially a naval battle on the
Bach-đằng River, the Chinese were defeated[28]; never again
did the Southern Han threaten Vietnam. Vietnamese historians
in later centuries considered this victory as the beginning of
independence. Vietnamese resistance to the ambitious
Southern Han was an important step toward full independence.
But the Sino-Vietnamese aristocracy was torn between the ties
of culture which held them to China and the growing reality of
anti-colonial Vietnam. The next step of this aristocracy was
more an expedient than a positive reaction.

Early in 939, Ngô Quyền claimed the title of king and, abandoning Đại-la, established a royal court at the ancient citadel of Cổ-loa, which dated from the third century B.C.[29] This was the first time that any leader had claimed to be more than an imperial governor, yet Quyền's pretentions to royalty were no more than an imitation of the Southern Han. The weakness of the Cổ-loa monarchy was characteristic of a disintegrating aristocracy whose bonds of class loyalty were being undermined by revolutionary forces. As the political situation gradually evolved toward the eruption of ancient anti-colonial traditions, the Sino-Vietnamese aristocrats, like men who belatedly discover that they have been basking on the back of a whale, began to look each to his own safety.

When Quyền died in 944, his brother-in-law, a son of Đinh Nghệ named Dương Tam Kha, took the throne for himself, setting aside Quyền's young sons. Tam Kha's authority did not extend beyond Giao. Quyền's eldest son, Ngô Xương Ngập, with the aid of several Ngô vassals, fled into the eastern part of the Delta and was protected by a powerful family established there.[30] In 950, Tam Kha sent Quyền's second son, Ngô Xương Văn, and two trusted generals against a pair of rebellious villages in Phong; these were probably the home estates of the Kiều family which had unsuccessfully attempted to supplant Đinh Nghệ in 937. Xương Văn persuaded the generals to return and depose Tam Kha whom they allowed to retire to a country estate.[31] Xương Văn immediately called for his brother and the two proposed to rule jointly. With two young princes attempting to share the throne, the time was propitious for local strongmen to assert themselves. Such a man was Đinh Bo Lĩnh.

Unlike other local lords who, while defending their estates against Ngô authority continued in theory to recognize Ngô suzerainty, Đinh Bộ Lĩnh represented a different force in the political scene, a force both new and old: new in the context of the tenth century but old in the traditions of the Vietnamese people. Bộ Lĩnh was the orphaned son of a man from the mountainous border between Trương and Ái who had served both Đinh Nghê and Quyền as a military commander in Hoan. With the passage of time, popular tradition erased Bộ Lĩnh's father and replaced him with a water creature who

joined with his mother as she bathed in a pond; Bộ Lĩnh's
success was explained by the burial of this creature's bones in
a spiritually potent cavern.[32] The official history states that
Bộ Lĩnh's mother lived in a cave beside the shrine of a
mountain spirit in Hoa-lư, a village in a narrow valley overlooking the Delta not far from the sea. The men of the region
were absent, having been conscripted into the aristocratic
armies. As a boy, Bộ Lĩnh tended water buffaloes with the
other village children. According to Vietnamese historical
tradition, his leadership abilities were demonstrated at an
early age as he induced his playmates to carry him about with
banners flying in the manner of a king. On leisure days he
led his followers to battle against the children of neighboring
villages. Eventually, all grew to fear him and competed in
gathering firewood and cooking rice to serve him. The old
people of the village counselled together: "This youngster,
with such spirit, will surely go places; if we don't follow him
now, later on it will be too late to repent." So he was made
chief of the village; after subduing neighboring villages, he
took the title "King of Ten Thousand Victories (Vạn-Thắng
Vương).[33]

The so-called Twelve Warlords who appeared as
rulers of petty estates began to assert themselves after 950;
they were all nominal vassals of the Ngô. Bộ Lĩnh was not
numbered among them.[34] In 951, the Ngô brothers prepared
to march against Bộ Lĩnh. Bộ Lĩnh sent his son Liễn with the
intention of negotiating. The Ngô, however, made Liễn
prisoner and, camping outside the mountainous enclave of
Hoa-lư, displayed him with threats of execution if Bộ Lĩnh
refused to submit. Bộ Lĩnh replied that he had no intention
of acting like a woman and shot a volley of arrows in Liễn's
direction. The Ngô bluff had been called and the brothers
retired in confusion, uncertain how to deal with one so
contemptuous of their claim to royalty. The two brothers
subsequently fell out, with the elder pushing the younger
aside.[35]

The Twelve Warlords were all located in the Red River
Delta except for a grandson of Ngô Quyền who had found refuge
in southern Ái. Nine were in Phong and Giao; most of Phong
remained in the hands of the Kiều family while the Ngô and

their most loyal men held western Giao along the middle course of the Red River. The two remaining men were in Trường along the lower Red River adjacent to Bộ Lĩnh's territory, which spread from northern Ái to southern Trường. These two lords of the lower Delta were Phạm Bạch Hổ of Đằng and Trần Lãm of Bố-hải, a seaport near the mouth of the Red River.[36] Bộ Lĩnh's first step to power beyond his local base was an alliance with Trần Lãm. Lãm was a Cantonese and it has been suggested that this alliance represented the linking of maritime commercial wealth with the manpower at Bộ Lĩnh's disposal.[37] The official history attests to the wealth and liberality of Lãm. At Đằng, Phạm Bạch Hổ was probably a middleman for moving trade up the Red River to the upper Delta; after the Đinh-Trần alliance was concluded, he quickly submitted to Bộ Lĩnh and received a title.[38] Thus, Bộ Lĩnh was in a position to seal the upper Delta off from the sea via the Red River. The northern sea route into the Delta via the Bach-đằng River had also been closed, either by Bộ Lĩnh's men or by local pirates, for when Ngô Xương Ngập died in 954, his brother Xương Văn requested the title of governor from the Southern Han, but the Chinese emissaries were unable to deliver the symbolic banner because "bandits from the sea were in rebellion."[39]

In 965, Ngô Xương Văn was killed while fighting the same pair of villages in Phong which had resisted Ngô control in 950.[40] In the wake of this debacle, there was a scramble for power in Giao. Three sons of a Chinese merchant and a Vietnamese woman took the name of their mother, Nguyễn, and consolidated control of northern and central Giao.[41] The Ngô and their most faithful vassal, the Đỗ family, were left in western Giao hemmed in between the Kiểu of Phong and Đinh Bộ Lĩnh in Trường. Đinh Liễn escaped to Hoa-lư signalling to Bộ Lĩnh that the time was ripe to move.[42] In 967, Bộ Lĩnh led his men into the upper delta, first defeating the combined Đỗ and Ngô forces and then the Kiểu.[43] Bộ Lĩnh sent Nguyễn Bặc, a trusted companion from Hoa-lư, to force the Nguyễn of Giao into submission.[44] With the leaders of the Sino-Vietnamese aristocracy fleeing in all directions, Bộ Lĩnh took possession of all Vietnam.

The following year, 968, Bộ Lĩnh claimed the title of emperor and founded the realm of Đại Cổ Việt (Viet of the

Great Watchful Hawk 大 瞿越) at Hoa-lư. In the palace yard he displayed a large kettle and caged tigers; trouble-makers would be boiled and fed to the beasts.[45] He established five queens, one of whom was the mother of Ngô Nhật Khánh, the surviving scion of the Ngô family. Bộ Lĩnh also married Nhật Khánh's daughter to his own son Liễn who received the title King of Nam Việt.[46] Hoping to adjust Nhật Khánh to the new situation, Bộ Lĩnh gave him a daughter in marriage; but in his anger the Ngô prince disfigured the Đinh princess and fled to Champa.[47]

In 971, Bộ Lĩnh established a court hierarchy. Nguyễn Bặc received the highest court position. Lưu Cơ, a man about whom nothing is known, was sent to oversee the key region of Giao. Lê Hoàn, a native of Ái and a companion of Liễn,[48] received the chief military post. Three men were placed in charge of religion; two represented the Buddhist community, one was a lay observer. Finally, a younger brother of Bộ Lĩnh's old ally Trần Lãm received a princess as well as a position that appears to have had something to do with supply.[49] In 972 Liễn went to the Sung court in China; he returned the following year with titles for himself and his father, thus normalizing diplomatic relations with the north.[50]

A seventeenth century observer recorded the following traditions concerning Bộ Lĩnh: "...after their [the Chinese] departure Dinh was king: Now, whether they made him so, or whether he usurped the regality, by the assistance of great numbers of vagabonds, and other scum of the nation, is differently delivered. They say that king Dinh had enjoyed the scepter but a small time before the great ones murmered against him."[51] Bộ Lĩnh was certainly rustic and the opposition he aroused among surviving elements of the Sino-Vietnamese aristocracy may explain his untimely death, but the characterization of him as a usurper and a leader of "vagabonds and other scum" is a prejudiced view. The official court history compiled by Confucian scholars noted his lowly origins yet praised him as a national hero who saved Vietnam from the disunity of local warlords. In their eyes his reign marked the beginning of the period of "our kings."[52] Furthermore, the court historians cited Bộ Lĩnh as the heir of an ancient political tradition. The official history states that Bộ Lĩnh "carried forward the rule of the Martial Emperor Thiệu."[53] In reference to Bộ Lĩnh, the thirteenth century commentator Le Văn Hưu posed the rhetorical question: "Was it not the will of heaven that our land of Viet again gave birth to a wise sage to succeed to the throne of King Triệu?"[54] Later, the great scholar of the fifteenth century, Nguyễn Trãi, cited Triệu and Đinh as founders of the nation.[55] This Triệu was Triệu Đà (Chao T'o), a Ch'in official who in 207 B.C. founded the kingdom of Nam Việt (Nan Yüeh) in the vicinity of modern Canton. Triệu ruled for 70 years, successfully resisting Han imperialism. In 111 B.C., Nam Việt was conquered by Han Wu-ti.[56].

The position of Triệu Đà in the historical self-image of the Vietnamese people is uniquely significant. The mythology of the Vietnamese people grew out of prehistoric traditions which included but ended with Triệu Đà. Triệu Đà defeated the local king established in the citadel of Cổ-loa and was recognized as suzereign by the indigenous aristocracy; this event was reflected in Vietnamese mythology by the story of the turtle claw, a magic symbol of military invincibility and political sovereignty, which belonged to the local king but was stolen by Trieu Đà, thus guaranteeing and legitimizing his his victory.[57] Elements of this story are related to the earliest myths of the Vietnamese people.[58] Most significant, however, is that it is chronologically the last addition to the ancient cycle of myths. Triệu Đà lived in the world of Sinic political concepts yet he made a career of resisting Chinese imperialism, taking a southern wife and willingly assimilating himself to the non-Sinic culture of what is now South China. Furthermore, he did not disturb the social and political life of the ancient Vietnamese.[59] Thus, he found a place in Vietnamese mythology as a legitimately accepted King and in Vietnamese history as a defender of local culture against Chinese imperialism. Lê Văn Hưu, the thirteenth century Vietnamese historian, made the following comment regarding the reign of Triệu: "Those who would be kings of the land of Việt after this, if they follow the example of the Martial Emperor...then they can successfully defend the frontier and the people of the North cannot be covetous."[60]

The importance of the Nam Việt period in Vietnamese

history is most obvious in the name Việt. Before this time, the ancestors of the Vietnamese people were known as the Lạc; the indigenous aristocracy retained the name Lạc until its final defeat in 43 A.D.[61] The appearance of the name Việt in ancient Vietnamese mythology cannot be regarded as genuine but rather as a later addition.[62] The Việt (Yüeh) culture which prevailed in South China during the Nam Việt period achieved a degree of political prestige as a result of Triệu's monarchy; in the culturally disorienting centuries of Chinese colonial control, the memory of the greatness of Nam Việt as an independent kingdom defending itself against Chinese imperialism was translated into a living political and cultural identity among the descendents of the Lạc people.

The name Triệu also reappeared in colonial times. Traditions associated with it survived in the less Sinicized areas of Ái and Trường. In the third century A.D., rebellions originating in Ái were on two different occasions led by persons with the name Triệu.[63] In the sixth century when Chinese dynasties were weakest and colonial rule lapsed, local strongmen struggled for control of the Delta. A man of the lower Delta, with the title King Triệu of Việt (Triệu Việt Vương) and the Lý family of Phong, who styled themselves Emperors of the South (Lý Nam Đế), negotiated and fought until the Lý eventually gained ascendency. This conflict was remembered in terms of the same story of the claw which had risen out of Triệu Đà's victory over the Cổ-loa monarch; other than names, the only altered detail was that the turtle claw had become a more Sinic dragon claw.[64]

Đinh Bộ Lĩnh was surely familiar with these traditions. He gave his son the title King of Nam Việt, earlier held by Triệu Đà. Like Triệu Đà he superseded a monarchy based at Cổ-loa, and like King Triệu of Việt of the sixth century he led the lower Delta against the more Sinicized upper Delta. More profound evidence of the traditions in which Bộ Lĩnh stood is the name he gave to his new kingdom. One of the oldest traditions of the Lạc was that of the Red Sparrowhawk clan based at Mount Tản-viên in Phong overlooking the point where the Red River flows into the Delta; Mount Tản-viên appears in Lạc mythology as a place of refuge in time of invasion and as the home of warriors who protected the people.[65] As Sinic pressure increased in the upper Delta, the name Red Sparrowhawk, Chu-diên (朱 鳶), appeared as a geographical name in the lower Delta, in what became the southernmost part of Giao adjacent to Trường. One of the sparks igniting the Lạc rebellion of 40 A.D. was the execution by the Chinese of the Lạc chief of Chu-diên.[66] During his campaign which crushed this rebellion and put a final end to the rule of the Lạc aristocracy, the Chinese general Ma Yüan reported that he saw a hawk fall into a river and drown while attempting to fly through the monsoon rains.[67] Did this symbolize the defeat of Lạc power? In the sixth century, King Triệu of Việt was the local chief of Chu-diên and it was in his name that the ancient claw myth was resurrected.[68] Thus, when Bộ Lĩnh named his kingdom Việt of the Great Watchful Hawk, he was not making up something out of the blue. Finally, in the realm of folk belief, the popular tradition of Bộ Lĩnh's power flowing from his association with the watery kingdom of aquatic creatures links him with the oldest and most consistent themes of Lạc mythology.[69]

Rather than simply didactic historiography, the link between Triệu Đà and Bộ Lĩnh signalled by Vietnamese historians represented a living tradition of resistance to Chinese imperialism. The Ngô monarchy utterly failed to rule Vietnam because it was more closely tied to the politics of South China than it was to the indigenous traditions of the Vietnamese people. Bộ Lĩnh was the starting point for the Vietnamese monarchy because he renewed the ancient traditions of a people long subjected to colonial rule and thereby provided the only viable basis upon which this people could begin to build an independent political life. Before these traditions could hope to survive in the old centers of Chinese control, they had to be given new legitimacy. Only after Hoa-lư had stood the test of resurgent Chinese imperialism and achieved recognition as a proper political entity was the throne transplanted to the upper Delta, near to the oldest centers of Vietnamese civilization.

Đinh Bộ Lĩnh was criticized by Vietnamese historians for not knowing how to take precautions.[70] This fault would seem to have led to his death. Late in 979, after a feast, he and his son Liễn were murdered as they slept off their drunkenness in a palace courtyard. The assassin, a servant named Đo Thích, hid in the roof of the harem for three days until he was discovered and killed by Nguyễn Bặc.[71] These events followed a period of palace intrigue. Bộ Lĩnh had two known sons besides Liễn. In 974, a queen of the Dương family gave birth to a prince named Toàn. This woman was very likely a member of the same family which had produced Đỉnh Nghệ and Tam Kha; she played an important role in the period following Bộ Lĩnh's death as the mother of the only surviving prince. What part if any she had in Bộ Lĩnh's assassination is not known. Sometime after 974, a son named Hạng Lang was born. In the spring of 978, Bộ Lĩnh was induced through "love" to make Hạng Lang his heir, thus setting aside both Liễn and Toàn. One year later, Liễn had Hạng Lang killed. It was just six months after this that both Bộ Lĩnh and Liễn were killed by Đỗ Thích whose identity and motives remain obscure.[72]

Five year old Toàn was immediately raised to the throne by Nguyễn Bặc, Lê Hoàn, and other men of the court. Eight months later, Hoàn took the throne for himself. The official history states that he was "adulterous in the royal harem, thus taking the country."[73] The liason that Hoàn established with the Queen Mother was his path to power. In the early months of 980, Nguyễn Bặc and two other men attempted to organize resistance to Hoàn. Hoàn defeated this group in Ái, killing one man in battle and capturing Bặc, who was brought back to Hoa-lư and executed. The third man was captured in Giao where he had gone in search of aid.[74] At this same time, Ngô Nhật Khánh, who had fled rather than submit to Đinh Bộ Lĩnh twelve years earlier, arrived with a Cham fleet, but he and the fleet were lost in a typhoon off the mouth of the Red River.[75] The greatest threat that began to materialize was from the north. Chinese officials in Canton informed the Sung court of the events in Vietnam and begged for an army of intervention; their words were heeded.[76] The Queen Mother and Hoàn sent their generals among the troops informing them of the Sung threat and counselling that in such a time of danger it would be best to have a tested leader like Hoàn on the throne. According to the official history, the response to this appeal was enthusiastic; thereupon, the Queen Mother sent the imperial regalia to Hoàn and Toàn became a mere prince one again. [77]

The final months of 980 were spent in preparing for the Sung invasion. During this time letters were exchanged between the Sung court and Hoa-lư. The first Sung letter is worth quoting at length for it vividly expresses the Chinese imperial mentality and its righteous horror at the impertinence of a long subjected people rising up on the edge of the imperial world.

> Chinese relations with the Southern Barbarians is like a human body with two legs and two arms which stretch and contract at the volition of the heart; thus, the heart is lord. If in an arm or leg the blood vessels are stopped up and the nerve is not peaceful, then medicine is taken for a remedy; but if no results are seen, then acupuncture is applied until health is restored. It is not that one does not know that medicine is bitter in the mouth or that the acupuncture needles make holes that hurt the skin; rather, a little pain but great benefit. The one who is Lord under Heaven also is like this. Therefore, our Great Ancestral Emperor, receiving the throne from the House of Chou, changing the dynastic title to Sung, declaring and clarifying civilization, returning to the ways of the past, sitting on the throne of all the former kings and emperors, saw the unhealthiness of the Southern Barbarians. In the first and second years, he administered medicine to the lands of Hupei, Szechwan, and Hunan; in the third and fourth years he administered acupuncture to the lands of Kwangsi, Kwangtung, Kiangsi, and Anhwei; the nerves and blood vessels appeared rather healthy: was not this possible because of the prince's spirit and intelligence?...Now, the nine regions and four seas are healthy and strong, peaceful and safe, there remains your region of Giao, far at the end of heaven, sprung up beyond the five regions [i.e. center and four cardinal directions of the empire], yet a land of inheritance for the arms and legs, comparable to a finger or toe of the body. Does a saint ignore one sore toe? If so, the only result will be to unloose your dark stupidity which will reach out to impregnate

our purity. Do you understand? Not to mention the
old days of Shang and Chou when you brought white
pheasants as tribute [apocryphal] and the days of Han
when the bronze pillars [erected in Vietnam marking
the southern frontier of the empire] gathered mould.
In the time of T'ang your land contined to belong to the
Middle Kingdom; because of the many troubles at the
end of T'ang the administrative districts have not been
restored. Now in our time, the civilized heart has
covered many lands, our inheritance of great peace is
prosperous, the laws are about to be made; hopefully,
you will come and submit so that our body can be
healthy. On the other hand, if you avoid turning your
shameful face into the corner but rather annoy us, our
command must be to cut up your corpses, chop your
bones, and return your land to the grasses; then it will
be too late for you to repent. Although your seas have
pearls, we will throw them into the rivers, and though
your mountains produce gold, we will throw it into
the dust; we do not covet your valuables. You fly and
leap like savages, we have horse drawn carriages; you
drink through your nose, we have rice and wine; let
us change your customs. You cut your hair, we wear
hats; when you talk you sound like birds, we have
examinations and books; let us teach you knowledge
of the proper laws. Your land is hot, muggy, foggy,
smokey, and poorly ventilated; we release the clouds
which sprinkle fresh rain. Pushed back by the sea air,
your clouds burn, causing your stones to melt; we
pluck the stringed instruments of ancient kings and a
fresh wind bursts forth. You do not know the stars in
the sky of your land; we will change the positions of
the stars to force your submission. You fear the
spirits in your land as monstrous demons; we cast
great vessels to avoid harm. Do you want to escape
from the savagery of the outer islands and gaze upon
the house of civilization? Do you want to discard your
garments of leaves and grass and wear flowered robes
embroidered with mountains and dragons? Have you
understood? Do not march out and make a mortal
mistake. We are preparing chariots, horses, and
soldiers; we are putting in order all ranks of gongs

and drums. If you submit, we will forgive you; if you disobey, we are determined to strike you. Obey or disobey, gentleness or ferocity, it is for you to consider and decide. [78]

Hoàn had the following reply composed in the name of Toàn.

Your servant's [i.e. Toàn's] father [i.e. Đinh Bộ Lĩnh] and elder brother [i.e. Liễn] both bore the favor of your land as guardians of the frontier, keeping with honor the outer regions, not daring to disobey. Their labors have but recently been published in the temples, for they disappeared as dew drops in the morning. In your servant's house there was murder; mourning clothes have not yet been discarded. The soldiers and generals in the provinces with all the elders and tribes came to your servant's straw mat and earthen pillow, requesting that your servant take authority for looking after military affairs. Your servant tried to refuse many times but was unceasingly forced; all the same, your servant has resolved to report and request orders. However, thinking that if orders are slow and are not received then the hearts of the people in the forests and mountains with bold and violent customs and all the crooked people in the caves and crevices may not be pleased, in which case your servant feared some calamity would arise; therefore your servant, respecting authority, took the title of Horse Commander of Moderation in Battle as temporary leader of military affairs in the region. Bowing down in anticipation of receiving true orders enabling participation among the ranks of your followers thus calming the heart of your insignificant servant; keeping true to the path of loyalty; receiving the books and laws of the royal court as a reward for ever and ever. [79]

In the spring of 981, Chinese armies entered Vietnam by land and sea. Hoàn defeated the invaders piecemeal before they had time to join forces. Then, turning south, Hoàn struck at Champa, capturing numerous prisoners including a portion of the Cham court. [80]

During the following two decades, Vietnam enjoyed internal stability and satisfying relations with its neighbors. Champa was weak, divided, and fearful of new Vietnamese agression.[81] Sung China quickly adjusted to the check it had received and normal diplomatic relations were resumed.[82] Buddhism prospered as monastic interests began to enter the arena of court politics. In the 990's a young man raised as a temple orphan at the Buddhist center of Mount Tiên in Giao found a position at court in the service of one of the royal princes; this was Lý Công Uẩn who would found a new dynasty and remove the court from Hoa-lư.

Hoàn had five official queens but the court history states that "concerning the customary laws of husband and wife, there were many affairs worthy of shame."[83] This may explain how by 995 he had at least eleven sons capable of filling administrative positions.[84] In 989, Dương Tiến Lộc of the old Dương family led Ái and Hoan in rebellion; Champa dared not respond to his appeal for aid and he died as his movement was brutally put down.[85] It was after this that Hoàn parcelled out strategic parts of the kingdom to his sons. The geographic distribution of these regional commands faced the mountainous frontiers and lay along the major riverine routes.[86] As Hoàn grew older, his sons assumed an increasingly larger role in local administration.

In 1000 and 1001, a series of events revealed that the court had grown lax. Rebels and bandits challenged the throne; Đinh Bộ Lĩnh's son Toàn, who was now an adult and an active member of the court, died attempting to put down one rebellion; a queen and Hoàn's eldest son died under undisclosed circumstances. Generals were sent to the northern and southern frontiers as a precaution against foreign intervention.[87] There followed a number of fresh initiatives designed to strengthen the government. In 1002, new laws were published, soldiers were recruited, and administrative sub-divisions were reorganized. An attempt to raise the prestige of the throne was reflected in the establishment of two ranks of generals and in six members of the court being permitted to wear special hats. However, in the countryside, the Hoa-lư monarchy was losing respect. In 1003, a canal was built linking Ái and Hoan; when the local population balked at being conscripted for the task, some were beheaded as an example. At this same time a man for undisclosed reasons and from an unlocatable district fled to China leading 450 people; sent back by the Sung authorities, he disappeared.[88]

After 1003, Le Hoàn's health began to fail. Hoàn wished his fifth son Đĩnh to succeed him but was prevailed upon by court officials to designate his third son Việt as heir. These court officials were very probably representatives of the Buddhist monastic community, for Việt was the prince in whose service Lý Công Uẩn had found a career. Việt is described in the official history as humane but impractical in military and political affairs.[89]

Following Hoàn's death in the spring of 1005, Việt was actively challenged by two of his brothers. Three other brothers sat tight in their local strongholds; one in Phong, one in the eastern Delta at Phù-lan, and Đĩnh at Đằng. After eight months, Việt defeated his rivals and claimed the throne. Yet, only three days later, Đĩnh succeeded in securing Việt's assassination. All of Việt's men fled except Lý Công Uẩn who, refusing to yield, obtained a high command under Đĩnh.[90] Đĩnh then reduced Phù-lan by seige and forced the brother at Phong into submission; he subsequently consolidated his position by clearing the coasts of pirates who had taken advantage of the political troubles.[91]

In 1006, Đĩnh established four queens, conferred titles on three infant sons, and set up a court modelled after the Sung. At this time, his brother Minh Đề, who in 1004 had served as an envoy to the Sung court, chose to go to China and live in exile.[92] According to Vietnamese sources, officials in Canton learned of the political disorders in Vietnam and again petitioned the Sung court for permission to recruit an army of invasion. The emperor refused, saying: "The House of Lê regularly sends its sons to make their submission, their portion of the coast is peaceful, they do not lack loyalty; now we hear news of a recent death; ambassadors have not yet arrived; to strike in a time of mourning with hurridly assembled troops is not the way of royalty." The Sung court then sent a letter to Hoa-lư admonishing the princes not to kill one another and warning that if peace were not soon restored envoys would be sent to find out whether all the surviving members of the house of Lê had not become incompetent. Đĩnh immediately sent a brother to demonstrate his submission. Officials in Canton once more urged action with hopes of using Minh Đề to advantage; this time the emperor's reply was more explicit: "Giao is a land of deadly climate; if soldiers are sent to take it, many will be killed and injured; therefore, let us be content with carefully keeping the land of our ancestors."[93] The imperial tide had turned and there was now room for the young Vietnamese nation to develop.

Đĩnh's short reign has suffered at the hands of later historians who accused him of elaborate cruelties in order to justify the rise of Lý Công Uẩn. There was certainly a measure of truth to the charges; cruelty had been a characteristic of the Hoa-lư monarchy from the time of Bộ Lĩnh with his kettle and caged tigers. If Lê Đĩnh relied unduly upon violence as a method of government it may have been because the Hoa-lư monarchy was losing its ability to command respect. Politics in Vietnam were outgrowing the limited perspective of Hoa-lư. Đĩnh, nevertheless, appears to have been a very energetic man. In three years he marched from one end of the land to the other pushing unruly mountain people back from the lowlands; he built roads, canals, and ferrying facilities in Ái and Hoan; he established excellent relations with Sung China resulting in a profuse exchange of gifts and the opening of trade.[94] Near the end of 1009, however, Đĩnh died of hemorrhoids at the age of 24. As he lay on his deathbed he was aware of the movement to place Lý Công Uẩn on the throne.[95] Công Uẩn was at this time commander of the palace guard.[96]

Lý Công Uẩn had been born in 974 to a woman residing at the temple of Mount Tiên. Popular tradition relates that she had conceived by the spirit of Mount Tiên who appeared to her in a dream; driven from the temple, the pregnant woman sought refuge with an order of forest monks among whom the emperor-to-be was born attended by miracles.[97] Công Uẩn was adopted at an early age by Lý Khánh Văn, head bonze of the Cổ Pháp temple in the vicinity of Mount Tiên.[98] He received his education from the bonze Vạn Hạnh; it was through Vạn Hạnh's influence at the court in Hoa-lư that he received a position in the service of Prince Việt.[99]

Buddhism in Vietnam dates from the turn of the third
century A.D. when the governor Shih Hsieh (Sĩ Vương) ruled
for forty years as the Han Dynasty declined and fell.[100] Shih
patronized Indian monks who came by sea and Chinese monks
who arrived overland.[101] Vietnamese Buddhism subsequently
grew out of the Dhyāna, or meditational, tradition (Chinese
Ch'an, Japanese Zen, Vietnamese Thiên). The first Dhyāna
sect dates from the last half of the sixth century when the
Indian monk Vinītaruci arrive from China. It was at this time
that Buddhism began to spread among the common people in
Giao.[102] It was also at this time that King Triệu of Việt and
the last Lý Emperor of the South were contesting the Delta in
the absence of a strong Chinese dynasty. The traditions
associated with King Triệu of Việt in the lower Delta have
already been examined. In the upper Delta, indigenous
traditions survived less strongly, and the Vinītaruci Sect may
have risen in response to the relaxation of Sinic pressure.
Indeed, the personal name of the last Lý Emperor of the South
was Phật Tử, meaning son of the Buddha. The remarkable
growth of Buddhism in Vietnam came as a surprise to Emperor
Kao of Ch'i (479-482). Intending to send missionaries, he
learned that Buddhism in Vietnam was equal to if not more
advanced than that in China, its temples and monasteries
were crowded with hundreds of monks. He accordingly
contented himself with sending officials to inspect the religious
centers.[103]

Near the beginning of this paper we saw how the Võ
Ngôn Thông Sect was founded in 820. This second Vietnamese
sect has been characterized as "pure Dhyāna"[104]; in contrast
to the more popular Vinītaruci Sect, it represented an ascetic
and scholarly tradition.

In the tenth century, monastic communities survived
as centers of learning while around them the political situation
became unstable. As the Sino-Vietnamese aristocracy declined
in Giao, the monasteries became havens for men seeking
economic and social security or the obscurity of a monk's
robe. Consequently, the role of administering monastic
estates evolved into a role of local political leadership.

When Đinh Bộ Lĩnh gave the Delta a new measure of political unity, the monasteries continued as centers of both culture and local politics. This would explain why Bộ Lĩnh contented himself with sending only one man to oversee Giao and why the most important administrative commands parcelled out to Lê Hoàn's sons were located outside Giao. This also clarifies the important position of the Buddhist community at the Hoa-lư court. In 971, Bộ Lĩnh gave the patriarch of the Vô Ngôn Thông Sect the title of Khuông Việt meaning "Builder and Protector of Việt."[105] Bộ Lĩnh's assassin Đỗ Thích may have had some connection with the Buddhist community.[106] Vạn Hạnh, a patriarch of the Vinītaruci Sect, was closely associated with Lê Hoàn as an advisor during the Sung crisis of 980-981.[107] The Hoa-lư court depended on monks for the scholarly expertise essential for diplomatic activities and for court affairs.[108] Lý Công Uẩn's career suggests that the Buddhist community may have reinforced its position by more practical expedients as well. As Đinh lay dying, Vạn Hạnh's activities at the court on behalf of his protégé became so embarrassing that Công Uẩn sent him back to Mount Tiên.[109] This is reminiscent of the situation five years earlier when Lê Hoàn was told which of his sons would succeed him. Although at that time Đinh eliminated the designated heir he still had to come to terms with Công Uẩn.

An obscure title occurred only three times during this period but each time in reference to particularly significant persons. The title is chi-hậu (祗 候) which means "one who serves"; what special meaning it had in the tenth century is uncertain, yet the three persons associated with the title either were or could possibly have been partisans of the Buddhist community. The title first appeared in connection with Bộ Lĩnh's assassin Đo Thích.[110] It appeared a second time in connection with the woman who was the mother of both Việt and Đinh and who became the Queen Mother after 1005.[111] Finally, it was the title of one Đào Cam Mộc who in 1009 stood out as Vạn Hạnh's man at court; he was apparently close to the royal family, for within two days of Đinh's death he had set aside the infant prince and removed all obstacles to the crowning of Công Uẩn. For his efforts he received a Lý princess in marriage and a special Buddhist cremation on his death in 1015.[112] Accompanying the smooth dynastic transition at the court was a propaganda campaign in the countryside on behalf of Công Uẩn. The Vinītaruci Sect, with which Vạn Hạnh and Công Uẩn were most closely associated, was near to the people in its acceptance of popular beliefs,[113] and Vạn Hạnh filled the land with miracles and oracles presaging the rise of the Lý.[114] The power of the Buddhist community had been growing throughout the Hoa-lư period. The events of 1009 were seemingly a consequence of this growth.

Seven months after his accession to the throne, Công Uẩn founded the new capital of Thăng-long at the site of modern Hanoi, in the vicinity of Đại-la. In proclaiming the change of capital, Công Uẩn criticized his predecessors:

> Sitting securely in their home district, they allowed a great disturbance to fill the land. Their destiny was short, the people were wasted, ten thousand evil deeds were committed which do not bear retelling. I am a man of compassion; I have no choice but to move to another place. Especially is it impossible for me not to move when there exists the old capital of Kao P'ien at Đại-la, in the region between heaven and earth, where the dragon-coiled tiger is able to sit, between south and north and east and west, with a favorable view of the mountains behind and the river in front, where the earth is spacious and flat and high and clear, where the inhabitants are not oppressed by flooding, where the earth is fertile and prosperous, a location overlooking the entire land of Việt; that spot is the best place imaginable. It is where the four directions meet, the location for a capital that will last ten thousand ages.[115]

The reference to Kao P'ien shows the broadening perspective of the Vietnamese monarchy as it settled into its new capital. The traditions of the upper Delta, deeply imprinted with the experience of Chinese colonialism, were added to the heroic but untutored traditions of Hoa-lư. Công Uẩn emulated the Hoa-lư kings when he honored his mother, named more than one queen,[116] and celebrated his birthday with an elaborate court festival.[117] The name Đại Cồ Việt was retained until the beginning of the reign of the third Lý king in 1054.[118] While preserving continuity with the Hoa-lư monarchy, the court now moved toward a broader synthesis of Vietnamese culture which encompassed the population of the upper Delta. One way this was done was to link the monarchy with the spirits of great men of the past who were objects of local veneration. One such personage was Lý Phục Man, a general of the first Lý Emperor of the South in the sixth century. Popular belief associated the spirit of Phục Man with victories against pirates during the T'ang period and particularly with Kao P'ien's victory over the Nan Chao invaders in the 860's; Phục Man was also believed to have assisted Ngô Quyền in 938 and Lê Hoàn in 981.[119] In 1016, when Công Uẩn was visiting the area associated with Phục Man's sixth century career, the old warrior appeared to the monarch in a dream with the promise of aid in future times of national danger. Công Uẩn immediately cast a statue and officially recognized Phục Man's cult.[120]

Of greater importance than local cults, however, was the Buddhist religion. Throughout the two centuries of its existence, the Lý Dynasty's most conspicuous source of legitimacy was its Buddhist piety. In 1010, Công Uẩn ordered the repair of all village temples and he built eight new temples in the vicinity of Mount Tiên and three in the new capital. Late in the year he ordered the casting of a bell to be donated to a temple near Mount Tiên.[121] In 1014, he donated bells to three temples and established a school at a fourth in Thăng-long. In 1016, two new temples were built in the capital and four statues were donated; also in this year ranks were established for more than one thousand monks in Thăng-long, and three years later monks were ranked throughout the land.[122] In 1020, the Tripitaka was received from China and delivered to the head of the monastic community; it was copied in 1023 and again in 1027.[123] In 1024, Công Uẩn had a temple built in Thăng-long for his private use.[124] While Buddhism's most lasting contribution was cultural, its political role in the early decades of the Lý Dynasty must have been great; what appear as acts of piety may in reality have been acts of administration. This is particularly so in the case of temple construction; the building of a temple would bring the authority of the throne to bear upon a local population both effectively and righteously.

Though praised for his virtue and piety,[125] Công Uẩn was criticized by later historians for lacking administrative ability.[126] The events following his death reveal that political realities had indeed been neglected. On the day of Công Uẩn's demise in the spring of 1028, the eldest prince, remembered as Thái-tông, found himself barricaded in one of the palaces surrounded by three of his brothers and their men. After deliberation, the palace guard rushed the beseigers. A warrior from Ái, the great Lê Phụng Hiểu, managed to unhorse one of the disloyal princes and killed him; the two remaining princes fled.[127] The next day, Thái-tông ascended the throne before his father's coffin; the two troublemaking princes appeared, begged forgiveness, and were pardoned. Soon after this, news arrived that Prince Bồ, who since 1013 had been in charge of Hoa-lư, was preparing to contest the throne; it developed that he had been harboring fugitives from Thăng-long and oppressing the local population by consorting with bandits. At the shrine to the Spirit of the Mountain of the Bronze Drum (Thần Núi Đồng Cổ) at Đại-la, each man was required to drink blood and beg the spirit to strike him dead if he were disloyal. Thái-tông declared that this particular spirit had forewarned him of the treachery of his three brothers.[128] When the king reached the vicinity of Hoa-lư, Prince Bồ surrendered without resistance. After clearing up affairs at the old capital, Thái-tông brought the prince back to Thăng-long and pardoned him.[129]

Buddhist leaders were shocked by the weakened condition of the throne revealed upon Công Uẩn's death. They demanded that Thái-tông immediately designate his five year old son as the crown prince to insure greater dynastic stability in the future. Thái-tông complied and followed this act with the naming of seven queens and the establishment of a festival commemorating his birthday. Only after these ceremonial duties were completed was Công Uẩn finally laid to rest, seven months after his death.[130]

Thái-tông was a patriarch of the Vô Ngôn Thông Sect. In the first five years of his reign he is said to have built nearly one thousand temples.[131] Images of Maitreya[132] and Avalokiteśvara[133] are first mentioned in his reign as is the practice of royal fasts[134] and an ascetic act involving monks

burning themselves to produce miracle-working relics.[135]
The surviving literature of this reign, all of it religious
poetry, was entirely written by members of the Vô Ngôn Thông
Sect, though a poem preserved from Thái-tông's own brush is
in praise of Vinītaruci.[136] In 1034, Thái-tông changed his
reign title on the occasion of two monks immolating themselves
by fire.[137] He personally deposited these monk's relics in a
temple at Mount Tiên.[138] Thái-tông's patronage of the Vô
Ngôn Thông Sect was advantageous from a political point of
view; this sect, with its tradition of scholarship, was more
responsive to royal authority than the Vinītaruci Sect and was
a more effective tool of the court in administering the monastic
life and thereby much of the political life of the land. The
1030's were unusually rich in temple miracles; perhaps they
reflected the rising fortunes of the Vô Ngôn Thông Sect which
probably caused bitterness among members of the Vinītaruci
Sect who had enjoyed royal favor under Công Uẩn. A
conspiracy to unseat Thái-tông by a prominent bonze and two
military men was discovered in 1035[139]; this might reflect
discontent caused by Thái-tông's religious and political
policies. The trend under Thái-tông was thus to downplay the
more popular but less controllable aspects of Buddhism and
to emphasize its scholarly and ascetic role.

In 1038, Thái-tông honored the God of Agriculture by
personally plowing three furrows. Some members of the court
criticized him for performing this unkingly act. However, a
fifteenth century Confucian commentator, Ngô Sĩ Liên, praised
the performance as a royal duty.[140] This is the first
indication that there may have been advisors with Confucian
ideas at the court. In the following year a mountain chief who
had been causing chronic difficulties was captured; a result
of this success was the discovery of gold and silver mines in
the mountains. A group of advisors requested that the reign
title be changed and that the king's personal dynastic title be
lengthened to commemorate the auspiciousness of these events.
Thái-tông declared that although he did not understand the logic
of his advisors' arguments he would comply in hopes of gaining
some advantage which their skills might afford. In this
instance, the thirteenth century commentator Le Văn Hửu
praised the king's trust in what he specifically identifies as
Confucian advisors.[141] In 987, Lê Hoàn had plowed paddy in

the mountains, uncovering gold and silver in the process, though without honoring the Confucian God of Agriculture.[142] Thái-tông's plowing thus appears to have been an indigenous custom which Confucianists were attempting to bring into conformity with their own ideology; perhaps it was Sinic additions to the older tradition which provoked the criticism. Likewise, Confucianists may have encrusted the discovery of gold and silver with their ideology of the state, an ideology that Thái-tông tolerated but did not care to understand. As Confucian theories began to circulate through the court, they appear to have met with resistance. In 1041, palace life was reorganized; within one month a plot by two palace guard commanders was uncovered.[143] Later in the year, Thái-tông seems to have been preparing for new initiatives when he visited Công Uẩn's tomb and built a new ancestral hall; this was followed by the casting of three statues, one of the Buddha Maitreya and two of irrigation gods. At the end of the year a new commander was sent to the southern frontier, anticipating the invasion of Champa three years later.[144]

In the following year the reign title was changed to Minh-đạo. The Minh-đạo period has been remembered as the beginning of Confucian influence. In 1042 and 1043, an attempt to rationalize all aspects of the kingdom was made. A law code was promulgated and stiffer penalties were imposed for disloyal behaviour; mourning regulations were instituted. New coins were minted and distributed to civil and military officials. Roads and bridges were built or repaired. Homeless persons were rounded up and put to work. The principle of group responsibility was imposed upon officials. Finally, conscription policies were tightened up and the army and navy were reorganized.[145]

The immediate effect of this campaign to strengthen the administrative powers of the court was preparation for an invasion of Champa. The security of the southern frontier had been a cause of concern for Thái-tông since early in his career. In 1020, as crown prince, he had led the Vietnamese in a border war with the Chams; at that time he had managed to kill the Cham general and to destroy half of the Cham army.[146] In 1031, he had personally quelled a rebellion in the border province of Hoan,[147] and in 1036 he had established a new military command there, changing the provincial name to Nghệ-an.[148]

In his proclamation declaring his intention of invading Champa, Thái-tông quoted from the Confucian classics to buttress his contention that the Chams had shown insufficient respect.[149] An important argument in favor of the invasion was that only if the Chams were humbled would the troublesome mountain peoples learn to respect the Vietnamese.[150] The young nation thus sought to win a measure of regional prestige sufficient to permit the unhindered development of its domestic life.

Early in 1044, Thái-tông distributed weapons and led his men south. The campaign was a total success with the Cham king being killed on the battlefield. The Vietnamese troops were so rambunctious that Thái-tông ordered punishments for those who "wrongfully" killed Chams. Over five thousand Cham prisoners were settled in Nghệ-an where they were allowed to retain their native customs. Nearly the entire Cham court including musicians and dancers was brought back to Thăng-long. When the Cham queen committed suicide to preserve her honor, she was praised by Thái-tông and subsequently entered the spirit pantheon of the Vietnamese people.[151]

During the last ten years of Thái-tông's reign, the borders were generally peaceful and the court turned to enjoying the respect it had earned. Palace women paraded in coaches guilded with gold and pulled by Cham elephants; a new palace was built for the exclusive use of the captured Cham harem. In 1048, an agricultural alter was erected for seasonal sacrifices.[152] In 1049, Thái-tông dreamed of Avalokiteśvara seated on a lotus blossom; he accordingly built the "one pillar pagoda" (Chùa Một Cột) which can be seen in Hanoi to this day.[153] Thái-tông had ascended a shaky and untested throne; he left it solid and tried. It is too much to attribute his success to the shadowy Confucian advisors whose administrative skills gave technical form to his leadership. Thái-tông's reputation as a great Buddhist king was genuinely earned.

When the king died late in 1054, his 31 year old son
Thánh-tông inherited a united and self-assured kingdom. The
new ruler's first act was to change the name of the kingdom to
Đại Việt meaning Great Việt.[154] The traditions of Hoa-lư
were being superceded. Thánh-tông's vision of himself and
his land was grander than that of his prececessors. Like his
father and grandfather he built numerous temples and stūpas.
Yet the momentum of power surrounding the court perceptibly
altered the quality of royal piety. The court history criticized
Thánh-tông for causing the people much misery by forcing them
to build palaces and stūpas.[155] As the power of the court
increased, relations with China grew more complicated. In
1059, Thánh-tông decreed that all court officials must wear
proper Chinese boots and hats when in the royal presence; at
this same time border incidents with China increased in
frequency and seriousness.[156] Attitudes were beginning to
harden which would lead to war fifteen years later.

In 1069, Thánh-tông invaded Champa. No explanation
of the campaign is preserved in the official history but it
would appear that the rationale behind the invasion of 1044 still
held with the added urgency of impending hostilities with the
Sung dynasty of China. Among the prisoners brought back to
Thăng-long was a Chinese monk found residing at the Cham
court named Thảo Đường (Hsiao T'ang). Thánh-tông used Thảo
Đường to found the third Dhyāna sect in Vietnam. The Thảo
Đường Sect has been called "Vietnamese Dhyāna."[157] Its
members were primarily of the royal family and their
protégés. This sect was more cosmopolitan and aristocratic
than the two older sects; in docrinal terms, it represented
some new trends imported from Chinese Buddhism.[158] A
courtly sect, three Lý emperors, of whom Thánh-tông was
only the first, were to be numbered among its patriarchs;
many princes of the royal house were also prominent. At
least two religious figures were active in both the Vô Ngôn
Thông Sect and the Thảo Đường Sect, indicating that there
was some continuity in relations between the court and the
Buddhist community during this period; yet the new emphasis
on a sect subordinate to the interests of the dynasty is
unmistakable. It is at this time that Phạn Vương (Brahmā)
and Đế Thích (Indra) were added to the Vietnamese
pantheon,[159] revealing a greater interest in the glory

of kingship. In 1070, Thánh-tông built the Palace of Literature
(Văn Miếu), a Confucian edifice filled with images of Confucius
and his disciples.[160] While Buddhism remained the
intellectual foundation of the kingdom, the court was
disentangling itself from the Buddhist community and asserting
a firmer control over it.

Characteristic of the new traditions being forged around
the throne was the so-called Great Buddha, a statue erected in
Thánh-tông's reign. The Great Buddha was conceived as the
reincarnation of all the heroes and spirits who had promoted
the glory of the Vietnamese people. Numbered among these
incarnations was the ancient peasant hero Dóng (Gióng) of Lạc
mythology who had defended the land from northern
invaders.[161] Equally significant, however, was the presence
in this august company of the Chinese god of war Chên Wu,
(鎮 武) under whose protection, in fact, Thánh-tông placed
Thăng-long.[162] As the threat of renewed Sung imperialism
loomed over the northern border, the Vietnamese throne was
fortifying itself not only with its own national heroes but with
the heroes of its enemy as well. The Vietnamese people had
faced the bitter realities of living with a powerful and
aggressive neighbor from the beginning of their history; now
the contest was entering a new phase.

When Thánh-tông died in 1072, his seven year old son
succeeded him without incident.[163] The Lý Dynasty and the
Vietnamese throne had stood the test of time. In the war with
China which broke out in the mid 1070's, the throne stood fast
as talented princes led the Vietnamese to victory under the
banner of a child king. When the Chinese and Vietnamese
armies faced one another in 1076, a temple dedicated to two
generals of the sixth century King Triệu happened to be
located near the Vietnamese encampment. The Vietnamese
commander, Lý Thường Kiệt, roused his troops by having the
following words sung in the temple as an oracle throughout
the night preceding the battle:

> The Emperor of the South reigns over the mountains
> and rivers of the South;
> So has it been written in the Book of Heaven.
> How do you bandits dare to invade our land?
> Your hordes will surely be annihilated without pity![164]

In conclusion, the heirs of Chinese colonialism in Vietnam were unsuccessful as long as they remained more closely tied to the world of their former colonial masters than to the indigenous traditions of the Vietnamese people. Only after these traditions had been revived and combined with an indigenous Buddhism was a synthesis of Vietnamese culture achieved. This synthesis provided the intellectual basis upon which Vietnamese independence was built and maintained.

NOTES

1. See Maps 6 and 7.

2. H. Maspero, "Le Protectorate General d'Annam sous les T'ang," BEFEO, 10 (1910), p. 681.

3. Edward H. Schafer, The Vermilion Bird (Berkeley, 1967) p. 71.

4. Maspero, op. cit., pp. 674-680.

5. Lý Tế Xuyên, Việt Điện U Linh Tập, trans. Lê Hữu Mục (Saigon, 1959), p. 148.

6. Ssu-ma Kuang, Tzu Chih T'ung Chien (Shang Wu Yin Shu Kuan, 1970), v. 13, p. 187. Đại Việt Sử Ký Toàn Thư, trans. Cao Huy Giu (Hanoi, 1972), v. 1, p. 133. Hereafter TT. Lê Tắc, An Nam Chỉ Lược (Hue, 1961), pp. 100, 148.

7. Trần Văn Giáp, "Le Bouddhism en Annam," BEFEO, 32 (1932), pp. 243-244.

8. Ssu-ma Kuang, op. cit., p. 195.

9. Ssu-ma Kuang, op. cit., pp. 293, 460. TT, p. 134.

10. Lê Tắc, op. cit., p. 153.

11. Ssu-ma Kuang, op. cit., pp. 559-560, 572. Lê Tắc, op. cit., p. 101. TT, p. 135.

12. Ssu-ma Kuang, op. cit., pp. 580-588. TT, p. 136.

13. Lê Tắc, op. cit., p. 102.

14. Ssu-ma Kuang, op. cit., pp. 608, 610-611, 612. Lê Tắc, op. cit., pp. 103-105. TT, pp. 138-142.

15. Lý Tế Xuyên, op. cit., pp. 43, 68, 101, 111, 117.

16. Lý Tế Xuyên, op. cit., p. 92.

17. TT, p. 142.

18. Lý Tế Xuyên, op., cit., p. 93.

19. L. Bezacier, L'Art Vietnamien (Paris, 1954), p. 138.

20. Wang Gung-wu, The Structure of Power in North China During the Five Dynasties (Stanford, 1963), pp. 23-25. Ssu-ma Kuang, op. cit., p. 736. TT, p. 142.

21. Wang Gung-wu, op. cit., pp. 47-84.

22. TT, p. 143.

23. Việt Sử Lược, trans. Trần Quốc Vượng (Hanoi, 1960), pp. 38-39. Hereafter VSL.

24. TT, p. 144; for a description of this family, see E. H. Schafer, "The History of the Empire of the Southern Han...," in the Silver Jubilee Volume of the Zinbun-Kagaku-Kenkyuso (Kyoto, 1954), pp. 339-369.

25. Khâm Định Việt Sử Thông Giám Cương Mục, trans. Hoa Bằng et al. (Hanoi, 1957), pp. 162-163. Hereafter CM.

26. TT, p. 144.

27. TT, p. 145.

28. TT, pp. 145-146.

29. TT, p. 147.

30. TT, p. 148. VSL, p. 46.

31. TT, p. 149.

32. Vũ Phương Đề, Công Dư Tiệp Ký, trans. Nguyễn Đình Diệm (Saigon, 1962), v. 2, pp. 67-70.

184

33. TT, p. 153-154.

34. TT, pp. 151-152. VSL, pp. 44-47.

35. TT, p. 150.

36. TT, pp. 151-152.

37. E. Gaspardone, Annuaire du College de France, 60 (1960), pp. 303-305. VSL, pp. 46-47.

38. TT, p. 152.

39. CM, p. 171. (Undoubtedly borrowed from Chinese sources.)

40. TT, p. 151.

41. VSL, p. 47.

42. TT, p. 151.

43. TT, p. 152. VSL, p. 46.

44. VSL, p. 47.

45. TT, p. 154.

46. TT, pp. 155, 160.

47. TT, pp. 160.

48. TT, p. 167.

49. TT, p. 155.

50. TT, pp. 155-156.

51. Samuel Baron, "A Description of the Kingdom of Tonqueen," in Churchill, A Collection of Voyages and Travels (London, 1732), v. 6, p. 19. Born in Vietnam of a Vietnamese mother, Samuel Baron was the son of Hendrik Baron, an employee of the Dutch East India Company in Hanoi during

the 1660's. Revue Indochinoise, 12, 7 (July, 1914), pp. 59-60.

52. TT, pp. 45-56, 154-155. The former reference is from Lê Tung's Việt Giám Thông Khảo Tổng Luận (1514).

53. TT, p. 153.

54. TT, p. 155.

55. TT, v. 3, p. 51; in the opening lines of the victory proclamation over the Ming, the Bình Ngô Đại Cáo (1428).

56. Lü Shih-p'eng, Vietnam During the Period of Chinese Rule (Hong Kong, 1964), p. 5-7. TT, pp. 71-88. G. Dumoutier, "Etude Historique sur Trieu-vo-de (Tchao-wou-ti) et sa dynastie," T'oung Pao, serie II, 7 (1906), pp. 413-436.

57. G. Dumoutier, "Etude Historique et Archeologique sur Co-loa," Novelles Archieves des Missions Scientifiques, 3 (1892), pp. 236-245.

58. Tatsuro Yamamoto, "Myths Explaining the Vicissitudes of Political Power in Ancient Viet Nam," Acta Asiatica, 18 (1970), pp. 87-90.

59. H. Maspero, "La Royaume de Van-lang," BEFEO, 18, 3 (1918), pp. 8-10. H. Maspero, Review of L. Aurousseau's "Le Premeir Conquete...," T'oung Pao, 23 (1924), p. 392. Cl. Madrolle, "Le Tonkin Ancien," BEFEO, 37, 2 (1937), p. 265.

60. TT, p. 78.

61. E. Gaspardone, "Champs Lo et Champs Hiong," JA, 243 (1955), pp. 461-477. Maspero, "La Royaume," pp. 7-8. H. Maspero, "L'Expedition de Ma Yüan," BEFEO, 18, 3 (1918), pp. 11-28. Bui Quang Tung, "Le Soulevement des Soeurs Trung," BSEI, n.s., 36, 1, 1 (1961), pp. 73-85.

62. Yamamoto, op. cit., p. 84.

186

63. TT, pp. 106, 109.

64. H. Maspero, "La Dynastie des Li Anterieurs," BEFEO, 16,
    1 (1916), pp. 1-26. M. Durand, "La Dynastie des Lý
    Anterieurs d'apres le Việt Điện U Linh Tập," BEFEO, 44,
    2 (1944), pp. 437-452. Yamamoto, op. cit., p. 91. TT,
    pp. 42-43, 121-126.

65. Dumoutier, 1892, op. cit., pp. 260, 266.

66. Bui Quang Tung, op. cit., p. 78.

67. Maspero, "L'Expedition," op. cit., p. 16.

68. TT, p. 121.

69. Yamamoto, op. cit., pp. 91-94.

70. TT, p. 153.

71. TT, pp. 157-158.

72. TT, pp. 156-157.

73. TT, pp. 166-167.

74. TT, p. 159. CM, p. 228.

75. TT, p. 160.

76. TT, pp. 160-161.

77. TT, pp. 161-162.

78. TT, pp. 162-163.

79. TT, p. 164.

80. TT, pp. 168-169.

81. TT, pp. 169, 171, 174, 177. CM, pp. 241, 243.

82. TT, pp. 169, 171-172, 173-174, 175-176. Maspero, "La Protectorate," pp. 168-172.

83. TT, pp. 166, 168.

84. TT, pp. 173-175.

85. TT, p. 173.

86. H. Maspero, "La Geographie Politique de l'Empire d'Annam sous les Li, les Tran et les Ho," BEFEO, 16, 1 (1916), pp. 28-30.

87. TT, pp. 177-178.

88. TT, p. 178.

89. TT, p. 179.

90. TT, p. 180.

91. TT, p. 181. CM, pp. 248-249.

92. TT, p. 181.

93. TT, p. 182.

94. TT, pp. 183-184.

95. TT, p. 186.

96. TT, p. 189.

97. Hoàng Trông Miện, Việt Nam Văn Học Toàn Thư (Saigon, 1959), II, pp. 34-36.

98. CM, p. 257.

99. TT, p. 189.

100. Lü Shih-P'eng, op. cit., pp. 11-12.

188

101. Trần Văn Giáp, op. cit., pp. 206, 209, 220, 256.

102. Ibid., pp. 235-236.

103. Ibid., pp. 208-210.

104. Ibid., p. 256.

105. TT, p. 155.

106. The Đỗ family had been particularly prominent in the Vinītaruci Sect since its beginning in the sixth century and a monk of the Đỗ family was important as an advisor to Lê Hoàn in matters of diplomacy. Trần Văn Giap, op. cit., pp. 236-238. The name Thích (釋子) might be understood as the title of a Buddhist monk.

107. Ngô Tat To, Văn Học Đời Lý (Saigon, 1941), pp. 28-29.

108. The role of the Buddhist hierarchy at this time has been emphasized by modern Vietnamese Buddhists. Nguyễn Hữu Chân Phân, Xã Hội Nhà Lý Nhìn Dưới Khia Cảnh Pháp Luật (Hue, 1971); Venerable Thich Quang Do, "A Summary of the History of Vietnamese Buddhism" (manuscript: Van Hanh University, Saigon); Thich Nhat Hanh, Lotus in a Sea of Fire (New York, 1967).

109. TT, p. 186.

110. TT, p. 157.

111. TT, p. 179.

112. TT, pp. 186-188, 195.

113. J. Y. Claeys, "L'autel de Thien-phuc," BEFEO, 28 (1928), p. 487; G. Dumoutier, "Choix de Legendes Historiques de l'Annam et du Tonkin," Revue d'Ethnographie, 8 (1889), pp. 189-191; Hoang Trong Mien, op. cit., pp. 32-34.

114. TT, pp. 185-186, 190.

115. TT, pp. 190-191.

116. TT, p. 188.

117. TT, pp. 182, 197.

118. L. Cadiere, "Tableau Chronologique," BEFEO, 5 (1905), p. 89.

119. Nguyễn Văn Huyên, "Contribution a L'Etude d'un Genie Tutelaire Annamite Ly Phuc Man," BEFEO, 38, 1 (1938), pp. 17-18.

120. TT, pp. 195-196. Lý Tế Xuyên, op. cit., pp. 85-87.

121. TT, pp. 191-192.

122. TT, p. 195.

123. TT, p. 197.

124. TT, pp. 198-199.

125. TT, p. 167.

126. TT, p. 189.

127. TT, pp. 199-201. Lý Tế Xuyên, op. cit., pp. 77-79. Chú, I, p. 248.

128. TT, p. 203. Lý Tế Xuyên, op. cit., pp. 99-100. R. Deloustal, "Code de Lê," BEFEO, 10 (1910), pp. 21-23.

129. TT, p. 204.

130. TT, pp. 204-205.

131. TT, p. 209.

132. TT, p. 218.

133. TT, p. 225. At this time the cult of Lokeśvara

(Avalokiteśvara) was of some importance in Champa and the Khmer Empire. Louis Finot, "Lokeçvara en Indochine," Publications de l'Ecole Francaise d'Extreme Orient, 19 (1925), pp. 227-256.

134. TT, p. 209.

135. TT, p. 210.

136. Ngo Tat To, op. cit., pp. 31-42. Anthologie de la Litterature Vietnamienne, I (Hanoi, 1972), p. 62.

137. TT, p. 210.

138. TT, p. 211.

139. TT, p. 212.

140. TT, p. 214.

141. TT, pp. 215-216.

142. TT, p. 171.

143. TT, p. 217.

144. TT, p. 218.

145. TT, pp. 218-222.

146. TT, p. 197.

147. TT, p. 208.

148. TT, p. 213.

149. TT, pp. 221-222.

150. TT, pp. 220-221.

151. TT, pp. 222-223. Lý Tế Xuyên, op. cit., pp. 61-62.

152. TT, p. 225.

153. TT, pp. 225-226.

154. TT, p. 228.

155. TT, p. 229.

156. TT, pp. 230-231.

157. Trần Văn Giáp, op. cit., p. 256.

158. Ibid., pp. 253-254.

159. TT, p. 230.

160. TT, p. 234. Trần Han Tan, "Etude sur le Van-mieu de Hanoi," BEFEO, 51, 1 (1951), pp. 90 ff.

161. TT, p. 61. G. Dumoutier, Le Grand Bouddha de Hanoi (Hanoi, 1888), pp. 44-45.

162. Dumoutier, 1888, pp. 9-11.

163. TT, pp. 234-235.

164. TT, p. 238.

Note:

The Vietnamese Confucian Scholar's View

of His Country's Early History*

by
John K. Whitmore

The fact that Vietnam was not a thoroughly Confucian
state throughout its history leads to the question of how the
Confucian literati of later times interpreted and commented
upon that earlier part of their history during which the
Confucian ideology was not yet dominant. This is also
interesting since each of our selected authors lived in a
different time regarding the acceptance of the Confucian
ideology by the Vietnamese. First of all, there are no known
Confucian works for the period of the Confucian Court cult in
the eleventh and twelfth centuries. Lê Văn Hừu then wrote
his history, the Đại Việt Sử Ký,[1] in the thirteenth century
when the Confucians existed in a Buddhist environment and
had no major policy role at the Court. His was a voice
seeking to establish a new doctrine. Ngô Sĩ Liên, on the other
hand, compiled his history, the Đại Việt Sử Ký Toàn Thu,[2]
during the initial triumph of Confucian thought in the fifteenth
century for an Emperor strongly imbued with this thought.
By the eighteenth century, Ngô Thĩ Sĩ was writing his private
history, the Việt Sử Tiêu Án,[3] during the time of renaissance
when both Vietnamese traditions and Confucian history were
being compiled by the literati. And finally the Tự-đức Emperor
in the following century made his comments in the Khâm Định
Việt Sử Thông Giám Cừơng Mục[4] at the apogee of Confucianism
as the ideology of the Vietnamese state and also when its
decline had already begun under French pressure.

Patterned on the chronological style of Ssu-ma Kuang,
the Vietnamese histories consist of the chronicling, year by
year, of the events of the state. Interspersed among the
entries are comments by the various historians concerning
the nature of the events and actions being recorded. We shall

concentrate on these comments in order to understand the
views of the Vietnamese historians, particularly those
comments dealing with the existance of a non-Confucian
Vietnam from the tenth to the fourteenth centuries.

Since there are many comments scattered throughout
the Vietnamese histories for these five centuries, particularly
by Ngô Sĩ Liên and the Tự-đức Emperor, those comments
made about certain key points in the development of the
Vietnamese state have been selected for discussion. This
will allow us both to see the point of view of the Confucian
writer and to examine significant changes in Vietnam.

The style of kingship existing in Vietnam at the end of
the tenth century and the beginning of the eleventh was quite
foreign to these writers. Both Đinh Bộ Lĩnh and Lê Hoàn
had five queens, and each had married the main queen of his
predecessor. These rulers tended to honor just their parents
rather than their paternal lines, and their posthumous names
were both carried over from their living titles. The first Lý
ruler, Lý Công Uẩn, in turn continued a number of these
patterns. Comprehension of these actions was difficult for
our writers. Lê Văn Hưu, the closest in time, could not or
would not tolerate such behavior. For him, having five queens
was against the natural order of the universe, a bad example,
and disruptive of propriety. Ngô Sĩ Liên agreed, seeing the
marriage of Lê Hoàn to the former queen as an example of
great impropriety for future generations, as did Ngô Thì Sĩ
who saw the bond of husband and wife being severed, bringing
a disruption of the natural way and the Sinic cultural
foundation. 5

The problems of ancestral reverence and posthumous
names also raised the condemnation of the Confucian writers.
The fact that both mother and father and not the paternal
grandfather had been honored upset Hưu and Sĩ. 6 While Hưu
merely blamed the deed on ignorance and let it go at that, Sĩ
thought that it boded ill for ancestor worship and contended
that the female element turned things upside down. In fact,
picking up a legend relating the spiritual nature of the Lý
founder's birth, Sĩ saw the ancestral temple as having become
a place of worship for the founder's maternal line, a cardinal

violation of proper ritual. Tự-đức, however, merely noted the confusion in the Lý ancestry and laid it to Heaven's will. [7] In addition, there was a strong feeling about the casual effort made in establishing the Lý ancestral temple at the same time that much energy was being put into the building of Buddhist temples. Lê Văn Hưu, himself living in a Buddhist age, had strong words to say about the situation and its effect on posterity. It strained the energies of the people and favored Buddhism over the royal position. [8] In this, Tự-đức heartily concurred. [9]

A major reason for such aberrant activities given by our writers was simply ignorance, a lack of the proper knowledge for carrying things out. Yet the fact that the ruler himself was uneducated was not so important as the inability or ignorance of the Court officials to set him right. A case in point was the use of Lê Hoan's royal title as his posthumous title, in a manner similar to that of Đinh Bộ Lĩnh. The reason for this occurrance, in Lê Văn Hưu's mind, was that "the son was worthless, and there were no Confucian ministers to give advice on the proper means."[10]

The ascension of the second Lý ruler in 1028 and the activities surrounding his taking the throne elicited more comments from our Confucian writers. This time we do not hear complaints on the number of queens (seven) or on the honor given to the mother of the new ruler. Again, however, there is Lê Văn Hưu's remark that the new king was unlettered and that the ministers either did not know enough, or did not have the ability, to look at past precedent, in particular concerning the name of the royal tomb. [11] Ngô Sĩ Liên, Ngô Thĩ Sĩ, and Tự-đức for their part castigated the ruler for reinstating a royal birthday festival when his father had abolished it, even before his father had been buried. [12] The new ruler's filial piety was again questioned by Liên when the king took the year of his ascension (and his father's death) as the first year of his own reign period, not waiting until the following year as was proper. To quote Liên, "One year cannot have two rulers."[13] For the son to infringe on his father's reign period was a definite violation of propriety. Tự-đức also remarked on the blood oath taken by all officials, saying that there was no need for such an oath since Heaven had given its mandate. To build a temple and require an oath to its spirit was irrational, foolish, and unrighteous.[14]

Thus the extent of understanding among our Confucian literati concerning the nature of the early Vietnamese monarchy was minimal. In the instances cited, our commentators could not, or would not, grasp what was being done and could only mumble about improprieties.

Over the following century, as various Chinese forms were adopted, including Confucian ones, the commentators were not faced with the dramatic differences of the early period of independence. Their attention now tended to focus on the extent to which the Vietnamese Court carried out the forms already adopted, particularly the activities surrounding the death of the ruler and the succession thereafter. Through the twelfth century, these Vietnamese activities gradually came to meet the proprieties of the Chinese model. In 1127, at the death of the fourth Lý ruler, the officials went into mourning, but only for as long as the funeral ceremonies and not for the prescribed three years. To Lê Văn Hưu, this was a rejection by the new king of both the example to be set for the people and the model to be upheld for the officials. But, as Hưu again noted, the new ruler was too young to know anything, and the blame fell once more on the Court officials, though Hưu speculated that there perhaps were none in the Court who knew any better. Ngô Sĩ Liên fully agreed, while Ngô Thĩ Sĩ again saw the bad example this would set for posterity and Tự-đức's remark was a simple "That's wrong!"[15]

The new king did, however, begin his reign only the following year (actually less than a month later), though he soon thereafter celebrated a military victory with a ceremony at a Buddhist temple rather than at the ancestral temple. Lê Văn Hưu thought this to be quite wrong.[16] Also, the dead king's tablet was placed in the ancestral temple only in 1129, after having resided in a "spirit house" for a month. This upset the commentators, particularly because of what they saw as an extraordinarily long wait of over a year. Ngô Sĩ Liên also complained that in past times the dead had been revered as though they were yet alive.[17] At the following ruler's death in 1138, matters appear to have slipped a bit as the reign period of the new ruler began on his succession, a month after the former ruler's death. Ngô Sĩ Liên's comment, however, paid no attention to this and concentrated on the intrigue surrounding the heir apparent.[18] The next succession, in 1175, on the other hand, went quite smoothly. The infant crown prince took the throne, honored his mother, waited until the new year to establish his reign, and had a three year period of mourning, all in accordance with the direction of a particular court official, Tô Hiên Thành. This elicited a favorable comment from Liên, particularly for the official.[19]

During the twelfth century, Vietnam was also strongly drawn into the political struggle throughout the eastern third of the Southeast Asian mainland. Khmers, Chams, and Vietnamese became involved in the Angkorian effort to spread its hegemony up the eastern coast. The commentators were quite leery of such involvement with the "barbarians" and showed no comprehension of the political intricacies of the time. In 1154, when the Cham king offered a girl as a gift and the Vietnamese ruler accepted her, both Lê Văn Hưu and Ngô Sĩ Liên reacted strongly.[20] The difference in their reactions is significant, however. Where Hưu felt that the pattern of political involvement between the two was correct and only objected to the weaknesses shown by the Vietnamese, Liên rejected this pattern and insisted on "righteousness" in their relations. The latter, drawing on cases from the Chinese Classics, condemned the Vietnamese handling of the matter, feeling that a high-minded Confucian approach should have been used. Tự-đức, on the other hand, responding to two different events (1119 and 1202), refused to take the Chams seriously, classifying them, the Khmers, and the Thais with mountain peoples, all vastly inferior to the Vietnamese and not to be worried about. In his mind, borrowing Cham patterns, such as music, was merely frivolous.[21]

The effects of just such a cultural mixture were a prime concern of our commentators as they examined the thirteenth century. The varied elements making up Vietnamese culture at the time of the first major Confucian scholarly development drew a number of adverse remarks from the writers. At the beginning of the new Trần dynasty, Ngô Sĩ Liên promptly equated its Buddhist efforts with those at the beginning of the previous Lý dynasty and saw both dynasties as being responsible for the worship of the Buddha existing in Vietnam, [22] as Lê Văn Hưu no doubt would have readily agreed. Ngô Thỉ Sỉ, on the other hand, saw the Trần as greatly surpassing the Lý in this regard. [23] Taoism and geomancy also appeared on the Vietnamese scene. In the 1250s when, we are told, a Taoist adept correctly foresaw the birth of a prince, Liên responded that the way of Heaven was distant and could not be known. Such a thing might have been possible if Heaven were behind it, but he remained skeptical. [24] Some years earlier, the ruler had sent geomancers out to supress all appearances of "Princely air." Liên retorted that no such action could ever keep a "sage" down, [25] and Tự-đức felt that this showed what little learning the Trần ruler possessed. [26]

The events that really demonstrated the lack of morality in the Vietnamese state of the thirteenth century for our writers were the marriages of the royal family. First of all, the Trần founder had taken one of the last Lý ruler's wives as his mistress, and she later became a major figure in the early Trần period. For Ngô Sỉ Liên, this woman may have served Heaven's way, but there was no virtue in her. [27] Then when the first ruler took his elder brother's pregnant wife as his queen in order to gain a son and this woman was later given a posthumous honorary title, the Confucians roared: Duty had been shattered and royal example destroyed! Liên pointed to the affair's dangerous precedent and moral consequences[28]; Ngô Thỉ Sỉ flatly stated, "An entire generation of the Trần royal family was without proper rites"; and Tự-đức thought the Trần morals to have been even worse than those of the T'ang dynasty in China, a consequence of the Trần founder's illiteracy and craftiness. [29] Amid such immorality, the small matter of not waiting to start a new reign period until the following year again went without comment.

Meanwhile the Confucian establishment had started its climb out of this cultural heterogeneity, and during the first quarter of the fourteenth century began to come in conflict with the ways of the Court. The first major instance was the celebrated affair of princess Huyên Trần being sent as a wife to the Cham king. Both the Confucians of the time and our commentators spoke strongly against the act, comparing it to the classical Chinese case of the Han princess given to the Huns.[30] Ngô Sĩ Liên asked why the abdicated Vietnamese ruler had done it in the first place and why the decision had not been reversed. In a Court that may well have had more in common with the Cham aristocracy than with their Confucian brethren, the impression of a debate given by the History (written by Sĩ Liên) may be wrong. Instead a policy discussion took place and the decision was made according to the political interest of the Court, not the moral interest of the Confucians.

The Confucian effort continued, however. When the abdicated king and Patriarch Nhân-tông died, a Court struggle arose over the cremation and Buddhist disposal of the royal body. Ngô Sĩ Liên felt that the Court should have been stern and solemn, but instead it had been overly lax,[31] while Ngô Thî Sĩ thought the combination of the son's reverence for his royal father and the Trần worship of Buddhism to have been a very odd combination.[32] Finally, in 1312 and 1315, came two acts that show the emerging Confucian influence. When the Trần ruler honored the three members of his paternal line who preceded the dynastic founder, both Liên and Sĩ strongly approved, though they wondered why it had taken the Trần so long to perform the ceremony and why only three ancestors had been thus honored.[33] Three years later appeared the first known Vietnamese proclamation enforcing the Confucian social order: father and son, husband and wife, master and servant were not to make accusations against each other. Liên's response was in a philosophic vein and predictably favorable: a good heart meant good government in the state.[34]

Despite such favorable signs, the Confucian state had yet to arrive. At the burial of the next ruler, Liên complained of the excessive delay before the burial and wondered whether Yin-Yang doctrine might have been responsible.[35] As the century progressed, the Confucian presence at the Court rose and fell. Whatever effect this presence may have had in the administrative realm, it seems not to have influenced foreign policy at all. Where Liên could see no value in dealing with a distant people like the Chams who spoke a different language and were treacherous, [36] the Vietnamese Court continued its tolerance toward its neighbors. When a strong Cham attack took the Vietnamese Capital in 1371 after a decade of raids, Liên could chide the Vietnamese ruler for having been so unobservant of his powerful foe and so unprepared in defense. [37] Writing shortly after the crushing defeat of the Chams a century later, Liên supported the member of the royal clan, Trần Nguyên Đan, who had unsuccessfully advocated treating Champa like a child and Ming China like a father. [38]

So our Confucian commentators came to grips with the non-Confucian reality of earlier Vietnamese history, chiding the rulers on point after point. Their frustrations and disagreements should act as guideposts for our examination both of the reality of the Vietnamese state and society of these centuries and for the prevailing ideology of the later centuries. A Chinese influence did exist, but the extent of its penetration must be re-examined. The existance of these histories shows this influence, written as they were in the Chinese style. Yet the history they show us, while dealt with in Confucian terms, does not hide the non-Confucian nature of the society it describes.

NOTES

* This essay is the second half of a paper, "The Confucian Scholar in Vietnam and His View of Early Vietnamese History," presented at the annual meeting of the Association for Asian Studies in Washington, D.C., 1971.

1. This text is now absorbed in the Đại Việt Sử Ký Toàn Thư, henceforth TT. Hưu's comments come from the TT (Hanoi, 1967), and Phan Huy Chú, Lịch Triều Hiến Chương Loại Chỉ (Hanoi, 1961). The latter is an early nineteenth century encyclopedia.

2. This now forms the bulk of the present text of the TT. Some of Liên's comments are found in Chú as well.

3. Việt Sử Tiêu Án (Saigon, 1960). Sĩ's comments are drawn from Chú and from the Khâm Định Việt Sử Thông Giám Cương Mục, henceforth CM (Hanoi, 1958).

4. CM.

5. Chú, II, p. 150. TT, I, pp. 155, 168.

6. Chú, II, pp. 124-125, 153. TT, I, p. 158.

7. CM, III, p. 48.

8. TT, I, p. 179.

9. CM, III, p. 42.

10. TT, I, p. 174.

11. TT, I, p. 205.

12. Chú, II, pp. 144-145. TT, I, p. 205. CM, III, p. 56. E. Gaspordone, Sinologica, 6, 1 (1959), p. 7.

13. Chú, II, p. 158. TT, I, p. 202.

14. CM, III, p. 55. See also his response to the Trần oath of 1227, CM, V, p. 6.

15. Chú, II, pp. 153-154. TT, I, pp. 258-259. CM, IV, p. 17.

16. TT, I, p. 262.

17. Chú, II, pp. 172-173. TT, I, p. 265.

18. TT, I, p. 274.

19. TT, I, p. 293. See Chú, I, p. 183, for a biography of Thành.

20. TT, I, pp. 285-286.

21. CM, IV, pp. 11, 57.

22. TT, II, p. 11.

23. CM, V, p. 33.

24. TT, II, pp. 25-26.

25. TT, II, p. 21.

26. CM, V, p. 27.

27. TT, II, p. 30. For Tự-đức's adverse comments, see CM, V, p. 5.

28. TT, II, p. 15.

29. CM, V, pp. 27 (Ngô Thĩ Sĩ), 15-16.

30. TT, II, pp. 92-94.

31. TT, II, p. 98.

32. CM, VI, p. 4.

33. Chú, II, p. 125. TT, II, p. 102.

34. TT, II, p. 104.

35. TT, II, p. 111.

36. TT, II, pp. 92-93.

37. TT, II, p. 162.

38. TT, II, p. 191.

Kingship, the Saṅgha, and Society in Pagan

by
Michael Aung Thwin

This paper is an attempt to reconstruct the nature of
state and society in Pagan (Pugān) in relation to the problem of
labor scarcity in early Southeast Asia, and to examine how
this scarcity of labor led to the decline of Pagan within the
framework of saṅgha-state relations.

One of the main themes in early Southeast Asian history
has been the struggle for, and effective organization of, labor.
Since land was plentiful, the key to economic growth and
political power was the effective control of human resources.
Much of the warfare of early Southeast Asia witnessed the
victor carrying off half the population of the vanquished foe
and later resettling them on his own soil. In Burma, this input
of labor was organized and placed in a structure that best
manipulated the human resources of the state. In many
instances, pre-existing patterns of social organization based on
village communities, such as clan and tribe, were used. With
the subsequent socio-economic development of the state and
the growth of these labor resources, administrative patterns
also had to change in order to accomodate this influx, while
still maintaining the old hierarchy. New communal bonds,
such as occupation, class, and religion, began to replace those
of clan and tribe--and perhaps even of the extended family.

The implications of these new bonds for the pre-existing
hierarchy of headmen and chieftains were significant in that
leadership, legitimacy, and authority had to be redefined in
light of the growth of the state from a small, loosely organized
entity of petty chieftains and fortified towns to one that had
imperial dimensions. Status in particular was no longer a
local matter, to be defined by (say) the village, but one that
concerned the whole nuclear area in and around the capital of
Pagan, and at times even the whole kingdom. For instance,
pride in "this country called Arimaddana" of "this country
called Pugān," a phrase found often in the inscriptions,[1]

205

now superceded pride in one's clan and tribe.

The increase in population, the growth in the number of communal bonds, the crystalization of the institution of kingship and royalty, and the development of new classes forced status to be redefined and hierarchy to be reorganized. Within an imperial context, social status now meant a title which only the king could confer. Thus change in structure, from "feudal" to imperial, was qualitative as well as quantitative.

This is what Pagan witnessed. As labor was obtained from neighboring states and adjacent areas by warfare and by internally generated growth, the society changed both in terms of the number of people as well as in the nature of its organization. Yet due to a basic institutional weakness the state lost its control over its labor force to the religious sector of society which was dominated by the Buddhist Church. Put another way, labor and land which initially helped develop the civilization eventually slipped through the hands of the state into the religious and private sectors of society. Although temple building and religious endowments at first stimulated the economy and significantly contributed to the growth of Pagan, such generosity eventually destroyed the economic base of the kingdom and consequently its political power. The flow of wealth from the state to the sangha, in short, was the crucial factor involved in the "internal decay" of Pagan.

When the Mongols, Mons, and Shans gave Pagan the coup de grâce in the thirteenth and fourteenth centuries, the state was already weak and the temples and monasteries were gorged with wealth. This theme, of sangha-state relations and the rise and decline of dynasties, became the primary factor in the dynamics of Burmese institutional history.

Background

The state of Pagan was established in the mid-ninth century and survived until the end of the thirteenth. Located in the dry belt of Burma, the tattadesa or "parched land" of the inscriptions, Pagan depended mainly upon irrigated agriculture for its economic base. Land was plentiful but labor was extremely difficult to obtain. In the eleventh century, Aniruddha provided the kingdom with additional labor from Thaton in lower Burma and began the process of centralization. To enhance his power in the expanded state, Aniruddha integrated the Theravāda Buddhist sangha from Thaton into Burmese society as well as the former's aristocracy, artisans, and other miscellaneous persons. [2]

He achieved this by endowing the sangha with land and people, by building temples and monasteries for the monks, and in general by providing royal patronage. Although this was upper Burma's first contact with Buddhism, [3] it was probably the first time that the sangha was established in a role which enhanced the cultural and economic development of the growing civilization. Consequently, wealth was to flow into the sangha for the next two centuries. These endowments were a great stimulus to the economy, but the result was that Aniruddha's successors in the late thirteenth century paid dearly for it.

Almost every king after Aniruddha had to regulate religious endowments in some manner, without at the same time rendering the sangha irrelevant. For, after all, the king's own legitimacy as a Buddhist king depended upon sanction by the Religious Order. We must keep this problem in mind as we now proceed to reconstruct the nature of state and society in Pagan. For our purposes, the presentation will be largely synchronic, i.e., without reference to change. Only when we discuss the late thirteenth century will change be emphasized.

The structure of Pagan society reflected the need for effective organization to overcome the shortage of labor. It also provided the socio-economic framework for sangha-state relations as well as for institutional change in Burmese history. There were three general aspects to this organization: a) society in Pagan was cellular, being organized into professional communities, or cells, each headed by a leader; b) the economy was redistributive being based upon the principle of centricity; and c) the religious ideology in Pagan favored a kammatic to nibbānic form of Buddhism. [4]

The analysis of Pagan society suggested here must be regarded as tentative. Although many sentences in the inscriptions can be interpreted several ways, the context of each inscription helps isolate the meaning. Moreover, bits and pieces of evidence which are alone inconclusive must be analyzed in the context of later Burmese institutions since the latter should not be considered to have evolved from a vacuum. On the whole, the evidence suggests strong continuity of institutions, and those of Pagan should be considered as embryonic forms of later institutions.

The Society

The population of Pagan was divided into classes of communities (cells) according to their occupation and ethnic background.[5] The leaders of these cells, generally called sukrī (modern thugyi), held each group together and provided the link between the central government and the people.[6] This categorization was not only by status, ethnicity, and occupation but also by habitation; residential groups were fundamental to the administration of the nuclear areas of the kingdom. Occupation and habitation were practically synonomous: all the masons lived in one place, all the sculptors in another, all the locksmiths in another, and all the cowherds in another. In addition, villages were often named according to the ethnic background of their inhabitants. For example, Mons generally lived in Mon Rwā or Mon village, Poṅ Loṅs (Palaung) in Poṅ Loṅ Rwā, the Syaṁ (Shan or Thai) in Syaṁ Rwā.[7]

Because status was defined by one's birth, and occupation and ethnicity were measures of status, heredity played a major part in determining one's occupation. For example, sons of cavalry officers (mraṅ khoṅ) had to remain in their own groups, as did the descendants of brick masons, scribes, potters, and especially purā kywan, those who took care of monasteries and temples. Hereditary status was strictly enforced to maximize effective control of labor.[8]

The general populace was also divided into hereditary categories of public (amhū) and private (asañ, modern athi) functions, although these distinctions were still in their early forms.[9] The former served in official occupations and carried out government functions (military, irrigation, granaries, tax collection, etc.), while the latter were the artisans, merchants, and peasants who could work for anyone and had no service obligations. A third category circumscribed the above two, viz., the class called kywan. This term has been wrongly translated as "slave." Its economic status generally suggests something more like indentured workers and its social status does no more than suggest inferiority to the king--a category which would include everyone.[10] Kywan pledged their services, skilled and unskilled, to a patron in religious, private or governmental service, for payment in kind. Usually, they received a fixed amount of produce from the land they worked, while the rest of the land's output was given to the patron-owner. Whenever an owner donated his property to the saṅgha, he normally included the service of his kywan and stipulated the amount of produce to be donated for specific purposes. If kywan were pledged in perpetuity, they became known as purā kywan or temple servants. Several instances suggest that some prestige was attached to this status as purā kywan since they served the Buddha. However, in time this term must have acquired a stigma of sorts, as civil law forbade a purā kywan's entry into any other class or category except the religious order.[11]

The indentured relations between kywan and their patrons were relatively simple. If the kywan pledged himself as a result of debt, he had but to pay the price of a male worker, fixed at thirty ticals of silver, to redeem himself. But if one's parents had been indentured and were unable to redeem themselves, their offspring could not be redeemed unless they became monks; even then, they still had to pay the price of thirty ticals of silver.[12] The guiding principle behind these laws was to maintain hereditary occupation and status. In later centuries, the word for "redeem" (to lhan) came to mean "rebellion," which clearly indicates that it became increasingly difficult to gain social mobility as society became more structured and rigid. In general, social mobility was permitted in Pagan, but only within a class and not between classes. The only option available in normal times was via the saṅgha. When one became a monk, all previous secular ties were broken.

The large "working class" (asañ) can be divided into four categories for purposes of clarity: a) agriculturists, comprising most of the populace; b) those in military service; c) artisans; and d) a miscellaneous group whose occupations differed widely. [13] They were paid either in kind or in cash, depending upon their skill. [14]

Agriculturists apparently comprised the largest segment of the populace; indeed, all common men who were not skilled artisans probably worked the land to some degree. Their functions varied: some were guards of paddy fields, others reaped while some planted paddy, and others were gardners. Semi-agriculturists included cowherds, goatherds, elephant keepers, tenders of ducks, etc. They either depended upon a patron for their upkeep or worked these occupations independently. Their varied functions as agriculturists were more than mere "divisions of labor"; each function carried with it a certain status. As we have noted above, each group lived separately in its respective village and, chances are, each group had a distinct ethnic background. [15]

The private entrepreneurs among the asañ had a variety of professions with varying socio-economic status. [16] Included in this group were mid-wives, launderers, boat men, palanquin carriers, water carriers, canal diggers, salt makers, barbers, and nga pi (fish paste) makers. [17] They either worked freely on the labor market or contracted themselves to patrons. Suffixed to their occupations was the word sañ, which indicated their private status. This suffix was equivalent to the -er ending in English, as for example in bake and baker, dance and dancer, drum and drummer. Thus those who played the cañ (drum) were called cañ sañ and those who worked with rhuy (gold) were called rhuy sañ. The whole class was collectively referred to as asañ as early as 1184 A.D. [18]

The artisans who built the magnificent temples of Pagan were of this asañ class, and they probably held the highest socio-economic status in this class as well as among the populace at large. They were paid in gold, silver, lead, land, horses, elephants, clothes, and agricultural produce. [19] They were not corveé labor as we normally understand the term. The temples of Pagan were thus built by paid labor and

not by forced labor.[20] The highest paid artisans were the
carpenters, masons, wood-carvers, and painters. Others
included scribes, clerks, artists, and various workers of
metals. Lower in socio-economic status, but still in the asañ
group, were the musicians, dancers, singers, cymbal
players, horn blowers, string players, and drummers who
performed at various festivals.[21] Some of the latter pledged
themselves to religious patrons and became purā kywan. Food
vendors and cooks, hunters and butchers, milkmen and keepers
of game were similarly employed.

The military belonged to the public sector and was
similarly divided into functional groups with their own leaders.
Each group lived with its families on lands granted to it by the
king and was distinct from every other group.[22] The members
of the cavalry, for instance, had their own villages, usually
prefixed by the word mrañ or "horse," controlled by their
own leaders--the mrañ mhū.[23] Apparently they lived together
in fortified stockades, keeping whatever produce they tilled
in exchange for military service.[24] The standing army (sū ray,
"braves") was kept distinct from the conscript army (cac swā
so sū ray, "braves that go to war")[25] which probably consisted
of the populace who fulfilled their service obligations in times
of war.

That socio-economic distinctions had to be made
between workers of similar occupations--as between reapers
of paddy and planters of paddy, between painters of temples
and painters of monasteries, between planers of wood and
carpenters in general, between string players and cymbal
players, between dancers and singers, older drummers and
younger drummers--indicates an intensive specialization of
function not unlike the process of "involution" as described
by Clifford Geertz.[26] Whether or not all the implications of
agricultural involution were present remains an open and
stimulating question, especially for early Southeast Asia; but
what is clear is that this situation reflects a regimented
society with little or no mobility between classes.

The headman or sukrī of such occupational groups
controlled his cell by the power of his personality and the
personal loyalty given him by his followers. His control over

his cell was personal, not territorial. That is, he controlled
people of the same occupation, not everyone who happened to
live in a given territory. He was in charge of revenue
collection and maintained records which prevented the
movement of his followers from one status or class to another.
In general, then, these sukrī enforced hereditary occupation
and class.[27]

The cell leader in turn pledged his loyalty to an "eater"
above him. The "eater" was a client of the king who gave
him a "fief" to "eat" (cā); i.e., he received the revenues of a
given town or other such unit, some of which he passed on to
the capital as tax, the rest of which he kept and shared to
maintain his own political power. In return he pledged his
personal loyalty to the king.[28] The "eater" (perhaps called
mriuw cā or myosā)[29] was thus the link between the king and
the cell leaders, as the cell leaders were the link between the
"eater" and the populace. In such a way did personal loyalty
and rewards hold together the key links in the chain of political
authority and centralized government.

Pagan society can be likened to a number of circles of
such professional groups, each organized along lines of
occupation and ethnic background, inhabiting a set geographical
location, and headed by an overseer presumably chosen by the
group. The King and his court, physically and ideologically,
unified the whole society of individual cells. Since there was
necessarily no loyalty between one cell and the next, and since
few kinship ties probably existed among the cells, communal
bonds such as religion and the institution of state and
kingship--with all their ideological manifestations--held these
communities together. The bonds were epitomized by kingship
and symbolized in the monumental architecture, court
ceremonies, dress, titles, language, etc.

Whatever one's class, whether private or public,
secular or religious, one brought some land under cultivation.
The main problem for the state was to tap these resources,
centralize the process, and build up a solid and stable
economic base. This was done by regulating the flow of
revenue to the center, from which point it radiated into the
various segments of society and levels of leadership as

payments and rewards, either physically or by appropriation. More specifically, to centralize the process meant winning the allegiance of each of the cell leaders to an entity that superceded their individual work force and to a concept that went far beyond mere group leadership. The king became the "group leader" par excellence.

The Economy

The type of economy that best performed this task worked upon the principle of centricity--of political and social structures--and is called a redistributive economy.[30] It is characterized by: a) a central point to which revenue flows, for example the capital, from which it is again redistributed; b) a "fixed" or "stable" supply of wealth (since there was a fixed or stable relationship between the population and irrigated land), with "fixed" equivalencies rather than prices determined by supply and demand; c) a policy of self-sufficiency, not gain, for development; and d) an economy embedded in society, that is, operating within the legal, political, and social structures and strictures. The laws of such an economy are not autonomous from society, but are subject to certain cultural factors, such as kinship and community good will. "Price," for example, may not be an objective result of supply and demand, but is dependent upon communal bonds.[31] In such an economy, "scarcity" must be culturally defined, which may perhaps not be a completely empirical process. In other words, Pagan's economy was unlike "market" economies governed by market principles; indeed, the supply-demand-price mechanism had little to do with the economy in Pagan.

In practice, the redistributive system operated something like this: land was worked by numerous small groups (cells) whose produce found its way to the government treasury as tax. This revenue was used to pay the military, ensure loyalty, and glorify and unify the state; the symbols of this process are still standing today as monuments in stone. Revenue due the state was often rechanneled to the saṅgha. A cook, for example, would provide the monks of a monastery with food for the year, in lieu of tax. Town "eaters" would do likewise. Thus, invariably, fiefs, rewards, and other such patronage eventually found their way to the saṅgha.

Pledges to the saṅgha in the form of religious endowments provided for the upkeep of the Order, but more importantly stimulated the economy. Workers were hired to grow crops, build and maintain temples, repair and service monasteries, and provide food for the monks. Scribes were employed to copy old and worn manuscripts and to keep records of land ownership as well as statistics on population growth. Revenues from endowed land paid for the construction of schools and libraries and for the food, shelter, clothing, and books of students. Wells were dug, two layered reservoirs (or tanks) were constructed for large temple-monastery complexes, sluices and canals were built, and palm trees and gardens (very important economic assets) were planted. All these acts were derived from the religious endowments. [32]

In addition, social welfare, in the form of theaters, festivals, dancing and singing, and feasts, was provided in these endowments. Those who performed these tasks were given land, a percentage of the revenue collected from a piece of land, or cash. The religious endowment, in short, had several economic functions, the most important of which were providing jobs and cultivating land. Massive temple construction was the primary material outcome of these endowments and tended to attract people into Pagan where jobs were available, rather than to drive people away as it would have under a corveé system. Because labor constituted wealth, the patronage of the Religion and the fine arts which drew people into Pagan was sound economic policy. Indeed, the group that most benefited from this policy was the artisan class. These artisans were the ones who received the wealth used to build the monuments, and they came to form a class of well-to-do landowners whose interests were maintained by this redistributive system. [33]

Furthermore, certain values of the society, such as status, were directly related to economic redistribution. One's status was measured in terms of how much one redistributed, especially to the Religion, rather than how much one accumulated. Donative inscriptions by nature, let alone by their content, reveal the principle of this redistributive economy. Thus material wealth that came to the king and aristocracy from the cells and their leaders flowed to the saṅgha in return for merit and legitimacy--and from the saṅgha back to the people in social and material ways.

Religion

Reinforcing this economic pattern of redistribution was religion, particularly the idea of kammatic Buddhism as opposed to nibbānic Buddhism. As one may recall, in Buddhist thought salvation (nibbāna, or nirvāna in its Sanskrit form) must be attained by knowledge. Yet, except for the most devout, this difficult path to salvation was quite beyond the reach of the ordinary man or woman. Consequently, salvation through good works came to replace salvation through knowledge. The aim of the average Buddhist became not knowledge but merit. The idea of kamma (karma) was redefined. Bad kamma could be neutralized by good kamma, as well as by knowledge. The distinction, then, was between nibbānic Buddhism (practiced by only the most pious monks) and kammatic Buddhism (practiced by the average Buddhist.)

In addition, although each individual was theoretically responsible for his own salvation, kamma could be transferred or shared and the merit of one person could be used to enhance the merit of another.[34] For example, one could build a pagoda in the name of one's deceased husband to provide him with additional merit and thus release him from whatever state he was in.[35] Or a rich man could build a temple and ask that the merit thus accumulated be redistributed to poor people who could not afford such good works. The person who had the most merit to share with everyone was the king (otherwise he could not have been king). It was thus expected that he would redistribute more than anyone else; indeed, the more he donated, the greater was his merit. One can thus see how close the king was to being a person who could provide salvation for the average man, that is, to being a Bodhisattva. One can also imagine the economic dilemma he faced, trying to maintain the wealth of the kingdom while being required to give much of it away.

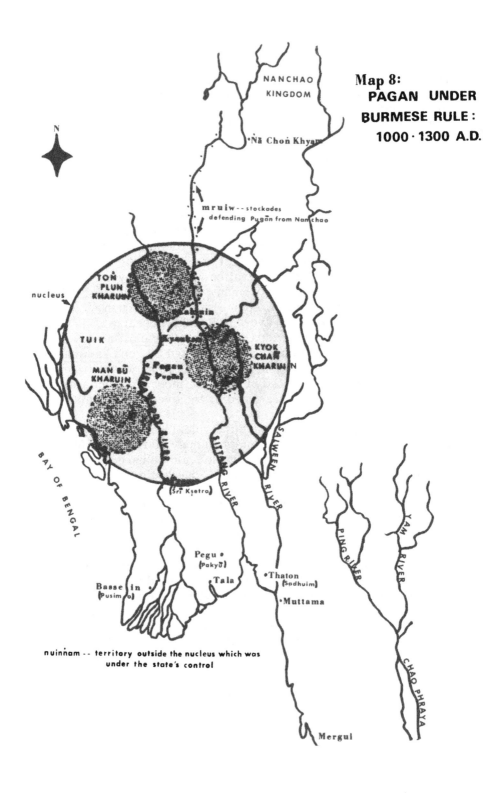

Map 8:
PAGAN UNDER
BURMESE RULE:
1000 · 1300 A.D.

NANCHAO
KINGDOM

Nā Choṅ Khyaṁ

mruiw -- stockades
defending Pugān from Nanchao

TOṄ
PLUN
KHARUIN

nucleus

TUIK

MAṄ BŪ
KHARUIN

Kyaṁ...

KYOK
CHAṄ
KHARUIN

Pagan
Pugām

BAY

OF

BENGAL

(Srī Kṣetra)

SALWEEN RIVER

SITTANG RIVER

PING RIVER

YAM RIVER

Pegu
(Pakyū)

Tala

Thaton
(Sadhuim)

Muttama

Bassein
(Pusim o)

CHAO PHRAYA

nuinnam -- territory outside the nucleus which was
under the state's control

Mergui

The content as well as the number of religious endowments in the inscriptions of Pagan which mention the sharing of merit testify to the wide-spread belief in, and practice of, <u>kammatic</u> Buddhism. Invariably, almost every donative inscription of Pagan ended in the following manner: "May I attain <u>nirvāna</u> for these my good works and may the King, princes, my relatives, and all those who uphold and support my good deed, equally gain merit like me. May those who destroy it cook in Avici hell."[36]

The average person in Pagan became a Theravādin not because he believed that Theravāda Buddhism was better than the earlier Mahāyāna Buddhism of Burma, but because a religion which emphasized merit as the path to salvation offered the kind of spiritual attitude that he needed. Because of the socio-economic realities of his envioronment, he was already thinking in terms of redistribution and communal sharing, and the religion promoted by the kings of Pagan provided further support for this world view.

Thus the doctrine of salvation through good works and the sharing of merit in <u>kammatic</u> Buddhism ideologically upheld the nature of the redistributive economy, while the pattern of religious endowments provided a practical method of achieving one's religious goals.

Administration

The administration of the Pagan Kingdom in theory reflected Buddhist and folk ideas of the world and cosmos and in practice showed the principles of centricity and cellularity necessary for a redistributive economy.

The settlement pattern of Pagan into cellular structures, with a city/urban complex on the one hand (Pagan proper, <u>prañ ma</u>) and communities of villages on the other, reflects the principle of centricity crucial to the maintenance of socio-economic and political structures, These communities all fed staples into the redistributive organization of the palace while the monastery acted as a secondary distribution center for the areas outside the capital. Thus we have the existence of a city-palace on the one hand and the temple-monastery on the other. Under a centralized government and a "purified" <u>sangha</u>, the administrative system ran smoothly.

The Kingdom of Pagan was divided into several administrative entities which changed slowly during the years, a change which can be detected in the use of different administrative terms for the same entity. The Kingdom consisted of 1) the nucleus, 2) secondary settlements or <u>tuik</u> areas, 3) <u>mriuw</u> (<u>myo</u>) or stockades in strategic locations, and 4) <u>nuinnam</u> or conquered territory in "foreign" areas.

The nucleus of Pagan was composed of three <u>kharuin</u>: north and east of the capital were Kyok chan (Kyauske) and Tonplun Kharuin, and southwest of the capital and west of the Irrawaddy lay Manbu Kharuin (see Map 8). All three shared the common feature of intensive irrigation. Pagan stood in the center of the three areas. The key to the effectiveness of the system is found in the word <u>kharuin</u>, "a center from which radiate spokes (like an umbrella)." Not only does it graphically describe a circle with "spokes" of loyalty-patronage reminiscent of a cell, but the association with the term "umbrella" bears special political significance. The phrase "wielder of the white umbrella" implies political autonomy and power and has done so throughout Burmese history. Prior to centralization, the eleven villages in Kyok chan and the six in Manbu were referred to as the "Eleven" and "Six" Kharuin. This usage suggests that these villages were once independent chiefdoms, each claiming sovereignty by associating itself with the word umbrella, until the leader of one of them managed to unify the whole group under his encompassing umbrella--a white one. He then would have become known as the "lord of the white umbrella."

Judson defined the word <u>kharuin</u> as "the single jurisdiction of a government, extended over several parts, and hence the parts collectively under one jurisdiction."[37] This definition fits well with what we have called the nucleus. When we speak of <u>kharuin</u> in the twelfth and thirteenth centuries, we are referring to the three areas of Kyok chan, Manbu, and Tonplun. Yet the eleven villages in Kyok chan and the six in Maṅbu were also individually called kharuin, apparently the remnants of the older usage. The eleven units in Kyok chañ were all fortified brick enclosures with a circular design, as if each were a miniature capital city. The area was also referred to as the "eleven kharuin of Mlacsā," which had probably been the seat of authority. Prior to coming under the centralization of the Pagan kings, the ruler or chieftain of Mlacsā must have claimed jurisdiction over the other ten kharuin or villages. When Pagan became the capital, it claimed authority not only over the eleven units of Kyok chañ but Maṅbu and Toṅplun as well.

Because of the economic importance of Kyok chañ, Maṅbu, and Toṅplun, each unit probably was assigned to a special appointee of the king. Kyok chañ certainly was governed by a minister (amāt) called the "sukrī of the eleven villages." He, in turn, had sukrī of each of the eleven villages under him. 38

All the tuik areas lay west of Pagan, across the Irrawaddy, as far south as Maṅbu, and stretched north almost halfway to the Nanchao border at Ñaṁsā Tuik. Tuik were less settled areas, perhaps similar to the "frontier" in any nation's history, which did however provide the state with revenue. The seat of authority in a tuik was again probably a fortified town (tuik means a "brick enclosure") governed by a tuik sukrī.39 Tuik, originally, may have been advanced frontier posts, at the limits of the nuclear area beyond which no Burman settled. Economically, they may have served as trading centers, where the wet rice of Pagan was exchanged for the produce of the hills.

Mriuw were stockades which encircled the rich Kyok chañ Kharuin and extended north on the banks of the Irrawaddy along Toṅplun Kharuin until they reached Bhamo on the Nanchao border. The defense of Pagan was clearly northeast oriented. Similar to the changes in meaning of kharuin, the term mriuw likewise went through various definitions. Originally, it must have meant "a stockade," as Professor Luce suggests. However, some mriuw were clearly more than just stockades and came to be associated later with the important administrative entity called "town." Yet their military origins were not forgotten, for even as late as the nineteenth century an authentic mriuw had to possess a moat, a fortress or stockade, and a market place. [40]

Forty-three mriuw were built by the Pagan kings and were probably begun during Aniruddha''s reign. Since most were only stockades during the Pagan period, with few exceptions they must have been governed by the leaders of the military units which inhabited them, such as mraṅ khoṅ, mraṅ cañ, or mraṅ mhū. Those stockades that became towns most likely had a mriuw sukrī over them. [42]

The three kharuin, the approximately eighteen tuik, and several of the mriuw made up Tampadipa Prañ or Arimaddanapura Prañ. The word prañ not only referred to this area, but to the capital city, the whole kingdom, and to specific places like Śrī Kṣetra as well. More than these physical entities, prañ also referred to concepts such as "state," both in religious and political contexts. For example, prañ was used as "state" as in "a state of religious experience" and also as a physical, geo-political entity like "nation." In addition, the word was used in statements such as "the affairs of state."[43]

Outside Tampadipa Prañ lay the nuinṅam, "conquered territories," in places distant from the capital, as Prome, the Delta, the Shan States, and the Kra Isthmus depending upon the particular period. Politically, they were tributary states, which pledged military levies in times of war, concubines for the king's court, and duties if they were commercial ports. Some were ruled by appointees of the king[44]; others probably had their own local rulers who paid nominal allegiance to the person of the Pagan king. By 1196 A.D., the concept of nuinṅam had changed with the expansion of the state. King Narapatisithu's description of his nuinṅam indicated that they were regarded as more than tributary states for they included areas which Pagan controlled directly. During his time nuinṅam must have meant a "state under one jurisdiction," that is, an entire realm, and the characteristics of his reign seem to verify that claim.

If one places the use of these administrative terms in

the context of later Burmese history, there seems to be a
trend suggesting growth and change in the following manner:
the nuinnam were originally only conquered outposts or towns;
later the term came to include the whole kingdom, the limits
of which were these outposts or towns; a kharuin was once a
village and later encompassed a whole province; a mriuw
began as a stockade but later developed into a town; and a tuik
was an outpost which developed into a district. These changes
in meaning reflect changes in structure and indeed show us
the transition that took place from the loosely organized
political situation of the early centuries to the centralized
kingdom with its stable territorial administration in the later
period.

At the center of the kingdom, in the prañ mā or capital
city, wielding the royal umbrella that covered all other
umbrellas, was the king and his court. Like its proto-type,
the kharuin, the capital city began as a fortified town or
village, but later grew well beyond its physical and conceptual
confines. The court was most likely composed of four chief
queens (ami phurā), a number of concubines (moṅ mā), princes
(maṅ sā), princesses (maṅ samī), ministers (amat), officials
(kalan-saṁbyaṅ), military officers (buil pā), and senior monks
(sakhaṅ or arī). Ministers were divided according to function
and were identified by suffixes added to their title of amat, such
such as Amat Mahāsenāpati (Minister General of the Armed
Forces) or Amat Mahāsaman (Minister of Land Affairs).[45]
The Mahāthera or Dhammarājaguru, usually the preceptor of
the king, headed the religious sector of the court. The
functions of princes differed, but in several cases they were
in charge of military affairs, possessed ministerial titles,
and were given important port cities as fiefs.[46]

The whole scheme of the Kingdom of Pagan can be
compared to concentric circles in a pond. At the center was
the palace of the king and his court, next came the capital
city, then the three irrigated kharuin (this was the nucleus).
Outside the nucleus (conceptually and partially geographically)
was the next concentric circle, composed of tuik and mriuw.
Encompassing the whole kingdom were the boundaries of the
nuinnam.

Within each ring of the nucleus were the smaller circles, the various cells headed by their respective leaders. The revenues of these cells circulated among the members of the cell, and their surplus moved to higher levels (from the village to the town) until it reached the capital (from the kharuin to the pran mā). Subsequently, in the form of patronage (fiefs) and rewards, this "surplus" radiated out into the kingdom in exchange for military service and loyalty. Of course the produce itself need not have moved physically anywhere; only the rights of appropriation were parcelled out. Thus a well functioning cellular administration enhanced, and was crucial to, the centricity of the redistributive economy, which in turn helped fulfill the ideals of kammatic Buddhism.

Kingship and Polity

The political structure was a replica of the cellular nature of society. The king, in effect, acted as the leader of his cell, which was the court. His personal abilities welded his followers together, while their functional distinctions provided balance. Both his authority and his legitimacy were culturally defined, being derived from Hindu-Buddhist ideas of kingship and the cult of the Nats. Kamma-derived authority was found in Buddhism, while territorial chieftainship (a chief's inherent right to a given territory) was found in the Nat cult. [47] These ideologies combined to forge the essence of kingship.

De facto rule, for example, supplied legitimacy when birth did not, as long as the king acted in ways that ensured the promotion, protection, and preservation of the Religion. At the same time, real and symbolic genealogical ties had to be made with the female side of his predecessors. [48] The maternal line was critical in determining legitimacy since the paternal side had far too many claimants to the throne. Because the king had many wives, a large number of princes could claim their father as king, but only a few could claim their mother as chief queen; therefore, the crucial factor to legitimacy was determined by one's mother, not one's father.

All of the above were justified by the doctrine of kamma, for without good kamma, one could never become a king. Heine-Geldern was correct in making the important distinction between the Kamma Rāja and the Deva Rāja conceptions of kingship.[49] The Kamma Rāja achieved his status by the merits of his past kamma; the Deva Rāja, because he partook of the divine. Thus the office holder, not the office, legitimized and authorized kingship. The behavior best suited for this position was one which generated personal charisma. The social foundations for such charismatic leadership point to the cellular structure of society, where a cell leader received his authority and legitimacy primarily from the personal loyalty given by his circle of followers.[50] The Buddhist ideology of kamma-derived leadership and the territorial element in the Nat cult thus combined with the social pattern and acceptance of charismatic cell leaders to form the foundations of kingship in Pagan.

The person of the king, not the administration, held together the society. The stabilizing factor in Burmese political structure, then, was the existence of a charismatic leader, not an efficient (or inefficient) administration. In the final analysis personal loyalty (however obtained and to whomever given) was the key to power and to a centralized state in the absence of a stong administrative structure.

Because the person of the king demanded loyalty and generated authority, at his death these bonds of loyalty became tenuous and were not automatically redirected to his successor.[51] Admittedly, such potential discontinuity affected the ruling elite at the court more than it did the populace as a whole. Stability was guaranteed during a king's reign because it was in the interests of his immediate followers to ensure his survival. Bonds such as loyalty, titles, position, and even ownership of property became ambiguous when a king died. There was, consequently, a conceptual instability in Burmese political culture between reigns that invited rebellion, but generally not during a reign. Thus, there was a sensitive relationship between a cellular social structure and the concept of a charismatic king, between a redistributive economy and kammatic Buddhism, and between a cellular social-political administration and a redistributive economy, which tied all three elements together.

Effects of Labor-Land Devolution
in the Thirteenth Century

Religious endowments and political fiefs resulted in one major situation: wealth flowed into the <u>sangha</u> for two centuries--wealth in the form of land and labor. The kings of Pagan acted in different ways to reduce this trend. They insisted, for example, that the king's permission be granted prior to any large donation; but in such instances the king found himself more or less helpless, since as the promoter of the Religion, he was not only not supposed to hinder gifts to the Religion, but was required to give more than anyone else. The spiritual worth of a person was equal to his <u>dānā</u> (donation). Since the king was superior to all people, he was expected to surpass everyone in <u>dānā</u>. Nevertheless, the kings of Pagan, like Aloncañsū, did require that their permission be granted for large donations.[52] One feels that this had a regulatory effect, but the state nevertheless did not get any land back.

Another method of control exercised by the king involved his freeing of secular property for religious donations. The <u>bona fides</u> of a grant remained under royal authority; that is, only if the king performed the water consecration ceremony of releasing (<u>lhwat</u>) property from secular ties such as taxation, could it legally be considered a religious donation (<u>alhū</u>).[53] The ceremony of pouring ritual water was performed in the presence of monks reciting <u>paritta</u> and of high officials. After the ceremony, the <u>Mahāsaman</u> would record the donation as legally released and affix his seal to the document.[54]

The institution of fiefs as political patronage also had similar destructive effects on the principle of centricity. Ironically, the "eater" system of loyalty-patronage was the institution <u>par excellence</u> upon which the political power of the state rested; yet centrifugal tendencies were inherent in this very system. To counteract these tendencies, confiscation was resorted to as a means of getting back some of this wealth. All those properties without valid proof of their tax exempt status were confiscated by King Klacwā in the mid-thirteenth century. century.[55]

To avoid such confiscations, however, people would endow the services of their chattels and the revenues of their lands--not the property itself--to a specific monk or monastery rather than to the sangha in general. According to Burmese civil law, if a person dedicated property to a specified monk rather than to the Church as a whole, when the monk died, the property right reverted to the donor.[56] He could then redonate this property to another monk. This method ensured the survival of one's property right, keeping this right in the family and out of the hands of the state--especially if the owner had received his property as a gift (Mahādān) from the previous king who might well have been the present king's political opponent.[57]

In addition to the drain on state resources, religious endowments and the grant of fiefs tended to diffuse land and labor. Inevitably, this pattern created numerous centers of economic and political power and patronage, instead of just one (or at most, two) center(s) required for the efficient functioning of the system. The necessity for the state to maintain its prerogative as the primary patron of the sangha (and thus maintain centricity) was being undermined by the growing artisan landed class whose new found wealth made them major supporters of the Order.

There was one alternative: "religious purification." This was to become the method par excellence of insuring that the economic resources of the state returned to its control. By this method, the king "purified" the Order, reduced its wealth, and regained some of its economic base. "Purification" in Burmese history, although perhaps motivated by religious reasons, has had very important economic and political implications. It has periodically reduced the sangha to a small, unified, "other worldly" oriented group with few riches and controlled by the king's Mahāthera. As a result of such "purification," more land and labor have been brought back under secular jurisdiction and hence have become taxable.

The fifteenth century Kalyani Inscription gives a vivid

and detailed account of the process of purification and is used here as the best available example.[58] According to the inscription, the king declared the saṅgha corrupt, lazy, worldly, and impure. By the power vested in him as a Buddhist king, he was expected to purify the Religion as well as the Order periodically, so as to perpetuate the Religion for 5,000 years, since everything, including the saṅgha, was held to be impermanent.[59] The saṅgha also possessed far too much wealth, unlike the ideal Order, which must be austere, even ascetic.

Kings like Kyanzittha deliberately dated their inscriptions from the years since the Buddha's parinirvāṇa to remind the people of the many years that still remained before the Religion would decay and to convince them that it would not happen during their reign. Thus "purification" enabled the saṅgha conceptually to exist indefinitely, while a "purified" saṅgha in turn showed the piety of the king. This quid pro quo of temporal self-survival became one of the major themes in the cyclical nature of Burmese history.

Since the Ceylonese tradition has always been regarded as the most "pure," the king would gather several chosen monks known for their spiritual qualities and send them to Ceylon to be re-ordained in the unbroken Mahāvihāra tradition. There these Burmese monks had to remove their saffron robes, don white ones, and admit their status as laymen. They confessed that they would no longer retain their previous ranks in the Order. Once re-ordained, they were given back their saffron robes, and became part of the "pure" unbroken tradition. However, regardless of previous status in the Order, they were then junior to those monks who ordained them--this was and is a law in the Ceylonese re-ordination procedure.

Having been purified, the monks returned to Burma, were welcomed by the king with great pomp and ceremony, and were given a sima (ordination hall) in which to officiate. The sima, of course, had gone through the proper purification rites, releasing it from all other spiritual ties and claims such as Nat rights over the soil. This was done by choosing a site where no sima had previously stood, erecting boundary

stones, digging a moat (since water purifies), and sanctifying
every inch of ground with recitations of various parittas, all
strictly prescribed by scripture. Roots of trees and
overhanging branches that touched the boundary were cut to
prevent contamination. [60] This land was called a visugāma and
the right of granting such land belonged only to the king.

Since the quality of one's merit depended upon the piety
of the monks that one gave gifts to and served, the Burmese
public was (and is still) always conscious of the relative purity
of the members of the saṅgha. When the purified monks
returned from Ceylon, their new status as well as royal
patronage turned public support and favor towards them. As
the rest of the monks in Burma did not want to be cut off from
state and public funding, and because relative seniority
depended on the order of re-ordination, there was a rush to be
re-ordained. As a result, petitions poured in to the king's
committee of purified monks.

Then, as now, precise records were kept as to when a
monk was re-ordained since even minutes could decide one's
relative rank in the Order. The crucial point, however, was
this: the monks that went to Ceylon to be re-ordained returned
to Burma higher in rank than anyone they re-ordained in
Burma, regardless of previous seniority. The king then chose
a Mahāthera to preside over this "purified" group. In effect,
the king, via the Mahāthera, now controlled a small, "pure,"
unified, "other worldly" oriented, and relatively austere
saṅgha--of which the senior monks were his chosen few.

Naturally, part of the criteria for accepting any monk
who wished to be re-ordained included giving up worldly
possessions such as cattle, land, and chattels to prove his
sincerity of purpose. Since saṅghika property as a whole
could not be inherited by any lay person, it reverted to the
state. In this way, much of the wealth of the state was
reclaimed periodically.

Once the new Order had gained enough members, the
king forbad any more re-ordinations without the expressed
permission of his committee. King Dhammaceti actually
instructed the saṅgha in the following manner: "First inform

us, so that the case [of an applicant] can be examined in the sīmā here.... When definite arrangements have been made, we will present the monastic requisites and will support the ordination. But if you do not act thus, but confer the upasampadā ordination privily, the mother and father of those who receive such...ordination, as well as their relatives, and likewise their lay supporters will be visited by us with royal penalties."[61]

When one was ready to be ordained, "our lords should inform us and we [the committee] shall support the upasampadā ordination. Let there be a single sect! Let not divers sects arise!" the King stated. Then, "His Majesty caused a message in these terms to be drawn up" and had an "investigation (and) search to be made throughout the whole extent of his...country regarding monks who were possessed of goods, paddy (and) rice, male slaves, female slaves, cattle or buffaloes, and His Majesty caused word to be sent to them in this wise: 'My lords, give up and surrender your goods if you would observe the conduct of monks. If my lords fail to do so, then with your goods follow the life of laymen' (whose property would be taxable)."

Then the king issued an edict naming the types of people who should not be allowed to enter or seek refuge in the monasteries. He declared that "the servants of the king and companions of the king...do not harbour them among you [in monasteries]."[62] Thus the apparent religious motive for the "purification of the saṅgha" had extremely significant social, economic, and political implications.

In the thirteenth century, however, "purification" ceased to work because the material interests of the large new landowning class which had grown out of the temple building projects coincided with the existence of a large, "this-world" oriented, sectarian, un-unified, and "impure" saṅgha: purification failed when the public refused to support it. For their social and material welfare, the public was dependent upon members of the artisan class who had become rather wealthy landowners. As we have seen earlier, the society as a whole was likewise dependent upon continuous and lavish patronage of the saṅgha. The larger the saṅgha was, the more it would receive, and the more wealth would spill over to the public, particularly to the artisans. The merit path to salvation was consistent with a wealthy, landowning saṅgha whose wealth grew along with that of the artisan class. There was thus a close economic tie between the latter's material well-being and the promotion of kammatic Buddhism.

The symmetry between the political power held by the state on the one hand and the socio-economic power of the saṅgha cum landowning classes on the other saw its first serious signs of imbalance in the late thirteenth century. In the eleventh and twelfth centuries, exchange of goods had been for the most part exchange of services. To make human beings thus disposed to serve as an outcome of their status (since status and occupation were hereditary) was an aim of political, as opposed to economic, power. "As long as dependent labor predominates as an element of wealth," Karl Polanyi wrote, "the economy has only a shadowy existence. That is, economic power is the countervailing power of political power, held by an aristocracy."[63]

By the thirteenth century, the artisan class had become independent rather than dependent labor and its economic power was now pitted against the political power of the state. Its advantage was enhanced by the support of thè saṅgha, at least structurally. Expansion in temple building had resulted not only in the growth of the saṅgha, but in the rise of socio-economic status for this class, whose members were recognized more and more by the suffix attached to their names--saṅ.[64]

That the saṅgha was not austere, ascetic, or "pure" as defined by scripture needs little documentation.[65] Buddhism in late thirteenth century Pagan abounds with a hodge-podge of ideologies and sects. Elements of Tantric belief permeated certain sects and monasteries; others absorbed beliefs from folk religion. The Church was involved in peasant uprisings, land disputes, land buying and selling, and throwing lavish feasts (consisting of whole cattle, pigs, and liquor) to celebrate legal victories. The saṅgha at this time could not be considered orthodox, although tantricism itself need not imply decay. According to Conze, tantricism was a phase in

the development of Buddhism and was in part the result of
Buddhism's integration with society.[66] Buddhism had indeed
spread to the masses and mixed its ideologies with animist
and other folk beliefs. The sangha was widespread,
uncontrolled, and nowhere near being unified under the sole
authority of the Mahāthera. The interests of the noveaux
riches now conflicted with the political and economic
implications of "purification," and the growth of the sangha,
once an asset, had now become a liability.

Centralization of the kingdom's numerous cells
depended upon the loyalty of their leaders. The loyalty of
their leaders depended upon social and material rewards given
by the king and his court. When wealth no longer remained a
monopoly of the state, loyalty likewise wavered. As soon as
centralization began to break down, the principle of centricity
so important to the effective functioning of a redistributive
economy also began to disintegrate. The state was thus unable
to affect the smooth functioning of the structure of loyalty and
patronage. All this encouraged the local autonomy of landed
nobles which added to the centrifugal tendencies inherent in
the system, as noted above. By losing its hold on the sources
of labor and land, the state lost the key to economic and
political power.

In short, the unique association of the Buddhist sangha
with the pattern of religious endowments and patronage did far
more to undermine the power of the state, and, ironically,
establish Theravāda Buddhism in Burma, than did the nature
of Theravāda Buddhism itself.[67]

Each of the Pagan kings from the eleventh to the
thirteenth centuries had tried to ensure survival of the state
in his own way, according to the needs of his own generation.
Aniruddha's reign revealed the need for supplementing the
short supply of labor and for centralizing it, both acts being
necessary to strengthen the kingdom. He solved both these
problems by military solutions. After securing his front--
which bordered the kingdom of Nanchao--with stockades, he
attacked his rear (Thaton), imported skilled and unskilled
labor, and instituted a hierarchically structured Buddhist
church.

Justifying his attack as <u>Dharmavijaya</u> or righteous conquest, Aniruddha left Thaton more or less intact, neither settling on it nor directly incorporating the port city into the Pagan administrative apparatus. Rather, Thaton was left as a neutral port with access to the outside world, an area which performed the economic and political functions of providing trade links with, and a buffer zone against, adjacent states-- much like the role of free ports in Asia today <u>vis à vis</u> the inland states. The control of Thaton as a semi-tributary meant that Aniruddha's agricultural empire was now integrated into a network of maritime trading empires with international connections (of which Thaton was one). On the other hand, a local nucleus was left intact from which the tributary state could re-emerge as an independent entity and in periodic cycles threaten the power of the mainland empire itself.

Aniruddha subsequently established cultural ties with Ceylon, thereby enhancing his prestige while providing his newly established <u>sangha</u> with older Buddhist traditions and the artisan class with new motifs in religious art.[68] Thus labor importation, military expansion and re-organization, social stability and economic development with the aid of the <u>sangha</u>, and finally overseas relations which added prestige and sophistication to the newly formed kingdom were Aniruddha's solutions to the demands of his generation.

Without fully realizing the implications, however, Aniruddha had sowed the seeds of self-destruction by making the <u>sangha</u> the main recipient for the flow of land and labor and thereby inviting the decentralization of economic and political structures, a process which was to have serious repercussions for the state in the thirteenth century. By his actions he had created a new situation that his successors had to face--by changing--or perish.

The challenges to the subsequent generation demanded form, order, and some sort of accommodation to the "chaos" of diverse cultural influences and inputs of Aniruddha's reign. Kyanzittha rose to meet these needs. Perhaps one word alone described the demands of his age as well as the age itself-- syncretism. Since no single culture was as yet completely dominant, there had to be an amalgam. It was an age

characterized by Burman military rule, Pyu traditions, Mon
"super-culture" and Theravādin spirit. To say that Pagan at
this time was an ethnic Burman civilization was to speak only
of the ruling class; to call it Pyu underestimated the changing
nature of institutions; to call it Theravādin oversimplified the
religious milieu. All these elements made up eleventh and
twelfth century Pagan.

Kyanzittha was the person around whom this amalgam
could unite. He cemented the fissures of decentralization by
appeasing all cultures and groups. He patronized Mon scholars
and artisans; their language became the lingua franca of the
court, and, in effect, the Mons emerged as the intellectual
elite. He satisfied the Burmans by maintaining their rule. He
provided a sense of continuity to the "old timers" of the
society, the Pyu, by linking his genealogy to the real and
mythical ancestors of the Pyu via Śrī Kṣetra, the symbol of
their "golden past." Lastly, he supported and favored
Theravāda Buddhism while tolerating all other religious
groups.

Art and architecture, religion, language and literature,
ethnic plurality--in effect the whole society during Kyanzittha's
reign portrayed assimilation and syncretism. At a time when
Sawlu, Aniruddha's son and short-lived successor, easily could
have brought the Pagan kingdom down to a premature death,
Kyanzittha injected new vigor into the civilization. This age
of syncretism, however, eventually yielded to a new one, itself
a response to patterns created by its predecessors. The new
age demanded not assimilation, cosmopolitanism, or
amalgamation. Because syncretism by nature had created
intellectual and structural uncertainty, there was now a need
for permanence. King Aloñcañsū did precisely that by
beginning the process which institutionalized what became
known as the Theravāda Burmese Buddhist Tradition.

Although many centuries laid the foundations of this
tradition, its establishment became evident only in the twelfth
and thirteenth centuries. This period witnessed the
disappearance of the Mon language from Pagan for several
centuries, replaced by Old Burmese language and literature[69];
Pali scholarship advanced to a degree of sophistication

heretofore unattained[70]; and the Burmese language acquired the status that Mon once held as the lingua franca. In art and architecture, the twelfth century evolved temple styles and motifs in ornamentation that became standards.[71] In administration, the state witnessed its most centralized structure, and the saṅgha was cohesive, small, and well controlled, especially under King Aloṅcañsū. Religious endowments at this time were relatively small and well regulated as wealth remained in the hands of the state.[72] The need for permanence created a durable tradition which posterity regarded as the classical model.

Because cultural permanence or institutionalization of a tradition occurred during a time when Burmans were ruling, when Pali traditions were supreme, and when Theravāda Buddhism was at its peak, this classical culture came to be associated with the (ethnic) Burman ruling class. It gave to posterity a rallying cry, a golden past with which emerging rulers could and did identify--whether they were Shan or Mon, efforts were made to link their genealogy with that of the Pagan Dynasty and its Burman kings.[73] Despite contributions from a variety of cultures, the synthesis at the right time and place supplied the intellectual raison d'être for the future unification of Burma by Burmans.

Since a society becomes most vulnerable to decay once cultural permanence (like a tradition) is achieved, conservatism, as a result of this permanence, hinders further change--and in essence, survival. The political and social institutions that once enhanced the economy, now stand in the way of, indeed oppose further economic development.

The reigns of Narasū, Narapatisithu, Natoṅmya, and Klacwā (1168-1249 A.D. collectively) were essentially responses to the trends begun by their predecessors. The continuity and climax of Pagan's architectural, political, economic, and religious achievements during this period were testimony to their success. However, their response which ensured survival during their own generation had serious repercussions by the end of the thirteenth century.

Military expansion and territorial acquisition (for

people, not land) was one reaction. It intensified the kingdom's military resources and caused the reorganization of its structure. King Narapatisithu (1174-1211 A.D.) epitomized this trend.[74] Under him the state had changed its policy from simple control of labor to acquisition of more labor and wealth, as Aniruddha had done. Although this strategy gave respite to his immediate successor, subsequent kings again found that labor and land continued to flow into the hands of the <u>sangha</u> in any case. The problem was that the king had to reward his military officers with land and labor, which invariably found their way to the Church as these soldiers donated to the Religion to acquire merit and obtain the type of prestige that military glory alone could not give.

The period during and following the reigns of Natonmya and Klacwā witnessed the symptoms of a declining kingdom as peasants revolted and civil suits and conflicts arose over land and labor. In general, the scene suggested the beginnings of decentralization and disintegration.[75] King Narathihapade (1255-1287 A.D.), although regarded by the chroniclers of the nineteenth century as a "bad king" for his apparent defeat by the Mongols, had a long and, on the surface, secure reign of thirty-two years as he tried to emulate the success of his predecessors. However, the period of grace that he provided for Pagan was the lull before the storm. His reign witnessed quantitatively more land and labor devolution by single individuals than did any other.[76]

Immediate causes that accelerated and confirmed the process of decentralization in the Pagan empire included the emergence of autonomous centers of power in the rich Kyok chañ area under the Shans, who had, during the course of the centuries, slowly integrated into the ranks of the Pagan aristocracy through marriage alliances and who now controlled a large part of the rich Eleven Kharuin[77]; the rise of Sukhodaya in the middle of the thirteenth century with its political support of Chiengmai and Pegu on Pagan's flanks[78]; the re-emergence of the Mons in Martaban with Wagaru; and the threat of the Sak-Kantū around the rich Six Kharuin of Manbū.

The Kingdom of Pagan had sown the seeds of its own destruction when it patronized and integrated the Buddhist sangha. Although the <u>sangha</u> gave Pagan its culture and "soul," and initially contributed to its economic development, it inadvertently destroyed the state's subsequent basis for survival. Since the wealth that had made Pagan was now in the hands of the sangha as well as of the artisan class, the state could no longer maintain its armies nor the loyalty of its aristocracy. Its control over the manpower resources of the kingdom had become ineffectual. At the same time, the sangha could not compensate for this loss, especially in terms of an army, without losing its raison d'être as a religious institution. In the face of all this, no able leader emerged to meet the challenges of the times. Minyiswasawke in 1398 A.D. with clear hindsight remarked in an inscription that the Burmese empire had declined because of civil war. [79] Thus the Mongol and Shan coup de grâce in the late thirteenth century merely confirmed and symbolized an institutional fait accompli.

It is not surprising that as a tradition as well as a city, Pagan survived well into the fourteenth and fifteenth centuries, as Paul Bennett has shown. [80] The tradition of Pagan continued because the cultural institution par excellence that could (and did) perpetuate this classic tradition, that is the sangha, now had the economic means to do so. As a city, Pagan remained the cultural center, the "museum" of the "High Tradition" in Burma, preserving the civilization's achievements and glory, while Pinya, Sagaing, and Ava in turn took the status of political and economic centers.

That the civilization of Pagan survived so long politically testifies to the ability of each generation of leaders to adapt to new socio-economic needs and circumstances, which were in part created by their predecessors. Great leaders provided this ability to survive while the environment furnished them with a context in which to do so effectively. But the dilemma that confronted the kings in the late thirteenth century was too difficult to resolve: the sangha represented the very essence that had made Pagan more than a simple military kingdom, although it had just as effectively drained the economic base that had created the civilization in the first place. Yet the state could not survive unless it destroyed the sangha and took back its sources of wealth, which it was both unwilling and unable to do. The sangha in Burma survived beyond the civilization that had first nurtured it to become the stabilizing pillar of continuity in the institutional history of Burma.

Symbols Used in Notes

ASB. Report of the Director, Archaeological Survey of Burma. (English and Burmese)

BODAW, I and II. Burma. Home Department. Inscriptions Copied from the Stones Collected by King Bodawpaya and Placed near the Arakan Pagoda, Mandalay. 2 vols. Government Printing Office, Rangoon, 1897. (Burmese)

EB. Epigraphia Birmanica. Edited by the Director, Archaeological Survey of Burma. Rangoon, Government Printing Office. (Mostly English translations of Mon inscriptions)

GPC. The Glass Palace Chronicle. Translated by Pe Maung Tin and G. H. Luce. Rangoon, 1922.

Jambu. Jambudipa U Saung Kyan. Edited by J. S. Furnivall and Pe Maung Tin. Burma Research Society Publication, Rangoon, 1960. (In Old and Modern Burmese: a collection of sittans or revenue inquests, edicts of kings and other material of a statistical nature kept by officials of the kings, approximately from the tenth century onwards)

JBRS. Journal of the Burma Research Society.

LIST. Archaeological Survey of Burma. A List of Inscriptions Found in Burma. Part I, compiled by Charles Duroiselle. Rangoon, Government Printing Office, 1921. (English and Burmese)

MKLYS. E. Maung. Pagan Kyauksa Let Ywei Sin. Panya Poneit Taik, Rangoon, 1928. (Selected Inscriptions of Pagan) (Old Burmese)

OI. Original Inscriptions Collected by King Bodawpaya in Upper Burma and Now Placed Near the Patodawgyi Pagoda, Amarapura. Rangoon, Government Printing Office, 1913. (Old Burmese and some Modern Burmese)

238

PPA. Burma. Home Department. Inscriptions of Pagan, Pinya, and Ava (in the Burmese Text) as Deciphered from the Ink Impressions Found Among the Papers of the Late Dr. E. Forchhammer (and Edited by Taw Sein Ko). Rangoon, Government Printing Office, 1892. (Old Burmese)

SIP. Selections from the Inscriptions of Pagan. Edited by G. H. Luce and Pe Maung Tin. Rangoon University, Department of Oriental Studies, Publication 1, Rangoon, 1928. (Old Burmese)

SMK. Shehaung Myanma Kyauksa Mya. Vol. I, edited by the Director, Archaeological Survey of Burma, U Aung Thaw. Rangoon, 1972. (Ancient Inscriptions of Burma) (Old Burmese)

TN. Inscriptions of Pagan, Pinya, and Ava. Translated by Tun Nyein. Rangoon, Government Printing Office, 1899. (English)

UB, I and II. Burma. Home Department. Inscriptions Collected in Upper Burma. 2 vols. Government Printing Office, 1900 and 1903. (Old Burmese and Modern Burmese)

NOTES

1. For example, see SMK, "The Dhammarajika Pagoda
   Inscription of 1196 A.D.," line 5b, and also SIP, no. 44,
   line 2. Other inscriptions use this phrase in a similar way,
   with a sense of community pride in the kingdom. Kyanzittha
   (Kalancacsā) used this term in his Mon inscriptions in EB,
   as did his son, Rājākumar, in the "Myazedi Inscription,"
   SIP, no. 5, line 3.

2. Aniruddha's conquest in 1057 and his following importation
   of labor from Thaton is supported by the GPC, the
   Sasanvamsa, p. 70, the Slapat Rājāwaṅ Datow Smiṅ Ron
   (The Mon Chronicle), p. 48. By 1058, Aniruddha had built
   shrines and dedicated a statue of Gavampati, the patron
   saint of the artisans he had imported from Thaton, in
   Pagan. See BODAW, II, pp. 627 and 633, and SIP, no. 1,
   p. 1.

3. Most of the evidence for pre-Pagan contacts with Buddhism
   can be found at Śrī Kṣetra (Old Prome), if not earlier at
   Beikthano Myo (Viṣṇu City). One should consult the
   Archaeological Survey of Burma from its inception to
   about 1939. Aung Thaw's Report on the Excavations at
   Beikthano (Rangoon, 1968) shows evidence of stupas of the
   Nagarjunakunda and Amaravati designs in the first century
   A.D. city. Ba Shin's article (in Burmese) entitled "Halin
   Gyi" (Great Halin) in Thekatho Pyiña Padeittha Sasaung
   (The Cultural Magazine), Than Tun's first two chapters of
   Khit Haung Myanma Yazawin (History of Ancient Burma),
   (Rangoon, 1964), and General L. M. E. deBeyliè's Prome
   et Samara (Paris, 1907), all deal with this subject.

4. The term "cellular" is taken from Edmond Leach's
   "Hydraulic Society in Ceylon," Past and Present, 15 (1959),
   pp. 2-25. The term "redistributive economy" is from Karl
   Polanyi, et al., Trade and Market in the Early Empires
   (Glencoe, 1957). The terms kammatic and nibbānic
   Buddhism are found in Melford Spiro, Buddhism and Society
   (New York, 1972).

5. Most of the data from the original inscriptions reinforce this contention that ethnic groups had certain occupations of their own (this practice continued into the nineteenth century), Musicians, for example, had Indian names, agricultural workers had Burmese names, and merchants had South Indian names. The latter were called setthi sikwray (rich Chettiyars). According to the Hobson-Jobson Burmese-English Dictionary (Rangoon, 1966, second printing) and to T.W. Rhys Davids' and William Stede's Pali-English Dictionary (London, 1966, p. 181), the term setthi applies to heads of trade guilds, today's Chettiyars. Sūkrwe, a term suffixed to setthi, meant "to be wealthy" and still does today. It is the term from which the modern word sūtthe "rich man" apparently originates. Names for skilled artisans were Mon in origin as were the skills themselves. "Stone mason," for example, was pantamo; tamo is "stone" in Mon, and pan was "he who did the work," like the Burmese sañ and the "er" suffix in English. For example, see SIP, p. 120, line 9.

6. BODAW, II, p. 656. Here the thugyi (sukrī) or leader of myedu "earth diggers" (also a place name whose inhabitants were those who "dug the earth") was mentioned. BODAW, II, pp. 643 and 656, mentions a leader of the asañ. SIP, p. 107, has a leader of the Sō (an ethnic group). Sukrī of the goldsmiths was found in MKLYS, no. 19, pp. 15 and 40. That they had personal rather than territorial jurisdiction over their groups is confirmed by MKLYS, p. 117, line 16, where a cell leader had control of a group of workers on land owned by someone else. In MKLYS, p. 140, line 11, there was a sukrī of purākywan (temple servants), and quite clearly, since only the monks owned the land on which the temple was built, he was merely in charge of the people on it. Personal jurisdiction meant that the sukrī had to keep strict account of where these people were, for sometimes they lived apart from where the sukrī resided. In these cases, kywan were prefixed with place names indicating their locality, as MKLYS, no. 57, p. 161 shows (here the kywan were Indians from Pagan). In many instances, kywan who lived far away were dedicated to a distant temple or monastery, which meant they did not reside in the territory or on the lands to which

they were to give their services. See MKLYS, no. 59, p. 171, and MKLYS, no. 44.

7. Mon Rwā, which means the "village of the Mons" was also the proper name of that village, as were the others. The occupants of Kwan Ma Cā Rwā (the village that does not eat betel," were apparently Chins (Professor Luce's personal communication; see also G. H. Luce, "Economic Life of the Early Burman," Burma Research Society Fiftieth Anniversary Publication, 2, p. 334). Other places took on occupational names, such as Mraṅ Mhu, "cavalry leader village," and Mraṅ Pugān, "village of Pugān cavalry." See for example MKLYS, no. 45, p. 120, where Mraṅ Cañ Rwā, "horse riding village" or "village of the Mraṅ Cañ" (a cavalry officer), is mentioned. One can get a picture of these early ethnic settlements in G. H. Luce, "Old Kyaukse and the Coming of the Burmans," JBRS, XLII, i (June, 1959), p. 81, the only work in English which treats this subject. See also Jambudipa, p. 69; BODAW, II, p. 656; SIP, p. 91; PPA, II, no. 2, p. 57; MKLYS, no. 38, p. 107; SIP, no. 16, p. 29; SIP, no. 34, p. 83; SIP, no. 26, p. 57; SIP, no. 49, p. 137, etc., where potters, earth-diggers, cowherds, goatherds, silversmiths, drummers, sweepers, and cooks all lived in their own villages.

8. Because Burmese do not have family or personal names, and since hereditary occupation and status were maintained, the only available method of controlling offspring was to keep registers of people, their occupations, habitations, ethnic backgrounds, and familial relations. Among lists of kywan, prefixes and suffixes would indicate a person's familial relationship to others in the group; for instance, a person would have "brother of..." or "husband of..." immediately preceding or following his name. Even "suckling babes" were listed. Sometimes "roll calls" were made (MKLYS, p. 70). Certain kywan had prefixes such as amuy, "inherited," some were noted to have been acquired--hap laṅ kon, "by natural increase," and others were noted for their marital status (see SIP, p. 91). In general, then, heredity was enforced.

9. BODAW, II, pp. 555, 643, 656. Leaders of the asañ (athi

of the eighteenth and nineteenth centuries) were called asañ
krī. In 1184 A.D., asañ were mentioned as a distinct group
(TN, 1, no. 11, pp. 4-5; PPA, I, no. 11, pp. 13-15). TN,
p. 9, showed likewise that asañ were referred to as a
group, in this case the kyunnwa asañ. Again PPA, no. 11,
p. 743, mentioned asañ as a group. Professor Luce feels
that asañ were "landowners," but I feel that owning land
was not a necessary condition. They probably came to own
land but other groups also owned land. In the context of
later Burmese institutions, moreover, the asañ, especially
in contrast to the amhudan or "service" class, were "non-
service" professionals or independent entrepreneurs. In the
nineteenth century, according to Hobson-Jobson, an asañ
was "a person of the common sort, who is under no
specific engagement to government, but is liable to be
called to occasional service..." (Hobson-Jobson's
Burmese-English Dictionary, p. 116). The second
definition (more obsolete, and hence probably closer to
Pagan's situation) went as follows: "an owner, proprietor;
combined with nouns, as kun sañ, a merchant, mun sañ,
a baker; one who continuously follows a particular trade...."

The term for the "public" group in post-Pagan times was
amhudan, "bearer of the duty or service," i.e. people with
service obligations to the state. In the seventeenth century,
amhudan were considered higher in social status (being
ethnic Burman) than asañ (being of other ethnic
backgrounds). The word amhudan in this combination was
not found until the fourteenth century, but the words amhu
and dan, separately and with the same meaning, were found
in Pagan (BODAW, II, p. 846, mentions "service" or dan
lands). It is true that many asañ in Pagan were indeed non-
Burmans, such as drummers. If they were Burman, it was
expressly stated, e.g., Mranma cañ sañ, "Burman
drummers" (SMK, p. 50, lines 20-21). The amhudan group
included military service people such as cavalry. The word
mhu, "gotten" or "not gotten by service," prefixed a
certain category of kywan (SIP, p. 91). Nevertheless, by
1369 A.D., an edict of Mingyiswasawkē used the word
amhudan in its seventeenth century sense and used it as if
it had long been known (Jambudipa, p. 62). Because the
inscriptions of Pagan were basically concerned with land

and labor and had little to do with service groups, little is found in them with regard to the amhudan.

10. The word "slave," used in the nineteenth century to translate the word kywan, has been quite misleading. At the time of that translation, no study, indeed no systematic compilation, of the inscriptions had yet been made by westerners. Some of these kywan were bought and sold as slaves, but "servants" or "indentured serfs," rather than "purchased kywan," describes their socio-economic status better. Marc Bloch's description of chattel slaves in European history, with certain small exceptions, fits kywan status rather well--particularly with regard to their service contracts vis-à-vis a lord [Marc Bloch, Feudal Society (Chicago, 1961), pp. 255-274]. In Pagan, however, unlike in Europe, these services did not include military duties. Edmund Leach's term "service tenure," as he described the Ceylonese situation, also fits well, although in Pagan the use of cash was much greater than in Ceylon at the time.

In addition to these economic attributes, the word kywan has a social dimension also. The impolite "i," used with those inferior in age and status, is "na." The former, kywan tō," implies a superior point of reference, in this case probably the king. Thus everyone is a kywan in relation to the king. It is interesting to note that in those Tibeto-Burman speaking areas where "na" is used as "i" and where no institution of kingship emerged, "i" remained in the "na" form and never became "kywan tō." People there use "na" for everyone, inferior or superior. I have a feeling that perhaps the development of kingship and hierarchy may have changed the polite "i" from "na" to "kywan tō" in Pagan, precisely because of the development of kingship.

Professor Hla Pe from the London School of Oriental and African Studies feels that the word kywan may have originated from the Mon word klon, "to work" and therefore "worker," since the word for kywan in the eleventh century was spelled with a subscript "l" rather than, or along with, a "y," enhancing the possibility of kywan being derived from klon. From my own work, this explanation seems to be viable.

11. The long "Min Anandathu Inscription" throws much light on law as practiced in Pagan. There were three levels of courts from preliminary hearings to appellate divisions. There were pleaders, recorders, judges, witnesses, and all the paraphenalia associated with civil courts. Two inscriptions, moreover, strongly suggest the existence of a civil code: 1) The edict of Klacwā and 2) Jeyyapikram's Inscription in 1247-1248 A.D. Klacwā was describing the legal procedure to be used to handle theft and in the process stated that judges, when deciding the penalty for such-and-such a theft, should refer to the amanwan cā, the book on civil law. Jeyyapikram's inscription was even more explicit. He had filed a suit and the investigators of the preliminary level handed their findings to King Klacwā, who said: "If that is the testimony, you Judges arrange the verdict according to the Golden Dhammathat..." (MKLYS, no. 58, p. 166, lines 41-42, and no. 59, p. 171, line 14).

Civil law as practiced in Pagan is suggested in the principles of the later law books. Forchhammer's Jardine Prize Essay (n.d.) argues well from internal evidence the existence of Dhammathats in Pagan. Apparently, Klacwā's edicts were yet undeciphered when Forchhammer wrote or he would have used these for inscriptional support. He shows, in great detail and with expertise, how the thirteenth century Wagaru Dhammathat and the Dhammavilasa Dhammathat of Pagan were practically the same; i.e., they were copies of each other. The later Dhammathats, of the seventeenth through the nineteenth centuries, were practically copies of these earlier two, with additional material added from their own times. The Dhammavilasa Dhammathat of Pagan is thought to have been composed by Dhammavilasa or Sariputtra, the Mahātherea possibly of Narapatisithu. The GPC, the Sasanavamsa, the Kālyani Inscription and several Pagan inscriptions confirm this person's historicity. For an inscription erected by this monk, see SMK, pp. 46-47.

12. MKLYS, no. 31, pp. 58-59, 71-72. This price was written into the Dhammathats of the nineteenth century unchanged,

as if the increase or decrease in labor mattered little with regard to thé price. For this concept of fixed equivilancies see note 31.

13. SIP, MKLYS, SMK, BODAW, PPA, passim. In English, see Than Tun's article "Social Life in Burma, A.D. 1044-1287," JBRS, 41, 1-2 (Dec. 1958), pp. 37-47, which enumerates the various types of occupations but draws no conclusions or generalizations.

14. Artisans were usually paid in gold and silver, while dancers and drummers received paddy and land. Payments did vary considerably, however, though in general skilled artisans, such as sculptors, carvers, masons, and carpenters received gold and silver. For a good example of an inscription that gives these details, see the article by Pe Maung Tin, "Buddhism in the Inscriptions of Pagan," JBRS, 26, 1 (1936), pp. 417-441.

15. See note 7.

16. See note 9.

17. Than Tun, passim.

18. See note 9.

19. See note 14.

20. One might add here that the conclusions offered by several historians of Southeast Asia, such as Harvey and Coedès with regard to the decline of these mainland empires have to be re-evaluated. Both suggest that the building of these great monuments was a drain on and exhausted the labor supplies needed for cultivation, etc., until finally the societies could not support these activities any more and decay subsequently set in. Their analysis is based on the assumption that the labor was forced, not paid. One can indeed argue the contrary, that temple building stimulated and developed the Pagan economy, attracting people into the capital from adjacent areas as well as abroad (India), and that monumental architecture brought about the growth

of the civilization, not its destruction. See G. E. Harvey, History of Burma (London, 1967 reprint), pp. 63, 331; G. Coedès, Angkor, An Introduction (London, 1963), pp. 105-107.

21. For example, see SIP, no. 11, p. 19.

22. TN, 11, pp. 55, 93; BODAW, II, p. 633; SIP, pp. 120, 133; MKLYS, p. 365. The military groups seem to have indeed lived on lands specially granted to them and were separated from each other according to function, i.e,, cavalry from infantry and so on. By 1442 A.D., royal elephanteers are mentioned as part of the military corps, and they were, in a similar manner, granted fiefs (TN, p. 40). The Jatabon Yazawin (p. 90), oldest of the Burmese chronicles, written by (at least) the sixteenth century and the most reliable, describes various miliatry contingents such as the Northern Cavalry and Southern Cavalry.

23. MKLYS, no. 31, p. 85; no. 56, p. 155. In the context of the later Burmese institution of Mraṅ mhu, "cavalry officer," this term in Pagan makes more sense. See also BODAW, II, pp. 397, 399; MKLYS, pp. 40, 346, where a Mraṅ khoṅ was mentioned. He seemed to be an officer under a Mraṅ mhu (khoṅ is "head" as in "leader").

24. See note 22. Most of the forty-three stockades are listed in G. H. Luce, Old Burma--Early Pagan, 3 vols. (Locust Valley, N. Y., 1969, 1970). See also Luce's "Old Kayaukse," p. 85.

25. The famous "Dhammarājika Inscription of 1196 A.D." in MKLYS, p. 66, lines 10-11. Narapatisithu was referred to as "Lord of 17,645 soldiers" in one of his inscriptions (TN, no. 11, p. 4). The Jatabon's estimate (see note 22) of cavalry came to about 10,000 horses, which seems to be a reasonable figure considering Narapatisithu's specific number. I think these figures referred to the conscript army, minus the standing guard, that is, all those who were obliged to take up military service in return for tax exemptions.

26. Clifford Geertz, Agricultural Involution, the Process of

<u>Ecological</u> <u>Change</u> <u>in</u> <u>Indonesia</u> (Berkeley, 1963), passim.

27. For example, see TN, 11, no. 9, pp. 34-36.

28. TN, 1, no. 16, pp. 9-11, and especially MKLYS, no 56, p. 155, lines 23b-27. On the whole, the inscriptions confirm the institution of "eater" or "fiefs." The word cā, "to eat," applied in this context to both secular and religious grants (see SIP, pp. 100, 131).

29. MK, p. 101, line 23, is the only <u>mriuw cā</u> that I have found thus far. In 1369 A.D., land records clearly use the term <u>mriuw cā</u> as if from experienced usage (<u>Jambudipa</u>, pp. 61-62). Many of the <u>mriuw cā</u> were also titled "umbrella wearers" or "those who bore umbrellas." Kyanzittha's inscriptional title <u>Hti duin Shin</u> could mean "the lord who wields the umbrella" rather than "lord of [the place] Hti'luin" as Professor Luce has suggested. Of course, it could be both, thus a play on words.

30. Polanyi, Part I. The description here is an adaptation of Polanyi's conceptual model from my own analysis of Pagan society in the context of the whole of Burmese history (the authors do not mention Southeast Asia).

31. Marshal Sahlins, "On the Sociology of Primitive Exhange," in Marshall Sahlins, <u>Stone</u> <u>Age</u> <u>Economics</u> (Chicago, 1972), pp. 185-275. The concept of "fixed" equivalencies is a characteristic of redistributive economies, to be discussed below. It implies, for a redistributive economy, all that supply and demand price does for market economies. The price of paddy, for example, was fixed and measured in absolute terms: the reason for differences in prices was not factors concerned with supply or demand, but with the type of paddy, i.e., wet rice, dry rice, sweet rice, etc. The prices for elephants, boats, gardens, etc., were all fixed in relation to paddy, as if an increase in either supply or demand were of little consequence (see MKLYS, pp. 72 and 120, where one boat was equivalent to eight <u>kywan</u>). In another donation (SIP, p. 121), instead of letting supply or demand determine price, the donor stipulated that "as for this estimate of mine, if there is rice in excess [larger

supply] , let there be as I said. But if there is ten
[smaller supply] , let the proportions be calculated before
dividing it out." One of the main characteristics of a
redistributive economy is to adjust supply and demand by
either redistributing more or less, without raising and
lowering the price. Revenue was likewise fixed. Thus a
sukrī had to pay a set amount as tax. People were paid
fixed equivalencies for assessing the tax (MKLYS, p. 35).

32. TN, 7, p. 91. SIP, no. 26, pp. 55-59, 106-110. MKLYS,
no. 51, p. 144; no. 44, p. 120; no. 53, p. 150; no. 48,
p. 135. These are but a few examples that document the
economic function of religious endowments. Also dependent
upon these endowments were moneylenders, bankers,
lawyers, etc., who were all indirectly supported by the
existence of these religious establishments (SIP, pp. 106-
110). Kings sometimes dedicated and endowed temples in
those areas from which they came, as if to repay their
constituents. In the nineteenth century, when the British
government cut off royal funds to the Shwesandaw temple in
Pagan, the entire area around the temple witnessed
economic and social decay (see A List of Monuments Found
in Burma, n.d., compiled by the Director of the
Archaeological Survey of Burma, Meitila Division, p. 12).
This monument had enjoyed Rs.5,000 yearly from its
endowments. These rents were subsequently appropriated
by the British government for public services, and the
temple fell into disrepair. In other words, the temple
brought socio-economic activity into that area and its
endowed existence was crucial for the vitality of life--both
socially and economically--of that location.

33. Evidence abounds in the inscriptions. Almost all the major
dedications of the thirteenth century were made by persons
whose titles and names reveal their original professional
standing as artisans. For instance, see EB, no. 14, p. 28;
no. 12, p. 237; no. 41, pp. 113-115. Many artisans did in
fact receive land as payment (for the best example see
SIP, no. 32, p. 75). Others undoubtedly bought it with
their earnings.

Furthermore, we can see that members of this group
married into the royal family, one of whose descendants

(Narathihapadi) in fact became king (see EB, p. 144 and SIP, no. 28, p. 64; no. 35, p. 86). Thus we may surmise a major jump in social status and landed interest by members of these families.

34. Melford Spiro, p. 124.

35. SIP, no. 24, p. 49; no. 27, p. 60.

36. An ambiguous sentence, this invariably concludes each donative inscription. For a typical example, see SIP, no. 25, p. 54, lines 39a-39b.

37. Hobson-Jobson, p. 266.

38. For a list of appointees who controlled the Eleven Kharuin in the thirteenth century, see MKLYS, no. 56, p. 155.

39. Among many, see SIP, no. 49, p. 133 and MKLYS, no. 9, p. 17.

40. Hobson-Jobson, p. 796.

41. G. H. Luce, Old Burma--Early Pagan, has identified over forty of these locations (see note 24).

42. See note 29.

43. For references to prañ, see SIP, no. 47, pp. 128-129; no. 3, p. 3; no. 44, p. 119; no. 31, p. 73; no. 24, p. 49; no. 40, p. 103; no. 38, p. 93; no. 19, p. 38. These include the variety of usages that we have mentioned.

44. During Kyanzittha's time, the Burmese section of the Kra Isthmus was governed by two officials with Pagan titles [Ba Shin, Lokahteikpan (Rangoon, n.d.), p. 23]. Ṅa Choṅ Khyam at the Nanchao border likewise had a governor responsible to the king. Talā (near modern Rangoon) had an appointee as did Peku (Pegu) (MKLYS, no. 56, p. 158).

45. SIP, pp. 35, 98, 107; MKLYS, no. 35, p. 95; no. 45, p. 121; no. 56, pp. 154-155. Witnesses at royal dedications

included a variety of officials, most of whose titles reveal their function, and whose order in the lists indicated rank. One should also see EB, particularly the "Saraba Gate Inscription" of Kalancacasā (Kyanzittha).

46. Aloncañsū was Kyanzittha's general, while Natonmya was Narapatisithu's. King Kalawswā, also known as Talā Sukrī, had this important port city as a "fief." Klacwā was also called Peku Man Krī, indicating his fief of Pegu (MKLYS, no. 56, p. 158). See also note 44.

47. H. L. Shorto, "The Dewatau Sotāpan: A Mon Prototype of the 37 Nats," BSOAS, 30, 1 (1967), pp. 127-141. See also Michael Mendelson's "Observations on a Town in the Region of Mount Poppa, Central Burma," France-Asie, 19, 179, (May-June, 1963), pp. 780-807. According to Shorto, the cult "united the worship of a male ancestor with that of a chthonic goddess by whose favour the tribe laid claim to its land..." (p. 140).

48. See the Mon inscriptions of Kalancacsā (Kyanzittha) as translated in EB, 1, 2, p. 148, where he traced his genealogy to the real and mythical ancestors of Śrī Kṣetra. He traced his father to the solar line (Buddhist-Indian implications) and his mother to the vilva (or velu, "bamboo") line (with indigenous implications, i.e., of the soil.) C. O. Blagden's and R. Winstedt's Malay Reader (Oxford, 1917), describes the folklore which associates the birth of a child from a vegetable substance to family names, that is, people took their names from particular plants, which suggests a totemistic origin. These families held these particular plants in reverence and imagined themselves to be descended from them. Kyanzittha's genealogy, represented by the bamboo genre, may be interpreted as an attempt to integrate the folk culture with the Buddhist culture, as represented by the solar elements.

49. Robert Heine-Geldern, "Conceptions of State and Kingship in South-East Asia," Far Eastern Quarterly, 2, 1 (November, 1942), pp. 15-30. This has also been republished as Cornell University Southeast Asia Program Data Paper no. 18 (Ithaca, New York, 1956).

50. Edmond Leach, passim.

51. The personal nature of kingship manifests itself in various other aspects of social relations. Although we cannot deal with it here, the principle behind penalties and fines in civil law was based upon personal rather than impersonal relations and conceptions of justice, unlike Roman law. Personal conceptions of justice are as intimately related to a society with an embedded economy as impersonal concepts of justice are to a contractus type of society, where everyone is considered equal before the law (and the economy). These types of personal relations in all aspects of society continued well into the nineteenth century. In the Konbaung period, Alaunpaya had to issue edicts to remind the public that a law made under his reign retained validity under the reign of his successors [Edicts of Alaungmin Tayagyi, in Burmese (Rangoon, n.d.)]. Thalun's successors in the seventeenth century had similar problems. In Pagan, the same emphasis can be seen at the end of each donative inscription, which warns future kings, princes, and others about violating the bona fides of a grant once the donor died. Even kings themselves put such curses in their inscriptions.

52. As early as 1144 A.D., King Aloncansū had instituted this policy. TN, pp. 63-64. SIP, pp. 18-19, 138. MKLYS, no. 61, p. 179; no. 17, p. 35.

53. SIP, pp. 18-19, 45-47, 106. MKLYS, p. 3; no. 24, p. 46. TN, p. 156. Kyanzittha, in the presence of royal witnesses and monks, consecrated his dedication. In 1183 A.D., Narapatisithu called the Mahāsaman to witness as he himself poured the ritual water. In 1229 A.D., Natonmya confirmed the decisions of previous kings and stated, "in my reign, wherefore should the decision be reversed?" and poured the ritual water. In 1271 A.D., King Narathihapade, at a precise and auspicious time, poured the ritual water to validate the offerings and legalize their religious status. In 1369 A.D., when King Mingyiswasawke ascended the throne, one of his first acts was to "rededicate the religious lands offered by ancient kings," as if to assure the sangha that he would indeed

promote the Religion and that they in turn had endorsed him as legitimate by their presence at the ceremonies.

54. SIP, pp. 71, 91. MKLYS, pp. 47, 79, 93, 102. PPA, no. 26. Than Tun, p. 163.

55. SIP, pp. 45-47, 106, 134. MKLYS, no. 24, p. 46; no. 42, p. 115. Sasanavamsa, p. 72.

56. Kinwun Mingyi U Gaung, A Digest of the Burmese Buddhist Law Concerning Inheritance and Marriages, Being a Collection of Texts from Thirty-six Dhammathats Compared and Arranged Under the Supervision of U Gaung (English title, text in Burmese), 2 vols. (Rangoon, 1902), p. 467. The Dhammathats that were quoted include two attributed to Pagan times, namely, the Pyu-Min-hti Dhammathat and the Dhammavilasā Dhammathat. A noble lady in the thirteenth century made good use of this law and donated all her lands and people to a specific rahan (her grandfather) thus keeping the property in the family. SIP, p. 134. MKLYS, no. 42, p. 115.

57. Mahādan (from Mahādāna, "great gift") was both secular and religious, but more examples of the former are found in the inscriptions. The late Professor Pe Maung Tin had suggested that Mahādan referred only to religious grants in his article (see n. 14 above). Professor Luce, however, has confirmed the belief that Mahādan was both secular and religious via personal communications to this author. See MKLYS, no. 20, p. 40; no. 33, pp. 92, 102.

58. EB, 3, 2, pp. 137-184. Other kings in Burma apparently resorted to this method. The tradition was carried on by Hsinphyushin, Bayinaung, and Thalun. The latter specifically forbade people to enter the monkhood. Alaunpaya and particularly Bodawpaya carried out "purifications." Even King Mindon had the Order purified.

59. Edward Conze, Buddhism: Its Essence and Development (New York, 1959), p. 114.

60. EB, p. 136.

61. EB, p. 137.

62. EB, pp. 183-184. Quite clearly, the monastery as a sanctuary for political exiles and potential pretenders to the throne was also being eliminated.

63. Karl Polanyi, p. 77.

64. Professor Luce feels that people with the san ending were those who were "freeborn." Most of them were wealthy and indeed owned and dedicated land. With a very few exceptions they never appear in kywan lists, but frequently appear in lists of royalty.

65. G. H. Luce, "Aspects of Pagan History--Later Period," in Tej Bunnag and M. Smithies, eds., In Memoriam Phya Anuman Rajadhon (Bangkok, 1970), pp. 129-146. There were apparently at least three identifiable sects in the thirteenth century. Ba Shin, Myanma Minsa Su (Rangoon, 1964?), p. 140, mentions one. The Sasanavamsa, p. 74, mentions four. In SIP, no. 27, p. 60, a donor specified three distinct monasteries to which she could donate, with strong implications that each was being run by a different sect.

66. Edward Conze, p. 104.

67. George Coedès, Angkor, p. 107, and L. P. Briggs, The Ancient Khmer Empire (Philadelphia, 1951), p. 259, argued that Theravāda Buddhism's submissive ideology stimulated a mass movement to bring down the autocratic "God-Kings" and elite religion in thirteenth century Southeast Asia. I have tried to show that Theravāda Buddhism's doctrine of the kammatic path to salvation and its relationship to the social, economic, and political structures did more to establish Buddhism and promote the development of the state than did the nature of Theravāda Buddhism itself. The devolution of land and labor brought about the downfall of the Pagan dynasty, not the "super-bolshevism" of the Theravādin.

68. Professor Luce's argument is that not until the 550 Jātakas were brought to Burma were Buddhist motifs expanded

beyond the ten major Jātakas. See G. H. Luce, pp. 61-62.

69. G. H. Luce, p. 96.

70. See Mabel Bode, The Pali Literature of Burma (London, 1909), pp. 14-30.

71. G. H. Luce, pp. 384-422.

72. Compared to the reigns of thirteenth century kings, Aloncañsū's reign witnessed few dedications and effective administration. He was consequently given the epithet "canal digger" by his contemporaries (SMK, p. 33, line 2) as well as by the nineteenth century chronicles (GPC, p. 113). More precisely the GPC stated that Aloncañsū "fixed the measure of the cubit and the ta. He marked off fields with the pē (pay) measure....He made reservoirs, canals, dams, and channels." The sangha during his time seemed to be closer to the Doctrine, as revealed by art and architectural motifs, particularly the austerity shown by the Sabbaññu and the Rhuyku temples that he built. There certainly were none of the feasts, lawsuits, indulging in secular businesses, and such non-religious activity which occurred in the second half of the thirteenth century. There was a sensitive relationship between the austerity and purity of the sangha and the strength of the state and, conversely, between the secularity of the sangha and the weakness of the state. Michael Mendelson's article has a similar argument, but with the inclusion of Nat worship.

73. Paul Bennett, Conference Under the Tamarind Tree: Three Essays in Burmese History. Yale University Southeast Asian Studies, Monograph Studies no. 15 (New Haven, 1971), pp. 3-53.

74. "The Dhammarājika Inscription of 1196 A.D." epitomizes the military and secular genre of Narapatisithu's reign. He did not attempt to disguise his military expansion with religious euphemisms, but was rather candid about it. The boundaries during his reign were the largest in Pagan's history (perhaps even in Burmese history). The kingdom stretched as far west as East Bengal's Patiekkara, as far

east as the east bank of the Salween, as far north as the Nanchao border in Yunnan, and as far south as Mergui in Tenasserim.

75. Although Natoṅmya reaped the fruits of his father's victories and accomplishments and was thought to have had a prosperous and relatively peaceful reign, his successor Klacwā certainly did not. Klacwā was plagued, as seen above, by peasant revolts and <u>saṅgha</u> power.

76. SIP, no. 13, p. 23; no. 18, p. 33; no. 19, pp. 35-36; no. 26, p. 58; no. 28, p. 63, just to name a few and to give us an idea of the amount of wealth that ended up with the <u>saṅgha</u>. In 1196 A.D., Narapatisithu's dedication came to 44,027 <u>klap</u> of silver (one <u>klap</u> of silver was one <u>tical</u> of silver). In 1248 A.D., a noble lady dedicated 5830 <u>klap</u> of silver--in addition to paddy, gold, and other precious objects. In terms of land, one donation in 1255 A.D. gave 1459 <u>pay</u> of land (one <u>pay</u> equals three-quarters of an acre). In 1264 A.D., a donor gave 386 persons (SIP, no. 49, p. 132). Another (SIP, no. 40, p. 97), in 1265 A.D., gave 1459 <u>pay</u> of land and 458 persons. These are but a few examples.

77. All three "Shan Brothers" were ministers in Klawcwā's court (see Paul Bennet, pp. 6-12, 31-32). The Shans had, moreover, married into the Pagan aristocracy rather early, as early as So Lū's (Aniruddha's son) reign in the eleventh century. <u>So</u> is the Shan title (<u>Saw</u>) equivalent to the Burmese <u>maṅ</u> (<u>min</u>), meaning chief, ruler, lord, king. In the twelfth and especially the thirteenth centuries, many names in Pagan's royalty and aristocracy had Shan titles (SIP, pp. 111, 123, 138). By 1241 A.D., a Syaṁ (Shan or Thai) had the title <u>saṁbyaṅ</u> (a high official) (MKLYS, p. 119, line 17b; p. 115, line b). Concubines and princes of Pagan kings also had Shan names (MKLYS, no. 14, p. 28).

78. <u>L'inscription du Roi Rāma Gāṃheṅ de Sukhodaya</u> (1292 A.D.), edited by George Coedès, trans. by H. R. H. Prince Wan Waithayakon (Bangkok, 1965), p. 12

79. TN, p. 164.

80. See note 73.

The Devolution of Kingship

in Twelfth Century Ceylon

by
Keith Taylor

Historians have tended to view twelfth century Ceylon with a certain amount of ambivalence. The reign of Parakkamabāhu I (1153-1186) is generally seen as one of the high points of Ceylonese civilization. Yet, it is this same reign which is identified as the immediate cause of the disintegration of the Ceylonese state early in the thirteenth century. The kingdom of Parakkamabāhu II, in the thirteenth century, was profoundly different from anything previously seen in Ceylon, in terms of its geography, economic base, and political organization. The problem of defining this transition, when and how it occurred, and why it came about, must be taken as a primary element of interpreting not only the reign of Parakkamabāhu I but also of interpreting the development of the Ceylonese monarchy during the tenth, eleventh and twelfth centuries. The symptoms which accompanied this transition have been enumerated in detail[1]; but the causes behind these symptoms have not been thoroughly explored. As a result of the transition itself being poorly defined, its chronology has been little understood. The transition is usually placed after the reign of Parakkamabāhu I. Yet, this is tenable only if Parakkamabāhu I is held responsible for the change. It is apparent that the transition which was completed by the thirteenth century has been viewed in a very narrow context. The purpose of this paper will be to place this transition in a larger framework, both in terms of chronology and of interpretation.

This paper will yield three conclusions. First, the transition can be broadly identified as one which sees the end of the traditional organization of Ceylonese society and politics and the emergence of new, more fragmented, social and political patterns of which the imperial rule of Parakkamabāhu I

257

is only the first and most successful example.
Parakkamabāhu I's empire, though not an example of political
fragmentation, was only possible by the destruction of the
traditional order and the welding together of the resulting
fragments through sheer physical force. Second, since the
nature of Parakkamabāhu I's rule shows more continuity
with what follows than with what went before, the breaking-
point of the transition must be placed prior to his accession.
Finally, the central theme of the transition was the struggle
of the Ceylonese monarchy to survive in the age of Cōḷa power.
Yet, while the continental pressures cannot be denied, they
cannot be used as an excuse for the demise of the Ceylonese
monarchy. This paper will emphasize the decline of the
monarchy as a result of primarily internal difficulties. That
the monarchy ran out of alternatives at this time does not
reflect the overwhelming power of external forces, forces
which in previous centuries had been successfully overcome;
rather, it reflects a new era in which traditions became
progressively irrelevant. Parakkamabāhu I was the first
Ceylonese ruler to perceive this. It was with more political
insight than bravado that he chided his retainers: "Have ye
not heard that one looks up to splendid might and not to age?"[2]

The cultural traditions of the Mauryan Empire survived
in the Buddhist sangha of Ceylon. Until the twelfth century,
Ceylonese kings derived a major portion of their legitimacy by
accomodating themselves to these traditions.[3] The monarchy
rested on a large royal clan, united by cross-cousin marriage
alliances; kings observed the rule of brother-to-brother
succession.[4] In the twelfth century, the royal kinship and
succession pattern as well as the secular role of the sangha
were abandoned. In their place appeared a new rationalism.
This rationalism did not immediately extricate itself from the
old order. Thus, Parakkamabāhu I enjoyed a legitimate claim
to the throne according to the old kinship pattern and fulfilled
his Buddhist duties by reforming the sangha. Yet, the entire
royal family was either exterminated or forced into exile
during his reign, while his reform of the sangha resembled a
civil war. Within a generation, the reformed sangha was
forced to flee from an empire which had become the prize of
foreign adventurers. So, although Parakkamabāhu I posed as
a traditional Ceylonese monarch, we must look closer.

The Character of the Cūlavaṃsa

Chapters 37 to 79 of the Cūlavaṃsa, our principle source of information, are considered to have been compiled by a Buddhist bhikkhu called Dhammakitti.[5] Though more than one Dhammakitti is encountered in an examination of Pali literature, it is believed that the compiler of the first forty-two chapters of the Cūlavaṃsa wrote in the early thirteenth century at Polonnaruva.[6] If this be true, then the Dhammakitti in question wrote under the patronage of Līlāvatī, the widowed queen of Parakkamabāhu I, and was closely associated with the man who placed her on the throne for the third and final time in 1211, "Parakkama of the family of the Kālanāgaras," a leader of the non-Kaliṅgan faction of the time and a man highly regarded by the church for his piety.[7] This Dhammakitti was a disciple of Sāriputta, the most renowned scholar during the reign of Parakkamabāhu I.[8] Dhammakitti appears to have assembled the contents of Chapters 37 through 61 from pre-existing materials, while his personal contribution is confined to chapters 62 through 79, the chapters dealing directly with Parakkamabāhu I.[9] Chapters 37 through 61 should be viewed as being based on material inherited by Dhammakitti from pre-Parakkamabāhu I sources. This is apparent from the fact that these early chapters do not view the unreformed division of the church into three (sometimes four) vihāras as a matter of any concern; on the contrary, the prominent role of sects associated with the unorthodox Abhayagiri-vihāra and the seemingly indiscriminate royal patronage of all ecclessiastical factions is reported without the least consternation.[10] On the other hand, the extensive "reform" of the church by Parakkamabāhu I came immediately after an era of civil disturbance, during a time when monks were in hiding, and amounted to the suppression of the traditional organization and its replacement by a reformed saṅgha which came to regard the tolerant diversity of the traditional church with abhorrence. It is in this newly established tradition that Dhammakitti stands. Dhammakitti is pro-Parakkamabāhu I because he was raised in the prosperous church of Parakkamabāhu I's imperial Ceylon. When he expresses disgust with the divisions of the church which existed prior to Parakkamabāhu I, he dismisses the traditional Ceylonese church as it had developed up to the twelfth century.[11]

A second aspect of Dhammakitti is his position in relation to the various dynastic factions existing during and after the lifetime of Parakkamabāhu I. He is careful to show that Parakkamabāhu I was claimed by all existing factions on the island at the time of his birth. [12] In his narration of the wars which resulted in Parakkamabāhu I's unification of the island, Dhammakitti is especially kind to Gajabāhu II, the scion of the house of Kaliṅga. [13] On the other hand, he is especially hostile to Parakkamabāhu I's Pāṇḍyan cousin Mānābharaṇa and to Mānābharaṇa's mother, Sugalā, both of whom led stubborn Rohaṇa-based movements in resistance to Parakkamabāhu I's policy of unification. [14] Part of his hostility may be due to Sugalā's identification with the traditional church which can be inferred by her possession of the sacred relics. [15] Parakkamabāhu I's urgent desire to capture the relics was motivated by the need to legitimize his reformed saṅgha and to deprive the remnants of the traditional church of their sacred possessions. [16] Dhammakitti could ridicule the Rohaṇese resistance because by the time of his writing it had become a lost cause. The respectability of the Kaliṅgan faction, however, could not be disputed, partly because many of its princes were proteges of Parakkamabāhu I and partly because of their continuing presence on the island as powerful aspirants to, and keepers of, the throne.

It seems that no great importance should be attached to Dhammakitti's association with Līlāvatī and Parakkama of Kālanāgara, who were of the non-Kaliṅgan faction. The church was patronized by both major post-Parakkamabāhu I factions, [17] and Dhammakitti was careful to stay above the politics of his day. Further reason for caution is that if we take chapter 79 as the end of Dhammakitti's contribution, we must admit that he never once mentions Līlāvatī, whereas he devotes a long passage to the praise of Parakkamabāhu I's other queen, Rūpavatī. [18]

A further argument in favor of assigning the first 24 chapters of the Cūlavaṃsa to the pre-Parakkamabāhu I church is the prominent role of the Paṃsukūlin sect of the Abhayagiri-vihāra in those chapters. In fact, it is only in these chapters that we hear of the Paṃsukūlins at all. From the reign of Mānavamma, who was established on the throne with Pallava aid in the seventh century, through the reign of Vijayabāhu I, the Paṃsukūlins are portrayed in the Cūlavaṃsa as the most important sect, seemingly in a class of their own above all other religious groups.[19] In the reign of Sena II (851-885), the chronicle states that the Paṃsukūlika bhikkhus "separated and formed special groups," perhaps meaning that they were not considered to be subordinate to the Abhayagiri-vihāra.[20] Then, in the reign of Kassapa IV (896-913), the chronicle relates that a dormitory (pariveṇa) was built for the Paṃsukūlika bhikkhus in the Maha-vihāra.[21] Thus, we see that the position of the Paṃsukūlins as a sect with ties to both major religious organizations was well established by the beginning of the tenth century.[22] That they also wielded considerable political power at the court can be inferred from their successful contest during the 930's with Udaya III and Udaya III's two royal colleagues, the future Sena III and Udaya IV.[23] Sena III, Udaya IV, and Mahinda IV all paid special attention to the Paṃsukūlins.[24] As will be discussed below, the genealogy of Vijayabāhu I appears to represent a tradition linking the Paṃsukūlins with the royal line starting with the reign of Mānavamma when, as noted above, they are first mentioned in the chronicle. The last mention of the Paṃsukūlins in the Cūlavaṃsa is in chapter 61, the last pre-Parakkamabāhu I chapter, in which they are portrayed as being "wroth" at the "manifold evil" of the civil wars following Vijayabāhu I's death and, "taking the sacred Tooth Relic and the Alms-bowl Relic, betook themselves to Rohaṇa and settled themselves here and there in places where it pleased them."[25] Since the sacred relics are next heard of in the possession of Sugalā and the Rohaṇese resistance movement, it appears reasonable to tie the extinction of the Paṃsukūlins with the suppression of the Rohaṇese resistance. Furthermore, if the Paṃsukūlins actually were the leaders of the pre-Parakkamabāhu I church (and their possession of the sacred relics would appear to confirm this) then perhaps the traditional church went down to defeat with the Rohaṇese rebellion rather than as a result of Parakkamabāhu I's so-called church reform. In this light, Parakkamabāhu I's church reform appears as the establishment of a new ecclesiastical organization which could claim continuity with the scholarly traditions of the suppressed church yet did not have the political power of the old church.

Relevant to this discussion of the Cūlavaṃsa and its authors is an examination of the nature of the church established by Parakkamabāhu I.[26] The Gal-vihāra rock inscription is a record of Parakkamabāhu I's church "reform." The inscription is of five parts. First, the deplorable state of the church is described; it is portrayed as "disintegrated" and "decadent" from the time of the fourth century (i.e., the end of the Mahāvaṃsa and the beginning of the Cūlavaṃsa). Second, Parakkamabāhu I arrives on the scene, sees the condition of the church, and looks for someone to remedy the situation. Third, Parakkamabāhu I finds Mahākassapa, the head of the Udumbaragiri monastery of the Mahā-vihāra, and uses him and his bhikkhus to bring about "a coalition of the three fraternities into a single fraternity." Fourth, Parakkamabāhu I nurtures his newly established church and causes it to prosper. And fifth, strict regulations are established to govern the monks of the new church; the regulations appear designed to isolate the monks from political life and to force them into scholarly and meditative activities.[27]

The author of chapters 62 through 79 of the Cūlavaṃsa, Dhammakitti, was a disciple of Sāriputta who was a member of Mahākassapa's Udumbaragiri order.[28] Dhammakitti, then, can be expected to have very low esteem for the pre-Parakkamabāhu I church, he can be expected to view Parakkamabāhu I as the greatest Ceylonese king in nearly one thousand years, and he can be expected to be non-political in matters not related to the life of Parakkamabāhu I.

As will be shown near the end of this paper, factional identities of post-Parakkamabāhu I rulers should not be over-emphasized. It appears that the rulers who followed Parakkamabāhu I held complicated and ambivalent feelings toward him; all wished to identify themselves with his splendor, yet none wished to be tied to the less happy aspects of his rule. Dhammakitti wrote in a time when the greatness of Parakkamabāhu I was not in doubt; his use of traditional church records to fill in the chronological gap separating what his new tradition considered to be the last great era of church and state (i.e., the Mahāvaṃsa) and the appearance of Parakkamabāhu I is evident from an examination of the Cūlavaṃsa itself. A purpose of Dhammakitti in writing this chronicle/panegyric was undoubtedly to establish the church of Parakkamabāhu I as a legitimate restoration of the ancient greatness of the Mahāvaṃsa. This is reflected in the first part of the Gal-vihāra rock inscription, cited above, which asserted that from the end of the Mahāvaṃsa to the accession of Parakkamabāhu I, the church was in disarray.

To conclude this analysis of the Cūlavaṃsa, chapters 37 through 61 can be seen as reflecting the collective view-point of the church prior to Parakkamabāhu I, apparently as interpreted by the Paṃsukūlins, a leading sect with a dominant influence in the court. Chapters 62 through 79 are the work of a bhikkhu who reflects the viewpoint of the church established by Parakkamabāhu I; he emphasizes the correct pro-Parakkamabāhu I attitude with regard to the factions of Parakkamabāhu I's time while judiciously ending his narrative at Parakkamabāhu I's death, without venturing to record the rivalry of the two post-Parakkamabāhu I factions, both of whom had reason to claim Parakkamabāhu I as their own.

The Polonnaruva Period in Perspective

Polonnaruva first emerged as a city of strategic political importance during the reign of Sena I (831-851).[29] From then until its adoption by the Cōlas as their administrative center in the eleventh century, it increased in importance for two reasons. First, its distance from the northeastern coast, debarkation point for invasions from the continent, was greater than that of the ancient capital at Anurādhapura, thus granting more security from external threats. Second, strategically located overlooking the fords of the Mahāvāluka River which was the frontier between Rājaraṭṭha (the region of the traditional Anurādhapura kingdom) and Rohaṇa (the southern Mahāgāma kingdom), it was well situated to control both regions. This became especially important as new continental threats required a more unified deployment of resources on the island. Vijayabāhu I (1059-1114), though consecrated at Anurādhapura, ruled from Polonnaruva. During the one hundred years from his death until the arrival of Māgha in 1214, Polonnaruva was considered to be the natural seat of Ceylonese kings. The first important

Map 9:
TWELFTH CENTURY CEYLON

N

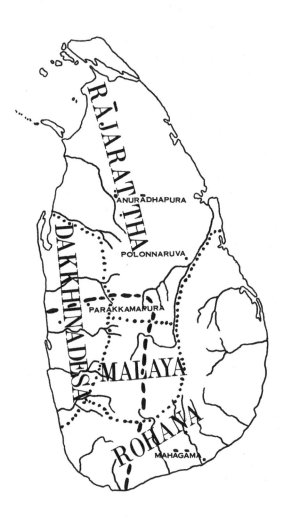

RĀJARAṬṬHA

ANURĀDHAPURA

POLONNARUVA

DAKKHINADESA

PARAKKAMAPURA

MALAYA

ROHAṆA

MAHĀGĀMA

REGIONAL BOUNDARIES
• • • • • • • • • • • • •

LIMIT OF WET ZONE
▬ ▬ ▬ ▬ ▬ ▬ ▬ ▬ ▬

king of the post-Polonnaruva era, Parakkamabāhu II in the
mid-thirteenth century, was consecrated in Polonnaruva, but
by his time Polonnaruva had no strategic value to the new
Ceylonese kingdom established in the wet zone at
Dambadeṇiya.[30]

The Polonnaruva period in Ceylonese history is a
period of transition. Polonnaruva's rise to prominence and
its abandonment are both directly tied to changing political,
social, and economic relationships on the island. The era of
dynastic warfare from the death of Vijayabāhu I to the
accession of Parakkamabāhu I (1114-1153) is the breaking-
point of this transition. Prior to this time, traditional
political, social, and economic patterns predominated; after
this time, non-traditional patterns are the rule.

Geographically, the transition was from the dry-zone
irrigation-based kingdoms of Rājaraṭṭha and Rohaṇa of the
north, east, and south of the island to the wet zone of the
south-west. In political terms, the transition was from the
traditional feudal order in which local power stood in a
contractual relationship with the throne[31] to a new situation in
which the old relationships were replaced by a pattern of
personal loyalty which was expressed both at the level of
vannī chieftainship and at the level of the imperialism of
Parakkamabāhu I. With regard to royal kinship, the transition
resulted in the abandonment of the pattern of collateral
brother-to-brother throne succession. In social and economic
terms, the transition was from the traditional peasant-based
agricultural pattern to the rise of a powerful merchant and
artisan (govi) class[32] as well as the appearance of a refugee
(vannī) culture out of which the post-Polonnaruva Ceylonese
kingdom would emerge.[33] In religious terms, it was a
transition from the traditional Ceylonese church with all of
its diverse elements wielding political and economic power
independent of the throne to a more homogeneous church
dependent on the throne.[34] Finally, in terms of nationalism,
the traditional Ceylonese nationalism associated with epic
heroes coming out of Rohaṇa was effectively crushed by
Parakkamabāhu I's brutal devastation and depopulation of that
old southern region. From the beginning of Ceylonese history,
Rohaṇa played a special and apparently essential role as a

reservoir of leadership and of Ceylonese national traditions.[35]
Parakkamabāhu I was the first unifier of Ceylon not to come out
of Rohaṇa; his original base of power being in the wet zone of
the south-west was indicative of the shifting political
relationships on the island.

The political equilibrium of South India, which had
been characterized by two hundred years of Pallava hegemony,
became unbalanced in the ninth and tenth centuries as the
weakened Pallavas and a rising Pāṇḍyan kingdom contended for
supremacy, both subsequently falling prey to the Cōḷas. The
wars attending these changing relationships on the continent
created new problems for the Ceylonese throne. Refugees and
exiles from the continent sought comfort and aid at the
Ceylonese court. Bits and pieces of defeated armies and
ousted dynasties found their way to Anurādhapura, forcing its
kings to consider Ceylon's situation vis-à-vis the resurgent
continent.

The influx of refugees which had reached proportions
making it impossible for Ceylonese kings to rule by the 980's[36]
certainly had its beginnings much earlier. It appears that at
least as early as the mid-tenth century, newcomers were
already in control of parts of the island north of
Anurādhapura.[37] Ceylonese kings not only were forced into
an aggressive policy toward the continent but also had to find
internal resources to support such a policy. In this light, the
policy of incorporating Rohaṇa into the Anurādhapura kingdom
by Sena I and his successors is understandable.

As the situation increased in seriousness during the
course of the tenth century, Mahinda IV (956-972) attempted to
strengthen the throne by downgrading the claims of his
numerous collaterals. He did this by means of a foreign
marriage alliance. Rather than aiding the Ceylonese throne,
however, the newcomers contributed to the growing state of
anarchy which led to the Cōḷa occupation of Rājaraṭṭha.

By the time of Vijayabāhu I (1059-1114), continental
adventurers had enjoyed free run of Rājaraṭṭha for almost a
century before finally being expelled. Vijayabāhu I sought to
increase the credibility and to insure the future of his throne

by a series of dynastic alliances with anti-Cōḷa continental powers. The results of this policy proved to be disasterous with the various dynastic factions brought into the island proceeding to divide it up and to war upon each other.

Up to this time, each king had responded to the various situations in a manner within the traditional feudal pattern. The gradual weakening of the throne's credibility over the centuries of Tamil hegemony and occupation, however, culminated in a disrespect for and abandonment of traditional patterns during the wars of 1114-1153. These wars saw the disintegration of traditional political and social patterns and were attended by a new philosophy proposing that success belonged to the strongest. [38] It is at this point that Parakkamabāhu I rose up with complete disregard for tradition. The empire which he and his successors ruled from the city of Polonnaruva was based on personal loyalty. The so-called disintegration of this empire must also be seen in these terms; without a strong tradition assigning rights and obligations, personal loyalty proved to be poor glue and failed to hold the island together in the face of continued external threats.

What is demonstrated by these developments is that actions of kings attempting to establish their credibility do have an impact on their political and social environment and can contribute to situations in which traditional assumptions no longer have any meaning. This is not to imply that the basic nature of a society is especially fragile in the face of actions by a ruling elite. On the contrary, Ceylonese society had, by the twelfth century, absorbed a number of significant shocks over a period of two hundred years of both external and internal origin before the cumulative effects of these shocks were great enough to bring about the discrediting of the traditional patterns in the midst of the dynastic wars of 1114-1153. It should also be remembered that external forces succeeded in occupying parts of the island only after the internal stability had been weakened, partly as a result of decisions made by Ceylonese kings and partly by the changing conditions on the island to which these decisions were addressed. It may be argued that under the circumstances, the Ceylonese throne had very few options and any course of action would have failed. Though this may be so, it cannot be proven; on the other hand the Ceylonese had survived previous eras of continental hegemony and lived to re-establish their distinctive civilization. Why they did not do so this time may be due to the longevity of Cōḷa pressure; but a more satisfactory answer would seem to lie in the political development of the Ceylonese throne itself, especially when evidence lies at hand with which to construct such an answer. Finally, though this lies outside the scope of our inquiry, it should be remembered that the Cōḷa era witnessed the appearance of new economic patterns on an international scale; the evolution of the Ceylonese monarchy occurred in the context of these larger forces.

Ceylonese Kingship
in the Ninth and Early Tenth Centuries

In the mid-ninth century, as Pallava power was shrinking, the newly envigorated Pāṇḍyan kingdom of Madurā invaded Ceylon. This was the first serious continental invasion of Ceylon in over 150 years. King Sena I (831-851) was forced to take refuge in Rohaṇa where he gathered resources with which to expel the invaders. These events confronted Sena I with two closely related problems: a rising external threat and the question of internal Ceylonese unity.

Prior to this time, Rohaṇa had existed as an autonomous kingdom dependent on Rājaraṭṭha for items of culture but politically independent and possessing its own local traditions. Anurādhapura kings had often turned to Rohaṇa as a reservoir of strength in times of continental invasion; however, geographic factors had made it virtually impossible for Anurādhapura to enforce any lasting political domination of the southern region. Nevertheless, Sena I realized that if Anurādhapura were to command sufficient resources to cope with a prolonged continental threat, closer ties with Rohaṇa were essential. A succession dispute in Rohaṇa presented the opportunity he needed to strengthen these ties.

The murder of the Rohaṇese king by his aunt sent his three brothers and three sisters fleeing to Anurādhapura. Sena I received the royal brood, married one sister to his eldest nephew, the future Sena II, and the other two sisters to Sena II's younger brother, Mahinda. This Mahinda later quarreled with his older brother and spent his remaining years in the south of the island; his sons, two of whom would be the first two Anurādhapura kings to consider themselves Rohaṇese (Udaya III and Sena III), later played a prominent role in further strengthening the political ties between Rohaṇa and Rājaraṭṭha. As for the three brothers of the murdered Rohaṇese king, Sena I sent an army to establish them in the southern region. The eldest of these, Kassapa, became the father of the third "Rohaṇese" king, Udaya IV. A daughter of this Kassapa, known in inscriptions as Dev Gon, became the consort of Udaya III and the mother of Mahinda IV.[39] The immediate effect of Sena I's Rohaṇese policy was to tie the southern region more closely to Anurādhapura within the socio-political pattern of the time; it was at this time that Polonnaruva, strategically located on the Rohaṇese border, first emerged as a city of political importance.[40]

Sena I's immediate successors pursued an aggressive continental policy. Sena II (851-885) allied himself with the Pallavas and sent an army which sacked Madurā. By the time of Kassapa V's reign (913-923), however, the Cōḷas had replaced the Pallavas, and he sent an army to aid the Pāṇḍyas in an unsuccessful campaign against the Cōḷas. In the fifteen years following the death of Kassapa V, Anurādhapura witnessed a crisis over this policy of continental intervention; the crisis was tied to the passing of the throne into the hands of princes who were identified with Rohaṇa and was resolved on terms dictated by the Paṃsukūlin sect.

The important position of the Paṃsukūlin sect in the Ceylonese state from the seventh into the twelfth centuries has already been pointed out. Later in this paper, a link between the reigning dynasty and the Paṃsukūlins will be postulated based on an examination of Vijayabāhu I's genealogy. The picture that emerges from the Cūlavaṃsa is of a religious-political order of bhikkhus in possession of the sacred relics (and perhaps other symbols of royal legitimacy as well) with connections to all religious establishments and a powerful position in the court. It appears that in the tenth century, not only was their approval necessary for a prince to take the throne, but they were also in a position to dictate national policy.

During the reign of Dappula IV (923-934), a son of Sena II, the Pāṇḍyan king and his court sought refuge in Anurādhapura after being expelled from the continent by the Cōḷas. Dappula IV was eager to pursue the interventionist policies of his father and half-brother and attempted to organize an expedition to restore the Pāṇḍyan throne to the refugee king. However, the project failed because, in the words of the Cūlavaṃsa, "the nobles dwelling on the island for some reason or other stirred up a sorry strife to the undoing of the Pāṇḍu king."[41] The Pāṇḍyan king was forced to flee the island in such haste that he left his royal treasure behind.

The identity of these nobles who "stirred up a sorry strife" is no mystery; they could have been no other than the "Rohaṇa" princes who successively occupied the throne after Dappula IV: Udaya III, Sena III, and Udaya IV. The Paṃsukūlin sect had supported the aggressive continental policy; this is reflected in their depiction of the crises under Dappula IV as a "sorry strife."

The question of continental policy, however, was still unresolved; the pro-intervention faction with the support of the Paṃsukūlins continued to wield considerable power in the court. Upon the accession of Udaya III, this faction was forced to flee the court and take refuge with the Paṃsukūlins. Udaya III and his brother, the future Sena III, broke into the monastery and beheaded the fugitive officials. In the uproar which followed this event, two princes, the future Sena III and Udaya IV, fled to Rohaṇa pursued by a division of troops loyal to the old court faction. The crisis was finally resolved when the king and his colleagues capitulated to the Paṃsukūlins. In the words of the Cūlavaṃsa, "from that time onwards the king observed the conduct of former kings," presumably meaning that he conformed to the policies espoused by the Paṃsukūlins and their allies.[42] In their successive reigns, Sena III and Udaya IV both followed a correct anti-Cōḷa line and assiduously patronized the Paṃsukūlins.[43]

Can any deeper significance be assigned to these events?

The most obvious conclusion is that the "Rohaṇa" princes came from a more provincial setting with no great interest in the continental politics which preoccupied the more geographically exposed Rājaraṭṭha. Evidence concerning the religious traditions is sketchy, yet it appears that Rohaṇa tended to be more orthodox and less sophisticated than the north. Certainly, the Rohaṇese were hostile to the cosmopolitan, heterodox atmosphere of Anurādhapura, seemingly dominated by the Paṃsukūlins, a sect originally part of the unorthodox Abhayagiri-vihāra.[44] The crisis of the 930's was resolved by the "Rohaṇa" princes submitting themselves to the established interests of Anurādhapura; this represented a further development of the policy of incorporating Rohaṇa as a means of strengthening the Ceylonese kingdom in the face of a resurgent continent.[45]

Breakdown of the Ceylonese Monarchy

A distinctive characteristic of traditional Ceylonese kingship was the pattern of brother-to-brother succession. This pattern required that all eligible claimants of each generation be given their turn as king before the throne passed on to the next generation. This practice of collateral succession, along with the relative importance of maternal patrilineage, appears to have given the traditional Ceylonese ruling nobility a great deal of cohesion by encouraging inter-marriage within the royal house. An aspect of this, however, was that the king was placed in the position of sharing his power with the other adult males of the royal family who were waiting for their turn on the throne. This sort of situation is clearly implied in the events, narrated above, of Dappula IV's reign during which his foreign policy was thwarted by the opposition of the three men who were to succeed him. The difficulty of a king attempting to rule in the face of external dangers under such unsatisfactory internal conditions provided the context for the reign of Mahinda IV as well as the subsequent break-down of the monarchy itself.

As Cōḷa power continued to increase throughout the tenth century, refugees and adventurers from the continent continued to find positions at the Anurādhapura court or to establish themselves in various parts of Rājaraṭṭha. [46] An inscription of Mahinda IV (956-972) declares that he "made the prosperous Laṅkā (Ceylon) a common ground for various peoples of various appearances who came from diverse countries."[47] The appearance of these various peoples may have been encouraged by Mahinda IV as a means of assembling a force of émigrés eager to aid in any anti-Cōḷa activity; it may have been that, in view of the continental situation, Mahinda IV had little choice in the matter; or it may have been that Mahinda IV, wishing to disentangle himself from dependence on princes in Rohaṇa, was purposely building a new base of support on foreign elements in Rājaraṭṭha. Caught between a bevy of royal collaterals and an unending stream of refugees and adventurers from the continent, he resorted to a foreign marriage alliance; by introducing foreign allies through the expedient of dynastic marriage, he hoped to dominate his royal collaterals at home and to bolster the credibility of his throne on the international scene.

The Cūlavaṃsa records that "although there was also in Laṅkā a race of nobles, the Ruler of Men (Mahinda IV) had a princess of the line of the ruler of Kaliṅga fetched and made her his first mahesī."[48] The official purpose of this marriage alliance is clear from both the Cūlavaṃsa and epigraphic remains; Mahinda IV and his Kaliṅgan Mahesī founded "the royal house of Sīhala (Ceylon)."[49] It may seem strange that the royal house needed founding after more than one thousand years of tradition to its credit. This simply reflects the weakened position of the throne. Mahinda IV was reaching back to the mythic origins of the Ceylonese dynasty, founded in the fifth century B.C. by Vijaya, a scion of the house of Kaliṅga; this was an attempt to renew the ancient, half-forgotten legends connecting Ceylon and Kaliṅga. By founding "the house of Sīhala," he was honoring his foreign consort and renewing the glory of his dynasty.[50] By symbolically reestablishing contact with the mythic origins of his dynasty, Mahinda IV hoped to strengthen his prestige and credibility in the face of not only continental threats but also of powerful rivals within the Ceylonese royal house itself. This theme was pursued in the Saint Mahinda festival instituted upon the donation of a golden image of Saint Mahinda by the Kaliṅgan Mahesī; a genealogy was inscribed on the occasion of this donation connecting the

Kaliṅgan house with Ceylon through Vijaya.[51]

Mahinda IV's experiment in dynastic renewal failed. His twelve-year old son, Sena V, succeeded him in 972; almost immediately, power fell into the hands of the Kaliṅgan Mahesī and a Kaliṅgan general, Senāpati Sena, who, apparently unable to rule in the face of resistance from the Ceylonese nobility, handed Rājaraṭṭha over to continental adventurers and set themselves up in Polonnaruva.[52] Upon Sena V's death nine years later, his younger brother, Mahinda V, attempted to rule for ten difficult years from Anurādhapura, "which was full of strangers brought hither by the Senāpati Sena," before being forced to flee to Rohaṇa.[53] The only alternatives remaining for Ceylonese kings were the roles of puppet or refugee. Ten years later, the Cōḷas occupied and restored order to Rājaraṭṭha upon the urging of a horse-dealer who informed them of the anarchic conditions prevailing there.[54] Thus began the much maligned seventy-year Cōḷa occupation.

The break-down of the monarchy appears to have grown out of the resistance of royal collaterals to the ascendance of an alien line which was introduced in an effort to lower the status of the collaterals. After the death of Mahinda IV the authority of the throne was undermined to the point where political life fell to the level of anarchy, and the Cōḷas subsequently stepped in to restore order. Prior to the arrival of the Cōḷas, the Cūlavamsa notes that in Rājaraṭṭha various groups of foreigners and local adventurers "carried on the government as they pleased."[54]

The Last Attempt at Revival

After the Cōḷa Empire had finally moved into the island and gained supremacy over the crowd of refugees and adventurers created by their conquests on the continent, Ceylonese traditions withdrew to Rohaṇa where the sangha had fled with remnants of the royal house. The sangha was undoubtedly anxious to find a suitable avenger to retake the north. Many adventurers tried their luck against the Cōḷas; two of the more prominent losers were men identified as being a Rajpūt and a Pāṇḍyan.[55] Vijayabāhu I (1059-1114) was the ultimate winner. It is reasonable to assume that his ancestry would reflect the conditions from which he arose; a crowd of contending adventurers hailing from many regions of the subcontinent mixed with survivors of the old Ceylonese dynasty. This assumption appears to be confirmed by the elaborate genealogy written to connect Vijayabāhu I with the royal line existing before the Cōḷa troubles.

The existence of this genealogy is important for three reasons. First, it reveals that Ceylonese traditions were not only alive but demanded formal acknowledgment; Vijayabāhu I's success may have partly rested on his ability to demonstrate a legitimate claim to the throne according to traditional definitions. Second, it reveals that the ancestry of Vijayabāhi I was sufficiently in doubt to require a genealogy; if his claim were obvious, there would have been no need for a genealogy. Finally, it reveals the role of the Paṃsukūlins on behalf of Vijayabāhu I; the genealogy appears to have been written by the Paṃsukūlins and to embody their claim to serve as royal advisers. Let us pause to examine more carefully this genealogy.

Vijayabāhu I's genealogy, found in the Cūlavaṃsa,[56] is designed to accomplish three purposes. First, it establishes his father's patrilineage. Second, it establishes his mother's patrilineage. And third, it connects both lines of descent with an ascetic order of royal advisers, apparently the Paṃsukūlins; it appears that the tradition of the Paṃsukūlins concerning their own origins and rise to power at the court was superimposed upon the lines of both the father and the mother of Vijayabāhu I. Both lines take their departure from the dynastic wars of the seventh century in which the Dāṭhopatissa faction fell under Pāṇḍyan domination and was expelled with Pallava aid by Mānavamma who re-established the Moriya clan on the throne and from whom all subsequent kings through Mahinda V claimed their descent. As noted in the introduction, it is during the reign of Mānavamma that the Paṃsukūlins are first heard of as an order associated with the Abhayagiri-vihāra.

The genealogy begins by telling the story of Mānavamma's elder brother, Māna, who is crippled while performing magic ascetic rites.[57] Renouncing his claim to the throne in favor of his younger brother, Māna is admitted to the Abhayagiri-vihāra and becomes head of an order of bhikkhus established by Mānavamma. This order is entrusted with the tooth relic and thereafter serves in the role of royal advisors; furthermore, "certain people who were of his (the king's) lineage, but had no desire for world renunciation, dwelt as they liked (with the bhikkhus) and were addressed by the title of Great Lord." All of this fits with what is known of the Paṃsukūlins, with the added intimation that the sect may have been founded specifically by and for the royal family. The next part of the genealogy establishes Vijayabāhu I's patrilineage from Mahinda V, the last pre-Cōḷa ruler. Following this is the story of "a grandson of King Dāṭhopatissa"; except for one significant detail, it is a pale imitation of the story of Māna. Dāṭhopatissa's grandson is an ascetic magician who establishes an order of bhikkhus at a place which became known as Selantarasamūha. He and his bhikkhus are made chief royal advisors by an unnamed king. The final section of the genealogy simply states that Vijayabāhu I's mother is the daughter of a Prince Bodhi and a Princess Buddha of the Dāṭhopatissa line.

A clue to the ancestry of Vijayabāhu I's mother is given in the name Selantarasamūha. In only one other instance is this name mentioned in the Cūlavaṃsa. On the occasion of the ceremonial elevation of Vijayabāhu I's daughter Yasodharā to the rank of rājinī (princess), Yasodharā celebrates the affair by donating an image house to the Selantarasamūha of the Abhayagiri-vihāra.[58] Yasodharā was the daughter of Vijayabāhu I by the daughter of the Rajpūt adventurer, Jagatīpāla, who briefly lead the Ceylonese resistance during the Cōḷa occupation.[59] The suspiciously sketchy nature of Vijayabāhu I's mother's genealogy coupled with the unique association of the Selantarasamūha both with her genealogy and with Vijayabāhu I's Rajpūt daughter can be construed as evidence of blood relationship between Vijayabāhu I's mother and the Rajpūt adventurer. This would explain why, although the following generation considered the Rajpūt line to be inferior and unworthy of kingship, Vijayabāhu I considered his Rājput Mahesī to be "of irreproachable descent."[60] It was only after his Rajpūt Mahesī failed to produce a male heir that he fetched Tilokasundarī from Kaliṅga.[61] In the light of this hypothesis, the importance of Vijayabāhu I's genealogy becomes clear; it is designed to obscure the Rajpūt origins of his mother by linking her with the royal clan ousted in the seventh century and replaced by the dynasty claimed by Vijayabāhu I's father. The genealogy also appears to be a reaffirmation of the traditional role of the Paṃsukūlins as an order of royal advisors.[62]

Vijayabāhu I is solidly within the Ceylonese tradition of epic heroism. After building up a power base in western Rohaṇa, he waged a victorious struggle to expel the Cōḷa occupiers and vigorously set about restoring the traditional Ceylonese monarchy, dividing the island according to the well-established system of Rājaraṭṭha, Rohaṇa, Dakkhiṇadesa, and Malaya, while using his brothers to unify this system more effectively than it had ever been previously. In spite of his unassailable position as a national hero, he nonetheless faced serious problems in establishing his newly won throne on a firm foundation. Cōḷa power continued to exist as a potential external threat while the royal house itself was ill defined and lacked the benefits of unblemished tradition. How could he insure that the independence and unity he had fought to win would not dissolve upon his death? He met this problem by concluding a series of dynastic marriage alliances with groups of foreign origin and by attempting to tie the various dynastic groups introduced by these alliances into a united royal house.

One of the characteristics of this new age which so severely challenged the Ceylonese throne was the increased tempo of diplomacy and war around the Bay of Bengal; this was a reflection of changing trade patterns in the area. The Cūlavaṃsa indicates that Vijayabāhu I maintained wide international contacts,[63] so it is no surprise to find that he sought marriage alliances with foreign allies. Refusing an alliance with the Cōḷas,[64] he turned instead to enemies of the Cōḷas. In addition to his Rajpūt Mahesī, the daughter of a man who fought for Ceylonese independence, Vijayabāhu I allied himself with the Kaliṅgan royal house, by taking the princess Tilokasundarī as his second Mahesī. If this house were the Eastern Gaṅgas, then ruling in Kaliṅga, Vijayabāhu I would have gained a powerful ally contemporaneously engaged in wars with the Cōḷas. Finally, he married his younger sister Mittā to a Paṇḍu (Pāṇḍya) prince.[65] The identity of this Paṇḍu prince is obscure, but he may well have been related to the Paṇḍu prince called Parakkama Paṇḍu I (1051-1053) who, like the Rajpūt Jagatīpāla, had led the Ceylonese resistance to the Cōḷa occupation until his capture and death.[66] Like the Rajpūt, Vijayabāhu I considered the Paṇḍu to be of "an unblemished line"[67]; it is clear from the Cūlavaṃsa that the intent of this marriage alliance was anti-Cōḷa.

The effect of Vijabāhu I's anti-Cōḷa dynastic alliances was to introduce a number of diverse elements into the royal family. He tried to tie these various elements together by a series of marriages within the royal family. His first concern was to link the Kaliṅgan element more securely to his own family; he accomplished this by marrying two of his Kaliṅgan daughters to his two younger brothers. Second, he sought to connect the Kaliṅgan element with the Pāṇḍyan element; this was urgent because his sister and her Pāṇḍyan consort had produced three ambitious sons: Mānābharaṇa, Kittisirimegha, and Sirivallabha. He married two more of his Kaliṅgan daughters to the two eldest Pāṇḍyan princes; a fifth Kaliṅgan daughter intended for the third Pāṇḍyan prince, however, died prematurely and was replaced by one of Vijayabāhu I's Rājput granddaughters, Sugalā.[68] Finally, Vijayabāhu I sought to tie all of the dynastic elements to Vikkamabāhu, his son by Tilokasundarī. Vikkamabāhu received a second Rājput granddaughter as well as a Kaliṅgan kinswoman of Tilokasundarī.[69] Unfortunately, there were no Pāṇḍyan consorts available to connect the three sons of Mittā to the interests of Vikkamabāhu. Vijayabāhu I's marriage policy failed to prevent the breaking out of dynastic war upon his death.

Dynastic War

It is possible that the marriage alliances of Vijayabāhu I reflected the coalition which succeeded in expelling the Cōḷas. The Kaliṅgans introduced by Mahinda IV's marriage in the tenth century appear to have cooperated with the Cōḷas in their conquest of Rājaraṭṭha; an alliance with these Kaliṅgans may

have been an important ingredient of Vijayabāhu I's success.
The Rajpūts and the Pāṇḍyans, on the other hand, were
localized in Rohaṇa where they were left high and dry after
the expulsion of the Cōḷas.

Vijayabāhu I's death was followed by two generations of
warfare between the Kaliṅgans of Rājaraṭṭha and the allied
Rajpūts and Pāṇḍyans of Rohaṇa. The sangha fled back to
Rohaṇa and attached itself to the Rohaṇese alliance. A new
power, however, rose in the south-west of the island, shielded
from Rohaṇa by rugged terrain and partially protected from
Rājaraṭṭha by mountainous Malaya. It was from here that
Parakkamabāhu I marched out to conquer and unite the island
in a great burst of economic and military activity.
Parakkamabāhu I was linked to all the factions contending for
control of the island, but he differed from each of them. He
had a different concept of the state than any previous Ceylonese
monarch. The interlude between the death of Vijayabāhu I and
the success of Parakkamabāhu I was fatal to the traditional
Ceylonese monarchy. A brief examination of this forty years
of war in terms of the contenders, the chronology, and the
results will help to clarify the appearance of Parakkamabāhu I.

Upon the death of Vijayabāhu I in 1114, succession to
the throne was disputed by his son Vikkamabāhu and the three
sons of his sister, Mānābharaṇa, Kittisirimegha, and
Sirivallabha. Vikkamabāhu's mother was Kaliṅgan; he claimed
the Solar dynasty to which the traditional Ceylonese royal
house belonged. [70] There is evidence that he tended toward
Śaivism and was generally hostile to the Buddhist religion. [71]
The three sons of Vijayabāhu I's sister considered themselves
Pāṇḍyan through their father; they claimed the Lunar dynasty
and were greatly influenced by Sanskritic learning. [72]
Vikkamabāhu successfully held Rājaraṭṭha while the three
Pāṇḍyan brothers divided Rohaṇa and Dakkhiṇadesa among
themselves. After the deaths of Vikkamabāhu and
Mānābharaṇa, a second round of hostilities erupted between the
two remaining Pāṇḍyan brothers and Vikkamabāhu's son
Gajabāhu, with neither side gaining an advantage. As
Kittisirimegha and Sirivallabha passed from the scene, their
holdings were inherited by Mānābharaṇa's son Parakkamabāhu I
in Dakkhiṇadesa and by Sirivallabha's son Mānābharaṇa in

Rohaṇa. This younger Mānābharaṇa, a cousin of
Parakkamabāhu I, was under the influence of his Rajpūt
mother, Sugalā; thus the basis of the Rajpūt-Pāṇdyan
alliance. [73]

Parakkamabāhu I, while raised in the Pāṇḍyan
traditions of his father and uncles, was also claimed by the
Kaliṅgan line through his mother. [74] However, he did not
cultivate nor depend upon dynastic identifications; he leaned
entirely upon the personal loyalty of his retainers. [75] By this
time, the cohesion of the old factions had loosened along with
respect for traditional values, and a new situation had
developed in which the old rivalries of the previous generation
had slight relevance. In the third and most decisive round of
warfare, Parakkamabāhu I defeated first Gajabāhu, thus taking
possession of Polonnaruva, and then defeated his cousin
Mānābharaṇa in Rohaṇa. [76] The Rohaṇese Rebellion, which
subsequently broke out under the inspiration of Sugalā,
Mānābharaṇa's Rajpūt mother, and which was joined by the
surviving remnants of the sangha, was in reality the last round
in this long era of warfare. Parakkamabāhu I's brutal
devastation of Rohaṇa completed the destruction of traditional
interests and the consolidation of his imperial power.

The effect of these wars is graphically portrayed in the
Cūlavaṃsa. [77] The physical devastation of the land was
unprecedented; tanks were destroyed, villages burned, forests
hewn down, and roads lined with impaled men. The social
order was turned upside down; slaves became men of power
and "people of good family" were forced into hiding. It is at
this time that first mention is made of vanni (forest)
refugees. [78] Tradition was discarded. [79] Bands of plundering
retainers roamed the land. Monasteries were handed over to
mercenary troops for their private maintenance; the
Paṃsukūlins joined the stream of monks seeking refuge in the
wilderness regions of Rohaṇa and Malaya, taking the sacred
relics with them. [80] None of the contenders during these forty
years of warfare was formally consecrated on the throne. The
destructive effects of these wars on traditional Ceylonese
society and on traditional Ceylonese notions of kingship was
more profound and cataclysmic than the Cōḷa occupation
during the previous century had been, for while Rohaṇa

successfully resisted the Cōḷas, it fell to Parakkamabāhu I.
This period of warfare was the breaking-point of traditional
Ceylonese civilization. The situation created by these wars is
of direct relevance to the rise of Parakkamabāhu I.

The Imperial Solution

After forty years of dynastic warfare, the credibility of
the Ceylonese throne was in serious doubt. The effect of these
wars was to make any return to traditional patterns of kingship
impossible. A new pattern had to be found if Ceylonese politics
were to rise above the level of regional and warring kingdoms.
The course taken was the imperial solution of Parakkamabāhu I.

Parakkamabāhu I united Ceylon after waging nearly ten
years of warfare. The bitterest resistance to his policy of
unification was in Rohaṇa, the traditional home of Ceylonese
heroes and national independence. After building up his power
in Dakkhiṇadesa and winning Rājaraṭṭha, he ruthlessly
devastated and depopulated Rohaṇa.[81] In place of the old semi-
feudal organization of the island, he created an imperial
administration of trusted men who ruled in both a civil and a
military capacity.[82] The core of the state was the army which
was kept occupied maintaining internal order and conducting
foreign campaigns. To support this army and to provide the
considerable outlay necessary to project the image of empire
in architectural undertakings, Parakkamabāhu I developed the
irrigated agriculture of the island with remarkable efficiency.
Parakkamabāhu I's prolonged military campaigns on the
continent served as a source of plunder as well as a first line
of defense against the Cōḷas.[83] Tamil prisoners were used as
laborers to build edifices on the island.[84] The Ceylonese army
was generally able to support itself by developing agriculture
in the occupied lands and by exacting treasure from wealthy
merchants.[85] Rather than being an economic drain on the
island, the continental wars appear to have been a source of
manpower and treasure as well as a means of keeping
ambitious generals occupied far from home.[86]

Parakkamabāhu I had built up a powerful army led by
men of talent personally loyal to him; this army was his

primary base of power. The maintenance of the army, however, rested on agricultural production. Consequently, he organized the agricultural life of the island along quasi-military lines, tying it directly to the army in its role as supplier. [87]

A feature of politics under Parakkamabāhu I is the extinction of the royal family. No male members of the royal family appear to have survived the wars of unification. [88] In their place, Parakkamabāhu I imported Kaliṅgan princes and set them up as his proteges. Thus, men with local bases of power were replaced by newcomers dependent on the patronage of the ruler.

The question of Parakkamabāhu I's so-called reform of the church has already been discussed at some length above. What must be further emphasized is that the church in the twelfth century was not the hotbed of sectarianism portrayed in the Cūlavaṃsa. There was no irreconcilable gulf separating the various vihāras; the traditional church as it had existed for hundreds of years had developed a sense of unity within which the various sects were able to retain their distinctive traits. Since the decline of Buddhism on the subcontinent in the ninth century, the Ceylonese church had been isolated; without the periodic importations of new heresies from the continent, the Ceylonese orders had adjusted to each other's peculiarities with some degree of tolerance and cooperation. [89] The Paṃsukūlins appear to have played an important role in binding the various vihāras and the throne together into a foundation for the traditional Ceylonese state. Furthermore, during the long years of warfare preceding the accession of Parakkamabāhu I, the church had become a refugee church, fleeing to the wilderness with its sacred books and relics. By the time of Parakkamabāhu I's "reform," the church was certainly in no mood for doctrinal disputes, having just passed through a difficult era in which survival itself was a primary consideration. Finally, it appears that important elements of the traditional church allied themselves with the Rohaṇese resistance and were exterminated with that resistance.

The church that emerged from Parakkamabāhu I's "reform" was built up around the nucleus of a Mahā-vihāra

monastery headed by an aged monk named Māhakassapa. [90]
Barred from any political role in the state, the church turned
its energies to scholarly activities. The spilling of ink which
resulted has left such a visible mark on surviving literature
that one modern writer has called this period the "Augustan
Age" of Pali literature. [91] Uncooperative monks were either
bribed into submission or forced to leave the island. [92]
Parakkamabāhu I built splendid edifices for his church, thus
creating an ornament for his empire which represented
cultural continuity with Ceylon's past.

The intellectual aspects of Parakkamabāhu I's imperial
solution represent a significant break with the traditional
ideologies of Ceylon. A Sanskritic rationality based on Manu
and Kauṭilya permeated every act of Parakkamabāhu I. [93]
He had no regard for the traditional Ceylonese version of
society and kingship based on mutually sanctioned
relationships. Old symbols such as the sacred relics and the
church itself were now used in a rational rather than in a
mystical or sacred function. Instead of being a necessary
element of the legitimizing process, they were now cultural
booty displayed to increase the splendor of the monarch and
his empire. [94] Without the old feudal system of rights and
obligations, there was a new reliance on physical force alone
for legitimization. The reign of Parakkamabāhu I was severe
to the point of cruelty; this is well documented both in the
Cūlavaṃsa and in the inscriptions of his successors. [95] He
kept the prisons full of dissidents as efficiently as he kept the
tanks full of water. It may be said, however, that
Parakkamabāhu I's application of cold, sometimes cruel,
rationality came after the traditional patterns had been
discredited by the effects of prolonged dynastic warfare;
society had lost its former cohesion, old loyalties had become
irrelevant, lawlessness was the rule. The imperial solution
was an unprecedented response to unprecedented disorder.

From Secularist to Infidel

The survival of Parakkamabāhu I's empire required a
continued momentum dependent upon strong personal
leadership. It may be argued that the island of Ceylon lacked

the resources needed to maintain an imperial momentum; but this cannot be proven without evidence which is not available. On the other hand, kingship can be examined from the Cūlavaṃsa and from epigraphic remains.

In attempting to gain a picture of throne politics in the thirty years following the death of Parakkamabāhu I, the first point that must be made is that the Pāṇḍyan faction of the dynastic wars in the first half of the twelfth century was dead; it was completely extinguished in Rohana during the reign of Parakkamabāhu I. Līlāvatī, one of Parakkamabāhu I's queens who was placed on the throne three different times by military men, could be considered as a scion of the old Pāṇḍyan faction. Her father was the youngest of the three Pāṇḍyan brothers who opposed Vikkamabāhu and Gajabāhu; her brother was the Mānābharaṇa who contested Parakkamabāhu I's rise to power; her mother, the Rajpūt Sugalā, and her nephews had led the prolonged Rohaṇese resistance, Yet, in an inscription, she claims not the Lunar line common to both the old Pāṇḍyan and Rajpūt factions and to which she was related by blood, but rather the Solar line claimed by her famous husband. Furthermore, in the same inscription, she specifically identifies herself with the greatness of Parakkamabāhu I.[96]

The situation is further clarified by an inscription of the Kaliṅgan Sāhasamalla who was placed on the throne by a pro-Kaliṅga court faction with Cōla assistance, thus bringing to an end Līlāvatī's first reign. The inscription criticizes the rule of Līlāvatī on the grounds that the island was kingless, then goes on to characterize those who placed her on the throne as men with vested interests on the island who opposed the strong centralized rule of kings (perhaps especially foreign kings who, having no local roots, would be less tolerant of vested interests).[97] These men were very likely surviving members of the old Ceylonese nobility who had successfully demonstrated their loyalty to Parakkamabāhu I. Parakkama of the Kālanāgara family, who placed Līlāvatī on the throne in 1211, was of an Ceylonese aristocratic line and is described by the Cūlavaṃsa as "the best among men of decision,"[98] perhaps hinting that he was a member of the old indigenous nobility which was greatly weakened by the events of the previous century. The so-called "Pāṇḍyan" faction was

nothing more than a coalition of the old Ceylonese nobility
which traced its origins back to "pre-Kaliṅga" times. It was
certainly in no position to disparage the memory of
Parakkamabāhu I; in fact, it attempted to use that memory for
its own purposes. No doubt plagued by the disunity to be
expected of the remnants of a feudal order, it was only able
to hold the throne for very short intervals. [99]

That the church was too weak in terms of political
power to play any role in these conflicts is apparent from the
fact that it was patronized in a perfunctory manner by every
faction and ruler during this time. Buddhism was undoubtedly
recognized by all contenders as an important theme of
Ceylonese culture and of national identity: thus it received lip
service from everyone. [100] The importance of church
patronage as a gauge of good kingship, however, fades during
this time; the Cūlavaṃsa indicates that the most that the church
could expect of rulers was that they follow the "political
precepts of Manu." [101]

If the church was in no position to play a political role
and the anti-Kaliṅgan elements were opposed to a strong
centralized rule, who, other than the Kaliṅgans, were in a
position to continue Parakkamabāhu I's empire? This question
has two possible answers. First were the merchants and
artisans known as the Govikula which had grown into a powerful
class by the last decades of the twelfth century. This class
was drawn from elements of the traditional society which had
been scattered by the wars of that century. In a time of
dynastic and imperial warfare, the Govikula prospered in the
role of serving and supplying armies. In addition,
Parakkamabāhu I's vast building projects gave further impetus
to the rise of this class. The revolt upon the death of
Parakkamabāhu I as well as the brief five day reign of Mahinda
VI in 1187 can be attributed to the Govikula. [102] That this class
continued to covet the throne is seen by the inscriptions of
Nissaṅkamalla (1187-1196), the strongest Kaliṅgan ruler of
this period. Nissaṅkamalla repeatedly warned the Govikula
against aspiring to kingship. [103]

A second source of imperial ambition was
Parakkamabāhu I's generals. [104] These generals invariably

allied themselves with the Kaliṅgan princes in opposition to the more entrenched and decentralized interests of the old nobility which rallied behind Līlāvatī. The most successful of these generals was Abonavan who ruled from 1200 to 1210, successively using three Kaliṅgan puppets.[105] The Kaliṅgan line (after Nissaṅkamalla) became subordinate to and dependent upon this class of generals who can without difficulty be identified with the army built up by Parakkamabāhu I.

The imperial leadership initiated by Parakkamabāhu I was carried on first by his Kaliṅgan protégés and then by his generals.[106] By 1211, the throne was ripe for foreign adventurers. The first of these was a Pāṇḍyan who apparently ruled in an acceptable manner for three years. He, however, fell prey to the greatly excoriated Māgha who "held to a false creed."[107] It appears that although the empire of Parakkamabāhu I contined to exist, and it could be argued that even under Māgha it existed albeit in a form totally unacceptable to the Ceylonese, it suffered seriously from the lack of any clearly defined conception of kingship. There was no agreed upon method of legitimizing one's rule, no established pattern for dealing with the problem of credibility. In terms of kingship, it was an empire up for grabs; anyone who had an army strong enough to take the throne could have it. This is a far cry from the traditional pattern of Ceylonese kingship still honored by Vijayabāhu I only a century earlier.

Ceylonese civilization continued to exist in the wet zone of southwestern Ceylon.[108] Yet, though basic religious and cultural themes endured, the new kingdom was drastically different from the traditional Ceylon that had developed for well over one thousand years in Rājaraṭṭha, not only in geographic and economic patterns, but in social, religious, and political patterns as well.

> The following page contains a "Reign List" of
> Ceylonese monarchs taken from Wilhelm
> Geiger, Culture of Ceylon in Medieval Times
> (Wiesbaden, 1960), pp. 225-226. Those rulers
> whose names are preceded by a capital letter
> are found on the genealogical chart which
> follows the "Reign List."

(A)	Sena I	831-851
(B)	Sena II	851-885
(C)	Udaya II	885-896
(D)	Kassapa IV	896-913
(E)	Kassapa V	913-923
(F)	Dappula III	923
(G)	Dappula IV	923-934
(H)	Udaya III	934-937
(I)	Sena III	937-945
(J)	Udaya IV	945-953
(K)	Sena IV	953-956
(L)	Mahinda IV	956-972
(M)	Sena V	972-981
(N)	Mahinda V	981-1029
(O)	Vikkamabāhu I	1029-1041
	Kitti	1041
	Mahālānakitt	1041-1044
	Vikkamapaṇḍu	1044-1047
(P)	Jagatīpāla	1047-1051
	Parakkamapaṇḍu I	1051-1053
	Loka	1053-1059
(Q)	Vijayabāhu I	1059-1114
(R)	Jayabāhu I	1114-1116
(S)	Vikkamabāhu II	1116-1137
(T)	Gajabāhu II	1137-1153
(U)	Parakkamabāhu I	1153-1186
(V)	Vijayabāhu II	1186-1187
	Mahinda VI	1187
	Nissaṅkamalla	1187-1196
	Vīrabāhu I	1196
	Vikkamabāhu III	1196
	Coḍagaṅga	1196-1197
	Līlāvatī	1197-1200
	Sāhasamalla	1200-1202
	Kalyāṇavatī	1202-1208
	Dhammāsoka	1208-1209
	Anīkaṅga	1209
	Līlāvatī	1209-1210
	Lokissara	1210-1211
	Līlāvatī	1211
	Parakkamapaṇḍu II	1211-1214
	Māgha	1214-1235

Chart 2

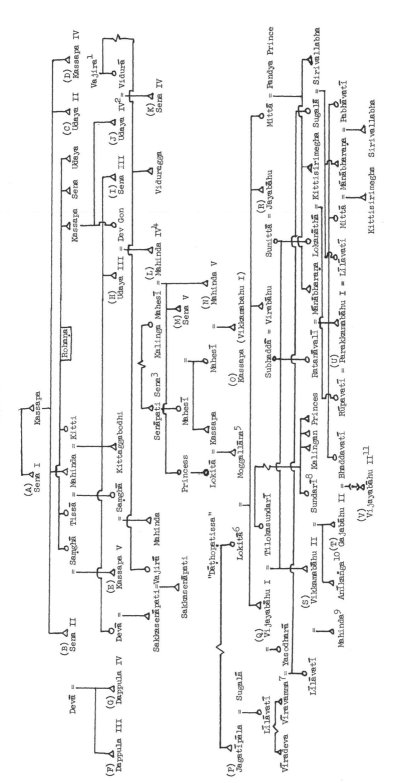

Notes to Genealogy

1. The postulated "Vajira/Vidura" family is based on the
   Cūlavaṃsa and on epigraphic evidence. This family first
   appears in the time of Sena I with high ministers at the
   court; it possessed great lands and wealth, patronized both
   the Mahā-vihāra and the Abhayagiri-vihāra as well as the
   Paṃsukūlins, and played a prominent role in bringing
   Rohaṇa into the Anurādhapura kingdom. After Mahinda IV,
   there is no further evidence of this family. See: Wilhelm
   Geiger, trans., Cūlavaṃsa (Colombo, 1953), 49:80;
   51:105; 52:63; 53:46, 50. (Hereafter, CV.) Epigraphia
   Zeylanica (London, 1904-1934), vol. 1, pp. 165-166, 171,
   175, 199-201, 205-207; vol. II, pp. 5, 13, 37, 51.
   (Hereafter, EZ.)

2. Udaya IV's ancestry is obscure (see CV, 54:48). The idea of
   of making him a brother of Sena III must be rejected not
   only because the two men are referred to as "friends" in the
   Cūlavaṃsa but also because Udaya IV's parents are referred
   to in inscriptions as annointed rulers, which cannot be said
   of Sena III's parents (EZ, vol. III, pp. 84-85). Epigraphic
   evidence that the name of Udaya IV's father was Kassapa is
   used by Paranavitana to postulate that Kassapa IV was his
   father (EZ, vol. III, pp. 294-300). In the context of Udaya
   IV's role during the crisis of the 930's however, it seems
   more likely that he was the son of the Kassapa set up as
   ruler of Rohaṇa by Sena I and later murdered by his nephew
   Kittaggabodhi (CV, 50:50-55; 51; 94-96). The idea that Sena
   IV was a son of Udaya IV and his consort Vidurā is based on
   an inscription of Sena IV (EZ, vol III, pp. 262-264).

3. CV, 54:14, 58-68; 55:2, 8-9. Postulating kinship between
   Senāpati Sena and Mahinda IV's Kaliṅgan Mahesī would
   explain the remarkably close relationship which apparently
   existed between them as well as accounting for the fact that
   both his daughter and granddaughter were Mahesī.

4. The lineage of Mahinda IV is by far the most obscure of any
   king in this period. Without going into all the ingenious
   methods used to make him the son of nearly every man to

hold the throne since Sena I (see CV, 54:48 with Geiger's note; EZ, vol. I, pp. 78-79, 98 note 4), suffice it to say that in almost every inscription of Mahinda IV, his mother is called Dev Gon. The only mention of a Dev Gon in an inscription other than one of Mahinda IV's is one which makes her the queen of Udaya III (EZ, vol. III, pp. 221-222). The only remaining difficulty is that another inscription states that Mahinda IV finished a religious edifice started by "the great king his brother" (EZ, vol. I, p. 228). The problem is to find a royal brother for Mahinda IV. This difficulty can perhaps be resolved by equating the mysterious brother with Mahinda IV's uncle, Udaya IV; according to the Cūlavaṃsa, Mahinda IV completed a religious edifice begun by his mother's brother, Udaya IV (54:48). For a different and perhaps equally valid version of the lineage of Mahinda IV and of his presumed father, Udaya III, see H. C. Ray, ed., History of Ceylon, vol. I, pt. II (Colombo, 1960), pp. 851-854 and EZ, vol. III, pp. 141-142.

5. The difficulties in ascertaining Moggallāna's ancestry have apparently been compounded by a mistranslation by Geiger of the pertinent portion of Vijayabāhu I's genealogy. For a full discussion of this problem, see Ray, op. cit., pp. 854-856.

6. The ancestry of Vijayabāhu I's mother, Lokitā, is discussed above in the section entitled "The Last Attempt at Revival."

7. For a hypothesis connecting Vīravamma with the Rajpūt Vīradeva, see note 61.

8. CV, 59:46-49.

9. CV, 62:59.

10. CV, 61:40.

11. On Vijayabāhu II's ancestry see CV, 66:147-149; 70:333; 80:1. EZ, vol. II, pp. 179-180. Ray, op. cit., pp. 507-508. A. Liyanagamage, The Decline of Polonnaruva and the Rise of Dambadeṇiya (Colombo, 1968), pp. 42-44.

NOTES

1. Most of the articles on this problem have been collected in
one volume: K. Indrapala, ed., The Collapse of the
Rajarata Civilization in Ceylon and the Drift to the Southwest
(Peradeniya, 1971). Also see: B. J. Perera, "An
Examination of the Political Troubles that followed the Death
of King Parakkamabahu I," JCBRAS, 5, 2 (July, 1958),
pp. 173-182.

2. Wilhem Geiger, trans., The Cūlavamsa, 2 vols. (Colombo,
1953), 65:20. (Hereafter, CV.)

3. Walpola Rahula, History of Buddhism in Ceylon (Colombo,
1956), pp. 59-77.

4. T. R. Trautmann, "Consanguineous Marriage in Pali
Literature," JAOS, 93.2 (1973), pp. 174-180.

5. See CV, vol. I, p. iv; G. C. Mendis, Problems of Ceylon
History (Colombo, 1966), p. 7. Properly, the Cūlavamsa
should not be distinguished from the Mahāvamsa of which it
is simply chapters 37 to 100.

6. Malalasekera and Wickramasinghe do not agree with this
identification; they prefer to make a later Dhammakitti the
compiler of chapters 37 through 90. See: G. P.
Malalasekera, The Pali Literature of Ceylon (London,
1928), pp. 142, 215; S. Wickramasinghe, "The Sources for
a Study of the Reign of King Parakkamabahu I," Ceylon
Historical Journal, 4 (1954-1955), p. 169. (Hereafter,
CHJ.) This view, however, is outdated. See: Mendis,
op. cit., p. 7; H. C. Ray, ed., History of Ceylon, vol. I,
pt. II (Colombo, 1960), p. 587; Wilhelm Geiger, Culture of
Ceylon in Medieval Times (Wiesbaden, 1960), pp. 71-72.

7. See: CV, 80:49-50; Malalesekera, op. cit., pp. 207-208.

8. See: Ray, op. cit., pp. 586-587; H. H. De A. Wijesekera,
"Pali and Sanskrit in the Polonnaruva Period," CHJ, 4
(1954-1955), p. 94.

9. CV, vol. I, pp. iv-xii. Concerning the nature of religious/ historical works such as the Cūlavaṃsa and their value to the historian, see Mendis, op. cit., pp. 18-22, 76-78.

10. On the major Ceylonese monastic orders, see: Andre Bareau, "Les Sectes Bouddhiques du Petit Vehicule," Publications de l'Ecole Francaise d'Extreme-Orient, 38 (1955), chs. 29-31.

11. On the heterogenous nature of the Buddhist intellectual world prior to the twelfth century, see: R. A. L. H. Gunawardana, "Buddhist Nikayas in Medieval Ceylon," Ceylon Journal of Historical and Social Sciences, 9, 1 (January/June 1966), pp. 55-66. (Hereafter, CJHSS.)

12. CV, 62:40-67.

13. CV, 70:272-280.

14. CV, 70:258-271; 71:9-11; 74:22-39.

15. CV, 74:38, 88.

16. CV, 74:108-109, 138, 159-160, 165-168, 183-248.

17. CV, 80:8, 11-14, 19-26. 35-41.

18. A possible explanation for this omission may be that whereas Līlāvatī was connected to the Rohaṇese resistance (and perhaps, thereby, with the pre-Parakkamabāhu I church) through her brother Mānābharaṇa and her mother Sugalā, Rūpavatī had no Rohaṇese connections and, like Parakkamabāhu I himself, could claim kinship with both of the major factions of her day (the Kaliṅgan through her mother and the Pāṇḍyan through her father). Līlāvatī was further tainted by her connection with the lowly regarded Rajpūt (Āriya) line through her mother. For example, Vikkamabāhu II regarded the son born of his Rajpūt consort as "unworthy of the crown" (CV, 62:59). Likewise, · Parakkamabāhu I's mother, a daughter of Vijayabāhu I's Kaliṅgan Mahesī, "protested over and over again" the marriage of her high-born daughter to Mānābharaṇa, whose

mother was of the Rajpūt line (CV, 63:6-17). The introduction of this Rajpūt line into the Ceylonese royal family and the possibility that Vijayabāhu I's mother was of this line are dealt with below in the discussion of Vijayabāhu I's genealogy.

19. The Paṃsukūlins invariably receive the cream of royal patronage. For example, Aggabodhi VII (766-772) "had rice by allotment distributed to the inmates of the three fraternities and delicious foods, fitting for himself, to the Paṃsukūlins" (CV, 48:73). Sena I (831-851), "for the Paṃsukūlika bhikkhus he built a monastery on the Ariṭṭha mountain, erected as if by magic, and endowed it with large revenues. He granted it also an equipment without flaw, worthy of a king, many helpers of the monastery and slaves as work people" (CV, 50:63-64). All orders were recipients of clothing donated by kings, but the Paṃsukūlins were the only group of bhikkhus to receive "fine garments" worn by the king himself (CV, 48:16).

20. CV, 51:52.

21. CV, 52:21.

22. The Cūlavaṃsa refers to the Paṃsukūlins of the twelfth century as "belonging to the two divisions" (CV, 61:59). If by the two divisions the Mahā-vihāra and the Abhayagiri-vihāra are meant, this indicates that the divisions of the church were not as unyielding as later portrayed by Dhammakitti (CV, 73:18-19).

23. CV, 53:13-27 and Geiger, op. cit., p. 206.

24. CV, 53:33, 48; 54:23-25.

25. CV, 61:58-61.

26. That the old church with its three vihāras continued to exist, in one form or another (perhaps in exile until the death of Parakkamabāhu I), could possibly be argued from Nissaṅkamalla's claim (1187-1196) to have "reconciled the clergy of the three Nikāyas" [Epigraphia Zeylanica (London,

1904-1934), vol. I, p. 134]. (Hereafter, EZ.) This claim
is made only once, however, and, appearing as it does
without details, seems to be more of an honorific formula
than a factual account.

27. EZ, vol. II, pp. 256-283. For an excellent discussion of
how monastic interests became important centers of
political and economic power in medieval Ceylon,
constituting in effect an ecclesiastical aristocracy, and how
rulers exercised their authority to protect the saṅgha from
decay by forcing these interests out of the political sphere,
see: Heinz Bechert, "The Theravada Buddhist Sangha:
Some Observations on Historical and Political Factors in
its Development," JAS, 29, 4 (August, 1970), pp. 761-768.
Also see: R. A. L. H. Gunawardhana, "Some Economic
Aspects of Monastic Life in the Later Anuradhapura
Period: Two New Inscriptions from Madirigiriya," CJHSS,
n.s. 2, 1 (January-June, 1972), pp. 1-49.

28. EZ, vol. II, p. 259; Ray, op. cit., pp. 586-587; Geiger,
op. cit., p. 209; Malalasekera, op. cit., pp. 190-195.

29. CV, 50:1-86. Polonnaruva is mentioned as a royal
residence as early as the reign of Aggabodhi IV (658-674);
see CV, 46:34-38; 48:74.

30. See: A. Liyanagamage, The Decline of Polonnaruva and the
Rise of Dambadeṇiya (Colombo, 1968), pp. 87-88, 173, 180.
Parakkamabāhu II delegated control of Polonnaruva to local
vannī (forest) chieftains.

31. See: EZ, vol. I, pp. 98-113, 187-190; vol. III, p. 78-81.
Also: L. S. Perera, "Proprietary and Tenurial Rights in
Ancient Ceylon," CJHSS, 2, 1 (January, 1959), pp. 31-32;
Edmund Leach, "Hydraulic Society in Ceylon," Past and
Present, 15 (1959), pp. 1-26; W. I. Siriweera, "Land
Tenure and Revenue in Mediaeval Ceylon," CJHSS, 11, 1
(January-June, 1972), pp. 1-49.

32. B. J. Perera, op. cit., p. 175.

33. Liyanagamage, op. cit., p. 85.

34. It is during this time that the Bhikkhunī-sāsana (order of female bhikkhus) disappears as well as the Paṃsukūlins and other heterodox sects. See: Malalasekera, op. cit., p. 165; also: EZ, vol. II, pp. 256-283.

35. For one of many examples of Rohaṇa as a rallying point for Ceylonese nationalism, see: CV, 38:38-40.

36. CV, 54:64-67.

37. EZ, vol. I, pp. 241-251.

38. This sentiment is revealed in an inscription of Nissaṅkamalla (1187-1196) who condemns those who "create discord by taking other's properties, like fishes who... (illegible)...each other in the water" (EZ, vol. III, p. 152), a stock literary image indicating that when the waters of just coercion dry up, the big fish eat the little fish, the strong devour the weak. Nearly all of Nissaṅkamalla's inscriptions indicate that robbery and general lawlessness were characteristic of his age. The Cūlavaṃsa gives a vivid description of the social effects of the dynastic wars (61:66-73).

39. This genealogy deviates from any previously proposed. It is based both on the Cūlavaṃsa and on epigraphic evidence. See Chart 2 for details of its construction.

40. For the events narrated in this paragraph, see: CV, 50:50-60; 51: 7-19. Sena I was not the first Ceylonese monarch to intervene in Rohaṇese affairs; indeed, there had been regular marriage alliances between the Rājaraṭṭha and Rohaṇese royal houses for at least three generations prior to this time. Yet from the reign of Sena I, the necessity of greater cooperation between the two regions became increasingly urgent.

41. CV, 53:7-9.

42. CV, 53:14-27.

43. CV, 53:33, 47-48.

44. CV, 47:66.

45. Rohaṇa continued to resist the overlordship of Anurādhapura throughout the ninth and tenth century. During the reign of Udaya II (885-896), an attempt by the "Rohaṇese" nephew of Sena II, Kittaggabodhi, to set himself up in Rohaṇa after murdering his uncle (Kassapa) who had been established there by Sena I, was crushed by a son of Kassapa V born of a Rohaṇese consort (CV, 51:94-119). An inscription reveals that Kassapa IV (896-914) "brought under one rule the Rohaṇa Province and the Malaya District" thus securing for himself "the enjoyment of the combined wealth, glory and prosperity that prevailed in the beautiful island of Laṅkā" (EZ, vol., III, pp. 275-277). Mahinda IV (956-972) also claims to have conquered Rohaṇa (EZ, vol. II, pp. 67 and vol. III, p. 224; CV, 54:8).

46. EZ, vol. I, pp. 154, 157-158, 1ᶠ'.

47. EZ, vol. I, pp. 254-259.

48. CV, 54:9. The question of Kaliṅga, its identity and the nature of its role in Ceylonese history has for the past several years been the object of considerable controversy. The most even-handed examination of this problem to date is perhaps W. M. Sirisena, "The Kalinga Dynasty of Ceylon and the Theory of Its South-East Asian Origin," CJHSS, I, 1 (January-June, 1971), pp. 11-67. Sirisena concludes on the basis of currently available evidence that the Kaliṅga in dispute was located in Orissa. There is one mention of Kaliṅga in the Cūlavaṃsa prior to the reign of Mahinda IV. During the reign of Aggabodhi II in the early seventh century, a royal family from Kaliṅga is received at the Ceylonese court after being driven out of its kingdom by the Chalukyas (609 A.D.). This event was followed by sixty-five years of dynastic war and foreign intervention (CV, 42:44-48; 44:1-154; 45:1-81; 46:1-46; 47:1-66). What connection, if any, the arrival of the Kaliṅgan refugees had with the subsequent internal upheavals cannot be known; in any case, it was not a felicious precedent. There is virtually nothing known of the dynasty or dynasties ruling in Kaliṅga during the reign of Mahinda IV; R. C. Majumdar,

general ed., The Age of Imperial Kanauj, The History and Culture of the Indian People, vol. IV (Bombay, 1955), pp. 61-62.

49. CV, 54:10-11. That the Paṃsukūlins may have been unhappy with the Kaliṅgan alliance may be inferred from the brief mention of the Kaliṅgan Mahesī in the Cūlavaṃsa; on the other hand, Mahinda IV's other queen, Kitti, and her son both receive lavish praise as patrons of the church (CV, 54:50-53).

50. Geiger, op. cit., p. 28.

51. No mention of this festival or genealogy is found in the Cūlavaṃsa, perhaps because of the reason mentioned in note 49 above. However, it is described in an inscription signalled by S. Paranavitana, Ceylon and Malaysia (Colombo, 1966), pp. 29 ff. The authenticity of this inscription has been questioned; yet it fits with other evidence.

52. CV, 54:57-67.

53. CV, 55:1-7.

54. CV, 55:12-14.

55. CV, 56:13-16.

56. CV, 57:4-44.

57. Magic ascetic rites are associated with the rise of two previous national heroes who hailed from Rohaṇa, rallied the Ceylonese, and expelled foreign occupiers; this theme seems to be an element of traditional Ceylonese nationalism, rooted in Rohaṇa. CV, 38:18, 26-27; 41:80-87.

58. CV, 60:83-84.

59. CV, 56:13-15, 59:23-28.

60. CV, 59:25.

61. CV, 59:29. Further support for this postulation may lie in connecting the husband of Yasodharā, Vīravamma, with the Rajpūt adventurer, Vīradeva, who intervened in the dynastic wars following the death of Vijayabāhu I. The Cūlavaṃsa gives no information about Vīravamma except for his name, the fact that Vijayabāhu I gave him the province of Merukandara as well as the hand of Yasodharā, and that he was the father of two princesses (one of whom became a consort of Vikkamabāhu II, the other being none other than the famous Sugalā who was the mother of Līlāvatī--the queen of Parakkamabāhu I who was later repeatedly put on the throne by the post-Parakkamabāhu I non-Kaliṅgan faction--and of Mānābharaṇa, who bitterly contested Parakkamabāhu I's rise to power; Sugalā herself led the Rohaṇese rebellion in the time of Parakkamabāhu I). The location of Merukandara is uncertain, but if Viravamma was able to set himself up on the island under the patronage of Vijayabāhu I, perhaps on the basis of kinship with Vijayabāhu I's mother, this may have strengthened Viradeva's claim, assuming he was a kinsman of Vīravamma, to play war and politics on the island. See: CV, 59:27; 61:36-47.

62. The genealogy is composed of four distinct sections. The first section, which tells the story of Māna (57:4-24), appears to represent the traditions of the Paṃsukūlins regarding the founding of their order and its establishment in a major role at the court. The second section is of two parts; first, a blood line is established from Māna (actually his brother Mānavamma) to Mahinda V (57:25-26), and, second, Vijayabāhu I's descent from Mahinda V through his father is established (57:27-30). The third section is apparently a retelling of the first section only substituting "a grandson of King Dāṭhopatissa" for Māna and leaving out many of the specific details reserved for the original version; the only new detail added to this account is mention of the Selantarasamūha which, in actuality, may have been connected with Vijayabāhu I's mother (57:31-39). The use of Dāṭhopatissa indicates that Vijayabāhu I's mother was not of the royal family which had ruled since the seventh century. Since the Dāṭhopatissa line was itself only an emphemeral branch originating with an ambitious minister (44:105, 128)

and ending with its absorption by Tamil adventurers
(45:11-22; 46:39-46), its use in the genealogy to mask the
true origins of Vijayabāhu I's mother was a safe device for
tying her into the Ceylonese royal line without attempting to
link her directly with the royal house as it had existed since
the seventh century, something which was apparently not
feasible. The vague manner by which she is linked to
Dāthopatissa in the fourth and final section of the genealogy
through means of a suspicious sounding Prince Bodhi and
Princess Buddha "of the line of Dāthopatissa" tends to
confirm this interpretation (57:40-42).

63. CV, 60:5-6, 24-26. On the unique relationship between
Ceylon and Burma during this period see G. H. Luce,
"Some Old References to the South of Burma and Ceylon,"
Felicitation Volumes of Southeast Asian Studies (Bangkok,
1965), vol. II, pp. 271-277; and C. E. Godakumbura,
"Relations Between Burma and Ceylon," JBRS, 49, 2
(December, 1966), pp. 145-162.

64. CV, 59:40.

65. CV, 59:40.

66. CV, 56:16.

67. Vijayabāhu I's tolerance of diverse blood lines seems to
come out of the context of his long struggle against the
Cōḷas; it is in strong contrast to the blood distinction made
by the following generation.

68. CV, 59:45.

69. CV, 59:45-50.

70. If these Kaliṅgans actually were of the Eastern Gaṅgas,
they had adapted to the Ceylonese scene, for the Eastern
Gaṅgas were of the Lunar dynasty. Majumdar, op. cit.,
p. 141.

71. EZ, vol. III, pp. 310-311. See also: P. Sarvesvara Iyer,
"Puranic Saivism in Ceylon During the Polonnaruva

Period," Proceedings of the First International Conference Seminar of Tamil Studies, I (Kuala Lumpur, 1966), pp. 462-474.

72. CV, 62:5-6, 45-46; 63:5. Inscriptional evidence indicates a possible alliance between Mānābharaṇa and the Cōḷas. EZ, vol. III, pp. 308-309.

73. CV, 70:266-267.

74. CV, 62:56-57.

75. CV, 65:17-20; 66:21, 128-145, 150-154.

76. The ambiguous nature of the relationship between Parakkamabāhu I and Gajabāhu indicates that they had common interests with respect to the threat from Rohaṇa and that an amicable relationship of some sort eventually came to be based on these interests. CV, 66:116, 147-150; 70:271-280, 327-336. EZ, vol. IV, pp. 1-8.

77. CV, 61:48-73.

78. Geiger, op. cit., p. 51.

79. The Cūlavaṃsa identifies the attempt of the Pāṇḍyan faction to prevent Vikkamabāhu from occupying the throne as the first act of turning away from "former custom" (61:4).

80. Inscriptions tell of benefactions made to bhikkhus during this period of warfare in the form of mountain cave retreats (EZ, vol. II, pp. 189, 195-196).

81. For example, see: CV, 75:185-193; in this passage, Rohaṇa is compared to "a forest burnt by fire."

82. Liyanagamage, op. cit., pp. 71-72.

83. CV, 76:31-32, 166, 176, 191. K. A. Nilakanta Sastri, "Parakkamabahu and South India," CHJ, 4 (1954-1955), pp. 47, 51.

84. CV, 76:103-104.

85. CV, 76:264, 286-287.

86. Sastri, op. cit., p. 51. Sastri's evaluation of Parakkamabāhu I's continental campaigns indicates a policy of "limited" warfare maintained at a profitable level which could be continued indefinitely.

87. This clearly described in the C̲ū̲l̲a̲v̲a̲m̲s̲a̲ (68:1-59 and 69:1-5).

88. Sastri suggests that one of Mānābharaṇa's sons escaped to the Cōḷas who subsequently attempted to use him in their wars with Parakkamabāhu I (Sastri, op. cit., p. 49).

89. V. Panditha, "Buddhism during the Polonnaruva Period," CHJ, 4 (1954-1955), pp. 128-129.

90. CV, 78:6-16. EZ, vol. II, pp. 256-283.

91. Malalasekera, op. cit., p. 175.

92. CV, 78:13, 19.

93. S. Saparamadu, "The Sinhalese Language and Literature of the Polonnaruva Period," CHJ, 4 (1954-1955), p. 98.

94. The three major relics were the tooth relic, the hair relic, and the bowl relic; a fourth, mentioned occasionally, is the right collar bone relic. There were many bodhi trees throughout the island, all venerated as descendants of the original. For how these various sacred items came to be introduced into Ceylon, see: Geiger, op. cit., p. 187; also CV, 37:92-95, 192, 207; 39:44-45.

95. CV, 80:2-4. EZ, vol. I, pp. 132-133; vol. II, pp. 80-83, 89-90, 115-122, 127, 130, 134, 136-137.

96. EZ, vol. II, p. 94.

97. The inscription refers to the men behind Līlāvatī as "evil

ministers who were causing obstructions with the object of
gaining personal power for themselves and so were not
desiring to have kings that would be powerful enough both
for granting rewards and for inflicting punishments."
(EZ, vol. II, pp. 226-229.) From this, it appears that
Līlāvatī was used by men whose interests were counter to
the strong rule of the Kaliṅgans.

98. CV, 80:49.

99. Liyanagamage (op. cit., , p. 57) posits a "Pāṇdyan" faction
and identifies it with Līlāvatī. However, he fails to identify
whom this faction consisted of or what interests it was
trying to promote or preserve by using the old queen.
There is neither sufficient evidence nor is there logical
justification for the existence of a "Pāṇdyan" faction if
what is meant is a group with interests other than on the
island. Also see: B. J. Perera, "Some Political Trends
in the Late Anurādhapura and Polonnaruva Period," CHJ,
10, 1-4 (Junly 1960-April 1961), pp. 69-70.

100. EZ, vol. II, pp. 235-236. CV, 80:8-14, 19-23, 35-40.

101. CV, 80:9, 41, 53.

102. CV, 80:15-17. EZ, vol. II, pp. 179-180. Liyanagamage,
op. cit., pp. 45-46.

103. Comparing the ambitions of the Govikula for kingship with
a crow aspiring to be a swan, Nissaṅkamalla declares,
"However powerful the people of the Govi caste may be,
they should not be elected to rule the kingdom. Those who
pay obeisance to persons of the same class as themselves
and render them the honors due to kings, and those, too,
who accept from them offices and titles shall indeed be
called traitors" (EZ, vol. II, pp. 122, 164).

104. For a detailed study of these generals, see: Liyanagamage,
op. cit., pp. 52-55.

105. Liyanagamage, op. cit., pp. 61-64.

106. The basic chronology of this period as well as a discussion of the interesting reign of Nissaṅkamalla will be waived inasmuch as neither is especially germane at this point. See: Ray, op. cit., pp. 507-528; Liyanagamage, op. cit., pp. 34-75; EZ, vol. II, pp. 115-122, 174-178; CV, 80.

107. CV, 80:56.

108. For a look at the new Ceylonese state founded in the thirteenth century, see Liyanagamage, op. cit., pp. 76-178.

Southeast Asian Trade

and the Isthmian Struggle, 1000-1200 A.D.[1]

by
Kenneth R. Hall and John K. Whitmore

The role of Southeast Asia in the international trade route has over the centuries been predominantly one of providing a key link in that route, rather than having been a source of goods for the route. The merchants on the route, directly or indirectly, focused on the wealth at both its ends, the riches of the Mediterranean and the Middle East and the greatness of China. All the points in between served as a series of links carrying the goods along and feeding in local goods at the regional entrepots. Certainly in the Chinese view, the waters stretching from the coast of China and the South China Sea to the Indian Ocean and the coast of Africa were in essence one ocean, the Nan-yang or Southern Seas.[2] The key fact of Southeast Asia in this context was that it lay astride this single ocean and its communications. In such a position, the Malay Peninsula and the islands adjacent to it possessed both negative and positive potential. On the one hand, any strife could disrupt the flow of trade; on the other, the maintenance of political stabliity and the establishment of entrepots could lay a proper foundation for and encourage this flow.

As O. W. Wolters has demonstrated, the history of the coastal regions in Southeast Asia has been intimately linked to this trade route and the ebb and flow of its commerce.[3] The Malay peoples of these coasts had long known far-reaching navigational techniques and had gradually become familiar with the peoples and cultures lying on both near and distant coasts. When the international route itself began to appear, over two millenia ago, these Malay peoples were in a position to learn about and to take advantage of the commercial possibilities. In particular, they appear to have supplied the ships and manpower needed to carry the commerce between Ceylon and China, thus forming a crucial link in the route. Gradually, as Wolters has described so well, the Malays took

303

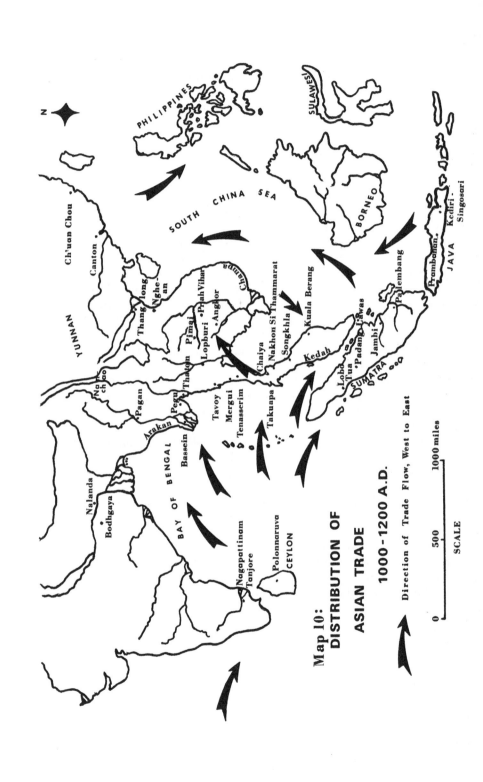

Map 10:
DISTRIBUTION OF
ASIAN TRADE
1000–1200 A.D.

Direction of Trade Flow, West to East

SCALE

0   500   1000 miles

a greater and more active role in the trade itself. [4]

Initially during the third and fourth centuries the international route had gone across the Kra Isthmus, disembarking on the west side around Takuapa and being carried over the peninsula to the Bay of Bandon on the east coast. It had then proceeded across the Gulf of Siam to the Funanese port of Oc-eo. The Chao Phraya valley seems to have received influence from the Kra in this period, while the Irrawaddy area undoubtedly had a coastal contact with the Ganges delta. By the fifth century, however, the Malays appear to have taken the initiative, and the route went through the Straits of Malacca to southeastern Sumatra, making direct contact with the richly endowed Java Sea area. [5] Out of this development rose the classic maritime state of Srivijaya. Based on the Malay role in the trade route and located on the "favored coast" of southeastern Sumatra, this power stood between the flow of international trade and the wealth of Java and beyond. In Wolters' terms, the rise of this state and its subsequent career were intimately linked to the rise and fall of the T'ang dynasty and the vast wealth that a unified and prosperous China meant. Having emerged from the mass of harbor states competing for a place on the trade route in the seventh century, Srivijaya gained control of the seas in the vicinity of the Straits of Malacca, put down piracy and competition, and established a cosmopolitan trading center, it would seem, at Palembang. The ports of Srivijaya then furnished supplies, local products, Chinese and Western goods, storage facilities, and hostelries for waiting out the monsoon season to the passing traders. The extent of this loosely knit empire covered the coasts of Sumatra and of the Malay Peninsula, and the trade that had existed for China with the Malay Peninsula and beyond to Java now came to be focussed on the Srivijayan ports. The ports of the Kra Isthmus remained secondary and under a loose Srivijayan control. [6]

Through the ninth and tenth centuries, when the T'ang state was slowly collapsing and China was splintering into numerous small political entities, the trade seems not to have dipped to any great degree due to the efforts of the Southern Han and Min regimes based respectively at Canton and Fu-chou. [7] Yet new pressures were building up along the sea routes. Where previously the political development of the region was such that there had been little conflict among major regional powers, the tenth century saw the beginnings of such conflict, particularly with the rise of maritime power in eastern Java and on the Tamil section of the east coast of India. Added to this inter-regional competition was the major upsurge in trade tied to the reunification of China under the Sung dynasty and its efforts to reopen the communications of the Southern Seas over the final third of the tenth century.

The hundred years following the upsurge along the trade route saw a serious weakening of the position of Srivijaya as the political and economic strains proved too great for it. First, the Srivijayan rulers sought to consolidate their position with diplomatic maneuvers in the direction of India and Ceylon[8] and then followed with a war against Java. The Javanese attacked Srivijaya in 992, but in 1016 suffered a devastating raid from their enemies, allowing the Srivijayan ruler to refer to himself when he sent a richly laden mission to China the following year as "king of the ocean lands."[9] Yet, within a decade, the Cōḷa power of the Coromandel coast had sacked the legendary riches of the Srivijaya capital and for the next fifty years was to play a role in the politics of the Straits area.[10] The attack of 1025 seems to have disrupted the concentration of the international route through the Srivijayan ports along the Straits, and by the last quarter of the eleventh century the trading pattern had become more diffuse. No longer were Palembang and its subordinate harbors the single focus of the international route in Southeast Asia. The ports of east Java began to surpass them in wealth, drawing traders from India and the mainland of Southeast Asia as well as from the eastern islands, and Chinese maritime vessels were for the first time sailing the Southeast Asian seas and going beyond them into the Indian Ocean.[11] Indeed, the small harbors of northern Sumatra began to act independently of the once great power to the south and to profit directly from the variety of traders now circulating along the sea routes.[12]

The 1025 Cōḷa expedition appears to have been critical in the expansion of several major states on the Southeast Asian mainland as well. By removing Srivijaya's presence in the ports of the upper Malay Peninsula, the Cōḷas cleared the way for the expanding mainland states to fill the resulting power vacuum. [13]

Stage One: The Khmers

By the first half of the eleventh century, the Khmers of Cambodia had pushed their control to the west into the Chao Phraya valley of present Thailand and towards the Kra Isthmus. Where tenth century Cambodia's commercial interest had been directed toward the eastern portions of its land, Sūryavarman I (1002-1050) reversed this pattern with his activities in the west. [14] Although his motivation may well have been in terms of conquest, Sūryavarman's extension of Khmer administration into the Lopburi region had strong economic implications. Control of the lower Chao Praya provided access to international commerce at Tambralinga on the eastern Kra, giving the Khmer a more direct contact with the international trade routes than had previously been the case. After the Cōḷas had eliminated Srivijaya's power over the Kra, the Khmer seem to have established their own influence over Tambralinga. [15]

In another article[16] Hall has speculated that a stronger Khmer relationship with the Kra allowed the development of commercial contact between Cambodia and South India. In 1020, before Rājēndra Cōḷa's Southeast Asian raid, Sūryavarman had sent presents to the Cōḷa king, an act which, based on other epigraphic records, must be viewed as a culmination to eleventh century Khmer commercial expansion. A Sūrya image found at Chaiya has been traced to the eleventh century style of the Cōḷa dynasty. [17] Other Cōḷa-style remains from the Vieng Sra area on the Isthmus appear to date to the same tenth and eleventh century period, reflecting a trans-peninsular route between the west coast port of Takuapa and the Bay of Bandon. [18] Archeological research by Alastair Lamb has shown that Takuapa was the terminus of the Persian-Arab trade until the mid-eleventh century, when it was shifted south to the Kedah coast. [19] "Kalah," as the Arabs called the Malay coast entrepot, was the center of Arab-Persian trade, while "Srivijaya" was the center of the China trade. Kalah's ability to handle the trade of two worlds was the source of its importance. The Arabs knew it as a place where a large amount of profit could be made, a fact reflected in the quantity of artifacts found at both the Takuapa and Kedah sites.

As the Khmer were developing commercial contacts with the west, the Burmese were pushing south into the delta of the Irrawaddy and were also moving toward the Isthmus. After establishing a base at Pagan in the tenth century, eleventh century Burmese expansion annexed the Mon kingdoms of Pegu and Thaton. Here the Burmese established control over the Mon commercial centers, one of which may have been Papphala, the Mon port sacked in the Cōḷa raid. Around 1050, the Burmese were expanding into the Malay Peninsula, where they seem to have encountered little resistence from the Khmer.[20] About that same year, the Chams were applying pressure to the eastern Khmer border, sacking Sambupura on the Mekong,[21] and Sūryavarman died. Thereafter Khmer epigraphy reflects a seeming lack of interest in the commercial development of the Cambodian empire until the late twelfth century. In this period the center of Khmer political power shifted north into the Mun River valley beyond the Dangrek mountain range. Internal political strife as well as external pressure may well have contributed to the lack of security adequate for generating the extensive commercial activity of the early eleventh century. We may speculate that after 1050 internal disorder prevented a Khmer presence in the Malay Peninsula, leaving the Kra to the Burmese.

Stage Two: The Burmese

In a recent article, Janice Stargardt has suggested that tenth century disorders in the Nanchao region blocked the overland commercial networks connecting the Irrawaddy plains and China and thus generated Burmese interest in opening commercial channels to the south.[22] Prior to the closing of the northern route, Burma had served as a center of exchange between northern India and China; overland trade to Bengal via Arakan had been of major economic importance to the Burmese heartland. If Stargardt's analysis is correct, then commercial centers on the Malay Peninsula provided an alternative source of foreign commodities for this India trade after the route to China had been closed. The Kra port of Takuapa was located well within the range of Mon coastal shipping. The Mon port identified as "Papphala" in the Tanjore inscription, located somewhere on the Pegu coast, could thus have connected the overland route to northwest India with this maritime route. This port's channel of communication with the Kra was undoubtedly disrupted by the Cōḷa raid.

Under Anirruddha (1044-1077), there was new interest in restoring commercial intercourse with the Kra. Around 1057, Anirruddha followed his conquest of Thaton by moving his armies south to Mergui. From Mergui, G. H. Luce believes that the Burmese forces crossed the Kra.[23] Burmese military success in this direction may be reflected in a request by King Vijayabāhu I (1055-1110) of Ceylon for aid against the Cōḷas, to which the Burmese king ("the king of Rāmañña") responded with "peninsular products," which Luce believes were used to pay Vijayabāhu's soldiers.[24] As interpreted by Luce, the Cōḷas did not look favorably upon this show of support. In 1067, they launched an expedition agains "Kaḍāram" (Takuapa), in "aid of its ruler" who had been forced to flee his country and had sought Cōḷa assistance: "Having conquered (the country of) Kadaram, (he) was pleased to give it (back) to (its) king who worshipped (his) feet (which bore) ankle rings."[25] Cōḷa administrative problems in Ceylon made this intervention short; by 1069-1070, South Indian control over Ceylon had been eliminated. The Cūlavaṃsa, the Ceylonese Buddhist chronicle, records that in 1070, after Vijayabāhu I had gained control over Ceylon, many costly treasures were sent to the Pagan king[26]; then in 1075, Buddhist priests from Burma were invited to Ceylon to purify the Order.[27]

Takuapa's position as the dominant port on the peninsula seems to have been dealt a death blow by this second Cōḷa raid. As reported by Lamb, the archeological evidence from the Takuapa area terminated in the second half of the eleventh century, a period corresponding to this raid.[28] It is significant that the Cōḷa inscription recording the 1067 raid states that "Kaḍāram" was the object of this attack. South Indian inscriptions from the early eleventh century were consistent in their reference to the King of Srivijaya as the ruler of Kaḍāram, the Malay Peninsula's trade entrepot,

calling him the K̲i̲ḍ̲ārattaraiyaṇ.[29] Thus George Coedès
interpreted the Perumbur inscription as a reference to a
revolt by Kaḍāram against Srivijaya's control in which the Cōḷa
ruler was called upon to put down this revolt and restore
Srivijaya's sovereignty.[30] In making such an interpretation,
Coedès ignored the possibility of a Burmese presence on the
Kra.

We have speculated that the 1025 Cōḷa raid resulted in a
loosening of Straits commerce, with new ports developing as
alternative entrepots to Srivijaya/Palembang. By the late
eleventh century the northern Sumatra coast was on its way to
being an important commercial center. The Kedah coast was
more strategically located to participate in this new pattern of
Malacca Straits commerce; there are even architectural
similarities between Kedah and northern Sumatra temples
constructed in this period, suggesting a direct contact between
the two coasts.[31] A Burmese military presence at Takuapa,
followed by the second Cōḷa raid may well have reinforced
Kedah's attractiveness--Takuapa was no longer a port which
could offer security to foreign merchants. Archeological
remains at Takuapa and Kedah support such a shift, with
evidence at Takuapa ceasing and that of Kedah showing a
dramatic increase during the second half of the eleventh
century. One could suggest that the port elites of Takuapa
transferred their operations to the new "preferred port" at
Kedah, which may help to explain the Arab geographers'
continued use of "Kalah" to identify their Malay coastal
entrepot. Similarly, even after Palembang had been replaced
by Jambi as the capital of the Srivijaya maritime state, the
name "Srivijaya" still identified the ports of the southeastern
Sumatra coast.[32] It is perhaps significant that in 1070 the
eastern Kra port of Tambralinga presented its first tribute to
the Chinese court since 1016.[33] This mission may be seen as
a response to the events of 1067: while the Cōḷa raid against
Takuapa and the shift of "Kalah" to the Kedah coast established
a new pattern on the west coast, Tambralinga's mission was
sent to reassure the Chinese that its east coast status was
unchanged.[34]

After the 1067 Cōla raid, the Burmese moved to insure
their external trade connections. The importance of

communication networks linking Burma with northern India was recognized by Kyanzittha (1077-1112) in his restoration of the Bodhgāyā shrine in Bengal. [35] An inscription from Bodhgāyā (1105/1106) recorded that ships laden with large quantities of jewels had been sent by the Burmese ruler to finance the restoration and the endowment of the Buddhist monument. [36] The fact that this mission was sent by sea is indicative of Pagan's new status as a participant in the regional trade of the Bay of Bengal. An inscription from Pagan records another mission which Kyanzittha sent to either South India or Ceylon:

> Then the king wrote of the grace of the Buddharathna, Dhammaratna, and Sangharatna (upon a leaf of gold with vermillon ink). The king sent it to the Chōli prince. The Chōli prince with all his array, hearing of the grace of the Buddha, the Law and the Church, from King Srī Tribhuwanādityadhammarāja's mission....he cast off his adherence to fake doctrines, and he adhered straight away to the true doctrine....[37]

Although stated in religious language, there are strong economic implications to such a mission. As Janice Stargardt has suggested, "campaigns which were clearly military in character, and probably economic in purpose, were recorded as religious missions."[38] Military campaigns became "quests for relics." By triumphantly carrying back relics and sacred treasures the expenses of campaigns whose "benefits might remain obscure to the people of the kingdom" were justified.

A network of Buddhist religious diplomacy actually pre-dated Kyanzittha's efforts. Srivijaya rulers had endowed vihāras at Nālandā in Bengal during the tenth century and at Nāgapaṭṭinam on the Coromandel coast in the early eleventh century.[39] In 1090, the Cōḷa king Kulōttuṅga I (1070-1122) renewed an endowment of village revenues to the Nāgapaṭṭinam vihāra. [40] In this inscription certain people who were occupying the previously granted lands were evicted, suggesting that the earlier (1006) grant had been ignored for some time. It is apparent that in 1090, Kulōttuṅga saw some benefit in restoring the original grant. It may be significant that by the early twelfth century the Nāgapaṭṭinam vihāra had come under the control of the Theravāda school of Buddhism, [41] the same school that was soon to become dominant in Burma. Since Kyanzittha's inscription indicates that Pagan was actively seeking a trade alliance with either South India or Ceylon in this same period, it is conceivable that the "Chōli prince" who received his mission may have been Kulōttuṅga himself. In this case the restoration of the earlier grant, the conversion of the vihāra to Theravāda Buddhism, and Kyanzittha's claim to have converted the "Chōli prince" may all be connected.

The last line of the Shwesandaw inscription quoted above includes the statement that the Chōli prince showed his gratitude by presenting to Kyanzittha "a virgin daughter of his, full of beauty," together with other presents. [42] Kulōttuṅga's pattern of beneficent diplomacy is also recorded in Chinese sources. A stone tablet inscription dated 1079, which was discovered in a Taoist monastery temple in Canton, states that the Cōḷa king ("Ti Hua Ka Lo"), also known as the "Lord of the land of San Fo Tsi" (i.e., Srivijaya), was the temple's benefactor. Kulōttuṅga's gift totaled 600,000 gold cash--a sizeable sum--which drew the praise of the Chinese court and bestowal of the title "Great General Who Supports Obedience and Cherishes Renovations."[43] While clothed in religious garb, it is difficult to resist the conclusion that the diplomatic efforts of both Kulōttuṅga Cōḷa and Kyanzittha were economic in motive. Closer economic ties by sea to South India and Ceylon would have provided new economic potential for Pagan, and, as Kyanzittha's inscription indicates, royal patronage was granted to efforts to open such new channels of communication.

Using these records to reconstruct the history of the late eleventh century, it appears that, as Burma came to dominate the Takuapa region and as "Kalah" shifted to the Kedah coast, the Burmese empire became a focal point of regional commerce. In this case, South Indian merchants who were formerly active at Takuapa may have moved their activities either south to Kedah or north to the regional commercial centers of the Burma coast. In the process, the old focus of international trade achieved by Srivijaya along the Straits of Malacca was shattered even more. Java and the northern Sumatra ports drew the major international route south and west, the Burmese drew the regional route of the Bay

of Bengal north, and the Isthmus came to exist essentially as a
transition area to the mainland states.

The Twelfth Century

In the following decades, the upper peninsula became the
the center of a multi-partite interaction among the Singhalese,
the Burmese, and the Khmers as the regional route developed.
Based on his study of Buddhist votive tablets and other
evidence, G. H. Luce believed that Pagan controlled the Kra
from 1060 until roughly 1200.[44] Examining the Ligor
Chronicles of Nakhon Si Thammarat together with additional
evidence, David Wyatt has revised Luce's dating, suggesting
that, from 1130 to 1176, Tambralinga was under Singhalese
hegemony.[45] To support his position, Wyatt cites Pali
literature from Ceylon which regarded Tambralinga
("Tamalingāmu") as an important twelfth century center of
Buddhist scholarship.[45] Indeed, a Polonnaruva inscription
from the reign of the Singhalese king Vikkamabāhu I
(1111-1132) may even record the "conversion" of Tambralinga
to the Mahāvihāra Theravāda school.[47] It describes a great
dignitary (thera) of the Ceylon saṅgha named Ānanda as being
instrumental in purifying the Order in that land.[48] In the Ligor
Chronicle story, the prince and princess of Tambralinga fled to
Ceylon after an invasion of their land. After a period of
exile, the king of Ceylon assisted them in their return home--
an event which Wyatt believes took place around 1130--
imposing his sovereignty on the new rulers in the process.
About 1176, King Narapati (Narapatisithu of Pagan, 1174-1211)
of Pegu (Hansavati) made an expedition into the Kra and
apparently established Pagan's control over the Tambralinga
area "with the permission of the King of Ceylon."[49]

Although the furthest extent of archeological evidence
documenting Pagan's control over the peninsula has been found
only at Mergui, the Pagan king Cañsū II (Narapatisithu) claimed
control over peninsula ports at Tavoy (a town near Mergui),
Tenasserim, Takuapa, and Phuket--all on the west coast.[50]
Burma's twelfth century influence on the upper peninsula is
substantiated by the Cūlavamsa.[51] When in the 1160's the
Burmese refused (or monopolized) the trade in elephants and

blocked the way across the peninsula to Angkor, the Singhalese responded with a retaliatory raid. In this account, five ships from Ceylon arrived at the port of "Kusumīya" (Bassein) in Rāmañña (lower Burma) led by a certain Nagaragiri Kitti. Further, a ship commanded by a goverment treasurer reached Papphala, the Mon port mentioned in the Tanjore inscription, where Singhalese troops fought their way into the country's interior to the city of Ukkama and killed the monarch of Rāmañña. This brought the kingdom under Ceylon's influence. The people of Rāmañña granted certain concessions to the Singhalese and envoys were sent to the community of monks on the island with the result that the Theravāda monks interceded with Ceylon's king on behalf of the Burmese.[52]

Since only six ships reached Burma, this could not have been the record of a large scale war but rather of a successful naval raid against lower Burma. Such a plunder expedition was similar to those undertaken by the Cōḷas in the eleventh century, with additional emphasis given to gaining trade concessions. It is unlikely that the raid penetrated to Pagan and killed the Burmese king. Gordon Luce has attempted to show that the death of king Alaungsitthu (1113-1165?) coincided with this raid, representing as he does the 1160's as a period of general disorder in Burmese history. However, recently published inscriptions indicate that Alaungsitthu ruled until 1169, four years after the date of the Singhalese raid.[53] Rather than a period of disorder, Pagan epigraphy reflects the 1160's as a time of great prosperity, with normal state affairs continuing vigorously. However, Burmese chronicles record that during Alaungsitthu's reign the lower Burma provinces were in a state of "anarchy" and "rebellion," suggesting that a local governor had become quite powerful and may well have attempted to assert his independence from Pagan. "Ukkama," the residence of the "king" killed by the Singhalese, has been identified as a commercial and administrative center of lower Burma--possibly Martaban, a later capital of the area--where a local governor could well have been put to death by the raiders.[54] Lower Burma governors derived considerable income from trade revenues generated by the regional commercial networks. Such an obstruction of commerce may actually have represented an attempt to establish independent control over this lucrative trade. It is notable that one of the attack ships was led by a Singhalese treasurer, an individual who would have had a great interest in increasing trade revenues. Herein we can see the raid of the Singhalese on lower Burma as the high point of the twelfth century competition for control of the Isthmus, and it is probably best explained in terms of an interruption and difficulties concerning the patterns of trade and communication in this area.

Epigraphic evidence from Ceylon supports such an economic interpretation of the raid. An inscription from the twelfth year of the Singhalese king Parākramabāhu I (1165) records a land grant to a certain Kit Nuvaragal (Kitti Nagaragiri) as a reward for carrying out a successful expedition against "Aramaṇa" (Rāmañña).[55] The expedition had been sent against "Kusumiya" (Bassein), which had been sacked. When the people of Aramaṇa sent envoys to conclude a treaty, Parākramabāhu granted favors to Kitti Nagaragiri--for forcing the envoys to be sent and not for a great military achievement. At the death of Parākramabāhu in 1186, his successor Vijayabāhu I concluded a final treaty of peace with Burma,[56] and through the remainder of the twelfth century the way to Cambodia remained open.

While the twelfth century relationship of Ceylon and Burma is relatively clear, that between Ceylon and Angkor is not. As indicated in the Cūlavaṃsa, the major reason for the 1160's conflict between Ceylon and Burma was Ceylon's concern that Burma was preventing free access to the communciation channels between Ceylon and Cambodia. This explanation is probably indicative of the peninsula's relationship to Angkor as well. The upper peninsula was significant as the intermediary between Ceylon and Angkor such that it was more important as a source of economic and cultural contact than as an area to be dominated politically. As a result Ceylon was willing to risk a war with Burma to preserve the peninsula's neutrality.

Further evidence of contact between Ceylon and Angkor is provided in two twelfth century inscriptions from Ceylon. One inscription from late in the century specifically states that friendly relations with Cambodia were maintained.[57] In the second inscription, one of the city gates at Polonnaruva was

called "Kamboja-vāsala," suggesting a possible Cambodian
settlement in the city. [58] Of particular interest is the
Cūlavamsa's reference to the interception of a Singhalese
princess en route to "Kamboja" by the Burmese, a story which
is presented as one of the events leading to the 1160's war. [59]
Such a marriage alliance between the Singhalese and the Khmer
is suggestive that such alliances were a common tool of the
Singhalese royal house. The cross-cousin marriage patterns
of the Singhalese royalty favored continuing relationships, and
to form such an alliance with Cambodia would have provided
long range benefits. [60]

Thus, as in the eleventh century, the northern peninsula
seems to have played an important role in such communication
between Cambodia and the west. From the other direction,
Chinese authors of the Sung period saw the upper east coast of
the peninsula as being within the Cambodian sphere of
influence, and one of them believed that its markets produced
some of the best incense available:

> Beyond the seas the Teng-liu-mei gharuwood ranks
> next to that of Hainan [where the price of incense had
> become too high] . It is first-rate. Its trees are a
> thousand years old....It is something belonging to
> the immortals. Light one stick and the whole house
> is filled with a fragrant mist which is still there
> after three days. It is priceless and rarely to be
> seen in this world. Many of the families of the
> officials in Kuangtung and Kuangsi and families of
> the great ones use it. [61]

The relationship of Angkor to the peninsula may perhaps
be seen in terms of the relationship between it and Tambralinga
on the east coast of the Isthmus. The last recorded embassy of
the latter to the Chinese court had been that of 1070, while
Cambodia was sending embassies in 1116, 1120, 1128/29, and
1131. [62] This suggests either of two interpretations: a) that
the Khmer came to dominate the upper coast between 1070 and
1130, such that they sent embassies and Tambralinga did not;
or b) that with Cambodia's internal political problems in the
late eleventh and early twelfth centuries Tambralinga became a
neutral port. In the twelfth century Chinese merchants were

dealing directly with the sources of supply on the peninsula, Sumatra, and Java, eliminating the earlier Chinese need for a dominant port of the Srivijaya type. Tambralinga, as a recognized source of forest products, would not have needed to advertise these products by sending embassies to the Chinese court. This differed from the case of the Chen-la (Cambodian) state of Lo-hu (Lavo) which sent elephants as a present in 1155 to the Chinese court in search of recognition.[63] If, as O. W. Wolters believes, Southeast Asian states sent embassies to China mainly in times of stress as in the case of Lo-hu, then the Khmer, who were more concerned with pressuring Vietnam and Champa in the east during the first half of the twelfth century, needed to undertake missions to reassure the Chinese that the disorders would not interrupt the flow of southern commerce.

Both Khmer and Chinese participated in the twelfth century China/Cambodia exchange network. Sūryavarman II (1113-1150) is said to have been personally involved in trade relations with China and to have possessed his own fleet.[64] The Sung hui yao kao contains references to Chinese trading vessels visiting Cambodia with cargoes of silk goods and porcelain.[65] In 1147, "specific favors" were conferred upon Cambodia by the Chinese.[66] Sung procelain has been excavated at Angkor, but there is a noticeable gap in the epigraphic evidence of any commercial relationship until the reign of Jayavarman VII (1181-1218) when the inscriptions of Ta Prohm (1186) and Prah Khan (1191) make reference to Chinese articles.[67] In addition, an inscription from the Phimānākas at Angkor mentions a flag made of colored Chinese silk.[68] The Prah Khan inscription also includes a reference to localities in the northern access zone to the peninsula, including Ratburi and Petburi, but there is no record of any specific relationship between Angkor and the Kra.[69] Using Cham inscriptions, E. Aymonier recorded an undocumented reference to a campaign by Jayavarman VII on the peninsula in 1195, which may indicate an attempt to restore a formal Khmer relationship.[70]

On the other hand, archeological remains suggest a cultural and economic tie between the Kra and Cambodia rather than direct Khmer political presence. Earlier historians used the Khmer inscription of the Grahi Buddha near Chaiya, which they dated to 1185, [71] as proof of Cambodia's administrative control over the upper peninsula, but since J. G. deCasparis depicted the inscription as a product of the last decades of the thirteenth century, [72] many historians quickly dropped this conclusion. However, when recently working on an eleventh century inscription from Pimai (1041), Hall's attention was drawn to the presence of an animal dating cycle typical of later Thai rather than Khmer practice. [73] It has been suggested that this may be early evidence of Thai speaking peoples who were administratively incorporated into the Khmer government of Sūryavarman I. [74] Significantly, this same animal cycle is used in the Grahi Buddha inscription. DeCasparis argued that this reference to the Thai animal cycle forced one to assign a date to the Grahi Buddha later than 1183. We would postulate, however, that, based on the Pimai inscription's earlier use of this animal cycle and on evidence of a communication network connecting Pimai and Lopburi in the eleventh century, it is indeed possible that Thai speaking peoples had reached the lower Chao Phraya valley and the peninsula by the late twelfth century and had taken their place within the mixed cultural configuration of that area with its international commercial routes and communications. [75] This may allow us to reestablish a late twelfth century date for this inscription and to show a definite Khmer cultural presence in this key area at that time.

Clay Buddhist votive tablets scattered between the Bay of Bandon and Nakhon Si Thammarat may provide further evidence of communication between the Kra and Angkor. These twelfth century tablets have been linked to the multiple figures of Angkor Thom, departing from earlier Mahāyāna style tablets of the eleventh century, and appear to have had more affinity to Theravāda Buddhism. [76] Thus, a common Theravāda Buddhist religious interest, as with Mahāyāna in the earlier centuries, would have encouraged regular communication among Pagan, Ceylon, and Cambodia. The Cūlavaṃsa records such twelfth century religious interaction between Pagan and Ceylon. By the the mid-twelfth century, Tambralinga had also become a center of the Theravāda Buddhist school. Legend records that Pagan was converted to the Singhalese Theravāda school at the end of the twelfth century when five monks returned to Burma from a pilgrimage to Ceylon and built the Chapata temple under the patronage of king Narapatisithu. One of these monks was said to have been the son of a Khmer king, probably Jayavarman VII. [77] Indeed, art historians believe that Preah Palilay at the Bayon, constructed during Jayavarman VII's reign, exhibits a Theravāda Buddhist style which may well have been introduced from Burma via the Menam valley. [78]

We have suggested that Burma and the upper peninsula lay on a more regional route of communication across the Bay of Bengal connecting Ceylon to Pagan and Angkor. While Luce and Wyatt postulate that the Isthmus was politically dominated by one or another of these powers at various times in the century, we have presented evidence that Burma, Cambodia, and Ceylon each had a real interest in the peninsula, but that this interest was probably more of a commercial nature, making making attempts to dominate the peninsula politically both unnecessary and perhaps undesirable. As we have stated, the raid of the Singhalese on lower Burma in the 1160's can best be explained in terms of an interruption and difficulties concerning the pattern of trade and communication in the area. The Burmese had come to dominate this trade and had blocked the way across the peninsula to Angkor, thereby bringing the retaliatory raid from Ceylon. Through the end of the twelfth century the way was reopened and rapidly became a path for the spread of Theravāda Buddhism to the western and central sections of the Southeast Asian mainland, establishing a cultural relationship of great significance for later centuries.

Thus, the upper Malay peninsula receded from the patterns of power and trade in the island world and was drawn into those of the mainland. In addition, where previously it had been the mode of outside contact with the islands and the international currents for the Mons of Rāmaññadesa and Dvāravatī in Burma and Thailand, now the Isthmus provided a more regional contact for the greater empires of Pagan and Angkor and, through their territories, to the northern mountain areas where the stirrings of the Thai-speaking peoples were becoming ever more important.

To understand the economic and cultural significance of the upper peninsula, let us put it in perspective by examining the other major trade routes of Southeast Asia in the early thirteenth century and the goods that flowed along them.

Southeast Asian Trade, c. 1200

By the end of the twelfth century, a major diffusion had taken place in the international route as it went through Southeast Asia. No longer was its chief focus on Srivijaya and the latter's control of the Straits of Malacca. The wars with the Javanese and the Cōḷas had opened up the Java Sea area to direct commercial contact and had left the straits region in a situation that would remain, until the fifteenth century and the rise of Malacca, a vague vacuum of commercial control. In 1178, Cho Ch'u-fei could write, in his Ling Wai Tai Ta:

> Of all the wealthy foreign lands which have great
> store of precious and varied goods, none surpasses
> the realm of Ta-shih (Arabs). Next to them comes
> She-p'o (Java), while San-fo-chi (Srivijaya) is third;
> many others come in the next rank. [79]

Indeed, the flow of trade moved toward the developing ports of east Java and the spices they offered. The route taken was apparently, from the west, along both coasts of Sumatra and, from the east, across the South China Sea and around the west coast of Borneo. Thus, the main thrust of international commerce moved away from the Isthmus directly toward the produce of Sumatra and the riches of Java.

On the mainland, only the east coast seems to have been involved, through a subsidiary route, with the international path. This secondary route was one of two which, besides the central route, connected Canton and the new ports of the southeastern coast of China, Fu-chou and Ch'uan-chou, to different parts of Southeast Asia. It appears to have gone by way of Champa down to Fo-lo-an (Kuala Berang in Trengganu) on the east coast of the Malay Peninsula[80] and on to the ports of of east Java. The other subsidiary route seems to have developed contemporaneously with the new China ports in the ninth and tenth centuries and extended along the coasts of the Philippine Islands. [81]

Paul Wheatley's work on the location and type of commodities involved in the Sung maritime trade demonstrates the above pattern from the Chinese point of view, both in terms of those areas which they knew and those which they did not know. His initial map[82] reconstructs the world as known to Chao Ju-kua, Superintendant of Maritime Trade at Ch'uan-chou and author of the Chu-fan-chih, a 1225 work on maritime trading patterns which must have derived much of its information directly from the seamen and traders themselves.[83] This map divides Southeast Asia into an Upper Shore (Shang An) involving the mainland and the peninsula, a region with which the Chinese had had contact in prior centuries, and a Lower Shore (Hsia An), covering Sumatra and the Java Sea, whose trading network had been controlled by Srivijaya. On the former were Champa, Cambodia, and the east coast of the peninsula; the latter included the old favored coast of southern Sumatra, the ports of Java, and the south coast of Borneo. Two areas are conspicuously missing from this Chinese view in any geographical detail, the hinterland of the Isthmus (including the expansion to the west of the Angkorian empire and to the south of the empire of Pagan) and the eastern islands beyond the Java Sea (Sulawesi and the Moluccas).

Yet where the latter, merely referred to en masse as the Ocean Islands (Hai Tao), were concerned, the Chinese still possessed an idea of the types of goods which the area produced and which it took in exchange. The Chinese record shows that this area, known later to Westerners as the Spice Islands, sent cloves, nutmegs, lakawood, and tortoise shell to the international route via Java and Sumatra in exchange for such goods as fermented liquor, porcelain, silk, and coarse salt.[84] Regarding the central and western mainland, on the other hand, the Chinese record leaves no such indication of goods produced or exchanged. Cambodia probably took some of the goods from the area of present-day Thailand and put them into the international trade along the east coast, but, as yet, archaeological work has shown little evidence of Chinese goods in central Thailand from this time and the Chinese mention nothing of any such occurrence. Whereas the Nakhon Si Thammarat area of Tambralinga is well described by Chao Ju-kua, the upper peninsula, known to the Chinese as

Teng-liu-mei, received only a confused description in Chao's work, [85] and the Chinese knowledge of Pagan was gained from the land route via Nanchao rather than by the sea route. [86] Indeed, the only product noted in the Chinese works which Wheatley can specifically trace back to this hinterland area is lead, a product seen by Chao as an export from India, but which undoubtedly was mined in the Shan Hills of northeastern Burma. [87] It would thus appear that this area north of the Isthmus was only linked in an indirect way to the main international trade route known to the Chinese and hence existed outside the realm of Chinese observation.

While one point of contact between the hinterland area and the international route was perhaps the east coast of the peninsula and its ports of Tambralinga and Kuala Berang, a more important point was probably the Ceylon/Coromandel area across the Bay of Bengal. Evidence of such commercial contact is provided in a thirteenth century Pagan inscription which notes that a native of the Malabar coast made a donation to a nānādēśī temple at Pagan. [88] The nānādēśī was one of several organizations of South Indian itinerant merchants in existence during the Cōḷa period whose activities also took them to the northern Sumatra coast in the late eleventh century. [89] A similar group is associated with the Takuapa Viṣṇu temple which has been dated to the ninth century. [90] The thirteenth century Pagan inscription indicates that the merchants' temple had been present there for some time; the recorded gift provided for the construction of a new maṇḍapa for the temple compound, which was also dedicated to Viṣṇu. Further evidence of a continuing economic relationship between Pagan and South India is reflected in Chou Ch'u-fei's note of 1178 on the Cōḷas: "Some say that one can go there by way of the kingdom of P'u-kan."[91]

The pattern of trade that followed these various routes, both international and regional, through Southeast Asia was essentially a luxury trade, though increasingly bulk items, such as ceramics, were becoming a part of the commerce. [92] As Wheatley has shown us, a Chinese trade inventory of 1141 listed 339 important items which can roughly be broken down into four general groups: aromatics and drugs, textiles, metal goods and minerals, and miscellaneous products. [93] The first group, that of aromatics and drugs, had been the most important through the T'ang period[94] and remained so under the Sung with at least forty different types, many of which derived from Southeast Asia. As noted above, nutmegs and cloves came from the Moluccas to join pepper and sandalwood in Java where they were injected into the international route itself.[95] A variety of forest products, such as camphor and sapanwood, came out of the hills in other locations through the islands (and on the eastern mainland)[96] and entered the international route by various ways, particularly as the north coast ports of Sumatra began to deal directly with the foreign traders. Just as impressive a list of products, including frankincense, myrrh, and indigo, flowed through Southeast Asia from various areas in the Middle East and India.[97] Rhinoceros horn, that famed panacea, was supplied by many different tropical regions, with the longest type coming from the black rhino of east Africa.[98]

The international trade through the first millenium A.D. was based on such goods as the above aromatics and drugs, together with other exotic forest and ocean products as kingfisher and peacock feathers, pearls and talking parrots, coral and ivory from both Southeast Asia and further west.[99] Yet, through Sung times and the growth and diffusion of trade routes within Southeast Asia, other relatively more practical and more bulky goods had become almost as important along the trade route. Textiles stood very high on the list, as they would in the centuries to come. While the luxurious silk continued as it had under the T'ang to play a major role in the exchange for the forest products of Southeast Asia,[100] cotton textiles, particularly from India, appear to have become a major part of the international system. These piece goods came mainly from the Coromandel and Malabar coasts of South India, but they also originated in northern India and the Middle East, with a variety of cruder local products being exported from various locations in Southeast Asia as Champa, Java, and the northern Philippines.[101] These centuries also saw the trade in porcelain grow much greater and penetrate Southeast Asia (and beyond, all the way to the African coast) much more deeply than had hitherto been the case. Fine Sung wares have been found, as can be seen throughout the Philippine Islands, in forms hardly less exquisite than those in China itself.[102]

Indeed, at the site of Santubong in present day Sarawak, a port which appears to have flourished greatly in the twelfth and thirteenth centuries, we see, to quote the archaeologist Cheng Te-K'un, "practically all the known ceramics of the T'ang and Sung periods." Products of all the major Chinese kilns have been found there.[103]

Beyond the trade for textiles and ceramics, the Southeast Asians sought a variety of practical objects, such as metal mirrors and scales,[104] yet the trade deficit was China's. For all the rich goods she produced, China still did not have enough to offer Southeast Asia and the other areas in exchange for the drugs and aromatics[105]; the gap was made up by a flow of metals, mostly copper cash, and was to a great extent illegal. Certainly Sung coins, like porcelain, have been found throughout Southeast Asia and all the way to Africa. During the twelfth and thirteenth centuries, prohibitions were constantly being promulgated by the Sung court against this flow, though with little effect.[106] The result was a great strain on the supply of metals within China, and ultimately the Sung dynasty had to use iron in its coinage. Thus the flourishing semi-industrial port of Santubong in Sarawak may have been a source of iron and even steel for Ch'uan-chou, the center of the iron industry during the Southern Sung as well as being one of its major ports.[107]

As noted, the hinterland of the Isthmus appears to have been linked only indirectly to the world trade routes of the early thirteenth century. Little evidence of Chinese porcelains and coins has yet been found in this area, and in their brief descriptions of "Teng-liu-mei" and Pagan the Chinese authors made no mention of any goods sought by the people of these two regions, though they did note that the products of the former were superb gharuwood, cardamoms, bee's wax, and lac.[108] Let us look at the products traded in this area approximately 250 years later in order to determine the commercial potential that existed there. Out of the hinterland came silver and lead, rubies and sapphires, benzoin and lac, besides the teak junks, supplies of rice, and other foodstuffs, in exchange for china, cloth, quicksilver, copper, vermilion, spices, pepper, and opium.[109] Earlier, lac of course had come from Teng-liu-mei, but of the other principal products only the barest of hints exist for trade in gems and lead[110] and, if commerce took place in either silver or benzoin from this area, the trade was well disguised by the Arab, Indian, or Malay merchants who acted as middle men.[111] It would thus appear that the regional trade which involved the hinterland of the Isthmus was rapidly absorbed into the economy of its partners, such that it was shielded from the eyes of the Chinese who have provided us with the above descriptions.

The period we are examining here stood midway in the development of the international trade route. Before it the trade had been essentially limited to luxury goods and was handled by Arab and Malay traders and shippers. The route itself within Southeast Asia had had a relatively narrow focus through the Straits of Malacca and the sea empire of Srivijaya. Then, during these centuries and after, the amount of trade (increasingly in bulk goods), the number and types of traders and shippers, and, through Southeast Asia, the areas directly and indirectly involved in the trade all become much greater than before. Hidden from our eyes though it is, the hinterland of the Isthmus must also have been brought more deeply into this growing international trade, where in earlier centuries it had existed merely on local coastal routes to Bengal and Tongking. Now the Chinese and, especially for this area, the Indians had begun to take a part in the trade itself rather than sitting and waiting for the goods to be delivered, just as the Europeans would do some three centuries later, and, like the European ships, those of China and South India took advantage of a diffuse trading situation, partly created by them, to gain more direct access to the goods they were seeking.

For Southeast Asia, the significance of these trade patterns lay not only in the greater penetration of the trade throughout its extent, but also in the interesting correlation that exists between the differing trade routes on the one hand and on the other the belief systems that were to develop in the following centuries. The Neo-Confucianism of Vietnam came from nearby China. Islam may also have come out of China, going along the eastern coastal route to Champa, Trengganu, and eastern Java[112] on the one hand and following the trade link south to the Philippines[113] on the other. In general, however, Islam followed the major international route from the west around Sumatra (perhaps both the east and west coasts) to Java and thence deeper into the island world. [114] As we have noted, the upper Isthmus and its hinterland lay on a more local route linked to South India and Ceylon, whence came Theravāda Buddhism to the Isthmus, Burma, Thailand, Cambodia, and Laos. For the different parts of Southeast Asia, a new age was moving along the sea routes of international commerce. Increasingly, in these and later centuries, Southeast Asia was being opened up, not only to the commercial possibilities and material goods of the international route, but also to the new modes of thought as the classical patterns of the Southeast Asian states were changing.

NOTES

1. Portions of this essay were originally presented by
   Whitmore in "Trade and Communications in Southeast Asia"
   on the panel, "Links East and West: Medieval Asian
   Maritime Trade, 10th-12th Centuries," at the Annual
   Meeting of the American Historical Association (New
   Orleans, 1972); and Hall in "Changing Commercial Patterns
   on the Malay Peninsula, 1000-1100 A.D.," D. C. Sircar
   Felicitation Volume (Mysore, India, 1975).

2. O. W. Wolters, "China Irredenta: The South," The World
   Today, 19, 12 (1963), pp. 540-552; for a more recent
   statement of this concept, see O. W. Wolters, The Fall
   of Srivijaya in Malay History (Ithaca, New York, 1971),
   pp. 20-22.

3. O. W. Wolters, Early Indonesian Commerce, A Study of
   the Origins of Srivijaya (Ithaca, New York, 1967), and
   Wolters, Fall of Srivijaya, op. cit.

4. Wolters, Early Indonesian Commerce, op. cit.

5. Ibid., chs. 2 and 5.

6. Wolters, Fall of Srivijaya, op. cit., ch. 2.

7. Ibid., p. 42; E. H. Schafer, The Empire of Min (Rutland,
   Vermont, 1954), pp. 75-78; and Wang Gangwu, "Early Ming
   Relations with Southeast Asia" in J. K. Fairbank, ed., The
   Chinese World Order (Cambridge, Massachusetts, 1968),
   pp. 47, 296, n. 27.

8. This activity is documented in several South Indian Tamil
   inscriptions which record the religious donations of the
   Srivijaya monarchs. See Annual Report on Indian Epigraphy
   (henceforth ARE) (1956-57), nos. 161, 164, 166; and
   Epigraphia Indica (henceforth EI), 22, pp. 213-281.

9. Wolters, Fall of Srivijaya, op. cit., pp. 1, 14; George
   Coedès, The Indianized States of Southeast Asia (Honolulu,
   1968), pp. 130, 142, 144.

10. For an extensive analysis of the 1025 Cōḷa raid see George W. Spencer, "Royal Leadership and Imperial Conquest in Medieval South India: The Naval Expedition of Rajendra Chola I, c. 1025 A.D.," Ph. D. dissertation, University of California (Berkeley), 1967.

11. See Wolters, Fall of Srivijaya, op. cit., pp. 42-48; and F. Hirth and W. W. Rockhill, Chau Ju-kua: His Work on the Chinese and Arab Trade in the Twelfth and Thirteenth Centuries, Entitled Chu-fan-chi (St. Petersburg, 1911), pp. 10-11.

12. An initial survey of surface deposits on the coastal areas of the northeastern Sumatra coast has shown large quantities of Sung ware present, reflecting this area's participation in the eleventh century trade routes. Previous archeological research has virtually ignored Sumatra's west coast, yet Bennet Bronson of the University of Pennsylvania Museum, who did a preliminary survey of potential sites during the summer of 1973, has found a considerable amount of surface material in the Barus area--particularly pot sherds and Sung porcelain which can be dated to the historical period being considered. When properly excavated this material may·well reveal that trade on a comparable level to that of the western Malay and eastern Sumatra coasts was being transacted on the western Sumatra coast as well. Indeed, in 1088, Tamil merchants were active at Lobo Tua near Barus [see K. A. Nilakanta Sastri, "A Tamil Merchant Guild in Sumatra," Tijdschrift voor Indische Taal-, Land-, en Volkenkunde, 72, 2 (1932), pp. 314-327]. Such evidence will no doubt indicate that by the eleventh century the Straits of Malacca was no longer the focal point of the island trade, as alternative routes were available and were being used by the various maritime traders. Hall wishes to thank Dr. Bronson for discussing this information with him.

13. The Malay Peninsula ports attacked by the Cōḷas are named in the Tanjore inscription of 1030. See South Indian Inscriptions, 2, pp. 105-109; this inscription has also been translated into English by K. A. Nilakanta Sastri, History of Srivijaya (Madras, 1949), p. 80.

14. See Kenneth R. Hall, "Khmer Commercial Development and Foreign Contacts under Sūryavarman I," JESHO, 18,3 (1975), pp. 318-336.

15. Past literature has presented Tambralinga as the scene of eleventh century conflict between the Srivijaya maritime empire and the expanding mainland power of the Khmer [see L. P. Briggs, "The Khmer Empire and the Malay Peninsula," Far Eastern Quarterly, 9, 3 (May, 1950), pp. 256-305]. In response to an expansion of the Sung China consumer market in the late tenth century, Tambralinga is believed to have made an attempt to free itself of Srivijaya's dominance. In 1001, a Tambralinga embassy brought a large quantity of sapanwood (an incense) to China in an attempt to impress the Chinese with the quality and quantity of local products [see O. W. Wolters, "Tambralinga," BSOAS, 21 (1958), pp. 587-607]. Embassies were also sent in 1014 and 1016, but in the latter year Tambralinga's hopes for recognition as a "first class" port were frustrated when the Chinese relegated the area to a "second class" status. These embassies have generally been seen as a reassurance to the Chinese in a time of internal disorder related to Khmer politics (see Wolters, loc. cit.).

George Coedès has interpreted the dynastic controversy surrounding Sūryavarman's ascension to the Khmer throne as involving the ruling family of Tambralinga [George Coedès, Inscriptions du Cambodge, v. 7 (Paris, 1964), pp. 164-189]. In translating the Prasat Ben inscription (1008), Coedès suggested that Sūryavarman I had expelled the Malay prince of Tambralinga, Jayaviravarman, from the Khmer capital in 1008 (Coedès had earlier believed that Sūryavarman was a Malay and Jayaviravarman a Khmer). In general, it appears that Khmer expansion and Srivijayan defeat coincided nicely and undoubtedly allowed Cambodian power to make itself felt more strongly in the area.

16. Hall, loc. cit.

17. Stanley J. O'Connor, Hindu Gods of Peninsular Siam (Ascona, 1972), pp. 60-62 and figure 34.

330

18. David Wyatt has told Hall of a Ligor Chronicle reference to
a Tamil inscription from Songkhla dated 983. In this
account, a monk states that he is copying this inscription,
which records an overland route to the west coast. Wyatt
has discussed the sources for Nakhon Si Thammarat's
eleventh century history in David K. Wyatt, trans., The
Crystal Sands, The Chronicles of Nagara Srī Dharrmarāja
(Ithaca, New York, 1975), pp. 45-47, which include what
seems to be an eleventh century Tamil inscription from Vat
Mahādhātu [Recueil des Inscriptions du Siam; deuxième
partie: Inscriptions de Dvāravatī de Çrīvijaya et de Lavo
(Bangkok, 1961), p. 38]. A. Teeuw and D. K. Wyatt, The
Story of Patani (The Hague, 1970), II, p. 263, notes a
Phatthalung chronicle version of the Malay tale "Lady
White-Blood" which apparently indicates such a trans-
peninsular route.

19. Alastair Lamb, "Takuapa: The Probable Site of a Pre-
Malaccan Entrepot in the Malay Peninsula," in John Bastin
and R. Roolvink, eds., Malayan and Indonesian Studies
(Oxford, 1964), pp. 76-86.

20. G. H. Luce, in his article, "A Cambodian (?) Invasion of
Lower Burma--A Comparison of Burmese and Talaing
Chronicles," Journal of the Burma Research Society, 12, 1
(1922), pp. 39-45, speculated that around 1050 there was a
Cambodian invasion of lower Burma to check the Burmese
expansion in the peninsula, but in his more recent work,
Old Burma, Early Pagan (Locust Valley, New York, 1969,
1970), vol. 1, pp. 21-23, 26, he asserts that the Burmese
attacked to stop Mon-Khmer expansion westward.

21. See Milton Osborne, "Notes on Early Cambodian Provincial
History: Isanapura and Sambhupura," FA, 20, 4 (1966),
p. 447.

22. Janice Stargardt, "Burma's Economic and Diplomatic
Relations with India and China From Early Medieval
Sources," JESHO, 14, 1 (1971), pp. 38-62. Michael Aung
Thwin's research indicates that the southern Burma
commercial centers at Bassein (Kusumī) and Tala (a port
near Pegu) became high priority administrative centers

under Pagan rule. Important ministers were allowed "to eat" (cā) a percentage of the revenues (trade revenues?) of these commercial centers. In 1058, Aniruddha erected a statue of Gavaruputi, not only the patron saint of the Mons but also of merchants and seaman, at Pagan after his 1057 sack of Thaton.

23. G. H. Luce, "The Career of Htilaing Min (Kyanzittha), the Unifier of Burma," JRAS (1966), p. 59.

24. G. H. Luce, "Some Old References to the South of Burma and Ceylon," in Felicitation Volumes of Southeast-Asian Studies Presented to His Highness Prince Dhaninivat (Bangkok, 1965), vol. II, p. 270. Luce used the Cūlavaṃsa as his principle source for this article.

25. Perumbur inscription, seventh year of Vīrarājēndra I, South Indian Inscriptions, 3, no. 84; and Charala Plates of Vīrarājēndra, Copper Plate no. 1 of ARE (1937-38), sixth plate, as discussed in EI, 25, pp. 241-266. On the location of Kaḍāram, see n. 29 below.

26. Wilhelm Geiger, trans., Cūlavaṃsa (Colombo, 1953), 58:8-9.

27. Luce, Old Burma, 1, p. 40.

28. Lamb, loc. cit.

29. See the "Larger Leiden Grant," EI, 22, pp. 213-266; and ARE (1956-57), nos. 161, 164, 166. There has been some controversy concerning the location of "Kaḍāram." General agreement places it on the western Malay coast, but many early historians considered the words "Kaḍāram" and "Kedah" and the Arab geographers' reference to "Kalah" to be the same, and therefore placed "Kaḍāram" on the Kedah coast [see K. A. Nilakanta Sastri, The Colas, 2nd edition,(Madras, 1955), pp. 217-218]. Alastair Lamb's archeological research has shown that the Kedah coast could not have been "Kaḍāram" in the South Indian references until the late eleventh century--a period dating later than all the inscriptions with references to "Kaḍāram" [see Alastair

Lamb, "Kedah and Takuapa: Some Tentative Historical
Conclusions," Federated Museums Journal, 6 (1961),
p. 84], and that, based on archeological evidence, Takuapa
had to be the "Kaḍāram" of these epigraphic and literary
references.

30. Coedès, The Indianized States, op. cit., p. 148.

31. Alastair Lamb, who conducted excavations at Kedah in the
late 1950's, suggested that a temple he had excavated at
Candi Bukit Batu Pahat in Kedah was similar in style to
Candi Biaro Si Topajan at Padang Lawas in north central
Sumatra, the center of a historically unidentified, but
seemingly important twelfth century state [see Alastair
Lamb, op. cit., pp. 2-9, 76]. Lamb's view is supported
with new evidence in B. A. V. Peacock, "Pillar Base
Architecture in Ancient Kedah," JMBRAS, 47, 1 (1974),
pp. 66-86.

32. O. W. Wolters, Early Indonesian Commerce, p. 266,
fn. 33; and "A Note on the Capital of Srivijaya During the
Eleventh Century," Artibus Asiae Supplementum 23
(Felicitation Volume Presented to Professor G. H. Luce)
(Ascona, 1966), vol. 1, pp. 225-239.

33. Wolters, "Tambralinga," op. cit., p. 595.

34. O. W. Wolters has seen the Tambralinga mission of 1070,
sent to inform the Chinese of its status as an independent
port, as evidence of the shift of the Srivijaya center to
Jambi. To him Tambralinga's mission symbolized the
decline of Srivijaya's old economic control over the China
trade. See Wolters, " A Note," loc. cit.

35. Shwesandaw Pagoda Inscription, Epigraphia Birmanica
(henceforth EB), I, viii, p. 163.

36. EI, 11 (1911-12), p. 119.

37. EB, I, viii, p. 165, the Shwesandaw Pagoda Inscription.

38. Stargardt, op. cit., p. 52.

39. EI, 22, pp. 213-266.

40. "The Smaller Leiden Grant," ibid., pp. 267-281.

41. S. Paranavitana, "Negapatam and Theravada Buddhism in South India," Journal of the Greater India Society, 11, 1 (January, 1944), pp. 17-25.

42. Luce, Old Burma, op. cit., I, p. 63.

43. Tan Yeok Seong, "The Sri Vijayan Inscription of Canton (A.D. (A.D. 1079)," JSEAH, 5, 2 (1964), pp. 17-24. Tan wrongly follows an earlier interpretation of Indian historians (see R. C. Majumdar, Suvarnadvipa, 1937, pp. 182-190) that Kulōttuṅga had served in a high position in the conquered country of Srivijaya before ascending the Cōḷa throne. Neither this inscription nor other evidence which Hall has examined substantiates this claim. Such interpretations consider the Cōḷas to have exercised considerable control over Srivijaya's government on a continuing basis during the eleventh century. The Chinese themselves were not quite sure of the relationship between the two; some Chinese chronicles represent the Cōḷas as being subordinate to Srivijaya (see a passage from the Sung Shih which is quoted in the Tan article, p. 21).

44. G. H. Luce, "The Early Syam in Burma's History: A Supplement," JSS, 47, 1 (June, 1959), pp. 60-61.

45. David K. Wyatt, "Mainland Powers on the Malay Peninsula," a paper presented to the International Conference on Asian History (Kuala Lumpur, 1968).

46. See S. Paranavitana, Ceylon and Malaysia (Colombo, 1966), p. 80.

47. Epigraphia Zeylanica (henceforth EZ), 4, pp. 66-72, as cited by Wyatt, loc. cit.

48. The inscription also states that this same monk was instrumental in the establishment of the Buddhist religion in the Cōḷa country. See S. Paranavitana, "Negapatam," op. cit., p. 24.

334

49. "Episode of the Tooth Relic," see Wyatt, The Crystal Sands, op. cit., pp. 26-28, 38-39, 42, 59, 66-71, 72-79, and Wyatt, "Mainland Powers," op. cit., pp. 13-14. The dating of Narapatisithu is based on the recent research of Michael Aung Thwin, as cited in n. 53 below.

50. G. H. Luce, "Some Old References," op. cit., p. 276. The "Dhammarajika Inscription" of 1196 A.D. commemorates Narapatisithu's conquest of the south.

51. Cūlavaṃsa, 76:10-75.

52. Ibid., 76:59-75.

53. Burma Archaeological Department, She Haung Myanma Kyauksa Mya, 1 (1972), pp. 33-37; the "Cañsū Maṅ Krī Inscriptions," and the "Mrat Krī Cwā Khai Toṅ Inscription of 1169." Michael Aung Thwin has discussed these inscriptions and other evidence relating to the Singhalese raid in his article, "The Problem of Ceylonese-Burmese Relations in the 12th Century and the Question of an Interregnum in Pagan: 1165-1174 A.D.," JSS (forthcoming).

54. Sirima Wickremasinghe, "Ceylon's Relations with South-east Asia, with Special Reference to Burma," Ceylon Journal of Historical and Social Studies, 3, 1 (1960), p. 48. See also C. E. Godakumbura, "Relations between Burma and Ceylon," JBRS, 49, 2(1966), pp. 145-162.

55. EZ, 3, no. 34, p. 321.

56. Cūlavaṃsa, 80:6-8.

57. EZ, 2, no. 17.

58. EZ, 2, p. 74.

59. Cūlavaṃsa, 76:35.

60. Thomas R. Trautmann, "Consanguineous Marriage in Pali Literature," JAOS, 93, 2 (1973), pp. 158-180.

61. Wolters, "Tambralinga," op. cit., p. 600, translated from the <u>Ling</u> <u>wai</u> <u>tai</u> <u>ta</u> (1178).

62. Ibid., p. 605.

63. Wolters has argued that this may represent a temporary independence of the Chao Phraya valley from Khmer control. Wolters, loc. cit.

64. Ibid., p. 598, n. 5. Possible Khmer ports have yet to be discovered. This fleet may well have been confined to river transport on the Mekong and the other major rivers of the Khmer domain. In the eleventh century one of the major commercial routes to China seems to have gone north on the Mekong to a point near the Ha-trai pass, where goods passed to Nghe-an on the Vietnamese coast. Nghe-an in turn had contact with commercial developments of the Red River Delta and the Vietnamese capital at Thang-long. That this would seem to have been the case comes from the 1128 Khmer attacks on Viet Nam which followed this route. One of these attacks is even noted as involving over seven hundred boats, which may be an indication of the extent of travel involved in the upstream area on the Vietnamese side [<u>Dai</u> <u>Viet</u> <u>Su</u> <u>Ky</u> <u>Toan</u> <u>Thu</u> (Hanoi, 1967), I, pp. 263, 347].

65. Ibid., p. 606, n. 5.

66. Ibid., p. 605.

67. Ibid., p. 598.

68. IC, 2, p. 178.

69. George Coedés, "La stele de Prah Khan d'Angkor," BEFEO, 41 (1941), pp. 255-301.

70. E. Aymonier, <u>Le Cambodge</u>, iii (Paris, 1904), p. 528.

71. See Pierre Dupont, "Le Buddha de Grahi et l'ecole de C'aiya," BEFEO, 42 (1942), pp. 105-113.

72. J. G. deCasparis, "The Date of the Grahi Buddha," JSS, 55, 1 (1967), pp. 31-40.

73. IC, 7, pp. 124-126.

74. Hall wishes to thank Hiram W. Woodward, Jr., Assistant Professor in the History of Art at the University of Michigan, for calling his attention to this inscription's use of the twelve year animal cycle and its implications.

75. In a recent article Michael Vickery establishes that the language of the Grahi Buddha is not linguistically Thai [Michael Vickery, "The Khmer Inscriptions of Tenasserim: A Reinterpretation," JSS, 61, 1 (January, 1973), pp. 52-53, n. 8], and in his doctoral dissertation Hiram Woodward argues on stylistic grounds that the Grahi Buddha does in fact date to this earlier period [Hiram W. Woodward, "Studies in the Art of Central Siam, 950-1350 A.D.," (Ph. D. dissertation, Yale University, 1975), 1, pp. 91-102]. Woodward presents evidence that the Grahi Buddha not only is a copy of a twelfth century Khmer image but also incorporates stylistic influences from Burma and the peninsula.

76. S. J. O'Connor, "Si Chon: An Early Settlement in Peninsular Thailand," JSS, 56, 1 (1968), pp. 1-18.

77. Taw Sein Ko, The Kalyāṇī Inscriptions (Rangoon, 1892), p. 53. In 1181, according to this inscription, four monks returned to Pagan with the Burmese monk Chapatai--Sīvali from Tamalitthi; Ānanda of Kāñcīpuram; Rāhula, a Singhalese; and Tāmalinda, the son of the Khmer king.

78. J. Boisselier, Le Cambodge (Paris, 1966), pp. 94, 275-76, et al.; and in general Woodward, op. cit., pp. 104-107.

79. Paul Wheatley, The Golden Kersonese (Kuala Lumpur, 1966), p. 63; see also Wolters, Early Indonesian Commerce, p. 251.

80. Paul Wheatley, "Geographical Notes on some Commodities involved in Sung Maritime Trade," JMBRAS, 32, 2 (1959), pp. 10-11, 65-66; Wheatley, The Golden Khersonese, op. cit., pp. 68-70.

81. Wu Ching-hong, "The Rise and Decline of Ch'uan-chou's International Trade and Its Relation to the Philippine Islands," Proceedings, Second Biennial Conference of the International Association of Historians of Asia (Taipei, 1963), pp. 475-476, 480-481; H. Bielenstein, "The Chinese Colonization of Fukien until the End of T'ang," in S. Egerod and E. Glahn, eds., Studia Serica Bernhard Karlgren Dedicata (Copenhagen, 1959), pp. 108-111; Hirth and Rockhill, op. cit., pp. 17-21, 159-162; R. Fox, "The Archaeological Record of Chinese Influences in the Philippines," Philippine Studies, 15, 1 (1967), pp. 41, 52, 54; L. and C. Locsin, Oriental Ceramics Discovered in the Philippines (Rutland, Vermont, 1967), pp. 2, 6.

82. Wheatley, "Geographical Notes," op. cit., pp. 16-17; see pp. 69 and 111 as well.

83. Ibid., pp. 5-8; Hirth and Rockhill, op. cit., pp. 35-39.

84. Wheatley, "Geographical Notes," op. cit., pp. 45, 73, 83, 98, 100, 119, 124.

85. Wheatley, The Golden Khersonese, op. cit., pp. 64-67; Hirth and Rockhill, op. cit., pp. 57-58.

86. Hirth and Rockhill, op. cit., pp. 58-59.

87. Wheatley, "Geographical Notes," op. cit., p. 114. Two other such cases might have been carnelians, which are found in Burma and Mergui, but which Chou Ch'u-fei saw as a product of Syria (ibid, p. 93), and amber, seen by the Chinese as coming from India's Coromandel coast, which to quote Wheatley (ibid., p. 81), "was probably a re-export from the Middle East but conceivably may have come from mines in the Hukaung Valley in the Myitkyina district of Burma."

88. EI, 7, pp. 197-198.

89. Nilakanta Sastri, "A Tamil Merchant Guild," loc. cit.

90. K. A. Nilakanta Sastri, "Takuapa and its Tamil

338

Inscription," JMBRAS, 22, 1 (1949), pp. 25-30; Lamb, Takuapa," loc. cit.

91. Hirth and Rockhill, op. cit., pp. 94, 98.

92. Wang Gungwu, "The Nanhai Trade," JMBRAS, 31, 2 (1958), pp. 112, 117; J. Gernet, Daily Life in China on the Eve of the Mongol Invasion, 1250-1276 (New York, 1962), p. 84; L. J-C Ma, "Commercial Development and Urban Change in Sung China," Ph. D. dissertation, University of Michigan, 1971, p. 38.

93. Wheatley, "Geographical Notes," op. cit., pp. 31-39.

94. Wolters, Early Indonesian Commerce, op. cit., pp. 95-138; Wang, "Nanhai Trade," op. cit., p. 113; E. H. Schafer, The Vermilion Bird (Berkeley, 1967), pp. 77, 194; E. H. Schafer, The Golden Peaches of Samarkand (Berkeley, 1963), pp. 5, 13, 15, 18, 124-125, 136-138, 150-152, 158-160, 163-175, 180-194, 210-211, 241-242.

95. Wheatley, "Geographical Notes," op. cit., pp. 32, 45, 65, 100-101.

96. Ibid., pp. 32, 101-103, 108.

97. Ibid., pp. 32-33, 46-49, 120-121.

98. Ibid., pp. 32, 33, 77.

99. Wolters, Early Indonesian Commerce, op. cit., pp. 40-42, 77, 138, 150, 243; Schafer, Vermilion Bird, op. cit., pp. 77, 238-239; Schafer, Golden Peaches, op. cit., pp. 16, 24, 39, 44, 47, 81, 83, 96-102, 110-112, 174, 239-241, 242-249; Ma, "Commercial Development," op. cit., p. 33, notes that in 987 the Sung ruler sent missions overseas seeking aromatics, rhinoceros horns, pearls, and Barus camphor (from the Sung Hui Yao).

100. Wolters, Early Indonesian Commerce, op. cit., pp. 40-42, 78-79, 82-82, 150; Wang, "Nanhai Trade," op. cit., pp. 91, 95; Schafer, Vermilion Bird, op. cit., p. 77;

Schafer, Golden Peaches, op. cit., pp. 12, 15, 18, 24, 64, 65, 195-204; Wheatley, "Geographical Notes," op. cit., pp. 96-98.

101. Wheatley, "Geographical Notes," op. cit., pp. 35-36, 59-61. 59-61.

102. Ibid., pp. 39-40, 83-85; Fox, "Archaeological Record," op. cit., pp. 54-56; Locsin, Oriental Ceramics, op. cit., pp. 2, pp. 2, 6, 9; Gernet, Daily Life, op. cit., p. 84; Wolters, Fall of Srivijaya, op. cit., p. 42.

103. Cheng Te-k'un, Archaeology in Sarawak (Cambridge, 1969), p. 17; see also T. Harrisson and S. J. O'Connor, Excavations of the Prehistoric Iron Industry in West Borneo (Ithaca, New York, 1969), pp. 18-20, 262-274.

104. Fox, "Archaeological Record," op. cit., pp. 49, 55; Wheatley, "Geographical Notes," op. cit., pp. 114, 117.

105. Wheatley, "Geographical Notes," op. cit., pp. 35-36.

106. Ibid., pp. 37-38, 100-101, 113, 115; Gernet, Daily Life, op. cit., pp. 84, 110; Ma, "Commercial Development," op. cit., pp. 32, 37; Fox, "Archaeological Record," op. cit., p. 43.

107. Cheng, Archaeology, op. cit., pp. 18-21; Harrisson and O'Connor, Excavations, op. cit., pp. 68-74, 183-186, 198-204, 273-275.

108. Hirth and Rockhill, op. cit., pp. 57, 58; Wheatley, Golden Khersonese, op. cit., p. 65; Wheatley, "Geographcial Notes," op. cit., pp. 69-71, 87, 95, 125-126.

109. Tomé Pires, The Suma Oriental of Tomé Pires (London, 1944), I, pp. 98-99, 101, 107-108; M. A. P. Meilink-Roelofsz, Asian Trade and European Influence, 1500-1620 (The Hague, 1962), pp. 69-72, 111; D. F. Lach, Asia in the Making of Europe (Chicago, 1965), I, pp. 525, 526, 541-542, 545, 546-547.

110. Wheatley, "Geographical Notes," op. cit., pp. 81, 93, 114.

111. Ibid., pp. 58-59, 114-115.

112. S. Q. Fatimi, Islam Comes to Malaysia (Singapore, 1963), pp. 35-69.

113. C. A. Majul, "Islamic Influences in the Southern Philippines," JSEAS, 7, 2 (1966), pp. 65-66, 69; C. A. Majul, Muslims in the Philippines (Quezon City, 1973), p. 54.

114. G. W. J. Drewes, "New Light on the Coming of Islam to Indonesia?" Bijdragen tot de Taal-, Land-, en Volkenkunde van Nederlandsch-India, 124 (1968), pp. 433-459; H. J. de Graaf, "Southeast Asian Islam to the Eighteenth Century," in P. M. Holt, et al., eds., The Cambridge History of Islam (Cambridge, 1970), II, pp. 123-239; Fatimi, op. cit., pp. 11-36.

Appendix

Southeast Asia to 1300:

A Course Outline and List of Suggested Readings

The following is a topical bibliography on early Southeast Asian History which is intended to suggest directions for future research. The bibliography is organized into six sections as a matter of convenience and does not represent clearly defined breaks in the area's history. At the beginning of each section is a list of readings which provide an overview of the period; under each section heading is a list of readings which explore the various aspects of a geographical entity or topical problem and which, hopefully, will suggest the need for future research. The bibliography is also organized so that it may be used as a course outline. Readings which we consider most appropriate for classroom use are starred (*). We have also cross-referenced the articles in this volume in an attempt to express our conception of how each essay fits into the overall pattern of early Southeast Asian historiography.

As per convention the complete title of a reference is listed only once, with listings by author. Following the full title in square brackets is the short form of the title as it appears in later citations. Symbols used to denote journals are consistent with the list of symbols preceding the text. Books readily available in paperback are noted by (P).

342

Topical Organization

Reading List

General Texts

*H. J. Benda and J. A. Larkin. The World of Southeast Asia
  [World]. New York, 1967. (P)
 R. Burling. Hill Farms and Padi Fields [Hill Farms].
  Englewood Cliffs, 1965. (P)
 J. F. Cady. Southeast Asia, Its Historical Development.
  New York, 1964.
*G. Coedès. The Making of Southeast Asia [Making].
  Berkeley, 1966. (P)
*G. Coedès. The Indianized States of Southeast Asia
  [Indianized]. Honolulu, 1968. (P)
 Ed. Conze. Buddhism, Its Essence and Development. New
  York, 1959. (P)
 C. A. Fisher. South-east Asia, A Social, Economic, and
  Political Geography. Oxford, 1964.
 B. P. Groslier. The Art of Indochina [Indochina Art]. Art
  of the World Series. New York, 1962.
*D. G. E. Hall. A History of Southeast Asia, 3rd ed.
  [History]. London, 1968. (P)
 F. A. Wagner. Indonesia, The Art of an Island Group. Art
  of the World Series. New York, 1959.
 H. Zimmer. Myths and Symbols in Indian Art and
  Civilization. New York, 1946. (P)

Regional Works

A. L. Basham. The Wonder That Was India [Wonder]. New
  York, 1959. (P)
J. Boisselier. La Statuaire du Champa [Statuaire]. Paris,
  1963.
L. P. Briggs. The Ancient Khmer Empire [Khmer Empire].
  Philadelphia, 1951.
J. K. Fairbanks, E. O. Reischauer, and A. M. Craig. East
  Asia, Tradition and Transformation. Boston, 1973.
H. J. deGraff. Geschiedenis van Indonesie. The Hague, 1949.
  1949.
D. G. E. Hall. Burma, 2nd ed. [Burma]. London, 1960.
G. E. Harvey. History of Burma. London, 1925.
C. Holt. Art in Indonesia, Continuities and Change [Indonesia
  Art]. Ithaca, 1967.

Htin Aung. History of Burma. New York, 1967.

N. J. Krom. Hindoe-Javansche Geschiedenis. The Hague, 1931. For an English translation of the initial sections of this work, see H. B. Sarkar, Journal of the Greater India Society, 13 (1946), pp. 1-72; 16 (1957), pp. 1-82.

Le Thanh Khoi. Le Viet-Nam, Histoire et Civilisation [Viet-Nam]. Paris, 1955.

J. D. Legge. Indonesia. Englewood Cliffs, 1964. (P)

K. A. Nilakanta Sastri. A History of South India, 3rd ed. [South India]. Madras, 1966.

C. W. Nicholas and S. Paranavitana. A Concise History of Ceylon. Colombo, 1961.

*P. Wheatley. Impressions of the Malay Peninsula in Ancient Times [Impressions]. Singapore, 1964.

P. Wheatley. The Golden Khersonese [Khersonese]. Kuala Lumpur, 1961.

I. Introduction

1. Historiography

*H. J. Benda. "The Structure of Southeast Asian History, Some Preliminary Observations." JSEAH, 3, 1 (1962): 106-138. This also appears in a somewhat abridged form in R. O. Tilman, ed., Man, State, and Society in Contemporary Southeast Asia [Man] (New York, 1969), pp. 23-33. (P)

G. Coedès. "L'avenir des etudes khmeres." BSEI, n.s., 40, 3 (1965): 205-213.

G. Coedès. "Some Problems in the Ancient History of the Hinduized States of Southeast Asia." JSEAH, 5, 2 (1964): 1-14.

B. P. Groslier. "Our Knowledge of Khmer Civilisation, a Reappraisal." JSS, 48, 1 (1960): 1-28.

D. G. E. Hall. "Looking at Southeast Asian History." JAS, 19, 3 (1960): 243-253.

D. G. E. Hall. "Problems of Indonesian Historiography." PA, 38, 3-4 (1965-66): 353-359.

D. G. E. Hall. "Recent Tendencies in the Study of the Early History of Southeast Asia, Notes and Comment." PA, 39, 3-4 (1966-67): 339-348.

D. G. E. Hall, ed. Historians of Southeast Asia. London, 1961.

M. E. Osborne. "History and Kingship in Contemporary Cambodia." JSEAH, 7, 1 (1966): 1-14.

*L. Sharp. "Cultural Continuities and Discontinuities in Southeast Asia." JAS, 22 (1962): 3-11. This is also in Tilman, ed., Man, pp. 45-54.

Soedjatmoko, ed. An Introduction to Indonesian Historiography. Ithaca, 1966.

"Vietnam, An Historical Outline." Vietnamese Studies, 12 (Hanoi, 1966): 4-26.

O. W. Wolters. Early Indonesian Commerce [Indonesian Commerce], ch. 1, "Some Problems of Srivijayan History," pp. 15-29. Ithaca, 1967.

Wang Gungwu. The Use of History [Use of History]. Athens, Ohio, 1968.

2. Lands and Peoples

D. G. E. Hall. "Introduction." In Atlas of Southeast Asia. London, 1964.

S. D. Ripley. The Land and Wildlife of Tropical Asia, esp. pp. 165-174. Life Nature Library. New York, 1964.

Burling, Hill Farms, pp. 1-39, 40-63.

*Coedès, Making, pp. 1-33.

*Coedès, Indianized, pp. 3-13.

C. Geertz. Agricultural Involution, pp. 1-11, 12-37. Berkeley, 1963. (P)

Groslier, Indochina Art, pp. 13-28.

*W. G. Solheim II. "New Light on a Forgotten Past." National Geographic, 139, 3 (1971): 330-339.

*W. G. Solheim II. "An Earlier Agricultural Revolution." Scientific American, 226, 4 (1972): 34-41.

K. C. Chang. Archaeology of Ancient China, 2nd ed. [Ancient China], pp. 73-83. New Haven, 1968. (P)

J. M. Treistman. The Prehistory of China [Prehistory], pp. 36-40. Garden City, New York, 1972. (P)

3. Cultural Development (c. 2000-500 B.C.)

A. H. Christie. "The Sea-locked Lands." In The Dawn of Civilization, edited by S. Piggott, pp. 277-300. London, 1961.

*Chang, Ancient China, pp. 175-181, 183-184, 376 ff.

J. M. Treistman. The Early Cultures of Szechuan and Yunnan, pp. 63-74. Ithaca, 1974.

B. and R. Allchin. The Birth of Indian Civilisation, pp. pp. 170-178, 197-199, 208-215, 220-232, 264-266. Penguin, 1968. (P)
*Wheatley, Impressions, pp. 17-24.
Groslier, Indochina Art, pp. 28-31.

II. Protohistory (500 B.C.-600 A.D.)

*Coedès, Making, pp. 39-70.
*Coedès, Indianized, pp. 14-35.
*Wheatley, Impressions, pp. 24-51.
Hall, History, pp. 12-40.
Groslier, Indochina Art, pp. 31-68.

4. Cultures of the Land

*Treistman, Prehistory, pp. 62-71, 105, 116-128.
*Chang, Ancient China, pp. 429-440.
*Vietnamese Studies, 21 (Hanoi, 1969): 9-24.
Pham Huy Thong. "Finds from North Vietnam." Arts of Asia, 4, 6 (1974): 32-36.
W. Eberhard. The Local Cultures of South and East China. Leiden, 1968.

5. Cultures of the Sea

R. O. Winstedt. The Malay Magician, Being Shamen, Shaiwa, and Sufi [Magician], pp. 1-26. London, 1951.
*Holt, Indonesia Art, pp. 11-33.
R. C. Suggs. The Island Civilizations of Polynesia, pp. 34-46, *57-85. New York, 1960. (P)
K. Taylor. "Madagascar in the Ancient Malayo-Polynesian Myths." In Explorations in Early Southeast Asian History: The Origins of Southeast Asian Statecraft [Origins], edited by K. R. Hall and J. K. Whitmore. Ann Arbor, 1976.

6. Asian Contacts

*R. Thapar. History of India [India], v. 1, pp. 109-124. Penguin, 1966. (P)
"A City of Gold." In Tales of Ancient India, edited by J. A. B. van Buitenen, pp. 74-95. New York, 1959. (P)
"The Country of the Cannibals." In A Treasury of Chinese

Literature, pp. 81-89. Fawcett, 1972. (P)
C. Maloney. "The Beginnings of Civilisation in South India."
JAS, 29, 3 (1970): 603-616.
L. Malleret. "The Buried Town of Oc-eo...." Annual
Bibliography of Indian Archaeology, 15 (Leiden, 1940):
7, li-lvi.
*Wang Gangwu. "The Nan-hai Trade." JMBRAS, 31, 2
(1958): 3-30.
Wolters, Indonesian Commerce, pp. 31-61, 154-156.
Wheatley, Khersonese, pp. 8-25, 123-157, 177-198.

7. Establishment of the Mainland States

*Coedès, Indianized, pp. 36-64.
Briggs, Khmer Empire, pp. 12-36.
Boisselier, Statuaire, pp. 1-32.
S. J. O'Connor. Hindu Gods of Peninsular Siam, pp. 11-51.
Ascona, 1972.

8. China and India, Commerce and Culture

Thapar, India, pp. 136-166.
Wheatley, Khersonese, pp. 185-198.
Wolters, Indonesian Commerce, pp. 63-85.
*F. D. K. Bosch. "The Problem of the Hindu Colonisation of
Indonesia." In Selected Studies in Indonesian Archaeology,
pp. 1-22. The Hague, 1961.
A. Lamb. "Miscellaneous Papers on Early Hindu and
Buddhist Settlements in Northern Malaya and Southern
Thailand." Federated Museums Jounnal, 6 (1961).
A. Lamb. "Takuapa." In Malayan and Indonesian Studies
edited by Bastin and Rolvink, pp. 76-86. Oxford, 1964.
*Wang, Use of History, pp. 31-61.
Khoi, Viet-Nam, pp. 115-121.
E. H. Schafer. The Vermilion Bird, T'ang Images of the
South [Vermilion], pp. 9-17. Berkeley, 1967.

9. Development of Religion

*P. Mus. "L'Inde vu de l''est, Cultes indiens et indigenes au
Champa." BEFEO, 33 (1933): 367-410.
R. Grousset. In the Footsteps of the Buddha [Footsteps],
pp. 140-201, 257-269. London, 1932, 1971.
Tran Van Giap. "Le Bouddhisme en Annam"

["Bouddhisme"] . BEFEO, 32 (1932): 203-232.
*Benda and Larkin, World, no. 1.
Wheatley, Khersonese, pp. 37-45.
W. Pachow. "The Voyage of Buddhist Missions to Southeast
   Asia and the Far East." Journal of the Greater India
   Society, 17 (1958): 1-22.

10. Development of Political Control

Wolters, Indonesian Commerce, pp. 159-196.
Wheatley, Khersonese, pp. 282-289.
J. Minattur. "The King of Kundungga of the East Borneo
   Inscriptions." JSEAH, 5, 2 (1964): 181-183.
C. Jacques. "Notes sur l'inscription de Vat Luong Kau."
   JA, 250 (1962): 249-256.
J. Boisselier. "Recentes recherches archeologiques en
   Thailande...." AA, 12 (1965): 144-145.
M. Durand. "La dynastie des Ly anterieurs d'apres le
   VDULT." BEFEO, 44, 2 (1947-1950): 437-452.
P. Levy. "Thala Borivat or Stun Tren: Sites de la capitale
   du sourverain Khmer Bhavavarman I." JA, 258, 1-2
   (1970): 113-129.

III. Political Growth (600-1000 A.D.)

*Coedès, Making, pp. 77-82, 88-99, 110-113.
*Wheatley, Impressions, pp. 52-83.
Groslier, Indochina Art, pp. 69-118, 133-144.

11. The Island World

*Coedès, Indianized, pp. 79-85, 87-93, 107-109, 125-132.
*Wolters, Indonesian Commerce, chs. 13-14.
*Hall, "State and Statecraft in Early Srivijaya," in Origins.
*Benda and Larkin, World, no. 2.
Wheatley, Khersonese, pp. 292-297.
K. A. Nilakanta Sastri. A History of Srivijaya. Madras,
   1949.
Grousset, Footsteps, pp. 270-284.
J. G. deCasparis. Prasasti Indonesia, II [Prasasti] ,
   pp. 15-46, 258-261, 288-300. Bandung, 1956.
*Holt, Indonesian Art, pp. 35-64.
*Hall, History, pp. 41-55.
P. Mus. "Barabudur." BEFEO, 32 (1932): 269-439;
   33 (1933): 577-980; 34 (1934): 175-400.

12. Indian Contacts and Mahāyāna Buddhism

Thapar, India, pp. 167-193, 221-229.
*Coedès, Indianized, p. 96.
*J. G. deCasparis. "Barabudur." In Encyclopedia of Buddhism, II, 4, edited by Malalasekera, pp. 545-549. Ceylon, 1968.
J. Mirsky, ed. The Great Chinese Travelers, pp. 61-106. London, 1965.
L. C. Damais. "Les ecritures d'orgine indienne en Indonesie et dans le Sud-Est Asiatique continental." BSEI, 30, 4 (1955): 365-380.
F. D. K. Bosch. "The Old Javanese Bathing-place Jalatunda." In Selected Studies of Indonesian Archaeology, pp. 49-107. The Hague, 1961.
P. Zoctmulder. Les Religions d'Indonesie, pp. 262-286. Paris, 1968.
Giap, "Bouddhisme," pp. 232-238.
N. Ray. Brahmanical Gods in Burma. Calcutta, 1932.
J. G. deCasparis. "New Evidence on Cultural Relations Between Java and Ceylon in Ancient Times." AA, 24 (1961): 241-248.

13. Champa and the Khmers

*O. W. Wolters. "North-western Cambodia in the 7th Century." BSOAS, 37, 2 (1974): 370-384.
*Coedès, Indianized, pp. 65-76, 85-86, 93-95, 97-104.
Briggs, Khmer Empire, pp. 37-114.
Boisselier, Statuaire, pp. 33-85.
P. Dupont. "La dislocation du Tchen-la." BEFEO, 43 (1943-46): 17-55.
P. Dupont. La Statuaire Preangkorienne. AA supplement no. 15. Ascona, 1955.
*Schafer, Vermilion, pp. 72-76.
Wheatley, Kersonese, pp. 288-292.
*O. W. Wolters. "Jayavarman II's Military Power: The Territorial Foundation of the Angkor Empire." JRAS, 1-2 (1973): 21-30.
G. Coedès. Angkor, An Introduction [Angkor], pp. 68-83. London, 1963.

14. Angkor, the Mons, and the Peninsula

*Coedès, Indianized, pp. 76-79, 86-87, 110-125.

H. W. Woodward, Jr. "Studies in the Art of Central Siam, 950-1350 ["Central Siam"], I, pp. 2-56. Ph. D. dissertation, Yale University, 1975.

Briggs, Khmer Empire, pp. 114-144.

Boisselier, Statuaire, pp. 87-224.

H. G. Q. Wales. Dvaravati. London, 1969.

P. Dupont. L'Archeologie Mone de Dvaravati, pp. 1-23, 163-171, 226-228, 289-293. Paris, 1959.

H. G. Q. Wales. "Dvaravati in Southeast Asian Cultural History." JRAS, 1-2 (1966): 40-62.

J. Stargardt. "Southern Thai Waterways." Man, 8, 1 (1973): 5-29.

Nai Pan Hla. "Mon Literature and Culture over Thailand and Burma." JBRS, 41, 1-2 (1958): 65-75.

G. Coedès. "Les Mons de Dvaravati." In Essays Offered to G. H. Luce, AA Supplement no. 23, I, pp. 112-116. Ascona, 1966.

G. H. Luce. "Dvaravati and Old Burma." JSS, 53, 1 (1965): 9-25.

G. H. Luce. "The Ancient Pyu." JBRS, 27 (1937): 239-253. Also in 50th Anniversary Publication, Burma Research Society, II, pp. 307-321. Rangoon, 1960.

G. H. Luce. "Old Kyaukse and the Coming of the Burmans." JBRS, 42, 1 (1959): 75-109.

15. China and the Southern Border, East (Vietnam)

*Schafer, Vermilion, pp. 18-47, 76-78.

Ed. H. Schafer. Ancient China, pp. 165-172. New York, 1967.

*Wang, Use of History, pp. 62-117.

H. Maspero. "Le protectorate general d'Annam sous les T'ang." BEFEO, 10 (1910): 539-584, 665-682.

O. W. Wolters. "China Irredenta: The South." The World Today, 19, 12 (1963): 540-552.

Wheatley, Khersonese, pp. 26-36, 46-60.

Khoi, Viet-Nam, pp. 121-143.

16. China and the Southern Border, West (Nanchao)

*Coedès, Indianized, pp. 95-96, 104-107, 132-133.

*Schafer, Vermilion, pp. 48-77.
G. H. Luce, trans. Man Shu (Book of the Southern
Barbarians). Data Paper no. 44. Ithaca, 1961.
Hall, History, pp. 141-145.
W. Stott. "The Expansion of the Nan-ch'ao Kingdom (750-
860)." TP, 50, 1-3 (1963): 190-220.

IV. The Apogee of Classical Southeast Asia (1000-1200 A.D.)

*Coedès, Making, pp. 83-87, 99-109, 113-117.
*Wheatley, Impressions, pp. 84-100.
Groslier, Indochina Art, pp. 118-132, 144-187.
G. Coedès. "La 11e siecle dans la Peninsule indochinoise."
FA, 173 (1962): 247-253.
G. Maspero. "La geographie politique de l'Indochine ca.
960 A.D." Etudes Asiatiques, II, pp. 79-125. Hanoi,
1925.

17. Angkor

*Coedès, Indianized, pp. 134-139, 152-154, 159-164, 168-177.
*H. de Mestier du Bourg. "La primiere moitie du 11e s. au
Cambodge: Suryavarman I, sa vie et quelques aspects des
institutions a sa epoque." JA, 258, 3-4 (1970): 281-314.
Briggs, Khmer Empire, pp. 144-236.
L. P. Briggs. "The Genealogy and Successors of
Sivacharya." BEFEO, 46, 1 (1952): 177-185.
*Coedès, Angkor, pp. 84-107.
Woodward, "Central Siam," I, pp. 57-85, 103-112.
B. P. Groslier and J. Arthaud. Angkor, Art and
Civilisation, pp. 23-31, 162-167, and look at the
photographs. New York, 1966.
Hall, History, pp. 110-135.

18. Pagan

Coedès, Indianized, pp. 148-151, 155-158, 166-167, 177-178.
*M. Aung Thwin. "Kingship, the Sangha, and Society in
Pagan." In Origins.
*G. H. Luce. "The Career of Htilaing Min (Kyanzittha), The
Unifier of Burma, fl. A.D. 1084-1113." JRAS, 1-2
(1966): 53-68.
*G. H. Luce. "Aspects of Pagan History--Later Period"
["Later Period"]. In In Memorium Phya Anuman

Rajadhon, edited by Tej Bunnag and M. Smithies, pp.
pp. 129-137. Bangkok, 1970.
G. H. Luce. Old Burma, Early Pagan. AA supplement
no. 25, 3 vols. Locust Valley, New York, 1969, 1970.
*Benda and Larkin, World, no. 9.
Hall, History, pp. 145-154.
A. B. Griswold. "Burma." In The Art of Burma, Korea,
Tibet, pp. 13-60. New York, 1964.

19. Thang-long

*K. Taylor. "The Rise of Ðai Việt and the Establishment of
Thang-long." In Origins.
*Vietnamese Studies, 21 (1969): 27-41, 50, 54, 57-58, 62-66.
*Benda and Larkin, World, no. 13 (1).
Khoi, Viet-Nam, pp. 143-169.
H. Màspero. "La geographie politique de l'empire d'Annam
sous les Ly, les Tran, et les Ho." BEFEO, 16, 1 (1916):
27-48.
*T. B. Lam. Patterns of Vietnamese Response to Foreign
Intervention [Patterns], no. 1. New Haven, 1967.
L. Bezacier. L'Art Vietnamien, pp. 179-189. Paris, 1954.
Giap, "Bouddhisme," pp. 239-255.
Tran Van Khe. La Musique vietnamienne traditionnelle,
pp. 16-51. Paris, 1962.

20. Interstate Conflict

*Coedès, Indianized, pp. 139-141, 154-155, 164-166.
Boisselier, Statuaire, pp. 225-328.
H. Maspero. "La frontier de l'Annam et du Cambodge du
8e au 14e siecle." BEFEO, 18, 3 (1918): 1-36.

21. The Hill Peoples

L.P. Briggs. "The Appearance and Historical Usage of the
Terms Tai, Thai, Siamese, and Laotioan." JAOS, 69
(1949): 60-73.
J. Rispaud. "Introduction a l'histoire des Tay du Yunnan et
de Birmanie." FA, 17, 166 (1961): 1849-1879.
F. W. Mote. "Problems of Thai Prehistory." Sangkhomsat
Parithat (The Social Science Review), 2, 2 (1964): 100-109.
H. Woodward. "Who are the Ancestors of the Thai: Report
on the Seminar." Sankhomsat Parithat, 2, 3 (1965): 88-91.

F. W. Mote. "Symposium on the Prehistory of the Thai People, The View from the Discipline of Chinese History." Sangkhomsat Parithat, Chabap Phiset, 3 (1966): 24-31.

*J. M. Brown. "The Language of Sukhothai, Where Did It Come From and Where Did It Go?" Sangkhomsat Parithat, Chabap Phiset, 3 (1966): 40-42.

*G. H. Luce. "The Early Syam in Burma's History." JSS, 46, 2 (1958): 123-214; 47, 1 (1959): 59-101.

J. F. Rock. The Ancient Na-Khi Kingdom of Southwest China, 2 vols. Cambridge, Mass., 1947.

H. B. Chapin. "A Long Roll of Buddhist Images [Nanchao]." AA, 32, 2-3 (1970): 157-199.

22. The Island States

*Coedès, Indianized, pp. 141-148, 158, 167-168, 173-180.

*O. W. Wolters. The Fall of Srivijaya in Malay History, chs. 2-4. Ithaca, 1971.

G. W. Spencer. "Royal Leadership and Imperial Conquest in Medieval South India," ch. 6. Ph. D. dissertation, University of California, Berkeley, 1967.

Wheatley, Khersonese, pp. 61-74, 199-203, 216-232, 297-301.

Thapar, India, pp. 194-220.

Hall, History, pp. 55-62, 65-71.

*Holt, Indonesia Art, pp. 66-77.

B. Schrieke. Indonesian Sociological Studies [Indonesian Sociological], II, pp. 16-21, 287-301. The Hague, 1957.

P. Zoetmulder. Les Religions d'Indonesia, pp. 286-300. Paris, 1968; originally in German, 1965.

*Benda and Larkin, World, no. 3.

R. Fox. "The Archaeological Record of Chinese Influences in the Philippines." Philippine Studies, 15, 1 (1967): 49-62.

Wada Sei. "The Philippine Islands as Known to the Chinese before the Ming Period." Memoirs of the Toyo Bunko, 4 (1929): 121-166.

V. The Institutions of Classical Southeast Asia

Basham, Wonder, passim.
*Coedes, Making, pp. 218-230.
*Coedes, Indianized, pp. 247-256.

354

*Legge, Indonesia, pp. 20-41.
L. A. Sedov. The Angkorean Empire, Social, Economic,
and Government Conditions of Cambodia, 9th-14th
Centuries (in Russian). Moscow, 1967.

23. Trade and Communications

*P. Wheatley. "Geographical Notes on Some Commodities
Involved in Sung Maritime Trade." JMBRAS, 32, 2
(1959): 5-41.
K. R. Hall and J. K Whitmore. "Southeast Asian Trade and
the Isthmian Struggle, 1000-1200 A.D." Origins.
*K. R. Hall. "Khmer Commercial Development and Foreign
Contacts under Sūryavarman I." JESHO, 18, 3 (1975):
318-336.
Woodward, "Central Siam," I, pp. 86-102.
S. Wickremasingha. "Ceylon's Relations with Southeast
Asia, especially Burma." Ceylon Journal of Social and
Historical Studies, 3, 1 (1960): 38-58.
Wheatley, Khersonese, passim.
Schrieke, Indonesian Sociological, II, pp. 102-120.
L. and C. Locsin. Oriental Ceramics Discovered in the
Philippines. Rutland, Vermont, 1967.
F. Hirth and W. W. Rockhill. Chau Ju-Kua, His Work on
the Chinese and Arab Trade in the 12th and 13th
Centuries.... St. Petersburg, 1911.

24. Government, Authority, and Administration

J. Gonda. Ancient Indian Kingship from the Religious Point
of View. Leiden, 1966.
D. M. Brown. The White Umbrella, Indian Political
Thought....[Umbrella] , pp. 3-75. Berkeley, 1964. (P)
G. W. Spencer and K. R. Hall. "Toward an Analysis of
Dynastic Hinterlands: The Imperial Cholas of 11th Century
South India." Asian Profile, 2, 1 (1974): 51-62.
R. von Heine-Geldern. Concepts of State and Kingship in
Southeast Asia. Data Paper no. 18. Ithaca, 1956.
*C. Geertz. Islam Observed, pp. 36-39. New Haven, 1968.
(P)
*K. R. Hall. "An Introductory Essay on Southeast Asian
Statecraft in the Classical Period." In Origins.
Coedès, Angkor, passim.

I. Mabbett. "Devaraja." JSEAH, 10, 2 (1969): 202-223.

*Nidhi Aeusrivongse. "Devarāja Cult and Khmer Kingship at Angkor." In Origins.

P. Stern. "Diversite et rythme des fondations royales khmeres." BEFEO, 44, 2 (1954): 649-685.

M. E. Osborne. "Notes on Early Cambodian Provincial History, Isanapura and Sambhupura." FA, 20, 4 (1966): 433-449.

Schrieke, Indonesian Sociological, II, pp. 7-21, 76-95.

S. Sahai. Les institutions politiques et l'organisation du Cambodge ancien. Paris, 1970.

The Oath

*Benda and Larkin, World, no. 9.

DeCasparis, Prasasti, II, p. 29.

R. Deloustal. "Code de Lê." BEFEO, 10 (1910): 21-22.

25. Land and the Law

R. Lingat. The Classical Law of India. Berkeley, 1973.

R. Lingat. "L'influence juridique d'Inde au Champa et au Cambodge d'apres l'epigraphie." JA, 237 (1949): 273-290.

H. de Mestier du Bourg. "Le proces dans l'ancien droit Khmer." JA, 256, 1. (1968): 37-53.

B. P. Groslier. Angkor et le Cambodge au 16e siecle, pp. 101-121. Paris, 1958.

*M. C. Ricklefs. "Land and the Law in the Epigraphy of 10th Century Cambodia." JAS, 26, 3 (1967): 411-420.

Boechari. "Epigraphy and Indonesian Historiography." In Introduction to Indonesian Historiography, edited by Soedjatmoka et al., pp. 47-73. Ithaca, 1965.

Schrieke, Indonesian Sociological, II, pp. 211-217.

6. Social-Economic Institutions

*M. Aung Thwin. "Kingship, the Saṅgha, and Society in Pagan." In Origins.

*K. R. Hall. "Khmer Commercial Development and Foreign Contacts under Sūryavarman I." JESHO, 18, 3 (1975): 318-336.

*Chou T-kuan. Notes on the Customs of Cambodia. Bangkok, 1967. (P)

P. Pelliot. "Recollections of the Customs of Cambodia." In The Great Chinese Travelers, edited by J. Mirsky, pp. 203-233. New York, 1964.

Ma Tuan-lin. Ethnographie des Peuples Etrangers a la Chine, vol. II, "The South." Paris, 1883.

M. D. Coe. "Social Typology and the Tropical Forest Civilizations." CSSH, 4, 1 (1961): 65-85.

G. H. Luce. "Economic Life of the Early Burman." JBRS, 30, 1 (1940): 283-335. Also in 50th Anniversary Publication, Burma Research Society, II, pp. 323-341; notes, pp. 342-375.

Than Tun. "Social Life in Burma, 1044-1287." JBRS, 51, 1-2 (1958): 37-47.

Pe Maung Tin. "Women in the Inscriptions of Pagan." JBRS, 25, I (1935): 149-159. Also in 50th Anniversary Publication, Burma Research Society, II, pp. 411-421.

27. The Intelligentsia and Religion

Thapar, India, pp. 241-265.

*S. W. Desai. "The Ramayana, An Instrument of Historical Contact and Cultural Transmission Between India and Asia." JAS, 30, 1 (1970): 5-20.

C. Hooykas. "The Old Javanese Ramayana." Verhandelingen der Koninklijke Nederlandse Akademie van Wetenschappen te Amsterdam, 61, 1 (1958).

C. Hooykas. "Kamandakikya Nitisara in Old Javanese." Journal of the Greater India Society, 15, 1 (1956): 18-50.

T. G. T. Pigeaud. Literature of Java, I, pp. 47-75, 114-128, 175-211, 304-311. The Hague, 1967.

J. E. van Lohuizen-de Leeuw. "The Beginnings of Old Javanese Historical Literature." Bijdragen, 112 (1956): 383-394.

*Winstedt, Magician, pp. 27-38, 39-71.

*Nidhi Aeusrivongse. "Devarāja Cult and Khmer Kingship at Angkor." In Origins.

K. Bhattacharya. Les religions brahmaniques dans l'ancien Cambodge.... Paris, 1961.

N. Ray. Brahmanical Gods in Burma. Calcutta, 1932.

G. H. Luce. "Rice and Religion: A Study of Old Mon-Khmer Religion and Culture." JSS, 53, 2 (1965): 139-152.

H. Kern. "Java, Bali, and Sumatra." In Encyclopedia of Religion and Ethics, vii, "Buddhism," p. 475.

P. H. Pott. "Le Bouddhisme de Java et l'ancienne civilisation javanese." Serie Orientale, Roma V, conference (1952): 109-156.

P. Zoetmulder. "L'Hindouisme et le Bouddhisme." In Les Religions d'Indonesie, edited by W. Stohr and P. Zoetmulder, pp. 262-314. Paris, 1968.

F. D. K. Bosch. "Buddhist Data From Balinese Texts." In Selected Studies of Indonesian Archaeology, pp. 111-130, 137-152, 155-170, 173-196. The Hague, 1961.

N. Ray. "Theravada Buddhism in Burma." Journal of the Greater India Society, 8, 1 (1941): 17-60.

Than Tun. "Religion in Burma, 1000-1300." JBRS, 42, 2(1959): 71-80.

G. H. Luce. "The Shwegugyi Pagoda Ins., Pagan, 1141 A.D." In 50th Anniversary Publication, Burma Research Society, pp. 377-384. Also in Benda and Larkin, World, no. 9.

Pe Maung Tin. "Buddhism in the Inscriptions of Pagan." JBRS, 26, 1 (1936): 52-70. Also in 50th Anniversary Publication, Burma Research Society, pp. 423-441.

Nguyen Van Khoan. "Essai sur le dinh et le culte du genie tutelaire des villages au Tonkin." BEFEO, 30 (1930): 107-139.

Nguyen Van Huyen. "Contribution a l'etude d'un genie tutelaire annamite: Ly Phuc Man." BEFEO, 30 (1930): 1-110.

Tran Van Giap, "Bouddhisme," pp. 191-268.

L. Finot. "Lokesvara en Indochine." Etudes Asiatiques, I (Hanoi, 1925): 227-256.

L. P. Briggs. "The Syncretism of Religions in Southeast Asia, especially in the Khmer Empire." JAOS, 71 (1951): 230-249.

28. Patterns of Interstate Relation

Brown, Umbrella, pp. 38-48, 58-63.

*E. Leach. "The 'Frontiers of Burma.'" CSSH, 3, 1 (1960): 49-68.

Schrieke, Indonesian Sociological, II, pp. 121-152.

O. W. Wolters. "Chen-li-fu,...." JSS, 48, 2 (1960): 1-36.

H. G. Q. Wales. Ancient Southeast Asian Warfare, chs. 1-4. London, 1952.

VI. Change (The Thirteenth Century)

*Coedès, Making, pp. 121-134.

*Coedès, Indianized, pp. 180-217.

358

Briggs, Khmer Empire, pp. 237-250.
Groslier, Indochina Art, pp. 189 ff.
Hall, History, pp. 121-125, 154-159, 169-175.
Boisselier, Statuaire, pp. 328-348.
Khoi, Viet-Nam, pp. 170-191.
Hall, Burma, pp. 22-29.
G. Coedès. "Une periode critique dans l'Asie du sud-est:
le XIIIe s." BSEI, 33, 4 (1958): 387-400.
L. Olschki. Marco Polo's Asia. Berkeley, 1960.
C. Jack-Hinton. "Marco Polo in Southeast Asia." JSEAH,
5, 2 (1964): 43-103.

29. New Religious Systems and New Peoples

*Benda and Larkin, World, nos. 4, 11, 13 (2).
*Luce, "Later Period," pp. 137-146.
*M. Aung Twin. "Kingship, the Saṅgha, and Society in
Pagan." In Origins.
P. Levy. "Les traces de l'introduction du Bouddhisme a
Luang Prabang." BEFEO, 40, 2 (1940): 411-424.
Woodward, "Central Siam," I, pp. 112-160, 176-179; II,
pp. 97-104.
*Vietnamese Studies, 21 (Hanoi, 1969): 41-49, 51-56, 59-60.
*Lam, Patterns, no. 2 (Tran Hung Dao).
*P. Bennet. "The 'Fall' of Pagan." In Conference Under the
Tamarind Tree, Three Essays in Burmese History,
pp. 1-11. New Haven, 1971.

30. Disappearance of the Old Political System?

*R. Murphey. "The Ruin of Ancient Ceylon." JAS, 16, 2
(1957): 181-200.
E. Leach. "Hydraulic Society in Ceylon." Past and
Present, 15 (1959): 2-25.
K. Taylor. "The Devolution of Kingship in Twelfth Century
Ceylon." In Origins.
D. Kaplan. "Men, Monuments and Political Systems."
Southwestern Journal of Anthropology, 19, 4 (1943):
397-410.

Printed and bound by CPI Group (UK) Ltd, Croydon, CR0 4YY

13/04/2025